MARTIN CLASSICAL LECTURES

* Out of print

MARTIN CLASSICAL LECTURES

VOLUME XIX

The Martin Classical Lectures are delivered annually at Oberlin College on a foundation established by his many friends in honor of Charles Beebe Martin, for forty-five years a teacher of classical literature and classical art in Oberlin.

ARISTOPHANES
AND THE COMIC HERO

BY

CEDRIC H. WHITMAN

Published for Oberlin College by
HARVARD UNIVERSITY PRESS
CAMBRIDGE · MASSACHUSETTS

SECOND PRINTING, 1971

DISTRIBUTED IN GREAT BRITAIN BY OXFORD UNIVERSITY PRESS, LONDON

LIBRARY OF CONGRESS CATALOG CARD NUMBER 64–22724

SBN 674–04500–9

PRINTED IN THE UNITED STATES OF AMERICA

TO
ANNE

PREFACE

Antiquity transmits its power, for us at least, primarily in forms imbued with high seriousness — the epic, tragedy, history, philosophy. Yet, there is a saying attributed to Anne de Lenclos, the famous Ninon, to the effect that the token of spiritual strength is gaiety; and in that case, Aristophanes must have been the strongest spirit of Greek antiquity, for he was surely the gayest. There is every reason to believe that it took a tough-fibered temperament to make merry during the grim years of the Peloponnesian War. The youngest of the great fifth-century dramatists, and the last to frame in poetry the heroic drive of the grand tradition, Aristophanes outlived his city's greatness, and therewith the art of Old Comedy. But before that happened, he created — or for us, at least, he created — a new kind of hero, the comic hero, who parodies his two solemn older brothers of tragedy and epic, but at the same time challenges their supremacy in expressing human aspiration in the face of the world's dilemma.

The present study had its beginning in the neglected question of the nature and value of Aristophanes as a poet, and if much of the answer was found to lie in the comic hero, that fact may explain some of the book's peculiarities. For one thing, the emphasis resulting from such an approach falls naturally on the fantastic rather than on the satiric aspect of Aristophanes; not that the satiric is unimportant, but that it is contained within the fantastic, not the other way around. For another thing, the last two extant plays have been excluded. This may be rather arbitrary. But it is commonly agreed that the *Ecclesiazusae* and the *Plutus*, whatever their intrinsic value, mark a departure from Old Comedy proper, and it was the spirit of Old Comedy which was the object of the search. The political and personal invective of the real Old Comedies is gone from them, though much of it had disappeared earlier. More important, the tremendous vitality of the plays of the fifth century, focusing most of the time, if not always, on a central heroic figure, the master of a transcendent fantasy, was lost in the more reflective and retired spirit of the postwar years. The poetry of these plays is different, and far more understandable in the light of later theories of comedy, practically all of which are based ultimately on the New Comedy of Menander and his followers.

But the fourth century can tell us little about the art of Old Comedy, except by contrast. The ethos of Menander is civilizing and philosophic; it affirms society, essentially, while deprecating the follies and selfishnesses which seek to corrode a structure possibly, and even probably, viable; it suggests common sense and deplores excess. No such gentility of purpose or creed can be said to underlie the work of Aristophanes; it may even be questioned whether he considered society basically viable. Society for him was a given fact, and when it frustrated him, he overturned it, and invented something he liked better. His mind was not philosophic; it was poetic and demiurgic. Yet if he lacked philosophy, Aristophanes possessed something almost totally lacking in New Comedy, namely the vital sense of the individual. To the fourth century and later, man was a piece in a puzzle which might comprise an intelligible picture. To the fifth century, man was still a microcosm. Hence Aristophanes is not "civilizing," at least not in the Menandrian sense; for a microcosm always is capable of asserting itself, to the peril of reason, systems, and ethical order. The concern of this study is with the last of the great and disturbing microcosms of Greece.

I have many friends and institutions to thank for their assistance in preparing this book. First, I wish to thank the veteran Aristophanean, Professor Charles T. Murphy, for the invitation to deliver the nucleus of the work as the Martin Classical Lectures at Oberlin College, in 1961, as well as for his patience in waiting for the expanded final version. His comments and encouragement both at that time and on subsequent reading of the manuscript have been of great value to me. I owe a debt of warm gratitude also to the John Simon Guggenheim Memorial Foundation for the fellowship which afforded me, in 1961 and 1962, the freedom to work, and to do research in Greece on the modern Greek shadow theater. To Harvard University my thanks are due for a sabbatical year and for further subvention from the Joseph H. Clark fund. I am particularly indebted to Professor George Megas, Honorary Director of the Greek Folklore Archive, and to other members of its staff, for permission to consult their collection, and for much kindly assistance with my work on the shadow theater. The American School in Athens also extended me every courtesy during my stay in Greece. I wish to thank Professor James A. Notopoulos for much good advice and information about Karaghiozes, and also Professor Kenneth J. Reckford, and Father T. J. Hoey, S.J., for careful critical readings of the manuscript and for many suggestions and timely corrections; also a most helpful unnamed reader for the Harvard University Press. To the Press staff I owe thanks, as always, for the warm concern with which my manuscript has been treated; in particular to Mrs. Margaretta Fulton, whose keen and vigilant eye has cleared my text of many faults and follies, both of style and of sense. The ones which remain are mine alone, except for two omissions attributable to fate. The excellent recent works on Aristophanes by Otto Seel and Eduard Fränkel are not referred to in my pages, the first because it was inaccessible to me until lately, the second because it appeared only when my manuscript was complete and ready for the press. The translations, except for two which are Rogers', are my own. They represent no theory, but were written simply as needed, partly for the fun of it, but chiefly because there is no single translation of all Aristophanes which would have served my needs.

C.H.W.

Cambridge, 1964

ix

CONTENTS

ARISTOPHANES
AND THE COMIC HERO

﹒I﹒

CRITICISM AND OLD COMEDY

ARISTOPHANES has always supplied his interpreters, both ancient and modern, with an abundance of problems. As the unchal-
lenged king of Old Comedy, and its only poet to survive in entire
plays, he represents the art at its point of splendid maturity, unique
among all other types of comic expression for its joyous vitality,
variety, and intricate form. The history of this extraordinary vehicle
can be traced back for three or four generations at most, after which
knowledge gives way to speculation about ultimate origins; and by
the time Aristophanes died, Old Comedy was already dead. The
fragments of his rivals, Cratinus, Eupolis, and others, teach us that
many of the themes and attitudes, even some of the jokes, which we
find in Aristophanes were common property, but this fact does
nothing to diminish the uniqueness of the form, and little to diminish
the uniqueness of Aristophanes himself; and the probability is that
if we had the complete plays of his rivals, the similarities would be
far less impressive than the differences formulated by the ancient
writers on comedy.[1] For us, in any case, the art of Aristophanes stands
forth as something *sui generis,* and any inquiry into its nature and
import must rely almost entirely upon a reading of the text. For,
apart from the abundant scholia, devoted mainly to the elucidation
of idiomatic jests and obscure allusions, ancient interpretive tradition about Old Comedy is neither copious nor particularly enlightened; and where antiquity offers little, it may be natural that modern
scholarship has discovered either little, or too much.

I

The reason is not far to seek: Old Comedy died essentially in-testate. The Middle and New Comedies adopted not only a new form, but a wholly different spirit, and one which was to dominate the conception of comedy for centuries to come. Old Comedy was identified with the extreme democratic society of fifth-century Athens, and could not be transplanted. It depended, obviously, upon a freedom of speech, especially of invective, impossible in later periods; even more, it depended on a social structure, or perhaps on an era in the development of this particular structure, when vast private fantasies, of cosmic dimensions, expressed something inherent in the time, albeit in the language of absurdity. It has been said truly that Old Comedy died after the Peloponnesian War because the polis no longer stood in close relation with individual lives.[2] It might be added, however, that comedy flourished most fully during that war, when the rupture between polis and individual was beginning to be felt; and the rupture itself seems to have contributed no little to the nature of Aristophanes' art. But once the break was complete, Old Comedy, though sporadically admired, almost immediately lost its meaning as a totality for later antiquity. Aristotle's taste inclined toward the new form, and he tended either to ignore the old or to identify it with buffoonery and impropriety of language.[3] For Horace, Aristophanes, together with his two chief rivals, Cratinus and Eupolis, is little more than the symbol of a by-gone freedom of satiric speech in the service of moral improvement.[4] Somewhat later, Plutarch in an essay compared Aristophanes and Menander, to the considerable damage of the former, whom he considered vulgar and irrational.[5] Though editions and commentaries of Aristophanes continued to be made from Alexandrine through Byzantine times, no general understanding of him appears at any point.

The judgment of Quintilian is perhaps an exception, and his remarks are worth quoting:

Old Comedy, for one thing, is almost alone in preserving the pure grace of Attic speech; for another, it is characterized by the most eloquent freedom, and especially in chastising vices; yet it possesses the greatest power in all other aspects as well. For it is grand, elegant, and charming [*grandis et elegans et venusta*], and I suspect that there is nothing, after Homer of course, of whom like Achilles it is always right to make an exception, more akin to the orators, or more suited to the making of orators.[6]

This is high praise indeed, especially the remark that the language of Old Comedy is "grand, elegant, and charming," adjectives which not everyone would instantly apply to some of Aristophanes' more redolent earthinesses. But it is clear that Quintilian is talking solely about style, and what an orator may learn about it from the comic poets, as well as from other classics; his brief entry offers no general critical perspective. Yet his three adjectives should be kept in mind, for they are entirely true of Aristophanes, and they perhaps represent, though they do not expound, a total response to him, such as was not shared, apparently, even by so sensitive a critic as the anonymous author of *De Sublimitate*, who only grudgingly admitted that Aristophanes could achieve elevation at times, despite his generally low-pitched idiom.[7] Quintilian's words are unique in antiquity for what they suggest about the real poetic power of Aristophanes, the power which it is the present task to discover. Certainly they are much more thought-provoking than anything which may be found in the late theorists of comedy, for the most part nameless, dateless, and thoughtless, whose quasi-Peripatetic formulations may rest, at some far remove, upon a lost *Poetics II* of Aristotle, *De Comoedia*, and certainly rest upon a precarious belief that Old Comedy had a moral end in view which justified its blatant indecencies.[8]

This notion has taken many forms, and has had far-reaching effects. We may justly smile when an ancient writer tells us that the nocturnal scurrilities of injured small farmers, under the windows of their rich oppressors, appealed so strongly to the Athenian magistrates as a corrective force that the songs were enshrined in comedy, and comedy enshrined in the Great Dionysia, henceforth to be a mighty moral elixir in the commonwealth.[9] But this statement is only a particularly unsophisticated romanza upon the theme, which

3

had prevailed from antiquity and to some extent still prevails, that comedy, for all its merriment, is a force for public and private good. The comic poets themselves claimed this for their art, quite as the Roman satirists claimed it for theirs. It was a persistent commonplace of criticism, admirably summarized by Tzetzes in the twelfth century in the following professorial verses:

> The comic poet in his comedies,
> Laughing at thief or villain or seducer,
> Thereafter brings him back to good behavior.
> So tragedy dissolves our human life,
> But comedy confirms and strengthens it.[10]

Such moralistic poetics were first framed in explicit theory by Aristotle, at least according to the usual view.[11] Actually, they are implicit much earlier, in the whole widespread conception of the poet as the teacher of the people; but when the age of criticism dawned, the attempts to say exactly what the poet taught were sometimes disappointingly flat. Ancient literary criticism, indeed, never quite developed tools adequate to the texts which it aspired to analyze, partly because of the moral bias, and partly because of the tendency to treat matter as separate from form.[12] One result is that modern criticism also, in the case of comedy, has labored under some anciently imposed shadows. The legitimate question "What is Aristophanes all about?" has usually been interpreted to mean "What serious message is Aristophanes trying to convey, albeit in a comic form?" Such a proposition clearly makes the form a stumbling block to its own meaning, which artistic form never is, except in the hands of a bad artist. For though comedy may take on a deeply serious coloring, and does so in the *Frogs*, it is at least questionable whether any calculated "meaning," moral, political, or intellectual, can be separated from any play, and identified as the positive good which the work is supposed to inculcate. Rather, the meaning which should be sought must be of a kind compatible with the form, even better, demanding the form, shaping it, and shaped by it. To put it simply, the real question is: "In what sense is Aristophanes a poet?"

For the most part, modern scholarship on Aristophanes has been divided into two kinds, technical and interpretive. In the technical category, the text, a notoriously happy hunting ground for linguists and emendators, produces a prodigious yearly crop of comment. Students of the Old Comic form also have analyzed and described in great detail the structure of the plays, following in the wake of Thaddeus Zielinski, who first revealed (and somewhat exaggerated) the elaborately symmetrical articulation of certain balanced parts, which he designated by the rather staggering term "epirrhematic syzygies." [13] Such studies, though often highly valuable, are for the most part extrinsic to the present one, for their concern is more with the exterior shape than with the interior dynamics of comic poetry. In the interpretive category, on the other hand, there has long been a wide divergence of opinion, arising, as said earlier, from the belief that Aristophanes' work contained an elusive "serious" (that is, "non-comic") message, which constituted his purpose in writing comedy. The usual method of discovering this message has been to align the plays with known historical events or situations, and then decide what Aristophanes thought about them — as if he always wrote plays as reflexes to Athenian public issues, which may be in part true, and as if he always took a definite, even didactic stand about them, which is far less likely.

On this basis, Aristophanes has become for one French scholar a strict conservative in the pay of the oligarchic faction; [14] for another, a rural democrat wholly opposed to the oligarchs. [15] For others, his purpose was to establish Panhellenic unity, [16] while for one great English scholar, himself a pacifist, he was a systematic partisan of pacifism. [17] One difficulty with these views lies in the fact that they ignore the manifest poet in favor of a hypothetical politician. Another is that they can all be supported to a degree, though the first, perhaps, but little. It is small wonder that recently some scholars have reacted against them all, and leaned toward a view of Aristophanes as a "pure" artist.

In a brief but resolute attack A. W. Gomme went far toward

demonstrating that Aristophanes can be identified with no political theory, that he was full of self-contradictions on all such subjects, but that as dramatist in each successive play he presented a probable and natural picture of Athens as he saw it.[18] Others who have followed in this refreshing line usually lack positive suggestions and have a tendency to go toward another extreme. Thus, Perrotta, responding with what is clearly fellow-Mediterranean feeling, finds Aristophanes "bizarre and sublime" and his work "above all a creation of fantasy"; at the same time, however, he gives the "poetic" aspect of Aristophanes a primacy which leaves poetry defined, if at all, by its remoteness from experience and reality.[19]

The problem with Aristophanes the pure artist recalls the remark of the man who said he wrote only poetry "because you have to know what you're talking about in prose." Another Italian scholar, rightly denying Aristophanes any specific political or moral purpose, describes his work, in a promising phrase, as "a celebration of individual autonomy," but then, in his enthusiasm for the pure artist, declares, "he knows not satire." [20] Now it is absurd to say that Aristophanes "knows not satire," though it may be justifiable to see in his work an element more central and unifying than the satiric one. But it is not very helpful to absolve a poet of moral or political tendentiousness, unless some attempt is made to suggest what actually is the content or meaning of his work. The remark about "individual autonomy," for instance, deserves fuller development than its author gives it, and a quite different one.

A number of more moderate critics, taking as their point of departure the actual dramatic phenomena of the plays rather than some theory of ultimate purpose, have emphasized the mingling of realism and fantasy. The late Werner Jaeger points to how the satirical element takes the form of fantastic allegory, and writes: "Again and again his picture of temporary reality dissolves into the timeless higher reality of imaginative or allegorical truth." Yet though Jaeger denies Aristophanes any political or moral didacticism, he sees comedy as a "critic of culture, with a strong educational mission," to be fulfilled on this high intellectual plane.[21] Whether or not some contradiction inheres in this view, it is clear that it places the fantastic aspect of comedy in the service of the critical, a fact emphasized by the word "allegorical." [22] To reverse this order, and to see the fantasy itself as the primary mode, to which satire and critical observation are foils, perhaps comes closer to identifying Aristophanes as an artist; at least it offers a new approach, some of whose advantages are apparent in the work of Hans Newiger, who rejects the term "allegorical" in favor of "metaphoric." [23] For fantasy is less akin to allegory, which communicates a pre-existent thought lying outside it, than to metaphor, which communicates an evolving thought and one which exists only in that form. For this reason too, the essay on Aristophanes by Karl Reinhardt is only partly satisfying: Reinhardt sees clearly the union of "real" and "fantastic," and calls the result a symbol, but then finds the symbol "political," and in the long run communicative of ideas which differ only in their greater vagueness from the ones attributed to the poet by those who consider him a propagandist.[24] But the mingling and interplay of fantasy and realism are, indeed, basic to Aristophanes, and have recently been recognized as such, by these and still other scholars.[25] It remains to be seen whether this view brings us any nearer to answering the question of what Aristophanes intended to convey to his countrymen, or to posterity.

The problem is of course complicated by the nature of comedy itself, whose relevance to the human condition is far more easily felt then analyzed. Perhaps laughter alone is enough, and there have been those who asserted that Aristophanes had no intention at all beyond raising a laugh, that he was a mere jester, and that whatever political or other views he held were to be attributed to the tradition of Old Comedy, which was by nature against most things, and especially against the government.[26] Yet, the reader of Aristophanes is haunted by a strong and subtle sense of real meaningfulness which makes it difficult to relegate him to the category of jokes for jokes' sake, while his impudent waywardness and frequent self-contradictions make it equally hard to pin him down to any recognizable scheme or drift. Be it said that the adherents of the "mere jester" theory have faced the latter difficulty and have not tried to force the text.

On the other hand, those who, after one fashion or another, make Aristophanes into a serious critic and educator have in their favor — besides the numerous assertions by Aristophanes himself that he was precisely that — the general consensus of antiquity described earlier, that comedy was a constructive and morally salubrious vehicle, admirably designed, through its mask of levity, to inculcate the most noble virtues, and effect without rancor or pain the most desirable reforms. Yet, history has recorded no social reforms or personal moral advances brought about by comedy, or by tragedy either, for that matter. One may at least doubt that Lycambes, Neobule, and all her sisters hanged themselves for shame at the lampoons of Archilochus; and neither did the work of Aristophanes have any outward effect whatever on the shape of Athenian society or politics, unless one believes that the *Clouds*, as Plato intimates, may have engendered a degree of public prejudice against Socrates, nearly a quarter-century after the play's abysmal failure. But the matter seems dubious. The character of Cleon seems not to have been improved by whatever constructive hints underlay Aristophanes' images of him, as a whale, a roaring cataract, a Paphlagonian slave, or a monstrosity whose attributes may not be repeated in polite company. For all the comedian's wickedly refined parodies of Euripides' style, music, morals, and versification, Euripides did not mend his ways. For all the numberless appeals for peace — from the half-serious deploring of the Megarian decree to the lighthearted suggestion that the government be turned over to women — Athens fought the war to its hideous end; and thereupon, the great reformer abandoned Old Comedy and adapted himself to an age of weaker stomachs and blander tastes.

It would seem, therefore, that a new approach is in order, and that such terms as "jester versus reformer," or "pure artist versus

moralist," might profitably be abandoned. Nor will it be quite sufficient to find some middle ground in the antinomy, for thus almost
any compromise case could be made, by manipulation of subjective
responses, without anyone's being much nearer to the poet.[27] Higher
ground, so to speak, rather than middle ground, may serve the purpose better, and by higher ground is meant simply an inquiry into
Aristophanes' poetry as identified with, not an accident of, his meaning. He, like every dramatic poet, deals essentially in terms of plot,
character, language, and imagery, both verbal and visual; and it is
remarkable how little scholarly attention has been given to these
elements. Certain lyrical portions have always been accorded high
praise as "poetry," of course, but as if these were fortuitous intru-
sions into a general scheme of satire, obscenity, and farce, and not
organic parts or aspects of a poetic whole. Yet few poets can be compared to Aristophanes for the wholeness of his poetic vision, a wholeness which indeed makes possible his baffling richness of texture,
and at the same time organizes it around the subtle interrelation-
ships of dominant motifs.

Nor is there the least truth in what is sometimes stated as virtually self-evident, that Aristophanes is deficient in plot construction
and character drawing.[28] Strictures upon Aristophanes' plots arise
chiefly from prejudice about what a plot is and what kind of coherence it must have; and the preconceived stereotype comes primarily
from the New Comedy. Sometimes, also, the belief in the multiple
origins of Old Comedy leads to the conclusion that Aristophanes
had to construct his plays badly because that was what the form
called for. Yet, whatever the source, or sources, of Old Comedy
may have been, Aristophanes' plays, as performed, satisfied public
taste well enough to win him many prizes in his own time, and it is
still hard to read any play, except possibly the *Ecclesiazusae*, and feel
that it is falling apart, at least, if one reads with an eye unprejudiced
and open to poetic coherence.[29] As for character drawing, one may
well ask if and why Peithetaerus, Agoracritus, Lysistrata, or Philocleon are failures. It is true that they do not correspond to modern

photographic taste in character imitation, and whatever is realistic about them is strongly modified by caricature and fantasy; but as dramatic images, they stand forth in clear, rounded individualism, and the mode of their characterization is appropriately pitched to the indecorous rumpus which is Old Comedy. Above all, it is untrue to say that Aristophanes creates only types.[30] New Comedy dealt in types; Old Comedy notoriously dealt in individuals, real or invented. And, as we shall see, the problem of the individual is of the utmost importance to Aristophanes' whole idea of drama; it is the individual who embodies the poetic core of his greatest plays.

Among other prejudices to be set aside are a number of half-truths which, though they perpetuate themselves openly for the most part in handbooks, appear as ground assumptions in the work of many critics. These statements concern what is thought to be the regular form of Old Comedy, and sometimes they are even pressed into service to reconstruct its archetype, or *Urform*. It is said that an Aristophanic comedy follows always the same general shape, to wit: an old countryman, faced with a dilemma, conceives an idea, and goes off on a quest in order to achieve it; he is opposed by the chorus (usually), and there follows the agon, in which he is successful, whereupon he sets up a whole new regime; then, after the parabasis, various "impostors" enter, and try to share in the benefits of the new scheme, but are beaten off by the hero, who concludes the play with a celebration, usually a marriage (*gamos*).[31] Not to say that there is no truth at all in this formula, yet one should observe that it is followed in any strict sense in only four of the extant eleven plays (no fragments of the other comic poets are extensive enough to establish their structure). These are the *Acharnians*, *Peace*, *Birds*, and *Ecclesiazusae*; in the last the series of impostors is lacking. Indeed, these impostors are by no means very much in evidence; they are clearly recognizable as such only in the *Acharnians*, *Birds*, and *Plutus*. Elsewhere there are representative types or individuals who have a legitimate claim or complaint, like the creditors in the *Clouds*, the plaintiffs in the *Wasps*, the armorers of the *Peace*, or the hostesses of the *Frogs*, and they should not be called impostors simply because they get no satisfaction, or because Old Comedy is supposed to have impostors.

As for the quest and the agon, some modification is needed here, too. If a quest is a journey into the unknown in search of an object of faith, then it can be found, strictly speaking, in only three plays, *Peace*, *Birds*, and *Frogs*. In the others, there is, of course, a big idea, or a big effort, and one might see the struggles of Dicaeopolis or Lysistrata as quests of a kind; but the term is hardly appropriate either to the *Clouds* or the *Wasps*, where another quite different comic notion has supervened. These two plays also illustrate the fact that the big effort is not always successful, and so does the *Thesmophoriazusae*. For indeed, the agon, like the quest, in Aristophanes is often handled with great flexibility, nor does it by any means always serve to put the hero in a triumphant position before the parabasis; it does so, in fact, only in the *Acharnians*, *Peace*, and *Birds*, the three which more than any others are built around a central hero.[32] In the *Knights* the contest continues throughout almost the whole play; in the *Frogs* and *Thesmophoriazusae* it becomes the action of the whole second half; in the *Clouds* it comes very late, as a set piece; in the *Wasps* it achieves only a partial success. In the *Lysistrata* it takes the form of two choruses contending intermittently throughout, while the *Ecclesiazusae* has no agon at all, unless the struggle of the hags and the girl for the young man be one. The *Plutus* reverts more or less to the "regular" form, but the agon is not crucial to the plot, and the figure of Poverty is admittedly, for once, an allegorical one, suited to Middle Comedy. Similarly too, only four plays, *Acharnians*, *Peace*, *Birds*, and *Lysistrata*, end with a true *gamos* or marriage, though the *Knights*, whose ending is lost, may have had one.

Finally, the old countryman, supposedly ever the same, actually varies considerably, and is not to be found at all in *Lysistrata*, *Frogs*, or *Ecclesiazusae*. Dicaeopolis and Trygaeus are much alike, it is true, but the dull Strepsiades is not to be identified with that sharp, inventive old paranoiac Philocleon. Mnesilochus and Demos represent still different, and less central, uses of the type, while in Peithetaerus the type reaches a climactic development which sets him quite apart. Moreover, it is never said or hinted that Peithetaerus is a countryman, but rather that he is all too much an Athenian. With these reservations, however, it may be allowed that the old countryman is a prevalent character in Aristophanes, and it should be observed that he is most pivotal to three plays: *Acharnians, Peace,* and *Birds.* These same three, it will be remembered, are also the ones which fulfilled most clearly the hypothetical "regular" form of Old Comedy, in the matter of the agon, the impostors, and the closing marriage. Whether or not there is an *Urform* to be recognized here, there is *a* form, and it will be found in succeeding chapters that this is also the form in which the idea of comic heroism is most completely dramatized. But there are other shapes as well, or at least important variations, which show that Aristophanes was not bound to only one.

Certain other habitual assumptions also can bear revision. We have become accustomed, for instance, to the picture of Aristophanes as a passionate conservative, agrarian and pacifistic, inexorably poking fun at everything new, whether political, intellectual, or artistic, contrasting the simple innocence of the country with the city's corrupt tumult, and striving constantly for peace. The love of peace is something which is inherent in civilized man, and it ran deep in Aristophanes, of course; but it should be remembered that no one can celebrate more fervently than he the wars which made Athens great.[33] His response to the countryside is indeed fresh, his descriptions of it lyrically tender and precise. But Aristophanes is also the most urbane of poets, a lover, and not merely observant critic, of Athens, and the masterly play which most fully exhibits his love of nature ends in the creation of a new and divine city. However comedy may have originated, partially at least, in rural celebrations, in its developed form it is the child of the city and the country, and cannot do without either; one could not imagine a man more bored than Aristophanes if he were forced to live exclusively amid the rustic joys which he praises so handsomely.

As for his conservatism, it is surely a comic convention, and it has been well pointed out that in Aristophanes the old is not always the right by any means, and that it is a new idea which regularly carries the day.[34] His attitude toward the rhetoric, philosophy, and music of his own generation has been shown to be not nearly so hostile as appears on the surface; indeed he seems to have had considerable technical knowledge of them all, a knowledge turned, no doubt, to parodic purposes, but betraying a man quite abreast of his time.[35] As for the new tragedy, he had at least enough in common with Euripides so that old Cratinus could coin the magnificent compound, to "Euripidaristophanize," [36] and it has been urged, in an argument strongly appealing to common sense, that Aristophanes was in fact very fond of Euripides.[37] Conservatism is a highly serviceable pose for one who wishes to wield, without seeming to, the powerful weapons of demagogic persuasion, even as it was an almost inevitable gambit for the clever speaker in a law court to protest his total ignorance of rhetoric.

There is much to be said, indeed, for the idea that Aristophanes, far from being a party-line conservative, was really permeated by the same spirit of demagoguery which he damned as so ruinous. The case, at least, has been put as follows:

The poet, who fought passionately against the deterioration of democracy brought about by demagogic leaders, was himself a demagogue. Frequently he used the very methods for which he blamed the political leaders — denunciation, overpraise, and appeal to the greed of the people. Witty and serious, rude and flattering, filled with fantasy and with emotion, Aristophanes, whom once again we take as the representative and the very culmination of Old Comedy, is one of the greatest seducers in all the history of literature. Even in his early comedies, when he was little more than a boy, his genius led him far beyond the stage of mere fun-making, however gorgeous. Comedy is permeated by the same spirit as that which led the people to the decisions about Mytilene, about the victors of Arginusae and about Socrates. It is this spirit of demagogy which persuaded the citizens to consider it intolerable if they were not allowed to do exactly as they pleased, even to the extent of cancelling laws and decrees sanctioned by themselves. It is the spirit which turned the sovereign people into a tyrant proud of not being accountable to anyone, either as jurymen or in the assembly. In the end, the people became the fool of their own sovereignty, and democracy was undermined for the sake of democratic principles.[38]

This view may be a little extreme, but there is much truth in it. If it fails to take account of Aristophanes' humane magnanimity as a poet, it nonetheless places him firmly in the intellectual context to which he belongs, and it recognizes his full comic duplicity about his stated and apparent values.

From the present attempt to reappraise him, it should appear that Aristophanes, far from having interest in inculcating any values, political or moral, created, as a poet ought, a myth of his own times, a myth which simultaneously required and transcended the methods, however devious, which contributed to its making. To create myth out of contemporary materials, without benefit of historical hindsight, demands that a poet think with his time, albeit with greater clarity and intensity; his understanding must then find expression in poetic terms symbolically inclusive enough to maintain the constituents of his vision in suspension, that they all may coexist in a fantastic counterimage of reality. Whether or not Old Comedy is a sound historical source for the study of fifth-century Athenian society, in Aristophanes' hands it is a powerful refractor of that society, more truthful, perhaps, about the passionate inner drives and aspirations than about the political or economic details; more concerned, at its best, with spiritual wholeness, as all true classic art is, than with moralizing about parts. Its mode is one of bursting generosity; it seems to use anything that comes to hand. Large sprays of wit, satire, slapstick, lyric, whimsy, realism, obscenity, and sheer nonsense come tumbling out in bacchanalian abundance, and in the midst of the cheerful tumult, it is vain, not to say absurd, to try to catch the poet, unmask him, and make him say his moral catechism. The effort to do so always leads to the same maddening and irresistible figure who avers that he is the best influence in Greece, constantly improving his fellow citizens by defending them from demagogues, sophists, and Euripides, and feeding them on the finest comic fare conceivable, in contrast to the vulgar and poverty-stricken offerings of his less fortunate rivals. This is what he says, and he would probably consider it one of his finest triumphs if he could know that Robert Browning took him seriously, or that sedulous professors were rooting about in his works, trying to pin down the essence of those prayerful and uplifting benefits to which he lays such bare-faced claim. If we could catch the poet, we ought, if we wish to learn something about him, to ask him a different question, as Plato did in the *Symposium.* Plato asked him to define love, and for answer he received a myth, mingled of Empedocles, impertinence, and hiccups, yet embodying a wistfully hilarious image of human desire. Even if Plato made it all up, as he probably did, it shows that he knew his man and the kind of language he spoke. Nor did Plato undervalue that language, if the memorial epigram attributed to him be genuinely his:

> The Graces, seeking a precinct imperishable,
> Found it in the spirit of Aristophanes.[39]

Grace, *charis*, is indeed a word often applied to Aristophanes in antiquity.[40] Sometimes it seems to mean simply "cleverness," but it could not be totally divested of its overtones of intellectual and spiritual refinement, urbanity, and artistic mastery. As here used, at all events, it seems to imply more than the keen satirist; rather the artist as a whole. Aristophanes is the grand master of satire, no doubt, yet only perhaps in the *Knights* is the satirical element really the preponderant one. In all the other plays satire becomes caught up in a more inclusive comic structure, and one must look beyond the satirist — as well as the moralist — if the real *charis* of Aristophanes is to appear. One must seek the fantasy, the comic myth, in all its rich complexity and embracingness; in short, one must read the poet.

Certain problems which are related to a study of Old Comedy must here be set aside; for instance, its origins. Highly important as this question is, its controversial nature demands that it be treated, if at all, in great detail, which space does not permit. Clear and certain knowledge on the subject would doubtless throw much light on the conventions of Aristophanes' art, and thus contribute to literary understanding. The lack of such knowledge, however, and the variety of existing theory, render the whole question of origins irrelevant here, and nothing will be said about it, beyond occasional notice of comedy's undisputed connection with some kind of fertility ritual.[41] Another, and even more tempting, subject which must be eschewed is theory of comedy. Although it is hoped that some general view of Aristophanes' art will take shape, there will be no attempt to evolve a comprehensive doctrine of comedy which would fit everything from the fifth century B.C. to the present, least of all to explore the psychology of laughter, and say what the comic is. Much has been written on these topics, and some of it has been helpful in the present study; but the question here is not "What is comedy?" or "Why is Aristophanes funny?" but rather, "What is Aristophanes' power as a poet?" Some generalities will inevitably emerge, but they are not intended to apply beyond the limits of the subject in hand, and where, for brevity, the word "comedy" is used, Old Comedy, often specifically that of Aristophanes, should as a rule be understood. Nor will this book add much, if anything, to the elucidation of historical or personal allusions, or of such problems as the staging of the plays, or the relations between Old Comedy and the state. All these questions have been ably treated; the matter which calls for attention is the purely literary one.

On the other hand, it is impossible to discuss a comedian without all trace of comic theory, or to criticize a literary figure without all reference to his historical context. To assert that fantasy, rather than satire, is the heart of Aristophanes' work requires that one speak of the workings and significance of fantasy; and to deny that Aristophanes was the firm conservative which he has been made out demands that something be said on the positive side about what his relationship was to the world around him. Hence, in the first matter, it will appear that Huizinga's brilliant insight into play as order has been of much help in the understanding of fantasy; so too has Baudelaire's essay on laughter, as well as certain aspects of Dalinian surrealism;[42] while in the second, the attempt to place Aristophanes in his intellectual milieu relies heavily on some recent reappraisals of the spiritual tides of the fifth century. Of primary importance to both these aspects of the poet is the concept of the comic hero, to be described in the next chapter. One may well ask in what sense an Aristophanic protagonist is a hero, and not, as has been stated, an anti-hero.[43] Yet he is precisely that, for he is the creative center of the comic fantasy on the one hand, and on the other he is a figure whose motivation, methods, and disposition reflect, in a mythic mode, a great deal of the collective psychology of the age. Even beyond that, the Aristophanic hero embodies something peculiarly Greek, a quality of boundless, magnificent artifice whose exercise amounts to an act of heroic self-fulfillment. In this respect, he parallels, rather than contradicts, his tragic brother, though it must be admitted that while the tragic hero's achievement may properly be called true selfhood, the corresponding term for comedy might be, with Mr. Potter's permission, "supreme selfmanship." This is not quite "selfishness," for that implies concerns too small and methods too direct; "selfmanship" connotes a world-encountering wholeness, complete with every kind of deviousness and audacious grasp.

One of the most revealing commentaries on this kind of comic heroism is to be found in the deathless hero of the popular modern Greek shadow theater, a certain Karaghiozes, whose significance will be described in what is to follow. Here be it said only, in reply to possible objections to the use of a modern Greek cultural phenomenon as a key to anything ancient, that there is a growing tendency to recognize the continuity of Greek culture from its beginnings to the present, especially as regards popular psychology. The belief that some radical changes in the ethnic composition of Greece, which took place during the Middle Ages, rendered such continuity impossible is not really tenable.[44] It is perhaps irrelevant that the creators of classical culture were a mixed people; the point is that ethnic purity ought not, in any case, to be regarded as a decisive factor in the maintenance of a cultural tradition. Greek civilization has assuredly undergone varying fortunes, but it has preserved its resilience and remained Greek; so that some scholars, at least, are turning with confidence to the contemporary Greek world in search of survivals from ancient times, whether of custom, idiom, temperament, or literary form.[45] In the case of the shadow theater, direct survival has been claimed, but doubtless mistakenly; what can be shown, however, is that Karaghiozes himself, though Turkish in name and origin, is the incarnation of a kind of comic heroism which is natively Greek, akin to, and in all likelihood derived from ancient tradition, albeit through very indirect channels. The support for this statement involves some rather specialized discussion, and it seemed best to place it in an appendix. But whether the truth be that there is any connection between Karaghiozes and ancient comedy, or simply that a fortuitous, but palpable resemblance between them may be legitimately used as a critical foil, the comparison may lead to some insight into the psychology of Aristophanes' times, and the conception of a popular hero whose combination of native wits and tenacity to life equips him somehow to become a symbol of national survival.

Of ancient Greek popular songs and entertainments little enough survives, but even that little bears out their kinship with comedy. In the next chapter we shall observe certain literary forebears of the comic hero, which seem to be at least as important for comedy's artistic development as its cultic origins, whatever they may have been. But certain fragments of a less literary nature, such as children's songs, drinking songs, and riddles, also played a part in the luxuriant growth of comedy. The parody of a famous riddle in the Wasps is well known.[46] The miscellaneous lists, so frequently found in Aristophanes, particularly lists of foods to be recited trippingly to the gratification of insatiable gastric drives, find their parallels in certain parlor games, where guests upon command must enumerate, in verse, as many things as they can within a stated category. Athenaeus quotes several examples, for instance, in the category of food:

> Pease porridge, lentil-soup, salt-fish, fresh fish, turnip,
> Garlic, meat, tunny-steak, salt, onion,
> Cardoon, olive, capers, iris-bulb, mushroom.[47]

One thinks at once, of course, of the endless supplies of food in the *Knights,* or the seventy-nine-syllable word for hash which closes the *Ecclesiazusae*; but also of other miscellanies, such as the activities in the Piraeus on the outbreak of war, described in the *Acharnians,* or the overwhelming catalogue of ladies' cosmetic articles in one of the fragments.[48]

Such childlike reveling in abundance and plurality has its erotic side too: the sexual readiness of Aristophanes' heroes, especially perhaps of Dicaeopolis with his two wenches at once, is echoed in a drinking song:

> A pig gets an acorn, and longs to get another;
> I've got a pretty girl, and long to get another.[49]

One recalls also the parody of the Megarian decree, which was written, says the poet, "like a drinking song," by which he means a well-known scolion of Timocreon.[50] The use of ithyphallic and phallophoric motifs is obvious, and perhaps dictated by cult considerations; [51] but one finds also that in many of the lyrics, especially those celebrating spring, the freshness of feeling, the mood of blessing, combined with an easy slipping into jest, find their nearest parallel in children's festival poems, like the Swallow Song, or the *Eiresione*.[52] Indeed, Aristophanes' much admired lyrical genius must have been formed to no small degree by the traditional songs of the people. A closer study might reveal much more, but it is perhaps enough to have pointed here to the popular songs, with their everyday concerns of food, animals, kitchenware, slander, and sex, as having added sundry patches to the motley of the comic muse.

But the hero claims first attention, for it is he who directs and controls the dramatic action, at least as a rule, giving it whatever coherence it has. As said earlier, he is not always the same, nor is his course of action always crowned with perfect success. At his most satisfying, he is wonderfully successful at accomplishing his bold and circuitous plan; but he can be just as funny, and perhaps just as representative, when the plan misfires, capsizing his imposture and reducing him to a fumbler. In that case, he is probably no longer to be called a hero; yet the heroic aspiration is there, and that is what counts, for though not all dreams come true, they are nonetheless the stuff that we are made on. We must first examine the hero in a general way, and in relation to some literary figures to whom he is akin; thereafter in his various dramatic avatars, in the context of individual fantasies with their controlling ideas and images.

COMIC HEROISM

As noted earlier, it is frequently said that Aristophanes' conservative agrarian beliefs are embodied in a recurrent character, the old countryman, and that this character is always essentially the same; and it was further observed that there is reason to doubt both the conservatism and the consistent sameness of the character. It cannot be denied that in many of the plays there occurs an elderly Athenian, of simple habits and sometimes simple mind, drawn very much to the pattern of the small farmer, and that this character seems to be a stable point in the teeming and variegated world which the poet paints. That Aristophanes was in sympathy with these figures is obvious; he drew them *con amore*. In the *Wasps*, for instance, he lavished on Philocleon some of his finest poetic invention, so that as a character he is by far the most vivid and individual of them all. But he is also least able to bear the weight of a serious message from his maker. What is the poet trying to teach us in the figure of a crusty old juror who gets cajoled, tricked, and bribed by his son to leave jury duty and enter high society, and does so, only to achieve a return of youth in the form of extreme pugnacious inebriation?

Philocleon symbolizes much, but he will not do as a mouthpiece for the poet. There seems to be, in fact, no evidence that the "smallfarmer" protagonist served as mouthpiece with any great regularity. In the *Acharnians*, it is true, Dicaeopolis steps out of character momentarily and recounts the law suit which had been brought against Aristophanes the previous year as if it had happened to himself; [1] but it would be as unsafe to conclude that Aristophanes means everything that Dicaeopolis says, as it would be to accept as sober truth some of the hair-raising assertions which occur in many a parabasis. Whatever these characters have in common, it is something different from a consistent moral platform. Morality implies limit, and Aristophanes' affinities are all with the limitless. True *joie de vivre* knows no bounds, and whatever sorrows or wistfulnesses are also implicit in the comedies — and they are numerous — there is always the illimitable, libidinous *joie de vivre*, transcending and glorifying the multifarious potpourri of comic experience, redeeming legions of bad puns from their native vapidness, and transforming the most unmentionable coarsenesses about sex and other bodily functions into an unoffending vision of hilarious nature. No holds are barred, and that is part of the secret; for had there been anything at which Aristophanes would have stopped — or even hesitated — the rest would have been inexcusable. It is the very extremity of shamelessness that puts it beyond shame.

For us today, who have had the advantage of admiring the unexceptionable life of Victoria and Albert, there may be a barrier or two. We may be shocked; or we may, if we are too tough to be shocked, make the worse mistake of accepting "dirt for dirt's sake." For example, the *Lysistrata* is periodically revived, usually as an example of high-class Greek pornography — a gravely erroneous misreading of one of Aristophanes' most delicate and charming texts. Pornography lurks, insinuates, and ambushes the sensibilities. There is nothing lurking or insinuating about Aristophanes. He is simply roaring out the facts of life, but lest he seem limited by the facts as they are, he sometimes invents a few new ones, piling Pelions of Gargantuan fantasy on Ossas of common, everyday indecency. It is not, of course, that the Greeks were a happy people with no sense of sin. Modern psychologists come nearer to the truth when they point out that there is a release of the spirit to be found in the periodic smashing of taboos, as it can be observed in the Times of Misrule, such as the Roman Saturnalia, the medieval parodies of the Mass, or the Greek festivals of Dionysus.

But Aristophanes' bawdry — or whatever it should be called — is not the essence of the matter; it serves merely to illustrate vividly the poet's devotion to the limitless, that kind of world view which, as said earlier, is almost the exact opposite of what we term morality. Boundlessness itself, one might say, is the essence of the Aristophanean comic impulse; and if that statement appears vague and undefined, perhaps it will, if kept in reserve, find qualification and meaning through some of the arguments to follow.

The heroes of Aristophanes are, more often than not, successful in their great schemes, and the successful ones must be our first concern. Each success is, presumably, to be regarded as the achievement of some kind of good, but what good, and whose, except the hero's own, is sometimes hard to say. Moreover, these triumphs evolve in extremes and excesses which would make Aristotle quiver.[2] In the *Acharnians* the hero's ultimate exploit is to win a first in the Feast of Cups, the yearly drinking contest, which was a favorite feature of the Anthesteria; and as he staggers off to collect his prize, supported by two wenches, the chorus follows him with hallelujahs. In the *Knights* the Sausage Seller is victorious in a contest of vileness, and proves his supremacy by outstripping Cleon in the attractive accomplishments of vulgarity, demagoguery, and bribery. The *Clouds* is a difficult play, in view of the confusion arising between the earlier, lost version and the one which we have; however the earlier one ended, our version ends with the hero, in whatever mood of regeneration and repentance, explicitly rejecting the idea of due legal process and squaring accounts by an act of premeditated arson, performed with the good will of Hermes, god of rogues. At the end of the *Wasps* the aged Philocleon, who has been persuaded to relax and enjoy life, has got magnificently drunk at a symposium, abducted the flute girl, and made his way home with her, punching people all the way. Trygaeus in the *Peace* marries

Opora, a divine figure representing the plentiful harvest, having obtained her by an act specifically forbidden by traditional Greek morality — namely, flying to heaven. But the supreme, climactic victory over all limits comes in the *Birds,* when the hero deposes Zeus and takes over the universe. After the *Birds,* things change; the comic potential begins to shrink, and the remaining plays do not have heroes in the same sense. But these six figures are perhaps enough to demonstrate that the comic hero's achievement is not of the sort which is usually called moral, but is an assertion, in one way or another, of boundlessness, a dethronement of limit, of reason, and even of the gods themselves.

Consistency is a virtue appropriate to philosophy, and Socrates was justifiably proud that his assertions about the same things were always the same.[3] But consistency may also be, as Emerson suggested, the "hobgoblin of small minds," and a truly fertile text for the study of Aristophanes might be that of Walt Whitman: "Do I contradict myself? Very well, I contradict myself; I am large, I contain multitudes."[4] One misses the largeness of Aristophanes unless one appreciates his gift for self-contradiction. After all, he must not be limited. And though, one might say, a pure consistency is perhaps the surest road to excess, the excess which an Aristophanean hero pursues cannot be one-sided, doctrinaire, or philosophical. Aristophanes has been called anti-philosophic, but he is more supra-philosophic. He is seeking to *include;* his ubiquitous negativities aim, indeed, at reducing to absurdity the phenomena of life, but not so much in themselves, as in the broad light of an experience which includes and transcends them. Old Comedy, according to an ancient anonymous writer, employed the "compelling and elevated kind of language" (τὸ δεινὸν καὶ ὑψηλὸν τοῦ λόγου), and it did so for a reason.[5] For Old Comedy is a heroic form. However it may comprise political or social satire and all the rest, these do not define it; they can, and do, exist in other forms. It is the heroic dimension, and the nature of the comic hero, which are decisive, and demand the grand style. Now whatever is heroic is individualistic, and tends toward excess, or at least extremes. It asserts its *self* primarily, and formulates its action and experience in isolation from society as such, and in relation only to the universe at large, whence its metaphysical implications. This unity of self-conception and self-assertion gives to the heroic spirit a kind of purity, but hardly what we would call consistency, for at any moment the hero may flout all expectation in deference to the private mysteries of his own will. He is, one might say, consistent with himself; but since he creates himself as he goes, the result cannot be foreknown, even perhaps by himself. Heroism is, one might say, "inner-directed," and though the directions may differ, the principle holds: appearances sometimes to the contrary, no abstraction ever controls the hero in quest of wholeness. And that is precisely what Aristophanes' heroes are.

It might be urged that these statements confound the fundamental distinction between comedy and the legitimate vehicles of heroic experience, tragedy and epic. Aristotle's view was that tragedy imitates the action of men greater than the norm, comedy that of men inferior to it. That may be true, but the point here is not the moral or even human worth of the hero; the point is his inner structure, and in this respect there is little to distinguish a hero of Aristophanes from one of Sophocles or Homer. Perhaps for this reason it is so natural for him to parody tragic heroes; he shares their largeness, their excessiveness, their representative individualism. His heroism may differ in content or in kind, but not in essential shape. As a kind of Everyman, he uses the grand style in his own right; it is appropriate to his nature, for the grand style is wayward, and seems to invent its own rules as it goes.

So too, the comic hero himself is wayward, and abides by no rules except his own, his heroism consisting largely in his infallible skill in turning everything to his own advantage, often by a mere trick of language. He is a great talker. Dicaeopolis' rags and rhetoric, borrowed from Euripides and the Sophists, Agoracritus' ferocious boastings, and the deft word play by which Peithetaerus wins over the birds are tokens of the comic hero's will and ability to use all things to his end. Whatever great good is supposed to arise from his actions, they are regularly motivated by a powerful, self-centered individualism, and once in command, the hero has no inclination to share his eminence with anyone. Dicaeopolis, whose name means "man of public justice," abandons the general public of Athens in disgust, and embarks on a course which for sheer individualism could scarcely be matched, a private peace with Sparta for himself and his family. He is very exclusive about it, as the chorus remarks:

> This man has made his treaty,
> And finds much sweetness there;
> As for the rest of us, he shows
> Small inclination to share.[6]

This and similar scenes illustrate the hero's unblushing determination to have things his own way. It is a mistake to reckon those who wish to share in the benefits as always "impostors," all the "wrong" sort, while the hero is entirely the "right" sort. To do so is to force the protagonist into too direct and simple a kind of goodness, and to forget that he and the "impostors" have much in common.

In his book on the origins of Old Comedy, Francis Cornford made great use of the two terms *eiron* and *alazon*, meaning respectively the man who pretends to less knowledge or power than he has, and the man who pretends to more. For Cornford, the comic hero was an *eiron*, an ironical buffoon who, by a pretense of dull-witted helplessness, manages to put to flight the boastful and pretentious *alazones*, or impostors, who seek to take part in his regime. The distinction is based solidly on a passage in Aristotle which foreshadows the *Characters* of Theophrastus, and there can be no doubt that in the fourth century the two ideas, or characters, were distinctly opposed.[7] Now one may find moments of ironical buffoonery in Aristophanes, for instance where Dicaeopolis pretends to cower before the apparition of the general Lamachus, but there seems to be more than irony involved, if one takes into account Dicaeopolis' total action. Is the man who makes a private peace treaty, to the baffled admiration of all, less of an *alazon*, or desperate impostor, than Lamachus? It is true, Dicaeopolis succeeds in his monstrous imposition, but only because he is allowed to do so by the poet, within the world of impossible happiness which exists for the hero alone. The irony of the comic hero, from one point of view, is merely a means to a greater and more inclusive *alazoneia*, impostorship; so that one might say that there is no real *eiron*, but only a variety of *alazones*, and the biggest fraud wins, on the theory that if the fraud be carried far enough, into the limitless, it becomes a template of a higher truth. Peithetaerus has few or no qualities of an *eiron*; but he is the most magnificent of impostors. Actually the word *eiron* occurs only once in Aristophanes, and then it is used in such close connection with *alazon* that the two clearly refer to the same kind of achievement. Strepsiades, hopefully entering the Thinkery of Socrates, says he will become

> An elusive ironical (εἴρων) slippery impostor (ἀλαζών),
> A difficult filthy twister of jibes.[8]

At bottom, the *eiron* and *alazon* are very similar, both looking out for their advantage, and neither much devoted to simple truth. It is a mistake to confuse the irony of the comic hero with that of Plato's Socrates, though Socrates, clearly and often, made use of it to get the better of his opponent, and not seldom with subtle comic effect. For the irony of Socrates leads the opponent, at least theoretically, toward ultimate submission before a philosophic logos; the irony of a comic hero leads to his own swaggering triumph over all reason or opposition, in the name of an impudent self which has become liberated from all small restraints of consistency or responsibility. The mere buffoon, says Aristotle, makes fun for the sake of getting a laugh from others; the ironical man makes fun for his own amusement, which is more worthy of a free man.[9] This is somewhat the case with the irony of the comic hero: he does everything for his own reasons, but his freedom from everything including morality is not quite what Aristotle meant. Hence this irony passes into *alazoneia* of a new sort, grand, excessive, and imperious.

There is good reason to think that the qualities of imagination and cunning went hand in hand with heroic courage as being the most admired traits among the ancient Greeks. The combination made practically the perfect man, and Homer's "doer of deeds and speaker of words" [10] doubtless does not exclude entirely the verbal dexterity which is so noticeable in Aristophanic heroes. Craft, and persuasiveness of speech, are means to achieving mastery, and if the comic hero is, in a way, merely the greatest and most successful of impostors, it is due to his imagination and his unscrupling cleverness, rather than to any higher gifts of courage or nobility. He begins as a little, ordinary fellow, to grow by his own absurd ingenuity into the great master of all, even a new Zeus. His royal progress varies to a degree according to the terms of the plot, but it is regularly a victory of shameless cunning and self-assertion over lesser and more stupid forms of much the same thing, of a Great and Representative Impostor over more partial and limited ones. It will be relevant to scan briefly some of the models to which Aristophanes might have looked in shaping his comic protagonist.

The spirit of consummate, individual, and perhaps rascally cleverness is traceable in much early literature, often combined with the loftier traditions of the heroes and the gods. One thinks at once of Odysseus, "knowing in all kinds of wiles and shrewd designs." [11] Ancient Greek did not, it appears, have any one word to express picaresque roguishness carried to heroic extremes, and the words for deviousness and craft are by no means always complimentary. Yet they could be so used, as in the line just quoted, where Helen is speaking of Odysseus with admiration. A better example is Athena's ironic, but approving, speech to the hero in the Thirteenth *Odyssey*:

> Crafty and cunning would he be indeed, whoever could outstrip
> You in all manner of trickery, even if a god should contend!
> Rascal, devious-minded, stuffed with guile! You would not
> Even in your own land leave off your deceptions
> And lying words, which are rootedly native to you.[12]

Athena's tone is bantering, but there is no mistaking the value she places on her favorite's gifts as a liar; she even goes on to say that in this respect he is among mortals what she is among the gods. One of the words which she uses is *kerdaleos*, which, together with its noun *kerdos* and other compounds thereof, implies both trickery and gainful advantage, and is very common in contexts of reproach.[13] Its transvaluation here arises simply from the point of view; Athena is on Odysseus' side, so that what elsewhere might be condemned as viciousness wins praise as a triumphant art.

Aristophanes, in similar fashion, is capable of reversing the ordinary implications of such a word, for example, πονηρός, "wicked." Generally used to condemn all sorts of delinquency, in the *Knights* the word becomes the touchstone of salvation and victory. Demosthenes and Nicias find a low sausage seller and tell him of the high destiny which, according to an oracle, awaits the man who can exceed the Paphlagonian Cleon in villainy:

S. S.:   But tell me, how shall I,
        A Sausage Seller, turn into a man?
Dem.:   Just for that very fact you shall be great,
        For you are a villain (πονηρός), right off the street, and brash.[14]

Somewhat later, in a violent exchange with Cleon, the Sausage Seller boasts that he need not yield to Cleon, for he himself is also a "villain," (*poneros*) and the chorus, cheering him on, cries "And if he won't yield to that, tell him you're also the son of villains." [15]

Such a use of the word may seem peculiar to the special circumstances of this play, where Aristophanes, unwontedly savage in his invective, sees the progress of demagoguery as fatally doomed to lower and lower depths of abomination. But there are examples where *poneros* seems to lose its overtones of real evil and imply something more like "cleverness," for instance where Philocleon in the *Wasps* is prevented from leaving the house by clinging to the underside of the donkey, like Odysseus escaping from the Cyclops' cave. His son's remark seems to acknowledge the old fellow's inventiveness: "You're a bad one (*poneros*), a past master, and a rogue." [16] The father's retort takes *poneros* in the more regular sense, but Bdelycleon's remark seems mild, and even a little admiring. One might compare the implications of skill as well as unscrupulousness in what the Unjust Discourse says of Hyperbolus' villainy, which gained him many talents; [17] or even better, though the word *poneros* does not occur, the Hoopoe's warm commendation of Peithetaerus in the *Birds*, all in terms of abuse used ordinarily to describe conycatchers:

> The subtlest, cunningest fox,
> All scheme, invention, craft; wit, wisdom, paradox.[18]

Such usages, especially of *poneros*, seem to foreshadow the modern Greek word *poneria*, which best expresses what the heroes of Aristophanes are up to. *Poneria* in modern Greek indicates not wickedness, but the ability to get the advantage of somebody or some situation by virtue of an unscrupulous, but thoroughly enjoyable exercise of craft. Its aim is simple — to come out on top; its methods are devious, and the more intricate, the more delightful. Moralists might disapprove of them, but the true *poneros* knows that they are justified by that heroic end so dear to every Greek — the joy of victory, "even for an eggshell." *Poneria* is wonderfully useful in politics, business, love-making, and family fights. Far from concealing its triumphs, one boasts of them; for though the word may be translated simply "cleverness," it also connotes high skill in handling those challenging aspects of life in which the agonistic tendencies of Greek psychology find a field of enterprise. It connotes further the qualities of protean resourcefulness and tenacity of purpose, and with all the world to gain, it can afford to dispense with any superfluous high-mindedness. Yet it has its own kind of transcendence, if one recalls that the isolated, helpless individual of the prologue to the *Acharnians* finishes by sweeping all resistance before him.[19]

One would like to know more about the tradition from which this kind of character comes. In modern times one may find an approximation in Falstaff, perhaps, and the figure of the Redeeming Rogue appears now and then, as in Azdak, the venal and whimsical judge in Brecht's *Caucasian Chalk Circle*. But it is less easy to discern the ancient sources. Protean resourcefulness combined with tenacity of purpose appear in the interchange between Odysseus and Athena quoted earlier, and certainly these qualities are in Odysseus, though they are not developed primarily for comic purposes. One does not, in fact, find the Aristophanean hero outside of Aristophanes; but one finds traces of some of his qualities scattered throughout the earlier literature in contexts which, to be sure, are not always comic; yet these traces suggest that when comedy developed as an art in the fifth century, it gathered to itself many themes, attitudes, and situations already existent in a variety of forms. One may leave aside the contents of Dorian mime, Megarian farce, and other popular entertainments which may have been included in the ancestry of Old Comedy, for these are of little help toward understanding the hero, who belongs with the grand tradition.

To continue with the *Odyssey*, as Athena took pleasure in Odysseus' wiliness, so also Odysseus takes pleasure in Penelope's, in the scene where she extracts gifts from the suitors. The passage has a number of levels, and is psychologically one of the profoundest moments in the poem, but what strikes Odysseus is his wife's *poneria*:

> So she spoke, and divine long-suffering Odysseus
> Rejoiced, that she got gifts from them, and bewitched their spirits
> With sweet words, while her mind had other intentions.[20]

The hero who invented the trick of "No-man" to fool the Cyclops might well appreciate the result of Penelope's little imposture. The phrase about her mind's ulterior intentions recalls her trick with the weaving, by which she had fooled the suitors for no less than three years. Penelope's actions are not, in either case, comic, but Odysseus' response to what he deems her deliberate guile is akin to the comic reaction.

The greatest exploitation of *poneria* in the epic corpus is, of course, the great *Hymn to Hermes*, god of rogues. Deviltry for its own sake, or rather, deviltry with an eye to ultimate mastery, could scarcely find a better paradigm than the story of how Hermes, the very day he was born, leaped out of his cradle and stole the cows of his illustrious brother Apollo. He was, so to speak, to the manner born:

> Then she [Maia] bore a child of many devices, crafty-minded,
> Robber, and rustler of cattle, conductor of dreams,
> Watcher by night and lurker by gates, who was presently destined
> To show forth wonderful deeds among the immortal gods.[21]

First, he invents the lyre, and there is a high comic, visionary quality about the words in which he apostrophizes the waddling tortoise, of whose shell he will make the sounding board: "Hail lovely-shaped companion at the feast, who strikes up the dance!" [22] He sees it already as that which it will presently become, somewhat as the Aristophanean hero, once the great conception has formed in his mind, transforms everything he encounters. The lyre complete, the god sings to its accompaniment, improvising "as young men do exchanging taunts at a banquet," and with a comic hero's characteristic self-centeredness, he sings of his own engendering and birth.[23] But all the while "his mind had other intentions."

And now the real *poneria* begins. At sunset he starts for Pieria, where Apollo pastured his cattle, selects fifty, and drives them off backwards, so that their hoofprints will appear to be going the other way, while on his own feet he ties some newly invented sandals of wicker work, designed to obscure his tracks. Arrived at the Alpheus river, he proceeds to slaughter two of the cows, and roasts them in twelve equal portions in honor of the twelve gods, of whom he himself is one. Then he returns to the cave of his birth, and gets back into his cradle. His mother scolds him for roaming around at night, "clothed in shamelessness," [24] and Hermes replies from his swaddlings, "Why do you scold me as if I were a little baby that knows very little?" He then reveals his motive for the theft. As long as he stays in the cave, he is without honor or account; the robbery asserts his claim upon a share in the world:

> Better to spend our days in converse with the immortals,

> Than sit in a mouldy cave; I will encroach on the sacred
> Honor Apollo possesses, I too.[25]

And if Zeus will not give him such a share, he will go to Delphi and steal everything Apollo owns. The god of truth and moral virtue is not, it appears, to have it all his own way; he must reckon with a dangerous young brother of quite opposite character. But throughout the poem it is Hermes who has all the reader's sympathy, and not least when, confronted by the wrathful Apollo, he shrivels himself down into his swaddling clothes and says: "Do I look like a strong cowhand? My business is milk and suckling, and blankets and warm baths . . . I was born yesterday!" [26] One recalls Dicaeopolis ironically pretending to cringe before the plumes and war gear of Lamachus, while secretly mocking him. And besides the irony and the *poneria*, there is a kind of Aristophanic absurdity in the situation of the infant thief versus the mighty Apollo, an absurdity which is carried to a climax, also Aristophanic in its way, when Apollo picks up Hermes bodily, and is promptly soiled.

The *Hymn* ends with a tactical, rather than an absolute victory for Hermes. Apollo is allowed to recover his dignity, Hermes gives him the lyre, and the two become fast friends. Old Comedy is prone to less civilized solutions, of course, for hilarity dies down when everyone modifies his pretensions, exchanges apologies, and becomes good. What is striking about the *Hymn* is the reveling delight in a clever and wicked exploit, the delight in an overweening *poneria* which sets aside all decorum — not to mention the usual limitations of infancy — flouts morality incarnate in the name of its own will to supremacy, and wins its case, at least in good part, before Zeus and all readers. And if it be objected that the hero is a god, and behaves appropriately to the god of thieves, be it remembered how the old jurors of the *Wasps* recall with wistful relish the days when they showed their young heroic mettle by stealing roasting spits and vine props.[27] Whatever use they may or may not have had for these articles is irrelevant compared with the deed well carried out.

Gay and humorous, the *Hymn to Hermes* offers a kind of archetypal tale of *poneria*; but it is not a joke or a travesty. It is the heroic exploit by which Hermes established his place and honor among the gods, corresponding to the slaying of the Python by Apollo, or Zeus's victory over the Titans. As such, it is part of the serious epic tradition which can on occasion, as in the examples from the *Odyssey*, find room for the appreciation of *kerdosyne*. Even in the somber *Iliad*, at the end of the high-flown, chivalric scene where Diomedes and Glaucus exchange armor, we are told that Diomedes got the better of the bargain in that he got gold armor for bronze, and Glaucus was a fool.[28] Propriety forbade that much be made of this aspect of the encounter, but its mere mention indicates clearly that the epic hero's will to supremacy did not always limit itself as to means, and that in the general tradition, as distinct from the exalted portrait of Achilles, to gain even the most niggling advantage had its satisfactions, since it made one, at least momentarily, superior to others.

The Homeric line "Always to be the best and superior to others" refers, doubtless, to heroic martial achievement in the main; but actually, it says nothing about how one should be superior, and it could be interpreted in terms other than the purely noble. Or, to put it the other way around, *poneria* could also be a form of heroism. The gods themselves, even apart from Hermes, can reflect this aspect of the Greek temperament, and the struggle between Zeus and Prometheus in Hesiod, regarded from the point of view of the methods employed, is a clear example of a contest in *poneria*.[29] It is perhaps significant that Prometheus can also, like the comic hero, become a figure representing human salvation. Indeed, as will appear later, the view of *poneria* as a kind of heroism is likely to arise during any struggle for survival against heavy odds, and it is not confined to literature. The hero of the Second Messenian War, Aristomenes, was famous for his cleverness as well as for his demonic valor; the story is told that once during the war he stole into Sparta by night and hung up a shield in the temple of Athena known as the

Brazen House, with an inscription dedicating it to the goddess and saying that he had captured it from the Spartans.[30] The exploit could have had little military significance, if any; but it points out the satisfaction which the desperate Messenians would take in thinking of the Spartans' livid rage at such boundless impudence. Even if the story is not true, for Aristomenes early became a legend, it nevertheless illustrates something close to the heart of comic heroism and comic victory.

It is a great pity that so little can be known of the *Margites*, the comic epic anciently attributed to Homer. The discovery of what seems to be a papyrus fragment of it has prompted at least two recent attempts at reconstruction, but the character of the hero, along with much else, remains obscure.[31] That he was some kind of fool seems clear, for it is reported that he did not know which of his parents gave him birth.[32] But one scholar reconstructs his folly as having in it a kind of ultimate, Quixotic wisdom, while another believes that, though ignorant in the extreme, he was driven by an overwhelming will to supremacy, and was therefore a kind of heroic failure.[33] It is doubtful if either theory can be proved ultimately, but it is at least probable that Margites was a sympathetic character, and his name, derived apparently from *margos*, rather than *moros*, suggests that his eccentricities were those of a passionate madman, rather than of a nincompoop. If so, then it is also possible that he resembled, to a degree, and foreshadowed some of Aristophanes' visionary lunatics whose sheer single-mindedness permits them somehow to transcend all. But the matter is highly speculative, and we are not even certain whether Margites was a comic victor or a scapegoat. It is tempting to picture him as what the Elizabethans would call a fantastic, with a broad streak of *poneria*, but that, though not out of the question, certainly begs it. Also, had he been in any sense clever, we would probably have heard about it, as we do in accounts of the *Cercopes*.

Aristotle's remarks about the *Margites* put us on firmer ground, however, and offer hints about a different aspect of the growth of comedy which will be relevant later. In the *Iliad* and *Odyssey*, he says, Homer foreshadowed what tragedy was to be, and in the *Margites*, which Aristotle believed to be genuine, he had fore-shadowed comedy; and he had achieved this by relying on what was purely ludicrous (γελοῖον), rather than on satire (ψόγος).[34] The distinction between these two kinds of humor is important for the study of Aristophanes. It is a reminder that Old Comedy does not depend primarily upon satire, political or personal, how-ever large these elements may loom in some of the extant plays, but on something else, something broader and more inclusively ab-surd. Satire, pure and simple, has no heroic dimension. It reduces its targets, but not by including them in a larger vision. The purely ludicrous, however, admits the possibility of heroic exaggeration, or boundless inflation of itself until it engulfs or transforms the world. This point will be further illustrated later, in connection with the meaning of the grotesque. For the moment it is enough to suggest that if the *Margites* was not satiric but "purely ludicrous," as Aristotle says, it may have comprised an element of the heroically comic; if not *poneria*, perhaps a Gargantuan grotesquerie such as is familiar enough in Aristophanes, perhaps something of the in-domitable individualism and self-assertion of the heroes of the *Acharnians* and *Birds*.

But if the *Margites* question is somewhat imponderable, com-edy's connection with the iambic poets is clear enough. Aristotle goes on to say that comedy is a higher art than the iambic lampoon, as tragedy is a higher art than epic, inferring, in his teleological way, that had comedy existed in the earlier days of the iambic poets, Archilochus, Semonides, and Hipponax would have written com-edy instead of satire.[35] Obviously, both comedy and iambic make much use of invective, against persons and situations in general; both use, ostensibly at least, the language of complaint. But be-tween Aristophanes and the greatest of the iambists there are other aspects of poetic affinity which are even more relevant to the present argument.

In antiquity Archilochus was identified with lampoon, but this view is clearly too narrow. Even in the meager fragments which remain there exists a variety little short of marvelous, a kaleidoscope of images betokening a mind peculiarly responsive to the immediacy of things. Such breadth of poetic awareness in itself suggests Aristophanes, but there is a more important factor, namely the kind of individualism which Archilochus represents. Εἰμὶ δ'ἐγώ, he begins, in a fragment which is perhaps a proem, certainly a self-presentation: "I, even I am the servant of Lord Ares, knowing the lovely gifts of the Muses." [36] The lordly air with which he introduces himself sets the tone for his whole self-oriented world. Despite his heavy dependence on the language of Homer, Archilochus is the most personal of poets, for he represents himself in direct relation with everything around him. One pictures him as constantly on a frontier of experience, reacting in splendid isolation to the buffets of fortune, war, the deaths of friends, the beauty of a girl, or betrayal by a comrade. The fragments teem with vignettes, concrete and fresh from the poet's observation: the repulsive chatterbox, the swaggering general, the halcyon bird quivering its wings, the drinking bout on shipboard, the swordsmen of Euboea, the figs of Paros, the courtesan, the uninvited guest, the perfumed hair and breast "enough to make an old man fall in love," the cremation funeral where the fire "toils about the head and graceful limbs of the dead, clothed in pure garments."

Archilochus is seldom really comic, but he consistently refuses to be tragic. His wide spectrum of response to the concrete things of the world suggests the wide, observant eye of Aristophanes, while his gift for denunciation often leads him to imagery which is akin to comedy; so, for example, he compares the silhouette of the island of Thasos to the backbone of an ass, or boasts of leading off the dithyramb when his brains are thunderstruck with wine.[37] He always assumes that his hearers are going to be fascinated by how he feels about something, and it is a dreary soul who is not. Full of the tough endurance that fights through to the end, he is a great believer in life, merriment, and camaraderie — but above all in himself. A plain man, or at least one who represents himself in plain terms, Archilochus is his own hero and his own measure of present experience; he leaves the ultimate view of things to the gods, or fortune, and meanwhile he lives somewhat as Aristophanes' heroes will do, combating his smallness and helplessness by the exercise of imagination, the relish of life, and the use of all his passions, in Christopher Smart's phrase, of which rage was not the least important. For pure *Schadenfreude* the great papyrus fragment might be cited:

> Lost on the sea,
> May the scalp-locked Thracians in kindest mood catch him
> Naked on Salmydessus,
> Where he will feel the fullness of many woes
> Eating the bread of slavery,
> Frozen stiff with cold, and heavily heaped with plentiful
> Seaweed out of the surge,
> His teeth chattering, and lying down like a dog
> Helplessly flat on his face,
> At the margin of the shingle among the waves.
> This I should like to see —
> He who wronged me, and stamped with his heel on our vows,
> He who was once my friend.[38]

In quite a similar vein, Aristophanes prays fervently for the future of a *choregus* who cheated him of a dinner, the unfortunate Antimachus, whom the poet supplies with the attractive patronymic Drivelson, or MacDrool:

> Oh may I see him yearning for octopus,
> Watching it roasting and sizzling salted,
> Coming to port on the festive board!
> And then, when it's just about done,
> And he reaches to get it, let a dog
> Grab it and run![39]

Aristophanes is funnier; Archilochus, one fears, means it literally. But there is the same sublimely self-centered rollicking in the imagery of revenge.

Above all, perhaps, one should point to Archilochus' willingness to overturn accepted standards. There was an occasion when he did not seize the opportunity to die nobly at his post in battle; instead, he threw away his shield, ran, and lived to fight another day, as well as to write some verses on the importance of staying alive.[40] The epigram in which he describes the episode is very famous, and indeed it founded a convention whereby ancient soldier-poets always threw away their shields. For us, the importance lies in the insouciance with which Archilochus reveals the disgraceful deed. It seems rather to confirm his self-respect than to damage it, though one has the feeling that the case would have been different if someone else had lost his shield. In his supreme self-confidence Archilochus can be two opposite things at once. Does he contradict himself? Very well, he contains multitudes.

Aristophanes himself makes use of the shield poem at the end of the *Peace* in a way which well illustrates the comic dissociation about moral values. Peace is restored and Trygaeus is preparing a feast; the son of Lamachus enters singing a martial song and is driven away. Then enters the son of the fat coward Cleonymus, who had lost his shield in battle; the son appropriately sings Archilochus' poem:

> One of the Saians is enjoying that shield of mine,
> Blameless weapon I left beside a bush;
> But I, I saved my life —

whereat Trygaeus breaks in and finishes the line for him: "Yes, and shamed your parents." Then he adds, "Well, come on in." [41] Here is no moral consistency. The shield-loser is admitted to the feast, but is taunted at the same time. Comedy eats its cake and has it too; or to put it another way: *your poneria* is disgraceful, *mine* is beautiful. Selfhood, not principle, is asserted.

As said earlier, the relationship between Old Comedy and iambic poetry is obvious, but the comparison with Archilochus serves to show that they had more in common than invective.[42] Besides the sheer poetic range, the concreteness of detail, and the emphasis on food, drink, and physical experience in general, there is above all the "inner-directed" individualism of the main character, be it Dicae-opolis or Archilochus himself, full of tough durability, self-contradic-tion, and shameless *poneria*. As for Archilochus, his tough dura-bility and self-assertion, as a small man against odds, are far more evident than any real *poneria*; but it is interesting to note also the contents of an inscription recently found in the Archilocheion at Paros, purportedly giving the biography of the poet.[43] It recounts that as a boy he was sent by his father to sell the cow at the local village, and on the way paused to banter with some peasant women; afterwards, when he looked around for the cow, it had disappeared, and a lyre was found in its place. His father sent to Delphi for an explanation, and received the answer that his son would be "im-mortal and famous in song." The inscription is Hellenistic, and the tale is probably a late invention, providing Archilochus with a kind of humorous consecration as a poet, analogous to that of Hesiod at the beginning of the *Theogony*, a favorite Hellenistic theme. What is interesting is that the imagery of the tale uncannily echoes that of the *Hymn to Hermes*, where a lyre is produced as a compensation for lost cattle. Nothing like parody is, of course, suggested; rather the episode suggests an analogy between Archilochus and Apollo, and perhaps a further one between Archilochus and the gay spirit of the *Hymn*.

It is unfortunate that we possess almost nothing of early Greek popular entertainments, for one may conjecture that we would meet therein with more characters of the sort, joyous adventurers prac-ticing "selfmanship" to impossible extremes. A striking analogue in the modern Greek shadow theater, to be taken up presently, sug-gests that the spirit of *poneria* was always a part of Greek tradition, though not always the part selected for preservation by fate and Byzantine editors. It would not, of course, have been regularly, or even often, developed to the degree here termed heroic, nor would it have been identified with any particular genre, necessarily. Rather it would have been diffused throughout various forms of cultural articulation, scarce in the high tradition, frequent no doubt in the lower-pitched forms of iambic, choliambic, popular farce, mime, beast fable, drinking songs, and even the *gnomai*, which, if Hesiod's work contains a fair sample, early took account of the necessity of wariness: "Smile at your brother — and get a witness." [44] It might crop up anywhere. Indeed, the tale of how the early orator Tisias cheated his teacher Corax of the price of lessons in rhetoric, whether true or a fable, is a perfect example of *poneria,* and stands at the beginning of the history of Greek oratory like a motif, which was to find enthusiastic development by the Sophists, both in theory and practice. [45]

Poneria, or whatever it should be called, is important, but it is not the only element in the comic hero's character. It provides the liberating wings, so to speak, but it may not seem sufficient in itself, though supported by the most determined individualism, to justify the term "heroic." There is another aspect, which takes us back once more to Aristotle and his remarks on the comic character. Aristotle said two things, first that comedy aims to represent people as worse than they actually are, and second, that it is a representation of inferior people, whose inferiority consists not of evil, but of ludicrous ugliness, involving distortion, but not pain. [46] One wishes that he had developed his thoughts, especially the second, a little further, for though both statements are applicable enough in a general way to comedy, it is hard to see how either applies to an Aristophanean hero. The poet represents many people as worse than they could possibly have been in actuality — Cleon, especially; and there are plenty of examples of the distortion and ugliness which occasion not pain but laughter. But how would the words apply to Dicaeopolis, Trygaeus, Peithetaerus, or Lysistrata? As invented characters, they cannot be said to be represented as worse than they were; and in what sense are they either ugly or distorted — unless, perhaps, the comic mask itself, to use Aristotle's own example, took care of that feature? As these characters go from victory to victory, they become objects of admiration and envy to the chorus, and the great point, in the last analysis, is not their inferiority, but their superiority. Even the Sausage Seller, though doubtless something of an exaggeration of the vulgarities of Athenian street vendors, is not merely an ugly-mannered fellow; he, too, rises into a figure of redemption, with whatever meaning or dramatic aptness. If the *Margites* were preserved, Aristotle's meaning might be clearer, since he used the poem as an archetype of comedy. Yet, in any case, his words point to the idea of the grotesque, which may help to clarify the comic hero's ambiguities, his "lowness" and his stature, his apparent insignificance and his supernal victory.

The word "grotesque," often used somewhat loosely in comic contexts, has gained a number of meanings since it was coined in Italy, around the end of the fifteenth century, to describe the style of certain Roman wall paintings which were unearthed at that time; the underground chambers where they were found were termed grottoes, and the paintings *grottesche*. They were characterized throughout by a free mixture of representational forms: men with legs of animals or terminating in fronded branches, horses adorned with leaves and having the hind quarters of serpents, winged *putti*, beast-headed men, monstrosities of all sorts deployed in a complex fecundity of designs. The style was imitated, became popular, and introduced into Europe a steadily progressing tradition which has been often studied, recently with great insight by the late German scholar Wolfgang Kayser.[47] Kayser's work, while taking account of the numerous connotations of the grotesque in different times and countries, finds its essence in the dark absurdity of the world viewed coldly as a puppet show. The grotesque is the "figuration of the alienated world," where the categories of our world orientation fail; it is both a "game with the absurd" and "an attempt to ban and subdue the demonic world," whether within the psyche or outside it.[48] Kayser, basing his study on the artistic phenomena of the last three centuries, from Hieronymus Bosch and the younger Brueghel, through the *Sturm und Drang*, to the surrealism of Kafka and Dali, is doubtless right in emphasizing the uncanny, dark incalculables of experience as the true subject of modern grotesquerie. But in antiquity, although certainly the demonic world is involved, its presence is invoked, one feels, not so that it can be banned and subdued, but for a different reason. In the late Roman *grottesche* themselves the minglings of animal, vegetable, and human do not suggest so much neurotic fear of the demonic as participation in it, so that if one traced the history of such forms backward through antiquity, one might discover a quite different implication in the term grotesque. The term still seems permissible, so long as it refers to forms of mixed and unrealistic ancestry.

The *grottesche* style, which arose in the first century B.C., was condemned explicitly by Vitruvius, and implicitly by Horace, on the grounds of its monstrosity and lack of relation to reality.[49] Official Augustan taste tended to follow Peripatetic lines and the doctrine of suitability, though Ovid's *Metamorphoses* is an extended study of the merging of different natural forms, and Vergil himself could send the daughters of Proetus mooing through the fields, like cows.[50] The new form may have been imbued with a certain irony, and certainly it went to extremes, but its essential materials were old, as a glance at mythology and earlier art shows. The so-called Orientalizing style of Corinthian pottery made comparably extravagant use of sphinxes, Gorgons, and other monsters in a profuse and close-packed idiom, and the hippocampi on which the sea gods rode were a frequent motif, in Hellenistic times especially. The bull-visaged river gods of Greek folklore, the winged horse Pegasus, the satyrs and goat-footed Pan, the Harpies, the centaurs and the Minotaur, the snake-legged or hundred-handed giants, not to mention the transformations of Proteus and Thetis, or the talking horses of Achilles, all attest well enough to an early appreciation of the possibilities of grotesque mixtures. What is important to notice, however, is that the mixtures, while always demonic in the sense of representing superhuman power or position, are by no means always threatening. If Gorgons, chimeras, and sphinxes are regularly dangerous, Pegasus offers Bellerophon a divine extension of his heroic gifts. Pegasus may be too shapely to connote the grotesque, but Aeschylus' four-footed bird in the *Prometheus*, whatever it was, seems to have been a helpful animal, and the certainly grotesque "horse-cocks," for which he was ridiculed, probably involved some beneficent magic.[51] Pan and his horse-tailed, rural friends, though touchy, are benignant deities.

More important for the argument perhaps is Chiron, who formed the exception to the usual turbulence and bestiality of the centaurs. The wise centaur of Mt. Pelion, the friend of Peleus, the educator of all the best heroes, and in part the liberator of Prometheus, Chiron is nonetheless a grotesque half-man half-horse, and, in contrast to all other centaurs, immortal. He has three levels, animal, human, and divine, and he clearly expresses a mythopoeic intuition for the wholeness of the world. In him nature and divinity are mighty, but benign and accessible: the heroes whom he trains are to have the strength of beasts, the understanding of men, and the aspiration toward divinity. Here is no vision of the alienated world, but of the world embraced in all its grandeur, the world as possibility, action, and transcendent power. In Homer the epithets which compare men to deities and the similes which compare them to wild animals doubt-less reflect a similar instinct for human range, for the drive to reach out to all aspects of life and to seize and make use of their essences. In early times it would seem that the grotesque, or at least the mingling of forms, could express the dangerous and incalculable forces, but it could also express a human kinship with the bur-geoning abundance of the demonic world; and the mummers dressed as goats or rams, known from Athenian vases, which are an impor-tant source for the origin of comedy, were surely striving, in the full tide of their merriment, to embrace that abundance through the magic of animals.[52]

All this may seem rather far from Aristotle's low character and the distortion which causes laughter but not pain; for surely Chiron is not funny, and it is a question whether distortion would be the right word for the peculiarities of his construction. The point is the complex of beast, man, and god which he represents, and the relation of that complex both to the high heroic tradition, whereof he was chief preceptor, and to the even more universal need of man to be one with nature, and to find wholeness in the penetration and command of its powers. Both aspects find their place in the scheme of Aristophanes, the penetration of nature in the Dionysiac rites from which, by whatever path, his art arose, and the heroic element in the figure which he staged, at least often, at the center of that art.

It is surely no accident that the beast-man-god structure is characteristic of Dionysus himself, at least in the two major classical texts in which he appears. Many Greek gods take animal forms; Apollo appears as a wolf, Zeus as a variety of animals. But these transformations, lacking as they are in the human interval, are associated with a specific end to be achieved. Dionysus' changes are more like weird mergings, or perhaps emergings, of the multiform nature of the great fertility god. Euripides catches their spirit skillfully in the *Bacchae* where Pentheus, already deluded and on the brink of ruin, sees the young and slightly feminine Dionysus as suddenly possessed of a bull's head.[53] Hitherto, the god had appeared simply in human form, as the leader of his own votaries, and only in the last scene does he reveal himself in his full divinity. The effect of Pentheus' vision of the bull's head is indescribably eerie, and not less so Dionysus' reply, "Now you see things properly," for a terrible hidden truth is emerging. The king is indeed a victim of an alienated world, a world which he has himself alienated, so that it has become only a chaos of violent forces which are about to tear him, literally, to pieces. Here is Kayser's grotesque, tragic and anticipatory of modern psychic nightmares.

Yet much the same story is told, though with anything but tragic force, in the Homeric *Hymn to Dionysus*, where once more the god shows himself in three avatars. First, as a princely young man he is captured by pirates to be sold for ransom. A touch of the uncanny begins to show through as they try to bind him; the bonds unwind themselves, while he lies there quietly smiling at them with his dark eyes.[54] When he is ready, he causes a grapevine to grow out of the sea, enveloping the ship in foliage and clusters; then he changes himself into a lion and roars from the poop deck; the pirates leap overboard and are changed into dolphins, while the god, now in his own divine shape, having produced a harvest out of the barren element, takes his ease under the mast which has become a vine prop. The spirit of the *Hymn* is distinctly akin to that of Old Comedy, though it is not actually comic. The figure who slips from youth, to lion, to a god creating impossible fecundity is grotesque in precisely the way here suggested, a demonic mixture of animal might and victorious divinity confronting and mingling with the human scene. Dionysus might be called the god of the grotesque.

If such figures as Chiron and Dionysus do indeed underlie the turbid mingling of natural forms which came later to be known as grotesque, the question rises, at what point the comic element entered. One might answer this in one way by saying that when the mummers in Bacchic festivals dressed themselves as animals, or impersonated the god himself, revelry overcame solemnity in the long run, and gave a new tone to the beast-man-god complex. But that answer, however right or wrong, is related to the problem of the origins of comedy, and the present inquiry is after the spirit and structure of the comic hero, specifically the comic hero of Aristophanes. For this, we may turn to two more Homeric characters, both of whom can be fairly described as grotesque in some sense. One of them, at least, provides a good example of Aristotle's low character, and is often thought of as comic to a degree.

In a deeply serious context, Thersites embodies formally much which we associate with comedy, though we may not find it to our taste to laugh at him, as the Achaeans did.[55] He is ugly to begin with, and in the end he is beaten, two features commonly exploited by the comic poets. He knows many things, but in a vain disorderly manner, possibly like Margites,[56] and he uses his dubious proletarian accomplishments to quarrel with his betters. One might compare the question of the irate Lamachus to Dicaeopolis: "Do you, a beggar, dare talk thus to me?" [57] Like many a comic hero, Thersites is a great talker ($\dot{\alpha}\mu\epsilon\tau\rho o\epsilon\pi\acute{\eta}s$); what he says is directed in good part toward getting a laugh from the Achaeans, so that in this respect he qualifies as a *bomolochos*, or buffoon, whose business it is to pick up everything and make a joke of it.[58] And yet, he is also a truthful buffoon, for the substance of what he says to Agamemnon differs very little from what Achilles says in the preceding book of the poem.[59] Thus he momentarily parallels the tragic truth of Achilles, echoing his actual words, and with him opposing, however ineffectually, the great kings, much as the comic hero (not to say comedy itself) is traditionally the opponent of the government. There is much dramatic irony in the role of Thersites, and with a little more detachment and refinement he might have been an early milestone on the way to the Shakespearean fool; as it is, he forms the sketch for the uniquely savage buffoon of *Troilus and Cressida*, the overturner of all order, the anti-Odysseus, shrieking hot enmity and cold derision.

Homer's Thersites is beaten into silence and sits down, "weeping and looking foolish," as the soldiers laugh. But he is not fully a comic character, least of all a comic hero. Thersites is pathetic, and closely resembles what Dicaeopolis would have been had he succumbed in the assembly to the herald's "Sit down and be quiet" and never taken his great decision. Thersites embodies something of the state in which the comic hero finds himself before he becomes heroic, before his nascent selfhood feels the conviction to assert itself, by *poneria*, in a Great Idea. He is merely Mr. Nobody, pinned to the wall, with only the brash buffoon's instinct for objection and articulation. Thersites could not develop further, for he lives in the *Iliad*, and it is hard to be a low character in a high tradition. But the fact that he, of all people, echoes Achilles' feelings causes him to approach that particular pattern of grotesquerie, of mingled forms and levels of existence, which is under discussion. Thersites comprises subhuman, human, and superhuman aspects simultaneously. To the Greeks, who in all periods considered a healthy and handsome body somehow normative for the human condition, such ugliness as Homer describes in Thersites could only seem subhuman, a misbegotten burlesque of a man; yet he is quite human in that he voices the feelings, to a good extent, of the army in general; and finally, the resemblance of his words to Achilles' implies an ironical connection with the superhuman transcendence of the hero. Here is not precisely the beast-man-god structure of the classical grotesque, but at least there is something of its range, a figuration of the human creature as reflecting simultaneously animality and divinity from a realistic, if scurrilous, middle ground of ordinary humanity.

Not to labor the point, yet one more example may be relevant. Most critics find more than a touch of comedy in the Cyclops episode of the *Odyssey*. Monster that he is, yet he has a very different effect from the anthropophagous giants of Laestrygonia, who, nameless and shadowy, spear men like fish from the heights of their dark, cliff-walled harbor. This is pure nightmare. Polyphemus has a kind of Gargantuan charm, and even though he eats his visitors, this bad habit does not entirely quench our sympathy for him as he cries out in pain to his neighbors, or addresses his bellwether tenderly while the men of Odysseus escape. One might even wonder why he should have taken kindly to finding his house and cheese bins invaded on his return, although the traditional hospitality laws of the Greeks toward strangers may have condoned such liberties. But Polyphemus laughs at Zeus's laws, and while that fact excludes him from the company of the good, it tends to align him with the Titans and Typhoeus, whom Zeus swept away, but only with difficulty, along with other antique portents. Polyphemus is no picayune fellow like Thersites, nor given to buffoonery; his olive-tree staff, his appalling voice, and his vigorous appetite recall Rabelaisian grandeur in particular, as well as comic exaggeration in general. Moreover, he has the comic hero's talent for turning someone else's claim to his own advantage: his guest favor to Odysseus will be the privilege of being eaten last.[60] This shows imagination, and hints at the kind of table-turning so frequently practiced by Aristophanes' heroes.[61] Yet massive and ferocious anti-god that he is, he is also an animal among his own animals, sharing his cave with them, and accommodating his activities to their needs. But his taste for wine is very human: "The Cyclopes make wine," he says, "but not like this. More!" [62] Drunkenness is a state denied to animals and gods, except for the rural companions of Dionysus. It is a basically human achievement, and a grotesque one, in that it combines ecstasy and brutishness, well illustrated by the dancing satyrs and sileni, with their goat feet, tails, and pointed ears. The Cyclops' drunkenness confirms his connection with humanity as well as with comedy. And here once more, we have the man-beast-god structure. For Polyphemus is bigger and grander than humanity, and deeply wounded at having been overcome by a "miserable little creature" like Odysseus; but he is also an animal in his ways. And if his humanity shows chiefly in his drunkenness rather than in any finer traits, yet somehow between his godlike bulk and beastlike jaws lies the scope of the comic hero.

Polyphemus does not, of course, exhibit the benignity of Chiron or of other grotesqueries discussed earlier; and unfortunately for him, the *poneria* was all on Odysseus' side. Yet it is easy to imagine a scheme — such as that of Euripides' satyr play — which would treat the values of a Cyclops with kindlier understanding, and Old Comedy seems to have done just that. Dicaeopolis shows little regard for the laws of hospitality, as pointed out above, when others try to invade his feast, and he is a monstrous drinker. Peithetaerus too is roasting several of his new winged subjects toward the end of the *Birds*.[63]

The transformations of the grotesque are many, as they must be, since the basic idea is one of mingled forms. The examples cited may serve to demonstrate what seems to be a regular classic structure, a complex union of what is at once human, subhuman, and superhuman. Mythological figures of this shape are quite separate from the Olympian aristocracy, for the most part; and even gods such as Dionysus, and human characters such as Thersites (or for that matter, the Aristophanean hero), in whom the structure is only implied, are not the same thing as the mythological creatures conceived as physically mixed forms of human and animal. But systematic classification is needless. For the study of comedy these figures are important in several ways. In whatever category, they point to a magical penetration of nature by the human consciousness, some intuition of unity with the abundant potency of the earth and natural things. Some are benign, some fearful, but all are figures which express, or magically effect, contact with the inner sources of power in the animal and vegetable world. The grotesque in this sense is therefore an obvious and inevitable companion of the fertility rites underlying comedy. More relevant to the present study, however, are the details which appear in connection with grotesque figures in the literary texts discussed. These show that many comic motifs, such as drunkenness, beating, talking too much, gluttony, and opposition to superiors, were already developed in early literature, albeit sporadically. They may therefore be classed with many other pre-existing elements of comedy, to emphasize that Old Comedy, when it took shape in the early fifth century, had literary roots in the grand as well as in the iambic and popular traditions.

But most important, this view of the grotesque, possessing as it does a likeness to myth, offers a framework, a kind of working structure, for the comic hero of Aristophanes. For this comic hero, sometimes only by implication but sometimes in actual staging, exhibits the man-beast-god complex which we have tried to trace. The best example is Peithetaerus at the end of the *Birds*, his human form adorned with wings, and a goddess-bride on his arm, acknowledging the chorus' jubilant celebrations of him as the new Zeus.[64] He has become both beast and god, though he began as a simple, and indeed, distracted citizen. Trygaeus, too, who first rides a dung beetle, marries a goddess, and so may be considered somewhat godlike. But matters need not be so explicit. It is enough to note the union of

opposites in the hero, the low depths and sublime heights to which
he extends. It requires an unwashed sausage vendor to become the
ideal Protector of the People. His sausages are made of dog meat, but
he produces two attractive and at least semidivine, abstractions, the
Truces, for the delectation of his master. Even when the actual
motifs of animal and god are absent, as in the *Acharnians,* there is
no mistaking the progress from something almost subhuman — Dicaeopolis in the rags of Telephus — to a transcendent liberation from
all restraints, a godlike freedom. Even poor old Philocleon, who was
formerly a wasp, has his moment of divine, if drunken, transcend-
ency. Whatever Aristotle meant by a low character, for Aristophanes
the words are not adequate. In Aristophanes the comic hero is a low
character who sweeps the world before him, who dominates all
society, and sometimes the gods themselves. The comic hero enjoys
the full range of all things, creating the world around him like a
god, and populating it in a manner less elevated. He is grotesque,
in intimate touch with nature and finally in control of it.

In connection with the comic hero's animal and divine imagery,
it must be admitted that the tragic hero also shares these spheres.
The Homeric heroes are like lions, bulls, rams, and so forth, and
they are also "godlike." Images of divinity play much the same role
in both types, but in the case of animal imagery there are differences.
For one thing, the kind of animal: epic animals are of the nobler
sort; at least, they are presented for ennobling effect, in contrast to
the mice, dogs, donkeys, birds, and dung beetles of comedy. But
more important, the epic animal is introduced not qua animal, but
as the epitome of a certain quality which the hero is thought to
have. Thus, the phrase "Achilles went like a lion out the door"
does not equate Achilles exactly with a lion (nor do lions frequently
go out through doors). It simply means that Achilles looked as ferocious as a lion as he went out. The lion's characteristic fierceness only
is added to the hero, as the stout compactness of a ram is added to
Odysseus in *Iliad* III, 197. These images pull in the same direction
as the epithets and similes implying divinity; they are all part of

the enlarging mirror of epic. But the animal imagery attending a comic hero pulls rather in the opposite direction and frames a paradox with his divine aspirations. The animal which enters enters qua animal, not to epitomize a specific quality, but rather to express the hero's relationship with nature at large. In the grotesque the animal side is functional and demonic, not merely decorative or illustrative.

We have no proof, and little evidence, that Old Comedy in general had to have such a figure as we have described. He is totally absent from the *Ecclesiazusae, Plutus,* and *Thesmophoriazusae*; he is hard to find in the *Clouds* as we have it; he turns female in *Lysistrata,* and he is greatly changed in the *Frogs.* The suspicion arises that he was a special creation, perhaps Aristophanes' own, framed in considerable part from earlier literature, both the grand and the more popular traditions. To the general structure of the grotesque was added the driving and liberating force of *poneria,* the unscrupling seeking of advantage, as well as the powerful instinct for self-preservation and self-orientation of Archilochus. The result was indeed a unique creature who brought into focus many elements that were hitherto only half-developed parts of other forms, a creature who, for a brief while in the late fifth century, represented something very important to the Athenians.

A desperate small fellow, inexcusably declaring himself for a social savior; an utterly self-centered rogue of *poneria,* representing a universal gesture of thumb-to-nose unto all the high and mighty; a coward who runs away from his enemies for the moment, and then dances on their graves with godless cheer; a fast talker, a hoper-for-the-best and a believer-in-the-worst; a creature of infinite ambition, infinite responsiveness, and infinite appetite — the comic hero, as represented in Aristophanes, somehow makes up a figure of salvation, survival against odds; he is the self militant, and devil-take-the-means. One may readily believe that he never existed complete before Aristophanes. The fragments of Cratinus and Eupolis give us little ground for thinking that these poets ever created such a vision, though, of course, they may have. In any case, Aristophanes did in his early plays. It is no small part of his genius that he was able to put together comic protagonists who represented so much of his people's psychology, and can still evoke full and sympathetic responses today. It was observed earlier that the Peloponnesian War, with its tensions, perhaps to some degree prompted and shaped a figure who was at once a release and a symbol of survival. The individual self was threatened in the late fifth century, not only by the war, but also by the many new philosophical doctrines and political events of the Periclean Age.[65] If Aristophanes did not advocate any specific program of salvation or reform, he repeatedly staged figures who represented salvation, not so much the political salvation of Athens, but a far deeper kind, the salvation of the self in all its individual waywardness, wickedness, and attachment to life. The result is a grotesque, appealing fellow, who extends one hand toward the blacker recesses of the psyche and the other toward the divine world of perfect supremacy and freedom. It is primarily this central and symbolic figure who raises the art of Aristophanes above mere satire and gives it a wider meaning. If he did not exist in the other comic poets, or not so effectively, perhaps this is one reason why their works became dated and were neglected.

When the war was ended a new world supplanted the Athenian Empire, and new political conceptions rapidly widened the breach, begun in the fifth century, between the individual and his city. The old form was no longer either possible or true, and the Aristophanean hero was not to have direct descendants. Yet some of the spirit out of which he was made must have continued. If the intense focus of Aristophanes was lost, the Greeks did not certainly lose their love of *poneria*, and the *phlyakes* and other mimes and the iambists, amid their buffoonery and social cartooning, doubtless made some capital out of it. It was, for the most part, considered below the level of the philosophic New Comedy. Somewhat later comes Juvenal's *Graeculus esuriens*, the ready-witted adventurer, available for any scapegrace enterprise. The man of *poneria* was always there, but there was no longer occasion to make him a hero.

53

One of the nearest approaches to the Aristophanic figure emerges in modern times, in the figure of Karaghiozes, the hero of the Greek shadow theater. Well known in various forms throughout the Balkans and Near East, Karaghiozes possesses a distinct and characteristic Greek form, which developed in the late nineteenth and early twentieth century, became a convention in its own right, and was regarded as something of a national symbol. Somewhat like Pulcinella, Karaghiozes is a small unshapely figure, with a hunchback, an enormous nose, and one very long and extra-jointed arm. He is intelligent, crafty, gay, opportunist, not overcourageous, and a thief. Barefoot and always hungry, he lives to get by, and to get the better of people, especially of the Turkish overlords; for though the shadow theater was not, apparently, brought to Greece from Constantinople until 1852, Karaghiozes himself was immediately turned into a Greek, and his adventures were reset in the time of the Turkish domination. He thus becomes the type of the Greek surviving under Turkish rule. All kinds of national heroes, not only from the War of Liberation but even from antiquity, including Alexander the Great himself, were imported into the shadow theater. But these worthies do not displace Karaghiozes from his central position in the plays and in the sympathies of the spectators. He is the strident embodiment of *poneria*, and though he does not always get the better of things, he always survives, an indomitable magpie. A number of other figures make up what is a kind of fixed cast of characters, into which anybody or any situation can be introduced.

Whatever may be the possible connection between Karaghiozes and antiquity (see appendix), the thing which concerns us here is the distinctive form which his Greek version possesses. The moment he came to Greece, he was approximated to a native tradition, the tradition of Greek *poneria*, and the result is something surprisingly like Old Comedy. One may leave aside, as inevitable comic types, the dull-witted but vigorous bumpkin, the *miles gloriosus*, the dandy, the gullible overlord, and the rest. Karaghiozes is a hero, a hero of shamelessness, of *poneria*, who lies, steals, dances, boasts, and jeers his way through life, adopting any trick or shift or rank absurdity in order somehow to beat the devil at his own game. He is appealing as the underdog is appealing; and yet he is a triumphant underdog because his spirit refuses to collapse. Under it all lurks an essential good, a heroic tenacity, which bespeaks the Greek, conquered and impoverished, but free in spirit. It is no accident that he attracted into his farces the heroes of the Revolution. But he is himself the real hero, the poor individual Greek of boundless aspiration.

A detailed comparison of the Karaghiozes theater with Old Comedy would reveal much common ground between them, but what is most relevant here is the central character himself, and the indication which he gives of the basic psychological ground for this kind of comedy, native to Greek minds, and having to do with the spirit's struggle with the intractability of life. Faced with the blank walls of hardship and unintelligibility, the spirit takes on a reckless bravado, which simultaneously dismisses life and asserts it. As Nikos Kazantzakis puts it, the philosophy of the Karaghiozes theater is "This world's a life-sentence; be damned to it." One is reminded immediately of Archilochus and his heroic declaration of independence from the heroic creed: "Let the shield go, I'll get another." It is an attitude which crystallizes in moments of great bafflement — not the bafflement of decadence, but of an inscrutable challenge — when a decision or stand must be taken; it has, moreover, its structural counterpart in tragedy, when the hero's course must be either held or abandoned. Oedipus, on the verge of ruin, cries out challengingly "Break forth what will, but I will learn my origin"; [66] and Eteocles, about to enter the duel with his brother, dismisses himself and his whole house in the fatal moment of identifying himself with the curse:

> Since the god drives the deed, let the whole race
> Of Laius, hated by Apollo, go
> Down wind and current on the stream of hell.[67]

In such moments the hero stands at a certain vantage point where his decision has become more important than the way things are, and where it legislates for the way they shall be. There is a perfect functional analogy in the decisiveness of Dicaeopolis when, baffled by the politicians and frauds in the assembly, he takes his stand: "Go to, I will make peace myself." The cure for a mad world is a more decisive madness; or, as Epicharmus puts it: "Against a villain villainy (πονηρία) is no mean weapon." [68]

Whether tragic or comic, the hero towers over life. He may, like Achilles or the Sophoclean heroes, outgrow it through the exalted gifts of the spirit, or *arete*. But if his gift is *poneria*, he will impose upon life a fantastic vision of his own making, in which little things like moral values are manipulated freely and dexterously in order to bring the world, kicking and screaming, under control. In both cases, one observes the individual being a law unto himself. In both cases, he is striving for the transcendent freedom and mastery of a god, while maintaining his ability to represent and communicate with humanity. The attempt is, perhaps, impossible, and for the tragic hero there awaits, as a rule, a bitter end. But nothing is impossible to the comic hero — perhaps because of the animal dimension. Peithetaerus deposes Zeus and thereafter runs the universe. Comedy makes life "work." All it takes is imagination, and an unwillingness to be hampered by scruples, consistency, and other kill-joy limitations.

The objection might be raised that this view of Aristophanes divorces him too much from reality, and in general represents him as irresponsible. But this is hardly the case, unless the only responsible poet is the one who is clearly committed to one side or the other of contemporary issues, and puts those commitments into his poetry. Aristophanes is not so committed in his poetry, though he may have been in his personal and civic life. Commitments and firm attitudes appear and disappear as the progress of the plays demands. Indeed, comedy as practiced by Aristophanes depends strongly on not letting your right hand know what your left is doing. The devious way of joyous wickedness leads on toward its goal through a series of unashamed dissociations, double perspectives, and the schizoid logic of brazen compulsions.

Is it, then, all quite immoral, or simply mad? Let us not, as critics have sometimes tried to do, deprive Aristophanes of his madness. The poet who allows women to capture the Acropolis, raises Aeschylus from the dead, builds brick cities in the air, and flies a hero to heaven on a dung beetle, must be allowed his share of lunacy. But the world is a case of lunacy too, and one answer to it is transcendence, not systematic or philosophic, but personal transcendence of the heroic sort. The world as it is perhaps cannot be transcended, but the comic hero is not stopped by that. He invents his own world and then subdues it. The Cleon whom Aristophanes trounces is his own, not history's; his Euripides is his own; his Socrates is his own. All are poetic inventions, parts of a fantastic analogue of the world as it is. The political and personal satire that seems so telling and realistic works only within this analogue, which is a personal structure, refabricated anew for each new comic hero's concern, as a larger and freer world whereby the real one is reduced to manageable size. This is, indeed, madness, but it is poetic madness, and it is neither directly moral nor immoral. It is a heroic absurdity, the absurdity of the helpless little self out-absurding the incorrigible world. If the comic hero, Dicaeopolis, Trygaeus, Peithetaerus, is a child of nature, and sometimes disarmingly and explicitly so, he transcends nature too, and arrives at a state like that of the gods, whose apparent freedom from moral or logical bondage formed one of the religious issues of the poet's time. As said before, the hero, whether tragic or comic, is a law unto himself. If Antigone is a type of law which transcends law, the personal vision which dwarfs the legal fact, the comic hero is a type of nature which transcends nature, personal nature dwarfing the nature of the world. And it is human nature, Greek human nature at least, to yearn for supremacy by whatever means. As W. K. C. Guthrie has well noted, the Greeks were always beset by the problem of whether the gods were unattainably removed from the human condition, or whether the human condition was rightly bound to the effort of being like the gods.[69] The problem was never really solved because, of course, both sides were true. No Greek ever became a god, and no true Greek ever gave up trying. The tragic hero tries it by the supreme moral sacrifice of *arete*, monolithic, grand and pure of will, however tangled in his humanity. The comic hero has *poneria*, a far more resourceful weapon, and by craft, bravado, and a wholly dissociative imagination, he achieves the quest and climbs the brazen heaven.

′III′

CITY AND INDIVIDUAL

Acharnians

THE earliest extant play of Aristophanes is one of his greatest works, surpassed in unity of design and poetic invention perhaps only by the *Birds*. Classified usually as a "peace play," it is sometimes treated as serious propaganda, sometimes as a document on the Megarian Decree, and sometimes as a source for the origins and form of Old Comedy. It has seldom been analyzed as poetry, and hence much of its singularly rich texture has gone unmentioned, while the attempt to fix it too narrowly in a single political or social purpose has obscured the whole range of larger meanings for which drama exists. The same might be said of the other plays as well; yet some of them, in fact, are of more limited import, and few make such full use of the comic hero. To approach the *Acharnians* as poetic drama is to see it as a structure of heroic fantasy, evolving through carefully elaborated images which themselves, as part of the action, help to maintain the basic conflicts up to the very end.

There are two kinds of Aristophanic prologue: either the poet begins with the hero alone, complaining and waiting for something or somebody; or there are two figures in a predicament, trying to find something or engaged in some undesirable task.[1] In the *Acharnians* the hero sits alone in the Pnyx, waiting for the Assembly to convene. His name, Dicaeopolis, may be derived from Pindar, and it is, like so many names in Aristophanes, a compound of the "grand" type, in that the single word stands for a whole phrase.[2] To judge by the sentiments which he utters, he is well named: he alone has arrived at the meeting on time; he is righteously disgusted with the tardiness of the magistrates, with the mismanagement of affairs, and with the length of the war. He yearns for his own country deme, and vows that he will make a great effort to establish peace when the meeting is finally brought to order. So far, he is a model of responsible citizenship, drawn in the pattern of peace-loving, agrarian conservatism. It is even noted that he admires Aeschylus, and hates the contemporary tragic poet Theognis. Above all, he hates Cleon: one of the few happy moments of his life arrived when Cleon, the previous year, was forced by the knights to disgorge five talents.[3] Within the space of the prologue the hero has been given, if not exactly a character, at least a significant name and a series of attitudes consonant with it; it should remain for the action to bear out these premises.

What actually happens is rather the opposite. When the magistrates finally do arrive, Dicaeopolis is helpless. His plea for peace is anticipated by the sudden outbursts of one Amphitheus, who claims that he is immortal and has been appointed by the gods to make peace.[4] Amphitheus is promptly suppressed and ejected, despite Dicaeopolis' protests, and no more is heard about peace at the meeting. Ambassadors who have spent eleven years luxuriating in Persia return with a purported emissary of the King, whom Dicaeopolis exposes for a Greek in disguise, along with his "eunuchs," who turn out to be in reality two notorious Athenian effeminates.[5] But Dicaeopolis' efforts go unheeded, and the fraudulent Persian emissary is escorted in all honor to dinner in the prytaneum, a favorite Aristophanean symbol for graft. At this point the "man of public justice" undergoes a change. He gives up society altogether, and summoning Amphitheus, sends him off to Sparta with eight drachmas and instructions to make peace for Dicaeopolis himself and his family. The man whose name sounded so politically promising has failed to accomplish anything in the sovereign Assembly, and has been told simply to sit down and be quiet.[6]

These opening scenes of the *Acharnians* are among the funniest in all Aristophanes. The Persian ambassador Pseudartabas, with his huge one-eyed mask and Greco-Persian gobbledygook, is succeeded by another emissary, just returned from Thrace with a troop of Odomantian mercenaries. If Pseudartabas' attendants were on the feminine side, these Odomantians are all too violently virile, and they proceed to rob Dicaeopolis of a bunch of garlic.[7] Cozening or outright plunder is seen as the net profit of Athens' foreign relations, and the government abets the fraud. The political satire is evident enough, but its chief purpose is to make clear the position of Dicaeopolis, the individual citizen. His helpless isolation is dramatized throughout, from the moment when he first appears, sitting all alone in the place of public assembly, counting his four joys and numberless woes. Amphitheus, who fares no better than he, underlines his predicament, but is also a foil to it, in that he does not react so decisively in the long run. Dicaeopolis' solitary and vain protests culminate in his decision to do something big,[8] and make peace himself; but before the negotiations are complete his robbery by the Odomantians evokes one final appeal, openly expressive of the citizen's plight:

> Look here, presidents, will you let me suffer this
> In my own country, at barbarian hands?[9]

But he is ignored again. Here is the self, trapped and mocked by the institutions of an alienated society.

Reduced to his individual anonymity, Dicaeopolis is confronted by an apparent yes-or-no situation: either he may accept his insignificance in the body politic and let himself remain the anonymous individual, or he may keep trying to make his voice heard, however vainly. But in fact, he does neither. He becomes a comic hero instead. He conceives an idea which transcends the Assembly with its corruptions, and at the same time startlingly liberates and exalts his own individual self. The private treaty with Sparta puts Dicaeopolis on a level with a whole polis, and even above it, for the city had refused to consider his ideas. When he nevertheless puts those ideas into action, he promptly ceases to be the small man crushed under the wheels of government; instead he towers over it.

When Amphitheus returns from Sparta with three wine skins of peace, the realities which had surrounded Dicaeopolis begin to yield to a world which becomes whatever he declares it to be. Rejecting the two wines which smell of pitch, ship gear, and embassies, he accepts the thirty-year-old wine of peace:

> O Dionysia!
> This smells of nectar and ambrosia,
> Instead of fetching rations for three days;
> And in the mouth it says, "Go where you please." [10]

The image of peace as an old mellow wine is, of course, fundamental, for drinking is a particularly prominent motif in the *Acharnians*. In essence, it is perhaps little more than a dramatization of the idiom φιλοτησίαν πίνειν, "to drink the cup of friendship," [11] but for the hero it is the primary token of his liberation, whereby, incidentally, he personally celebrates two festivals of Dionysus, apparently at such times as please him. His invocation "O Dionysia" leads at once to his celebration of the Rural Dionysia in the following scene, and by the end of the play he wins the drinking contest of the Anthesteria. Since these festivals fell two months apart, rationality might complain of putting so great a strain even upon dramatic time; but no matter. The liberty with time suits the liberty with space represented in a scene which includes the Pnyx, the house of Euripides (who lived in Salamis), and Dicaeopolis' own house in the countryside. Liberties with time, though less frequent than those with space, are fairly common in Aristophanes: it takes Amphitheus, for instance, only forty-five lines to get to Sparta and back. In the *Thesmophoriazusae*, for the sake of a joke about the frigidity of Agathon's verses, the time of year is said to be winter; thirteen lines later Euripides says that it is the third day of the Thesmophoria, which was celebrated in autumn. [12] On the other hand, the astronomer Meton's attempt to reform the calendar provokes the Moon's displeasure in the *Clouds*, and Meton is elsewhere treated as an outright impostor.[13] Apparently it makes a difference as to who takes the liberties. The hero has the magic wine of peace, and with it the mastery of all things. The original "Go where you please" has grown into "Have your will of the world," and the climax is, of course, the final drunken scene, where the triumphant Dicaeopolis will receive as prize a "wine skin of Ctesiphon," who in his vast obesity represented a generous supply of the grape. The chorus closes the play with a song in honor of the hero "and the wine skin," inseparably united.[14]

From the moment Dicaeopolis receives the wine he is consistent only with himself. He has dismissed the city with a contemptuous, "Go on with your embassies and your gaping"; [15] his desire for peace now is only for himself and his family, and his commitment to it is a decommitment from practically everything else. There could scarcely be a more vivid example of the insufficiency of public virtue compared with private imagination. But the private imagination is destined to have its struggles, and the hero must prove his mettle. The Rural Dionysia, with its lilting song to Phales, the deified phallus, is interrupted by the attack of Acharnian charcoal burners, who have smelled the wine and are outraged by the thought of peace with the Spartans who have cut down their vineyards. Now follows the agon, involving a whole new set of images, to be traced presently; [16] it also involves a new development in the character of Dicaeopolis. He is far from being any longer a simple countryman, a term now more applicable to the choristers. As one alone against many he must use persuasion and subtlety, and does so by having recourse to the great master of guileful rhetoric, Euripides, whose tongue is a god to be called upon in the hour of need.[17]

The Aristophanic Euripides is a wonderful invention, an image presented first here, to be constantly revised and refined throughout the comedian's lifetime, a man of straw meticulously set up, and uproariously knocked down. In three plays Euripides is a main character, and he is mentioned or parodied in nearly all the others.

He is always very much the same: we see nothing of the melting poet of the *Troades*, the demonic poet of the *Bacchae*, the subtle ironist of the *Alcestis*, or the heroic tragedian of the *Heracles*. What we see is a gloomy intellectual, composing, with the help of a slave, thin, doctrinaire, paradoxical verses designed to lower tragic solemnity to the level of kitchen gossip and ruin the taste and character of all who hear them; or we see a vacuous lyrist writing, in bravura style, a lament for a lost rooster; or a muddled philosopher dismally disintegrating moral values or gravely expounding the secrets of physical nature. He is always a misogynist; his plays are always about kings in rags and loose women; his mother is always a peddler of green groceries. The travesty must have been successful, for two of the Euripides plays got first prize, and the *Thesmophoriazusae* may have. Certainly its creator thought so. If Aristophanes could taunt Euripides that he could not write a tragedy without a king in rags, one might equally well taunt Aristophanes that he could not write a comedy without Euripides.

In the present play, however, Euripides represents, as often, the new rhetoric, and Dicaeopolis, by having recourse to him, allies himself with a whole series of figures who elsewhere are treated as incarnate powers of darkness, the spirits of *poneria*. If the comic hero ever was a conservative, he is evidently under no obligation to keep his conservatism pure; if he has need of the new rhetoric, he uses it, and Aristophanes is deterred from giving it to him neither by scruple nor by incompetence in the art.[18] Dicaeopolis' appeal to Euripides is important as a primary illustration of the fact that the comic hero, and the spirit of Aristophanic comedy in general, have more in common with the Unjust Logic which they condemn than with the Just Logic which they extol and pretend to represent. Moreover, in the present play, from the moment that Dicaeopolis makes his great decision, the controlling factor in the dramatic evolution is a series of word plays, verbal prestidigitations and dramatized figures of speech, which lift the play dizzyingly from the solid ground of issues and beliefs into a world which perhaps is best described as a metaphor of private reality. The matter of the relation of language to reality in the fifth century will be discussed more fully in a later chapter. It is enough to note here that Dicaeopolis' alliance with Euripides, however ironically conducted, is a real one, and it aligns the hero, in a way, not only with the impostor poet whom he so regularly assailed for filling his plays with clever chatter and moral perversity, but also with the impostor Socrates, who can win either side of a case, and probably also with those "foreign speeches," perhaps by Gorgias of Leontini, from whose deceptions Aristophanes claims to have preserved his fellow citizens.[19]

The role which Dicaeopolis chooses is that of Telephus, the beggar-king and rhetorician par excellence, who is described as "A lame, importunate, mouthing, artful talker." [20] The role seems to come naturally to him, even before he has visited Euripides. The Acharnians are pelting him with stones and shouting that they hate him even worse than Cleon.[21] As Telephus used the infant Orestes as hostage, Dicaeopolis seizes a coal basket and threatens to run it through with a sword. The Acharnians subside in sympathy for the "coal hod, their fellow demesman." [22] From here on, it is only a matter of filling out the role, staking his head, like Telephus, on his ability to persuade, and finally going to Euripides himself to borrow the necessary rags and other drab properties out of which tragedies are made. There is more than mere tragic parody here. It is a real shift of roles. Dicaeopolis becomes Telephus in his own right as comic hero, that is, a low character triumphant through *poneria*, and he confounds the simplicity of the peasant choristers, those men of the good old days,

> Acharnians, hard-tamped old oaken men,
> Tough Marathon warriors, made of maple wood.[23]

Throughout the scene with Euripides, Dicaeopolis shows all the characteristics of one of the typical impostors, the uninvited guest, as he extracts item after item of tragic equipment. He explains that he has to make "a long speech to the chorus," and needs rags; rags and rhetoric are apparently one and the same, and Dicaeopolis keeps begging until he begins to feel full of "little set phrases" with which to "thumb his nose at the silly choristers." [24] Euripides is at first sympathetic toward the cause of subtle devices; eventually, however, the poet in impatience drives him off, but Dicaeopolis has been just as "sticky and importunate" as Telephus.[25] It is with good confidence in the art of speech, therefore, that, now fully costumed, he approaches the chopping block:

> Have you not drunk down Euripides?
> Yes, and a good thing. Go thither now,
> Long-suffering heart, and offer up your head,
> And say whatever may come into it.
> Dare, onward, go; I marvel at my heart.[26]

And the chorus, in solemn dochmiac meter, comments on his heroic, shameless fortitude:

> What will you do? What will you say? Know you well,
> You are a shameless man, a man iron-bound,
> You who before the city, proffering your neck in pledge,
> Will speak alone in opposition to all.[27]

The terms are paratragic, but the situation of the isolated protagonist, in his "iron-bound shamelessness," tilting against all society has more in common with tragedy than the scraps from the Telephus or the solemn metrics. Something representative, albeit grotesquely representative, of the human condition here takes the stand on its own behalf.

What he actually says, however, may be a different matter. The man who had "drunk down Euripides" in order "to thumb his nose at the silly choristers" now does exactly that, in a speech whose sheer impudence ought to discourage anyone from trying to see beneath it any serious thinking about the war and its causes. After a proem in which Dicaeopolis-Aristophanes covers himself from the possible charge of attacking the city, comes the account of the troubles with Megara. But the cart is before the horse; according to this tale, the informers had been denouncing Megarian goods before there had been any decree making them contraband; in fact, all this was "trivial and local." [28] What really mattered was the Athenians' abduction of Simaetha the harlot from Megara, and the Megarian reprisals against the harlots of the court of Aspasia; only then was Pericles roused to write the Megarian Decree and start the war. It has long been recognized that the passage is a parody of the beginning of Herodotus' history, while the picture of Aspasia and Pericles was a well-worn comic theme begun probably by Cratinus and always good theater.[29] The only point in the speech which might lay claim to seriousness is the implication that the Peloponnesians were fighting in self-defense. But that implication, if it is really there, fits the role of Telephus, who had apparently used this claim in Euripides; it certainly fits no particular point made in the speech.[30] It is at most an implication, and as Dicaeopolis makes it, he refers to himself pointedly as Telephus, and lets what will follow. It is at least unlikely that Aristophanes thought that Sparta was fighting simply in self-defense, any more than he thought that Pericles and Aspasia were running a brothel. The whole speech was meant, as said, to befuddle the chorus, and it succeeds. They start fighting each other instead of Dicaeopolis. The power of speech has won the day, at least until the arrival of Lamachus, with which this supple and extended agon comes to a climax.

There is little or nothing historical about the ferocious figure who now leaps upon the stage. The real Lamachus seems to have been a brave officer, and he was certainly one of those entrusted to negotiate and sign the Peace of Nicias in 421.[31] His name, however, contained the word for battle, and it was used in a jingling word play in the Phales song. The image so lightly sketched there now springs forward in the flesh, fully armed; there is probably no other reason why he, of all possible generals, should have been chosen.[32] A similar jingle accounts for Dicaeopolis' greeting to him, "O hero Lamachus, O feathers and fights!" ($\tau\hat{\omega}\nu$ $\lambda\acute{o}\phi\omega\nu$ $\kappa\alpha\grave{\iota}$ $\tau\hat{\omega}\nu$ $\lambda\acute{o}\chi\omega\nu$), where the association of the feathers of a crest with battles instigates what will be an important active image later in the play.

In any case, Lamachus appears as a typical *alazon*, a braggart soldier, while Dicaeopolis, as said in the last chapter, plays the *eiron* briefly, only to emerge later as the greater *alazon*. Dicaeopolis is ironical enough at first as he pretends to cringe before the general's arms and waving plumes; tremblingly, he induces Lamachus to put down his shield, which he calls a "bug bear," and then vomits in it, borrowing a feather from the crest to assist his purpose. This is mere slapstick, and what follows might be called verbal slapstick. When Lamachus protests against the treatment of his shield, Dicaeopolis asks what kind of bird the feather came from — was it perhaps an "eagletist?" [33] It is important to note also that, at this point, Dicaeopolis drops the role of the beggar Telephus, and takes a more threatening stand against the general.

> Lam.: You talk like that to a general, you beggar, you?
> Dic.: Who, me a beggar?
> Lam.: Well, who are you then?
> Dic.: Who? A good citizen.

And thereupon he begins denouncing Lamachus in such terms as Spoudarchides and Mistharchides, comic patronymics both of which might be roughly translated "Son-of-ambitchon"; and condemning the whole tribe of profiteering officers as Teisameno-horse-show-offs, Cavalroblackguards and other grotesque and provocative combinations.[34] The role of the beggar, with the language of Euripides, is explicitly abandoned, and the long comic compounds suggest the "Lycabettus-sized" words for which Aeschylus, in the *Frogs*, is specifically condemned as an *alazon*.[35] Tragic or comic, such language has a fulminous grandeur, which in fact puts Lamachus to flight. The comic hero, though an *eiron* when occasion demands, can also roar and thunder like an *alazon*, with the difference, however, that his impostorship is too complete, and his imposition too enveloping, for anyone to unmask. Once he has overcome Lamachus, Dicaeopolis does not condescend to any further ironies.

The Lamachus scene marks also Dicaeopolis' victory over the disaffected half of the chorus, through his engaging their sympathies in the matter of embassies and military service. Old men, he says, like the Acharnians must fill the ranks, while the young ones go on embassies at three drachmas a day.[36] This is a theme which began earlier, and is subtly worked into the texture: the theme of youth reveling in unearned wealth and comfort, imposing on old age in its poverty and hardship. It is taken up at length in the parabasis which follows immediately, in the vignette of the old man in court, prosecuted by a young shark of a lawyer:

> Muttering in our old age we stand at the bar,
> Seeing nothing but the darkness of the case,
> While some young squirt, an eager advocate of himself,
> Speedily thumps and tangles one of us in periodic rhetoric;
> Then drags him up and questions him, and sets wordy traps,
> Rending, confusing, confounding a man as old as Tithonus.
> And he mumbles in his agedness, and goes off docked,
> Hiccuping and sobbing, and saying to his friends,
> "I've come off paying a fine with the money I'd saved for my coffin." [37]

There is an unmistakable note of real pathos here, though there may also be a *double-entendre* in the word for coffin.[38] But it is also well to remember that the poet represents the old men quite differently in the *Wasps*, where they are the merciless jurors, enjoying the writhings of their victims and not at all given to mercy. Dicaeopolis himself, a few lines before, had assumed the role of the clever talker in order to befool the silly chorus of old Marathon fighters; and in fact, by the end of the play it is Dicaeopolis who is rolling in wealth and comfort, while the young Lamachus has been out taking the brunt of the war, guarding the passes in the snow, with onions and salt pickle for ration. One may say that this is a satisfying table-turning, but it is also a case of comedy's freedom from consistency and its double view of everything.

Such consistency as there is in Aristophanes is to be sought, perhaps, in the progress of the imagery, for the plays are conceived as dramatic poetry and the images take part in the action. The term "image" is perhaps a vague one, but it is necessarily so, for all the elements in a drama, whether visual or auditory, are really images, the characters included. There is a distinct critical advantage, in fact, in thinking of a character as an image, for it emphasizes mimesis, as Aristotle would call it, the poet's representation of a thing; it categorizes the character — or whatever — as a unit of communication, and obviates the fatal hypostasis of treating a character as a real person. The poet makes his character seem real, but only within the milieu which he has created, and to treat a character as image is to reveal his relationship to the inner form of the drama, as part of a communicating whole. Within this whole, the various images may shift from one category to another, and an image, in one place verbal, may elsewhere terminate in an action or a character. From this point of view the principal image of any play might be said to be the protagonist himself, as he evolves throughout the action. Thus Dicaeopolis is an image of the small self, achieving the dream of authenticity through heroic *poneria* and gigantic impostorship, and he is surrounded by a series of other images which help to control and develop the fantastic structure.

There are two principal kinds of image relevant here, the controlling or dramatic image which moves with the action, and the lyrical image which is static, and seems momentarily to crystallize and even supplant it. Among the first kind, we have already spoken of the image of peace as wine, which generates the drinking scenes at the end. But there are other controlling images, and one of the most important is that of coal, with attendant images of cinders, smoke, and fire. The image arises, of course, from the charcoal trade of the chorus, who, it has been noted, are described in a passage already quoted as oak and maple men, in reference to the hardwoods used in the manufacture of charcoal.[39] One need not trace all the little smudges of coal dust in the poetic texture, but one of the chorister's names is Marilades, "son of a cinder," and it is tempting to accept the conjecture Anthracyllus, "Coalkin," for another.[40] The Acharnians in their rage are characterized as firebrands, so that Dicaeopolis cries out, as nearly as the pun will go in English, not "what a black-tempered," but "what a black-embered" outburst.[41] In the scene where the hero threatens the coal hod with a sword, the personification of the hod as the infant Orestes leads to puns on ἄνθραξ, coal, and ἄνθρωπος, human being; unless, of course, the word play prompted the scene.[42]

So far, the coals have been a threatening image, but once they are subdued they begin to gain different associations. As Dicaeopolis puts down the coal hod he remarks that in its terror it squirted soot all over him, like an inkfish.[43] Now squid is a delicacy, often praised in Aristophanes, and this simile provides a transition to what the coals are to become, namely something to cook a feast with. As the hero overcomes warlike opposition with his personal peace, so too the Acharnians' warlike coals are transformed to peaceful purposes. The image is complete when the Copaic eel, a great delicacy, is brought to the market by a Boeotian and introduced in a stately parody of Aeschylus, something roughly equivalent to "Daughter of a hundred eels." [44] Dicaeopolis embraces the eel, addressing her like a tragic heroine, and calls for his grill and charcoal to greet the long lost guest; from here on the cooking images are too numerous to list. It is a question somewhat like that of the chicken and the egg to ask whether the coal image has followed the plot, or the plot has followed the coal image. Both move together from strife toward peace, from hot resentment toward a hot frying pan, from a beleaguered Dicaeopolis toward a victorious one. Nor should one overlook the wonderful strophe where the coals, the fire, the oak logs, and the fried fish appear in a brilliant lyrical concentration, in honor of the Acharnian Muse:

Chorus: Hither, O flaming Acharnian Muse, strapping lass with the might of fire,
          Such as the spark springs up from oaken logs when stirred by the blast of the bellows!
             When the fish are laid by the coals for frying,
             And some stir oily pickle brine,
             And others dip,
          Come then, with a confident, thumping country song,
             With me, your fellow townsman! [45]

The Acharnian Muse is not one of the canonical nine; she was born of one of the play's chief images, red-faced, blowzy, and hungry.

A similar development can be found in the image of feathers. When General Lamachus enters, he wears a helmet, clearly with a very large crest of feathers, and Dicaeopolis exclaims: "O hero Lamachus, O crests and cohorts!" or perhaps, "O fights and feathers!" [46] The feathers, like the coals, must be subdued and brought into line. In the scene described earlier Lamachus is discomfited but not reformed, so that when the feathers fly again they have two contexts. Lamachus is still overshadowed by triple crests,[47] and when his marching orders come, he is specifically directed to take along his "crests and cohorts"; but Dicaeopolis goes into his house to prepare the feast to the accompaniment of "thrushes and blackbirds' wings," tasty stuff, and the chorus sings that he is "winged" with excitement as he flings the feathers of the plucked birds out the door.[48] Clearly the thing to do with feathers is throw them away and eat the bird. But Lamachus, incorrigibly preparing for his campaign, calls out: "Bring me the double wings of my helmet!" "Bring me," says Dicaeopolis, "the ducks and thrushes!"

> Lam.: The ostrich feather's beautiful and white.
> Dic.: The meat of ducks is beautiful and brown.
> Lam.: You creature, you, stop sneering at my arms!
> Dic.: You creature, you, stop leering at my thrushes.
> Lam.: Bring me the crest case with the triple crest!
> Dic.: Bring me the platter with the rabbit meat.[49]

The point is clear enough, but Aristophanes has still not finished with Lamachus' feathers. The one which Dicaeopolis had borrowed, the eagletist feather, comes to a tragic end: Lamachus in the next scene has been wounded leaping over a ditch, and bumped his head,

> And the great feather of the eagletist
> Fell on the rocks and uttered this dire song:
> "O glorious day, now looking last on you
> I leave my light, and I no longer am!" [50]

With the feather's fall Lamachus is fallen, and he limps off to the doctor. The image of overblown, nonsensical bombast has walked hand in hand with plot and character, to become in the end a symbol, like the coals, of war yielding to peace, and all things yielding to Dicaeopolis.

This passage, which has been condemned as ungenuine, calls for defense; but first, one more motif, a central one for the *Acharnians*, though not so fully developed. The invading Spartans had destroyed the vines of Acharnae, together with the long poles used to prop them up, and the villagers want revenge.[51] Throughout the play the vines and the vine props accompany the wine of peace as strict antinomies of war. One of the most moving and ingenious passages is the chorus wherein Polemos, War, is described as a brawling guest at a symposium:

> Never will I receive War (Polemos) into my house,
> Nor will he ever sing the Harmodius catch with me,
> Lying on my couch, for he is a rude, drunken fellow,
> Who, bursting in on people who had all good things,
> Did every outrage, overturned, and spilled,
> And quarreled, and though I begged him many times,
> "Lie down and drink this cup of kindly cheer,"
> All the more he burned my vine poles in the fire,
> And violently dashed the vintage from the vines.[52]

In the climactic last line, by supremely controlled ambiguity of language, Aristophanes has merged the image of wine spilled from a cup with that of a vineyard destroyed by the enemy, and the mingling of humor and pathos is incomparable. Yet it is the oppressed and stricken vine prop of the Polemos passage which brings about the final triumph of the vineyard over war. By a happy and natural *aperçu*, which he used again in the *Peace* four years later, Aristophanes contrasts the vine pole with the spear. Lamachus' spear has been in evidence before, and as he comes back wounded he cries out, in high tragic style: "Ah, hateful and chilling woes, these! Alas, ah me! I perish smitten by the enemy spear!" But the fact is, he was not wounded by a spear at all. He was wounded by a vine prop, as the messenger who came in just before him has related.[53] The image has become active, and the oppressed vineyard has taken its own revenge on the warmonger.

This messenger's speech is worth a digression, for it has been attacked as unworthy of Aristophanes.[54] It reads:

> O servants of the house of Lamachus,
> Water, heat water in a little pot,
> Prepare the linen bandages and salve,
> Wool soaked in oil, and bindings for an ankle!
> The man is wounded, leaping over a ditch,
> Speared by a vine pole, and he sprained his ankle,
> And fell and smashed his head upon a stone,
> And thus bestirred the Gorgon from his shield,
> And the great feather of the eagletist
> Fell on the rocks and uttered this dire song:
> "O glorious day, now looking last on you
> I leave my light, and I no longer am!"
> Having said so much he fell into a drain,
> And rose and met the runaways, driving
> And pressing the marauders with his spear,
> And here he is.[55]

The objections are three: (1) that the recurrence of the eagletist feather is an unsuccessful attempt to revive the earlier joke; and the same point avails about the bestirring of the Gorgon, which occurred before, l. 574; (2) that the feather could not utter a dire song, and if it could it ought to speak better Greek; and (3) that the closing lines, about falling into a drain, rising, meeting runaways, and chasing marauders, are "next door to delirium." These are matters of taste. It is perfectly possible to prove, no doubt, by due philologic process, that the lines do not make rational sense. But the revived joke about the eagletist, as said above, is the climax of the feather motif, the final fall of belligerent boobery; and one should hesitate to prescribe what kind of syntax a dying feather uses, as long as it makes all the tragic noises. The same is true for the Gorgon. If it was bestirred from its shield case earlier, it is bestirred right off the shield now, in full climactic flight. As for the last lines, they are not "next door to delirium," they *are* delirium, and they belong with equally delirious approximations by Aristophanes of the style of dithyrambic poets, or the learned twaddle of Meton, or Dicaeopolis bidding his heart lay its head on the chopping block.[56] If nobody knows just what is happening in those lines, neither did Lamachus, and we should be quietly grateful for the felicitous slapstick of having him fall into a drain. If Aristophanes did not write the passage, a major comic poet did.

In the case of the lyrical images, there is perhaps more to be said about them in connection with other plays than in the *Acharnians*. What is meant is not simply the kind of lyrical passage, such as the *aubade* to the nightingale in the *Birds*, which prompted Jebb to call Aristophanes one of the greatest lyrists of all time. This song, together with the praise of Athens in the *Clouds*, the songs of the Initiates in the *Frogs*, and others, are indeed some of the purest and most enchanting lyrics in the Greek language, and their beauty stands out in such contrast to much else which is, at least in content, quite different, that there sometimes seem to be two people at work, Aristophanes the poet and Aristophanes the satirist and muckrake. But Aristophanes is all poet, and he did not have to cease to be comic in order to be lyrical. Lyricism does not depend on birds, flowers, and sacred precincts. Lyricism implies singleness of feeling in an image, or a distillate of feelings which momentarily cohere to create a single, though prismatic, unity. It is meaning overreached by form, the fly caught in amber, the fixity whereby experience is preserved in clarity but can no longer move backward or forward. In drama a lyrical image differs from the controlling or dramatic kind in arresting the action, however briefly, in favor of a static and crystalline moment; as, for instance, the image of dawn in the first scene of Hamlet provides a moment of pause, while metaphors of disease, impostume, and rottenness move with the action.

The lyrical image differs simply in function and not necessarily in content from the dramatic. Indeed, two passages already discussed, the Acharnian Muse and War at the symposium, are momentary refocusings, in lyrical, albeit quite comic, terms, of the controlling images of coals on the one hand and wine and vineyards on the other. In this form the passages stand as tableaux, more for

75

their own sake than for that of the movement of the play, before they are reused in the dramatic working-out. Hence, they have a certain self-sufficiency, which tempts memorization and quotation. But the trick can be done also in a single word, sometimes a pun, usually a word play. In the speech denouncing Lamachus, Dicaeopolis lists three cities in Sicily where vain, expensive Athenian embassies have provided egregious examples of incompetence and graft. Two of them are real cities, Camarina and Gela; to these, however, Aristophanes adds a third, Katagela, a community which owes its sudden and full-blown existence solely to the illicit union of Gela with the verb καταγελάω, "to heap derision." It stands at the end of the passage as a kind of distillate of all that has been said, less in the context than the embodied essence of the context. This is wit, no doubt, but it is also wit with lyrical imagistic force: the city of Katagela has, in the uniqueness of its structure and significance, for the moment, a higher formal reality than the other two.[57] One might multiply examples, illustrative of the essential unity of Aristophanes' genius as comedian and poet.

Such are the principal images which both shape and adorn the central action of the hero in the *Acharnians*. All are well-established motifs in the forepart of the play, and in the later scenes they are transformed and find their fulfillment. Of the later scenes little need be said, except to emphasize the *poneria* of Dicaeopolis and the exclusiveness of the position which he achieves. It is often said that Old Comedies fall into two halves, the second being merely a series of genre scenes illustrating the hero's success and his ability to beat off impostors. The statement hardly does justice, however, to Aristophanes' dramaturgy. From early in his career Aristophanes had a genius for keeping his plays dramatically alive throughout. In the *Acharnians* the scenes in the market place, while a natural, illustrative consequence of what has gone before, also represent further extensions of the hero's *poneria*, and the tension with Lamachus, as shown earlier, is sustained through feather imagery to the very end. The scene with Lamachus even ends with two symmetrical speeches, of three lines each, pointedly aligning the issues of the remaining scenes:

> Lam.:   Well I, at least, with all Peloponnesians
> Will ever fight and everywhere confound
> With ships and infantry, most doughtily.
> Dic.:   And I proclaim to all Peloponnesians
> And to Boeotians and Megarians,
> To trade with me, and not with Lamachus.[58]

The structure of these lines, with Dicaeopolis mockingly echoing Lamachus, foreshadows formally the structure of the two last scenes where the same device is exploited to the utmost.

But there is something else. Dicaeopolis' proclamation of a market jars somewhat with what he had once said of his own, happy country deme, which provided all his needs, and never said "buy" anything.[59] That, however, was when he was still a simple countryman, before he became a comic hero. His high calling now prompts him to greater enterprise in trade, and he proves himself a master of the art of getting something for nothing. The two trading scenes, also symmetrical, present an impoverished and starving Megarian, balanced by an opulent Boeotian, both of whom are dexterously cheated; both also are denounced by informers, who are summarily disposed of. There is real pathos, as well as ingenious sexual equivocations on the Greek for "pig," in the scene with the Megarian, who sells his two little daughters in the disguise of pigs. Such is his destitution that he hands them over for a pint of salt and a bunch of garlic, and wishes he could sell his wife and mother too at similar profit.[60] But Dicaeopolis remains in possession of two pigs, or, if one chooses not to regard them as pigs, at least two items more valuable than salt and garlic. One wonders what he will do with them; their father had assured him they were appropriate for sacrificial purposes.[61] But no matter, the chorus sings an ode congratulating him on his shrewd bargain and on the advantages of his private market.[62]

The victory over the Boeotian is even more splendid. He arrives loaded with every delicacy, especially birds, which incidentally provide many of the feathers later on. Dicaeopolis buys the whole lot, taking the Copaic eel free, as market tax; in return for the rest he offers barter, Phaleric anchovies or pottery. But the Boeotian wants something unavailable in Boeotia. The answer is an informer. The Boeotian, like all Boeotians a clod according to Athenian judgment, is delighted and accepts the informer Nicarchus, who arrives just in time to be packed up in a crate and shipped off to Boeotia, with instructions that he be carried upside down. This happy touch seems to have been prompted by the mention of Athenian pottery, and throughout the ode wherein he is crated he is treated as a piece of ceramic; he has a tattle-tale ring, but he is a useful vessel, a bowl of villainies, a vat of law suits, a lamp for showing up magistrates, a cup of — but the text breaks off.[63] Not only is Dicaeopolis rid of the informer, he gains all the goods in Boeotia in exchange for him.

But, as said above, *poneria* is more than just cleverness in gaining the better of things; it is also a form of self-seeking and self-assertion. True to his promise, Dicaeopolis will not trade with Lamachus, "even if he should give him his shield." [64] Less explicable is the scene where the farmer from Phyle, whose oxen have been stolen by the enemy, begs for a little drop of peace in the hope that he may recover them; he gets not even sympathy.[65] One may conjecture that the farmer was really rich, and Dicaeopolis saw through the fraud. But it is more likely that *poneria* is the spirit of gain, whose first tenet is that it is more blessed to receive than to give. A bridegroom, who shares Dicaeopolis' aversion to war and wants to stay with his bride, sends his best man to beg for a little peace. He is similarly rebuffed, but in this case the bridesmaid prevails, "because she is a woman and had nothing to do with the war." [66] Yet one may wonder if her innocence of war was the only thing Dicaeopolis found to recommend her, as she whispered privately in his ear. By and large, it is made clear that the peace is his and his alone, enviable, joyous, and not to be shared by lesser people, as the chorus declares, hungrily gazing at the preparations for the feast.[67]

At the very end Dicaeopolis' victory has spread in a mysterious way to include more than had appeared. Not only does he win the drinking bout, but he is invited to dinner by the priest of Dionysus, with

> Couches, tables, cushions, mattresses,
> Garlands and oil of myrrh, whores, and hors d'oevres,

four kinds of cake and dancing girls.[68] No reason is given for this sudden burst of hospitality from the Athens which Dicaeopolis had abandoned. It is just that the whole world has collapsed before this almighty individualist, and no honor can be too great for him. It only remains for him to win the Feast of Pitchers, collect a couple of buxom trollops, and jeer in derision at the wounded, groaning Lamachus, while the chorus chants his glory. As a moral parable, all this is rather a failure; as a heroic adventure of the wishful self, it is superb.

"Heroism," says Emerson, "dances joyously to its own music." The music of the *Acharnians* is the song of personal and individual salvation, sung with loud and impudent cheer. The fantasy, spun of malleable images of wine, coals, feathers, and vine props, rises irresistibly around a hard core of that touchstone of survival, *poneria*, the wiles that can move mountains. If the hero in the rags of Telephus is as wretched and forlorn as that unfortunate king and as ludicrous as Thersites, it is not long before his ability to use words, which includes the ability to turn metaphors into facts, exalts him to a superhuman position. The whole grotesque range is there, from quasi brutality to quasi divinity, and in this broad picture one recognizes a basic image of man — the Great Impostor, Nature's exile, the absurdity of a self against the selfless Absurd, driving on somehow toward unity with, and mastery over, the world. If it is *alazoneia*, it is a kind with no limit, either to its aspiration or its demiurgic command of reality through words. It is a kind which somehow is Aristophanes' own, if one recalls the preposterous parabasis where, after declaring that he had never so sinned as to praise himself in the theater, he proceeds to list all the benefits he has brought the

Athenians, adding, for good measure, that the King of Persia is willing to favor only the cause assisted by such a poet, and that the only reason the Spartans wish to recover Aegina is in order to get Aristophanes away from the Athenians.[69] One would think better of the Spartans and of the Great King if we could believe him.

Knights

When Aristophanes produced the *Knights* in 424 B.C., he returned to a theme which two years before had involved him in some sort of indictment for slander before the Council. In the *Babylonians* of 426 he had represented the allies of Athens as grievously oppressed by Cleon, and since the play was produced at the Greater Dionysia, where foreigners were permitted, it was felt, by Cleon at least, that the dignity of Athens, not to mention his own, had suffered a public insult. So the youthful poet was summoned. All too little is known of this *cause célèbre*, though the meager details have been generously filled out by many scholars. The whole question of legal restraints upon the outspokenness of comic poets is a tangled one; the most thoroughgoing recent study of its leads to the conclusion that whatever laws of censorship existed were difficult to enforce, and perhaps this is the only explanation.[1] In any event, Cleon's indictment could have had little effect on Aristophanes, for in the *Knights* he unleashed one of the most savage attacks to be found anywhere in the history of literature, though he produced it, perhaps for reasons of circumspection, at the private Athenian festival of the Lenaea. Since, also, the *Knights* is the first play which Aristophanes produced in his own name, it may be possible to conclude that his former producer, Callistratus, was unwilling to risk further complicity in such libelous proceedings; and indeed it appears likely that there was further trouble over it.[2]

The *Knights* is unique among the plays for its vindictive violence. Aristophanes seldom restrained himself from free expression in matters which occasioned his disapproval, whether real or pretended, but nowhere else in his known works does he devote a whole play to such a systematic indulgence of ferocity. It might be added that the fragments of the other comic poets, even of the fiery Cratinus himself, have little comparable to offer. Indeed, it seems somewhat out of character for Aristophanes to abandon himself so fully to the luxury of sheer hate, for his poetry in general abounds in sweetness, whatever passing invectives it may contain, and its prevailing motive elsewhere is not hate, but love. It is hard to explain Aristophanes' rage on purely political grounds, for the play contains little, if any, sober criticism of Cleon's actual policies, but concentrates instead on his personality, by all accounts vulgar, his loud and blustering voice, his leather industry, his demagogic ways of maintaining favor with the people, and, perhaps above all, a venality which is historically hard, if not impossible, to substantiate.[3] There can be little doubt that the war against Cleon, however it had begun, had become by this time a thoroughly personal feud, and little else.[4]

This fact has consequences for those who wish to find in the *Knights* a serious political message. The *Knights* is a highly political play, the most political of them all, in that its whole action is concerned with the political scene in Athens, while the characters purportedly represent actual people in high civic or military office. Hence an air of specious realism and topical immediacy surrounds the play, and this impression is enhanced by the fact that the element of pure fantasy, so pervasive in other plays, is here suppressed in the welter of things as they are. Nonetheless, for all its dependency upon political satire — or perhaps one should say, scurrility — the *Knights* cannot be made to fit into any program of reform, or even of responsible criticism. It is a monument, and a vigorous one, to the personal animosity of Aristophanes, who was perhaps still of such an age as to behave rather like a Young Turk, toward an opponent formidable enough to be dangerous and for that reason, if for no other, the biggest comic fish that could be pulled ashore. It must be acknowledged that the poet landed his catch, gasping and flipping, a good many times before Cleon's death made the sport no longer amusing. And if the *Knights* relies less on fantasy than some other plays, it is still not wholly lacking in fantastic structure and elaboration; and in his treatment of the character of Cleon, Aristophanes gives full range to that visionary creativity which renders his work, one might say, of the world but not quite in it.

Moreover, it is surely a mistake to suppose that in this play the poet has formed a real political alliance, permanent or momentary, with the young aristocrats who formed the corps of the knights.[5] This impression can have arisen only from the opening lines of the parabasis, which have been interpreted as if they were spoken by the actual knights, instead of by a chorus dressed up to represent them. What they say smacks more of Aristophanean irony than of politics:

If ever someone of the old-hat comic producers had tried to compel us
To step to the fore of the theater here, and deliver parabasis verses,
He would never have got an easy consent; but this, this poet is worthy,
Because he detests the same folk we detest, and courageously speaks what is
    righteous,
Marching heroically forth in the hurricane's teeth, and the toils of the cyclone.[6]

It is hard to understand these words as anything but another example of Aristophanes' ingenuity in praising himself. As for the knights, they provided a natural not to say obvious chorus, since there was trouble of some undetermined sort between them and Cleon, as the beginning of the *Acharnians* makes clear. But the "alliance" can hardly have gone beyond that, and we have no reason to believe that the young knights had anything to say about Aristophanes' use of them. If they had, they would surely have objected to his representing them as supporting a sausage seller for prime minister, and they might have resented being teased about their elegance and their long hair.[7] For all the play's political orientation and subject matter, neither in the persons of the chorus nor in the action of the play as a whole can any serious political intention be discovered. The supreme good which is envisioned is simply the fall of Cleon. Once this is achieved, what follows is a finale representing the "good old days," a stock theme frequent in Aristophanes and in all the other comic poets.[8] It is rather pedantic to see in the reforms promised by Demos at the end the manifesto of a practicable program corresponding to the general moral beliefs of the rural democracy, and currently endorsed by the younger aristocrats.[9] All that Demos promises is to pay the fleet; prevent draft-dodging; hang Hyperbolus; and put an end to forensic impostures, rhetorical jargon, and beardless people in the market place. If the knights or the poet had practical aims in mind, they could not have failed worse; Demos' reforms were not carried out, Hyperbolus was not hanged, and Cleon continued in office. The play, however, was a rousing success.

It is not only the degree of savagery which makes the *Knights* unique. As said above, Aristophanes has relied less upon fantasy in this play than is usual with him, and has instead built a structure which approaches allegory. As a rule, Aristophanean fantasy does not merely provide a reply to the situation of which it is born; it goes further and answers the whole world, so to speak, in terms of the individual who invents it. Dicaeopolis' fantastic private treaty does not solve the international situation, but it provides him with a utopian structure of peace for himself, a transcendent new world corresponding to nothing but the dream states of a singularly uninhibited psyche. By contrast, the evil situation in the *Knights*, and the cure which is found for it, involve nothing transcendent, no new or private world which reduces the real world to unimportance. The Paphlagonian slave, Cleon, can only be deposed from his influential position with Demos by someone who can surpass him in vulgarity, impostorship, and corrupt demagoguery, and a Sausage Seller is found who performs these feats. Ludicrous as the proposition may seem, it is scarcely a real fantasy; indeed, when one considers the post-Periclean leaders who piloted Athens to her ruin, Aristophanes appears almost as a historical prophet. Nor do the two slaves who discover and support the Sausage Seller envision anything beyond the riddance of the hated Paphlagonian. It is true that in the last scene everything changes for the better, the Sausage Seller turns out to be a savior and a restorer of the old Demos of

Marathon days, so that in the very end a touch of the utopian enters. But it comes as a surprise, and it is rather feebly motivated dramatically, if at all. Moreover, the reforms which Demos promises, while some are ridiculous enough, are simply on the level of reforms, not of transcendence. Demos promises to be good and sensible hereafter, and the play ends with a kind of one-to-one cure for the evil with which it began.

Such a structure tends to pitch the *Knights* in a lower key than some of the other plays and to give it a flavor of superficial realism. If it cannot be said to offer any actual program of reform, it nonetheless presents with some fidelity the contemporary political scene of the rabble-rousing Cleon hoodwinking the Athenian demos, and eclipsing in power his more moderate and gifted colleagues, Nicias and Demosthenes.[10] The general picture corresponds well enough with Thucydides', and is far from fantasy. The Sausage Seller is, indeed, a wholly invented character, and as such, perhaps, a creature of fantasy, and certainly grotesque. But he is invented for a single purpose, and he does little beyond simply accomplishing it. On the other hand, as will appear, he possesses certain features in common with other comic heroes, and if these are less developed in his case than elsewhere, he is still not altogether different. Aristophanes' main characters are extremely varied, but their variations arise from the varying emphasis on the different elements in the comic hero's structure. In the case of Dicaeopolis, it was seen that his *poneria* could on occasion become *alazoneia*; in the Sausage Seller there is an enormous emphasis on this element — it is, in fact, almost his whole character. He is not, however, much interested in peace; indeed the *Knights* is scarcely a "peace-play." Though he does present Demos with the two *Spondai*, or Truces, at the end, the gesture is perfunctory, and is perhaps motivated chiefly by the attractions of staging the Truces, in the form of two strumpets, without which the "good old days" would be, in comic terms, unthinkable.

That the hero is the Sausage Seller, not Demos, should be self-evident. Those who believe that Aristophanes' hero must always be an old peace-loving farmer have sometimes tacitly assumed that Demos, who fits the description, is therefore the hero, though he appears only in the second half of the play, and then does very little.[11] In character Demos has much in common with some of the heroes, but in the *Knights* the small farmer's role is displaced from the center of action, and dexterously transformed into a symbol, and a very explicit one, of the sovereign people of Athens. In a brilliant monograph on Aristophanes' technique with metaphor and personification, Hans Newiger has devoted much attention to Demos, and has analyzed him as a metaphoric figure, simultaneously conceived as the people as government and an Attic countryman, with a name which, felicitously, was a fairly common personal one.[12] By skillful, almost imperceptible, shadings of language, Aristophanes makes his political and domestic aspects alternately emerge, so that there is a constant equivocation in the figure, an equivocation which keeps him from being purely allegorical. His irascibility, deafness, and intellectual shortcomings as a person subtly become identified with the disastrous legislations of the Assembly, while his altogether human devotion to eating beans shades off into the materialistic foibles whereby the people are cajoled and duped by demagogues. Thus, to go no further than his first introduction, he is described as

> A scratchy-tempered old bean-munching bumpkin,
> Demos of Pnyxville,[13]

where the beans indicate not only a staple of country diet — Greek bean soup is still called the "national dish" — but also glance at the use of beans in elections by lot; while the Pnyx is happily discovered to be the "deme" from which the whole *demos* comes.

Newiger's very detailed analysis confirms vividly the contention of the preceding chapter, that a character in a play is an image, a unit of communication embracing a wide range of experience in small compass and refracting it anew for the audience or the reader. Demos is a more than usually complex image, and a wonderfully successful one; for being himself both individual and mass, he captures the spirit of individual anonymity amid the masses, a feeling central for the era of Aristophanes. Yet, important as he is, he is not, in his passiveness, the hero; he is the background before which the Paphlagonian and the Sausage Seller play out their flagrant villainies.

It is the Sausage Seller who bears most of whatever fantasy the play contains, and it is a strange fantasy. Though at the end this creature of the market place brings about the "reform" of Demos, and thus the one-to-one cure spoken of earlier, he does not begin in any such way. Given the proposition "The demagogues are going from bad to worse," Aristophanes does not say, "Let us therefore revive the good old times in the form of a great man or two," as Eupolis seems to have done in the *Demoi*; [14] instead, with characteristic perversity he replies, "Then let us have the utter worst and be done with it." The proposal marks one of those leaps into outer darkness, acts of desperate pulling-free from things as they seem, which lay the bases for such structures as Nephelococcygia and Dicaeopolis' paradise. If what follows is no such structure, that is due to the limited end at which the play aims. The leap is there, and the Sausage Seller is the man of the hour, the hero with whom we are invited to invest our sympathies. It has been well observed that social and political conditions in the late-fifth-century democracy were such that the small burgers, in their inarticulate helplessness, depended progressively more and more on striking individuals in public life, with whom they identified their fading selves and interests.[15] Such a striking individual is the Sausage Seller, incredibly exaggerated, gross and obscene, yet cut in the pattern of those leaders who, after the death of Pericles, rose to eminence from the lower orders of trade and industry as representatives of the people. His force, however, lies not so much in his satirical relevance, which is sufficient only to authenticate him in the world of experience, but in his grotesqueness, the absolutism of his shamelessness, and his affinity for the boundless.

Comic heroes, it seems, are made not born. Their careers are the results of decisions framed in desperation and carried out with steadfast paranoia. Dicaeopolis had to find himself before he could take his great step, and the Sausage Seller at first has no intimation of what is in store for him. The two slaves of the prologue, maddened by the clever oppressions of the new Paphlagonian, have discovered oracles which reveal that Athens is to be ruled by a succession of merchants each worse than the one before; there have been so far an oakum seller, a sheep seller, and now a leather seller, who seem to represent respectively, Eucrates, Lysicles, and Cleon. The last and worst is destined to be a sausage seller. Scarcely has the oracle been spoken, when this apparition of dubious salvation enters, with his tray of sausage meat, κατὰ θεόν, "according to the god," a phrase which lends him a dignity greater than he knows.[16] The atmosphere of divine appointment develops as Nicias and Demosthenes hail him, and explain:

Nic.:   Come, take his chopping board away from him
        And teach him about the oracle of the god;
        I'll keep an eye on the Paphlagonian.
Dem.:   Come, first lay your utensils on the ground,
        Then greet the earth and gods with reverence.
S. S.: There y'are. What is it?
Dem.:   O blessed man, O rich!
        O Nobody now, tomorrow Supergreat,
        O Chieftain of all happy flourishing Athens!
S. S.: Look, fellow, why don't you just let me wash
        My guts and sell my sausage? You're laughing at me.[17]

When Demosthenes insists that he will become, in accordance with the oracle, a great man, the Sausage Seller wonders rather pathetically how a Sausage Seller can become a man at all.[18] Already one detects the theme of the subhuman and the superhuman playing subtly around the more immediate point that only a wicked and clever fellow can triumph:

Dem.:   Just for this fact you shall be great, because
        You're wicked, straight from the market place, and brash.
S. S.: I don't think I am worthy of great power.

Dem.: Oh my! Why do you say you are not worthy?
Don't tell me you've a virtue on your conscience? [19]

But the Sausage Seller has no virtues. When he has heard the oracle, he accepts the god's gift of demagogic rule, which is, as Demosthenes explains, as easy as making sausage, and a very similar hash. As allies he is promised an odd assortment: the thousand knights, all good and high-class citizens, anyone in the audience with brains, Demosthenes himself, and the god. At the first sight of the Paphlagonian, the poor Sausage Seller runs for his life, but the chorus of knights enters, and the long battle begins. Before it ends the Sausage Seller, now confirmed in his destiny, boasts that Athena herself has sent him to outdo Cleon in imposture; he has become a divinely appointed creature of bestiality.[20]

As Old Comedy developed the problem of giving it dramatic unity was one which was felt, apparently, more and more strongly. Pherecrates won notice, for instance, for relying less on invective than on original and skillful plot construction, and Eupolis also was concerned with structure.[21] What these two poets actually did is not clear, but Aristophanes, recognizing no doubt that conflict is indispensable to drama, frequently pulled a play together by expanding and developing the agonistic element. After one fashion or another, this is true of the *Acharnians, Birds, Thesmophoriazusae, Lysistrata,* and *Frogs,* wherein there is great freedom in handling this aspect. In the *Knights* the problem was simpler, and the agon becomes essentially the whole play, beginning instantly after the parodos, and continuing unabated beyond the parabasis, up to within a hundred lines of the end, when the utopian epilogue follows.[22] Aside from the end, which is a special problem, the *Knights* has thus a unity which is perhaps almost too strict; the play lacks a degree of the others' delightful variety. But, be it fault or virtue, such strictness of design is carried out also in the actual writing; the *Knights* is imagistically one of the most contrived and ingenious of the plays, conceived from beginning to end around a very limited number of images, the chief of which, as we shall see, is eating.

This fact perhaps accounts in part for the way in which certain things are represented, in particular the character of Cleon, and the profession of his opponent.

One need not be troubled about the historical accuracy, or lack of it, in the representation of Cleon as the conniving, toadying, ruthless slave of Demos. Aristophanes seems to have had only one scruple in the matter of staging his enemies, and that was to be sure he said everything bad he could think of. Yet it is relevant, perhaps, to ask why he here makes so much of Cleon's supposed corruption and susceptibility to bribes, when not even Thucydides, writing presumably well after Cleon's death, makes any such charge, though he regards him as brutal, incompetent, self-interested, and in general repulsive. Had Cleon ever been convicted, or even generally suspected, of bribery, it is hard to see how he could have maintained his prominence; one is forced to conclude either that Aristophanes had private information in the matter, or that bribery, and especially the swallowing and regurgitation of bribes, forms merely a particularly useful image in the general picture of a voracious monstrosity, gobbling down everything within reach. It is possible that the whole idea began with a scene in the *Babylonians*, but it is certainly a major theme here, and the probability is that we are dealing with an image run rampant, no less dramatically viable and expressive for being not literally true.[23]

The agon rages for about a thousand lines, with some interruptions. Throughout, it is a contest in *poneria* (clever wickedness), *anaideia* (shamelessness), *bdelyria* (disgustingness), *panourgia* (criminality), and *alazoneia* (impostorship). It falls into three main events: first, a bawling and boasting match by way of *proagon*; second, the contest for the control of the Council, which takes place offstage but is narrated by the victorious Sausage Seller; third, and most important, the contest for the control of the Demos. This last has three parts, a fawning and flattering match, an ordeal by oracles, and finally the contest in feeding and coddling. The words listed above, or words like them, summarizing the proper equipment of a demagogue, keep appearing in undisguised candor; the two opponents brag of what they will do to each other, while the chorus cheers its champion on:

> Ah, from of old have you not shown
> The shamelessness wherein alone
> Orators find defense?
> At the milking of fat foreigners, trustful in your quality,
> You're unrivaled; and the son of Hippodamus weeps to see.
> Now to my infinite joy has appeared
> Another, and fouler by far than you are!
> He will stop you, he will chop you off, he comes from where you
> come — the
> Gutter, and he'll master you in villainy,
> And wildness, and impudence! [24]

Shouting is the first accomplishment, excellence in which gives some promise of supremacy in shamelessness in general; stealing, lying, and bullying follow, all mixed up together in a perfect orgy of scurrility, as the two boast of the horrors which they can perform: analysis is futile.[25]

But presently the Paphlagonian, so called from the verb "to bluster," begins to take on the aspect of a great storm, and the texture is suddenly filled with images of seafaring:

Cleon: I shall come forth in mighty breadth, and furiously blowing
  Confound the earth and sea in one confusion and contusion!
S. S.: And I will furl my sausages right prudently, and sweetly
  Sail down my own nice breezy waves, and you can go to hell-fire!
Dem.: And I, if you should spring a seam, I'll tend the bilge and bailing.[26]

The imagery of the storm-tossed ship of state, already traditional, is unmistakable here, but with characteristic inventiveness, Aristophanes adds, as he added a new city to Sicily, a new wind to her troubles, the *Sycophantias*, the "Informistral," or "Sycophoon," the blast of the informers, a particular threat in the war years. The sailing images continue sporadically; if the Sausage Seller had "furled his sausages" before, the chorus urges him later to "let out his sheet with brave spirit and irresistible speech," and to "swing his ship alongside with his yard-maces ready." [27] The battle with Cleon has become a sea fight, and as Cleon gets the worst of it, he is left churning the sea and splashing his oars helplessly.[28]

The vision of Cleon as a storm is frequent. He is a typhoon, a whirlwind; he comes "shoving heavy waves before him, jumbling and confounding"; he blusters and "boils over." And the Sausage Seller is promised that, if he is victorious, he too can enjoy the power of the trident with which to "shake up and confuse everything." [29] It is through the confusion which he creates that Cleon maintains his power and obscures his wickedness, as men catch eels by muddying the water.[30] And finally, he is not only the storm itself, but a pair of instruments indispensable for stirring and pulverizing, a ladle and a pestle, figures which become more important three years later in the *Peace*.[31] Such images of Cleon are perhaps justified by what is known of Cleon's turbulent character, and his dependence on a state of confusion for the preservation of his own influence.[32] But Aristophanes does not leave it there; he transforms him into a series of monstrosities, a chasm, a Charybdis, a dog-faced baboon, the last perhaps partly arising from Cleon's designation of himself as the watchdog of the people.[33] Better still, he is a gigantic colossus overshadowing the whole Greek world:

> Impossible to evade the Paphlagonian!
> He watches everything. He has one leg
> In Pylos, and the other in the Assembly;
> And thus bestraddling, so great is his stand,
> His backside gapes toward Chaos, while his hands
> Reach Graftia, and his brain's in Peculasia.[34]

Grand as this vision is, it is only a trial run for the prodigy which appears two years later in the *Wasps*. But it well illustrates Aristotle's point, that poetry is more philosophical than history; here is real creativity, the myth-making force of the true poet.

Imagery of this sort tends to overtake the action of the play and direct it, as we have seen in the case of the imagery of coal and feathers in the *Acharnians*; and when this happens, the satirical aspect, with its immediacy of point and relevance, yields to a larger structure of the ridiculous. The *Knights*, however, offers an example of extreme economy in the use of images, most of which are of the dramatic, or controlling, kind. Besides the related metaphors of storm, confusion, and seafaring already mentioned, there are only a few major images, which are played again and again like recurrent notes in music, and all are associated with the basic idea of shameless knavery which motivates the play. Now food, as a rule, is a happy subject in Aristophanes, most of whose plays end in some kind of feast. But in the *Knights* it becomes a symbol of every kind of political corruption. To list the various foods mentioned in the play, or the cooking vessels, or the words meaning to eat, guzzle, or gourmandize would be lengthy indeed. What is interesting is the way in which the food images accompany and develop the characters and situations in the play.

One may pass over peripheral examples, such as the prompt conversion of the language of Euripides into a meal of bitter herbs;[35] the whole course of the plot takes place in terms of food. In his speech of exposition Demosthenes explains that old Demos is fond of the pleasures of the table, and his slaves do their best to provide him with fine fare. The Paphlagonian, however, steals all the credit by bringing the others' confections to the master as if they were his own, flattering and encouraging him to "fill up, munch, gobble!" Demosthenes, it seems, had baked a fine Laconian cake in Pylos, but Cleon had served it up as if he had made it — a not very subtle way of saying that Cleon's spectacular victory over the Spartans at Sphacteria had been really due to the generalship of Demosthenes.[36] Immediately, somewhat as in the case of the character of Demos himself, the action is conceived in terms of the blended images of politics and gluttony, suggestive enough of a greedy public body kept complacent by obsequious demagoguery.

With the arrival of the Sausage Seller, however, the food imagery becomes thicker and distinctly less pleasant. The fact that the climactic figure in the series of demagogic horrors is a maker of sausages is almost surely the result of the play's basic symbol. Low and illiterate, he was raised in the market place on scraps and offal, which he calls dog's meat, and out of similar materials he makes sausages.[37] The market place itself is a double symbol. The agora was the administrative center of Athens, but it also was a commercial center, the place where the various "sellers" have come from. This association of trade and low breeding is a fundamental idea which gives the adjective *agoraios* almost the simple meaning of "vile," even when it is used as an epithet of Zeus and Hermes, as gods of the market place.[38] And the Sausage Seller's name is, of course, Agoracritus, "Pick of the Market." But the main point is sausage. In a passage mentioned earlier, Demosthenes explains the art of government:

> Do just what you do now,
> Hash everything up into mishmash, make
> Sausages of it, and stick close to Demos,
> Sweetening him up with sugary, cookery talk.[39]

The verb here used for making sausage means literally "to stuff a gut," and it is fair to say that the image of a stuffed gut, a sausage, stands at the center of the dizzying whirl of gastronomic and alimentary images which keep constantly in view of the edifying spectacle of bloated gluttony and indefatigable sycophancy. The Sausage Seller will stuff the public gut with political confusion; Demos stuffs his own gut with the palliatives of demagoguery; Cleon tries to do both at once — a fact which in the end is his undoing.

In the succeeding tussles between the two contestants food images, especially in gluttonous context, keep flying about:

Cleon: This here fellow, I denounce him, I declare he exports soup
         To the triremes of the Spartans, so they're all souped up to fight!
S. S.:   I, by Zeus, denounce this fellow; let the prytaneum judge!
         He runs in with belly empty, and runs out with belly stuffed.[40]

In an odd scene, inexplicable probably except by the controlling quality of the eating image, the Sausage Seller and Cleon alternately threaten first to *eat* something, and then to *do* something great and wicked:

Cleon: With me, with me whom will you match? I am the sort that promptly
Gulps down hot slabs of tunny fish, anon a stoup of liquor
Unmixed, and then will bugger all the generals in Pylos!
S. S.: And I? A haunch of beef for me, and then a porker's belly;
I'll gobble all, and drink the broth; anon, unwashed and reeking,
I'll croak down all the orators, and give old Nicias spasms! [41]

The threats which follow grow more intestinal and less quotable. But as the Sausage Seller departs to win over the Council from the Paphlagonian, Demosthenes primes him with wine and tidbits, as fighting cocks were primed for battle with garlic, and sends him off "to bite and slander, eat crests, chew off cock's combs and return." [42]

The image disappears in the parabasis (except for the horses that eat crabs), but returns immediately thereafter. The Sausage Seller has won over the Council by telling them first that anchovies are cheap, and then passing out free coriander and leeks to eat them with.[43] Discountenanced, the Paphlagonian comes raging back, threatening to challenge his enemy before Demos:

S. S.: How fierce you are! Come, what do you want to eat?
What is your favorite dish? A leather purse?
Cleon: I'll pull your guts out with my fingernails!
S. S.: I'll trim your free feeds in the prytaneum! [44]

Cleon feels confident that he can win in a contest before Demos, because he "knows what tidbits" to feed him.

S. S.: You feed him tidbits poorly, as nurses do:
You chew up something, giving him a little,
And yourself swallow thrice as much as he.[45]

The Sausage Seller's reply obviously motivates the penultimate scene, where it is Cleon's attempt to combine simony with bribery which leads to his downfall. In the meantime, however, politics continue to be symbolized under the guise of all kinds of food, cookery, and voraciousness. Cleon gulps down magistrates under examination, and dips his bread in treasury soup; Demos' seal is a vine leaf stuffed with beef fat, where the word for "fat" is a pun on the word *demos*; the Sausage Seller's oracles will outdo Cleon's because they are not only about Athens and Lacedaemon, but also about pea soup, fresh fish and false barley measures.[46] Even Themistocles gets dragged into it, because he "kneaded the Piraeus into the city" by means of the long walls, having first made the city "full to the brim" — again, an image of stuffing.[47] The Sausage Seller's oracles are by Glanis, the older brother of Bakis, and a *glanis* seems to be a kind of fish.[48] Demos allows his politicians to batten on him until they are fat, and then sacrifices and eats them, or else tickles their throats till they regurgitate their evil gains.[49]

The image is ubiquitous, inexhaustible, almost monotonous; its climax is dexterously dramatized in the scene where the two adversaries bring out their sacks of presents for Demos. There are other kinds of presents, but for the most part they consist of food, and presumably Demos sits there eating goodies passed to him from each side, until the sacks are empty. The menu is generous; out come cake, barley, bread, pea soup, sliced fish, meat broth, tripe, entrails, another cake, wine, more cake, and rabbit. But Cleon has cheated. He has reserved the biggest cake for himself, and Demos fires him, taking in his place the Sausage Seller, whose sack is empty. Cleon struggles to the last, but finally collapses, in a fine parody of tragic recognition scenes, upon learning that his adversary is indeed the Sausage Seller divinely appointed to be his downfall.[50] Three final touches complete the culinary imagery: in the last scene Demos has been redeemed from his naïvete and, in a parody of the legend of Medea and Aeson, he is rejuvenated by being cooked; even in this uplifting picture food is not forgotten, for Demos is said to be such as he was once when he was "messmates with Aristides and Miltiades";[51] the Sausage Seller is invited to dinner, where food resumes its usual associations of festivity and social health, while Cleon is condemned to become a sausage seller, to make his wares of dogs' and asses' meat, and drink used bathwater.

The imagery of eating, cooking, and stuffing concretely embodies the action of the play, which is, as said earlier, a contest in political villainy. Following Francis Fergusson's suggestion that a play's action can be summarized as a rule in an infinitive phrase, one might summarize the action of the *Knights* in the phrase "to stuff a gut." [52] Gut-stuffing, in one form or another, constitutes the chief mode by which the two demagogues strive for supremacy; furthermore, a sausage is, in fact, a stuffed gut, the concrete token of the action. The approaching victory of the Sausage Seller is signalized by a final transformation, when the redeeming sausage becomes a belly-timber for a trireme:

> S. S.:   The goddess especially
> Sends you this belly-timber for the ships.
> She has a great regard for naval things;
> Take it and eat, with wine mixed three to two.[53]

Almost as important as stuffing, however, is the motif of speech, as a vehicle of persuasion, deception, and manipulation. The true *alazon* is a master of murky but specious rhetoric. It might be just noted that in the fifth century the word *logos* had as yet few associations with philosophical reasoning and pursuit of truth, and many with the rather opposite ideas of calculation, seeming (as opposed to fact), and even deceit.[54] Dicaeopolis, as we have seen, has recourse to Euripides in order to equip himself rhetorically for his speech to the chorus; and similarly, the Sausage Seller is advised by Demosthenes to sweeten Demos with "cookery phrases," $\dot{\rho}\eta\mu\alpha\tau\iota\iota\iota\varsigma$, the exact word used by Dicaeopolis, and elsewhere, of Euripides' language.[55] Verbal dexterity is the essence of the comic hero's power, and there is no real difference between the prayer of Euripides in the *Frogs* to the "swivel of the tongue," and the Sausage Seller's prayer as he is about to enter the Council:

> "Come then, ye lechers and ye quacks," said I,
> "Boobies and dunderheads, and Impudence,
> And market place where I a boy was reared;
> Now give me brazenness and provident tongue,
> And shameless voice." [56]

The tongue is the concrete image; it "mints grand phrases," and the Sausage Seller can even speak of Athens as "tongue-kissed" by Cleon into docility.[57] Speaking also unites with food imagery: "How dare you talk in opposition to me?" cries Cleon; "Because," replies the Sausage Seller, "I too can speak and make a rich sauce." [58] Cleon replies, "By means of my skill, I can make the *demos* wide and narrow," a line which, though in the form of a statement, suggests what will become the main theme of the *Birds*, the power of language to mould fact.[59] As yet, however, in the *Knights* the power of speech is less metaphysically treated, and the idea is developed simply for a satirical end, as a formal illustration of *anaideia* (shamelessness).

The oracle contest is a striking example of the delusive power of language. Demos is fond of oracles, especially of oracles about himself as an eagle in the clouds, a fact borne out by Thucydides.[60] The orator's task is to use the obscurity of oracular language to support himself and his case, and to hoodwink Demos with promises of power and wealth. There could scarcely be a better framework for the exploitation of the gifts of a fast talker, and the Sausage Seller makes full use of his native genius, first by reinterpreting the oracles of the Paphlagonian. If Cleon has an oracle bidding Athens preserve "the sacred watchdog" (Cleon himself), the Sausage Seller promptly turns the dog into Cerberus, the Hound of Hell, who fawns, but secretly eats the best morsels, licking up the dishes "and the islands." [61] If Cleon represents himself as a lion (who fights mosquitoes!), and urges Demos to guard him, building a wooden wall with iron towers, the Sausage Seller reinterprets the wood and iron wall as a pillory in which to "guard" him.[62]

The Sausage Seller's own oracles are lofty but opaque structures of nonsense, impenetrable without an explanation of the farfetched puns of which they are built. Demos is to beware of the "hound-fox," an image which clearly is intended to suggest Cleon, to begin with, but then by a deliberate confusion is made to mean a trireme full of soldiers collecting tribute. Staggered by such ingenuity,

Demos is ready to believe that the Sausage Seller will provide money for the fleet within three days.[63] The next oracle depends wholly on a pun on the city of Cyllene and the word for a hollow palm, denoting graft.[64] Cleon proves to be not so skillful in the art of reversing implications, and the Sausage Seller crowns his success with a flattering dream of Athena pouring ambrosia on the head of Demos, and on Cleon's head garlic pickle, a word which dexterously recalls an oracle quoted by Demosthenes to the Sausage Seller at the outset.[65] The oracle contest marks the climax of the motif of εὐγλωττία, specious talk, as the *sine qua non* of political knavery and power; as the chorus had said earlier to its champion:

> O you who have appeared, to all mankind the greatest blessing,
> I envy your glib running tongue; for if you thus can wield it,
> You will be mightiest of the Greeks.[66]

It was said earlier that such uses of language in other plays more often terminate in fantasy, while in the *Knights* the satirical purpose remains always in view. Nonetheless, there are verbal touches even here which illustrate Aristophanes' penchant for the detachment of pure fantasy, and the structural autonomy of lyric. The "Sycophoon" was one example, the dread wind that blows when Cleon blusters, an invention possessing something of the life independent of reality which gave the city of Katagela its charm. To call Cleon a "dog-faced baboon" is a simple sort of abuse; but the proper word for it is *cynocephalus*, and to spell it with two "l's" as Aristophanes does suggests a monster rare indeed, verging on the mythical: "the dog-headed phallus." Such constructions defy reason, but are tellingly imagistic, and structurally akin to lyric, however their contents may differ from what is commonly associated with the lyrical. Similar is the musical mode which is the only one that Cleon, in his "swine culture," could learn, namely the "Graspian," or "Bribian," mode.[67]

It might be objected perhaps that these are little more than word plays, and should not be dignified as either lyric or fantasy. Yet good word plays are metaphoric, and metaphors affect and modify reality, or at least the mind's grasp of it. For instance, what, if not metaphor, is the inspired behavior of the knights' horses in the parabasis? The knights first praise their fathers' and their own services to the city, and then proceed to praise their horses. These are remarkable horses: in a frenzy of patriotism they rushed down to the sea, manned the galleys themselves, and rowed off against Corinth, urging each other on with the cry "*Hippapai*," a delicate perversion of the sailors' "heave away" refrain, ῥυππαπαῖ. The passage as a whole is an amusing enough cadenza on the cavalry officer's horse-worship, but in the single nonsense word *Hippapai* the fantasy is crystallized unforgettably. By one shout of "Yo-heave-horse" the Athenian cavalry is transformed into a troop of high-spirited, seafaring Houyhnhnms confounding the distracted Yahoos of Corinth.[68]

Another example, only a little less inspired, might be found in the second parabasis, where the triremes of the fleet expostulate indignantly at the thought of being commanded by Hyperbolus. One is an older dame; another a "maiden who has never known man," but she would rather rot at her moorings than submit to Hyperbolus; another declares that if the Athenians vote such an outrage, the ships had better sail to the Theseion or the Eleusinion, both well inland on the slopes of the Acropolis, and take refuge with the gods.[69] Here the personification of the galleys and the dream image of sailing inland create a poetic level beyond the satire on Hyperbolus, while the delicate sexual overtones, especially of the young ship rotting at her dock, recall, or better perhaps foreshadow, the wistful images of war-widowed young girls in the *Lysistrata*.[70]

These are all essentially detached moments of fantasy, lyrical spurts with little or no relevance to the play in general. But sometimes a lyrical moment can evolve with significant summarizing force from a coagulation of the running images, previously designated as dramatic or controlling. Such was the passage on the Acharnian Muse in the last chapter. In the *Knights* there is a fine example, cast appropriately enough in the form of an oracle. Demosthenes is trying to persuade the Sausage Seller to rise to the occasion, and he quotes him a prophecy, "subtly and cleverly riddled":

> Yea, at what time soe'er shall an eagleather, crooked of talon,
> Seize in his jaws a boob of a serpent that drinks blood, verily
> Then is the garlic pickle of Paphlagonians ruined,
> Yea, and the god shows forth great glory to sellers of entrails,
> If but they choose not rather to be mere vendors of sausage.[71]

Here the fantastic eagle of leather, with his talon crooked for plunder and bribery, is tangled with a serpent (explained in succeeding lines as the stuffed gut of a sausage), together with images of stupidity, blood-sucking, selling, the garlic-pickle government of Cleon, and finally the divine dispensation by which the Sausage Seller is to assume the reins of power. All the major images of the play are here, concentrated into a single oracular image (itself a motif), and a parody to boot of the snake-and-eagle omens of epic. It is a construction which refracts the action of the whole play, itself static and unrepeated, while the "eagleather," the garlic-pickle policy, and the sausage-serpent all belong to the same world of comic metaphor as the seafaring horses of the parabasis, or the avenging vine prop which topples the mighty Lamachus of the *Acharnians*.

Such passages, which exercise the poet's gift for playing his subject to the full extent of imaginative possibility, bear the unmistakable stamp of Aristophanes, and relax the almost too severe economy of the play in general. Old Comedy had a native tendency toward inconsequential sportiveness. The *Knights*, by contrast, sticks peculiarly close to its subject, with the result that what fantasy there is, instead of expanding, enveloping, and measuring the world in the light of the poet's personal fullness of response, remains a fantasy *upon something*, less of an emancipating figure of thought than a simple ornament. Why Aristophanes should have written so on this and on no other occasion is a question. One reason must surely be his private hatred of Cleon; another may have to do with the possible influence of his contemporary, Eupolis. In antiquity it was regarded as common knowledge that Eupolis collaborated with

Aristophanes in the *Knights*, and there is a fragment of Eupolis in which he claims that he helped the "baldhead" write this play.[72] It is very hard to discover precisely what Eupolis did, and probably the effort to mark any certain passages as his is misguided; but he was, according to tradition, "elegant, and an excessively good marksman in satire." [73] The *Knights* is the most astringently satirical play of Aristophanes, and its elegance is evident in the tightness of its execution, if not in the nature of its subject matter and imagery; so that it may not be unreasonable to suggest that for the nonce Aristophanes had adopted some of his rival's technique, or perhaps actually profited by his suggestions. In any case, the familiar Aristophanean mixture of satiric realism and metaphoric fancy here is weighted heavily in favor of satire and the world of immediate relevance, and one looks in vain among the extant works for anything quite like it.

One important feature of the play, however, stands out in strong contrast to the rest, and poses a special problem. In the last hundred lines, Aristophanes turns the tables upon his audience, as well as upon the basic assumption of the play, and presents a picture of the *demos* redeemed and restored to the heroic freshness of the days when he defeated the Persians at Marathon. The Sausage Seller has changed character, and instead of being the worst of demagogues, has turned out to be a savior. This ending is rather a surprise, and something of a disappointment; one might have expected that Aristophanes could contrive a scene of final, triumphant celebration without altering his whole conception and introducing a happy ending, which seems little more than a quasi moralization upon the thumb-worn theme of the utopian past. The previous action has been built wholly around the necessary progress of bad coming to worst, and the Sausage Seller's prime dramatic function has been to exceed Cleon in every form of corrupt and vulgar practice. The chorus celebrates him as doing exactly that:

> The villain has found another, far
> Exceeding in mightier villainies,

And subtle wiles,
And crafty words.[74]

By what right does this creature of the gutter suddenly become a magician who boils Demos back to his pristine vigor and intelligence, a moral catechist who scolds his ways and approves his repentance, and finally reveals himself as an apostle of peace and order? What has become of shamelessness, impostorship, and *poneria?* The change seems unmotivated, and though it has been ably defended as a designed surprise, consistent with Aristophanes' usual inconsistency, yet it seems odd, and there may be another solution.[75]

The reformation of the city in general, or of the *demos* in particular, is regularly implied in Old Comedy, and the rejuvenation of an old man, usually the hero, is something which takes place ordinarily by imperceptible degrees as the play progresses. The only problems are the Sausage Seller's role, and the excuse for such a scene here. The scene may seem far less incongruous when staged than when read, for the chorus and Demosthenes have repeatedly hailed the Sausage Seller as a savior, and salvation now appears, in a satisfying, albeit unlooked-for, shape.[76] *Poneria* is always a means to salvation; the only thing new here is that it is the salvation of the polis which is achieved, rather than the transcendent salvation of the individual hero, as in the case of Dicaeopolis. But the *Knights* is not a play of personal transcendence of the polis, but of victory within it and on its own debased terms; so that by rights there should be no paradisiac vision at all.

Yet, somehow it works, and the answer may lie in the conception of the grotesque as advanced earlier. The Sausage Seller is, by the oracle's definition, the lowest creature in the city, and when first told that he is to be a great man, he replies, as we have seen, in terms which imply that he scarcely considers himself a man at all. Yet, nightmare that he is, he is divinely appointed, and throughout the play references to this higher sanction, and to oracles, continually contribute to his demonic stature, while the inspired horrors of his vulgarity, unscrupulousness, and personal filth constitute something which is both less and more than human. Or simply, to be that bestial requires genius, and the nearest Greek word for genius is *daimon*.[77] If, therefore, in the actual plot of the play there seems to be little motivation for the sublime though ridiculous reversal at the end, such motivation may exist in the imagery, or more precisely in the pattern of grotesquerie, in which the Sausage Seller is conceived. And this pattern finds completeness in the last scene, when the Sausage Seller remarks that if only Demos knew what his own former behavior had been like, he would think him, the Sausage Seller, a god.[78] The ability to do wonders had been implicit in the character throughout, and the divinely chosen beast has become the new god of Athens. Here, doubtless, is much irony, but also the complex of the grotesque, beast-man-god, running covertly beneath the action of the play and making possible, if not inevitable, the final scene. By way of completeness, be it noted that the superhuman colossus of Cleon, also a grotesque vision, in the end assumes the role and profession of the Sausage Seller, and sinks to subhuman stature. There is a kind of fullness in the grotesque which invites infinite transformation.

The *Knights* is not the most engaging play of Aristophanes, nor the most characteristic, but it is an extraordinary *tour de force*. If it lacks the charm of the *Acharnians* or of the *Birds*, it must be praised for the most sustained self-consciousness of technique, in dramaturgy, in humor, and in language. The language may be repellent, but it is nowhere slack; the wit may be tinged with sourness, but it is abundant. Still, in its topical concern and involvement with personal hate, the *Knights* remains but a poor example of what Aristophanes was capable of by way of broad sympathy and large symbolic structures. He had better things in store, but meanwhile, at less than thirty, he had gained the first prize for the second time, and Cleon was unable to do a thing about it.

Peace

The *Peace* has commanded less admiration in general than most of the plays of Aristophanes. Wilamowitz called it a hastily turned-off affair, the weakest of the lot, and a good many scholars agree.[1] There is doubtless some justice in this view. Aristophanes could scarcely have planned the work until the peace negotiations of Nicias had reached a point where their success was assured; and since, according to Thucydides, these negotiations began only in the winter, or toward spring, the *Peace*, in order to be ready for the City Dionysia, must have been written in a matter of weeks.[2] There is some reuse of earlier ideas, chiefly from the *Acharnians*: Trygaeus is a less interesting Dicaeopolis, Polemos is a less interesting Lamachus; the mockery of the armament makers, while amusing enough, is a little pale after the ingenious lampooning of crests and "bugbear" shields in the earlier work. Above all, there is little plot and no real conflict, no spirited agon, to give the play dramatic tension and shape. Yet withal, the *Peace* has extraordinary charms; its gaiety is the purest to be found in all Aristophanes, and its verbal and imagistic wealth is abundant. If it lacks conflict, that lack may in part arise appropriately from the nature of the occasion, and we should not be too captious if the poet celebrated such a long wished-for event, not with a comic drama, but with a festive masque.

The excuse for treating the *Peace* here, instead of in its chronological position, should be self-evident. Thematically it belongs with the *Acharnians* and *Knights* in that it is concerned directly with the political life of Athens, the dilemma of the war, the role of Cleon, the desire for peace. It is the last play, indeed, in which Aristophanes confined himself within the immediate scheme of the polis, so far as we know; in later works he seems to stand outside it, as we shall see, considering it with detachment and as a whole, rather than finding his themes in the specific manifestations of its daily life. In the *Peace* he writes as a citizen within a scheme which is, for all the ever increasing problems which it presented to the individual, still familiar, intelligible, and, at least in the spring of 421, hopeful and promising. Seven years later, in the *Birds*, one feels a degree of alienation, or at least a need for revaluation of the whole idea of the city; but in the *Peace* the magic circle is still unbroken, and the magician-hero an unqualified civic success. And indeed, if Trygaeus is less interesting than Dicaeopolis, it is precisely because his problem has been solved within the polis. Dicaeopolis failed as a citizen, and hence was driven to transcend the city. For Trygaeus there is no need; his flight to heaven in order to recover peace, "or else denounce Zeus for Medism," is heroic fantasy; but the treaty of Nicias was not, and the fantasy serves only to bring about what was in fact already true. It seems almost unfair that Nicias is never mentioned in the play, but fairness has little to do with the spirit of Old Comedy; Lamachus, too, is still treated as a warmonger, as he was in the *Acharnians*, though at the time of the play's production he was serving with Nicias as one of the peace commissioners.[3] But no matter: the peace had come, and in the second part of the play fantasy and fact coincide; the poignant and tormented dreams of the *Acharnians* and *Knights* end in a joyful wakening, to which Aristophanes was never to be able to return.

It has been shown that in both the preceding plays the hero is a creature of *poneria*, and a grotesque one, in the special sense of combining in himself aspects at once bestial, human, and divine. These elements appear to be almost indispensable in the earlier plays of Aristophanes, though the proportions in the mixture may vary. If strong emphasis fell on the godlike transcendence of Dicaeopolis, and on the subhuman bestiality of the Sausage Seller, Trygaeus is the most human of the three. He alone comes from a real deme; he is "Trygaeus of Athmone, a good vine dresser," and though there is symbolic significance in his personal name, which means Mr. Corn-and-vineyard-crop, there is none in his demotic. He announces himself to the chorus:

> A highly valuable man to you
> Am I, Trygaeus of Athmone,
> Who rid of all its terrible toils
>   The people's masses,
>   And farmer folk.[4]

The point in giving him such local habitation seems to be to unite him closely with the people, however he may surpass them in the gift for adventure; for as said earlier, Trygaeus does not need to transcend a city where fantasy is ratified by fact. For once, humanity is reasonably acceptable in its own shape.

And yet, this happy state is achieved, once more, only by one of those great leaps into outer darkness which mark the career of the comic hero. Trygaeus' great deed is perhaps the most grotesque of them all. He has been suffering from madness, according to his servant, madness of a brand new sort; he glares at the sky, expostulating against Zeus, and wondering how he can get up to heaven to thrash matters out with him.[5] Having tried ladders at peril of his skull, he now tries a giant *cantharus*, or dung beetle, an animal able, according to Aesop, to fly to Zeus. Mounted on this attractive steed, and addressing it as Pegasus, in a fine parody of Euripides' *Bellerophon*, Trygaeus flies off to recover Peace from the gods:

> Come, Pegasus, fare forth with joy,
> Shaking and jingling the golden bridle,
> On your shining ears;
> Hey, what are you doing, whither divert ye
> Your nostrils? To the sewers![6]

The dung beetle completes, in a way, the figure of Trygaeus himself, enabling him to achieve his quest and providing a symbol of the comic hero's range. A resolved and isolated individual, riding to the gods on an animal notable for its disgustingness, offers as full and rounded a picture of the grotesque as one could ask; he has found the secret key of nature, and the key unlocks the realm of the divine. The first interchange with Hermes is significant. Struck by the apparition of the *cantharus*, Hermes asks what it is. Trygaeus replies with dignity, "a hippocantharus," whereupon that earthly creature suddenly attains a mythic grandeur, analogous to the hippocentaurs, the hippocampi, and perhaps also the hippalectryons of Aeschylus. Trygaeus, however, momentarily undergoes an opposite sort of change, and when Hermes bursts out at him, presumably on the beetle's account, with a flood of abuse, Trygaeus sinks under it:

Herm.:   O filthy and presumptuous and shameless,
         Execrable, all-execrable and most execrable,
         How got you here, most execrable of execrables?
         What is your name? Speak!
Tryg.:   Most execrable.
Herm.:   Your ancestry! Speak!
Tryg.:   Most execrable.
Herm.:   Who is your father?
Tryg.:   Mine? Most execrable.[7]

One is reminded specifically of the Sausage Seller boasting that he is a villain and the son of villains, and in general that the comic hero unites the highest and lowest in himself, a "most execrable" fellow, who blandly says, at the gate of Olympus, "Go in and summon Zeus for me."

The transformations of the dung beetle, first into Pegasus, and then into a hippocantharus, are stages on the way to its final destiny. Trygaeus' little daughter had doubted that such a foul-smelling creature could approach the gods,[8] but it does. And when after Peace has been discovered Trygaeus looks for his mount in vain, Hermes explains that it has been hitched to the chariot of Zeus to draw the lightning.[9] It is the apotheosis of the dung beetle, completing not only the parody of the *Bellerophon* but also in a way the motif of heroic divinization, which would not be quite appropriate for Trygaeus himself, who has to get back to Athmone. The final transfiguration of the beetle fulfills an earlier suggestion of one of the servants in the prologue that the beetle was sacred to Zeus the Thunderer, or Kataibates, where the final "s" of Zeus is certainly intended to be carried over as the first letter of the epithet, so forming the Greek equivalent of a well-known four-letter word; one might translate, roughly, but politely, "Zeus of the Thundermug."[10] At any rate, the monster of disgust has been found worthy of lofty things.

Nor is this all. In the same passage of the prologue the servant had remarked that whatever deity this beetle was sacred to, it was certainly not Aphrodite or the Graces. Yet it is precisely the beetle, as emblematic of the play's whole quest, who brings about a victory for Aphrodite by restoring Peace and her two lovely companions, Theoria and Opora. As Trygaeus and the chorus gird themselves for the effort to pull Peace out of the cavern, they call on Hermes, the Graces, the Seasons, Aphrodite, and Desire.[11] All have associations with sexuality and fertility, while throughout the whole second part the principal image for Peace is sex, culminating, of course, in the wedding scene at the end. Old Comedy is a paradoxical affair, and within its scheme it is only natural for the "anti-social virtues," if one may so call them, to restore society to health and happiness. This paradox, ambiguity, or what you will, has been implicit in the beetle from the first. The two slaves who are feeding it have a further complaint beyond the simple repulsiveness of their task: the beetle is fastidious, and will not eat its manure unless it is made up into a neat round cake, "as if for a woman!"[12] The image of femininity adds somehow a basic touch; if not precisely aphrodisiac, the beetle is a characteristically Aristophanean blend of grossness and delicacy, setting the tone for the play, and corresponding aesthetically to the grotesque paradox of beast-man-god.

Few plays exploit this blend, or juxtaposition of grossness and delicacy, so freely as the *Peace*. Analysis runs the risk of dissolving the charm with which Aristophanes manages to mention the unmentionable in contexts of freshness and light. Translation does real violence, but the point can perhaps be illustrated. Flying, for instance, is a lofty business, regularly associated by Aristophanes with philosophy, dithyrambic poetry, and lunacy; these associations appear in the *Peace* when Trygaeus, having walked back down from heaven, gives a meteorological account of the phenomena of the upper air, and remarks that the only other people he saw there were the souls of two or three dithyrambic poets.[13] But the flight of the beetle, unwillingly turning toward the courts of Zeus away from the sewers and drains, offers a fine example of high, if maniacal, aspiration linked with *nostalgie de la boue*.[14] And furthermore, the play's basic structure is built around the related, though opposite, functions of eating and defecation, both simultaneously represented in the prologue as the two slaves make dung cakes for the monster.

One of the most basic image clusters is, not surprisingly, that of smell. The first part of the play fairly reeks. Offal and excrement are the smells of war, but with the return of Peace the world begins to smell sweeter. The progress is foreshadowed in Trygaeus' command, called out from beetleback, to the man who is relieving himself in the Piraeus:

> O dig it under,
> And heap over it mounds of earth,
> And over the top of it plant wild thyme,
> And pour on myrrh! [15]

The stenches of war must be buried under the earth, and the divine Peace must be hauled up out of it. The very extremity and explicitness of the stinks in the first part lend poignant contrast to the abundance of sweetness which bursts out as Peace rises from the cavern. She is described in terms of what she smells like, not like a military knapsack or onion hiccups, but "most sweetly round the heart," of "exemption from service and perfume":

> Tryg.: She smells of harvest, hospitality,
> The Dionysia, flutes, and tragedies,
> And melodies of Sophocles and thrushes,
> And little verses by Euripides —
> Herm.: Drat you, don't slander her! She takes no joy
> In a poet of forensic phrasicles.
> Tryg.: Of ivy, of wine strainers, bleating sheep,
> Of bosomy women bustling to the fields,
> And drunken slave girls, and the cup drained out,
> And all good things.[16]

If Aristophanes has dragged us through muck before, he makes up for it by this lovely kaleidoscopic romanza on the "smells" of peace. The motif now moves on to the wedding scene, where the bride is freshly bathed, and the bridegroom fragrant with sweet ointment.[17] Nothing malodorous recurs in the play except twice: once where the oracle-monger Hierocles, who opposes peace, enters and tries to stop the feast; one of his nonsensical oracles mentions, appropriately enough, a stink beetle.[18] The other is in the parabasis, where the chorus offers a description of Cleon, an absolute chef-d'oeuvre repeated from the *Wasps*, which lists among Cleon's other less quotable personal attractions the stench of a seal.[19]

The imagery of food makes a similar progress from the beginning to the end, from the ghastly fare of the beetle to the splendid marriage feast. More specifically, it goes from the dung cakes of the opening line to the wedding cakes of the last, cakes which go "wandering around alone," waiting to be eaten.[20] Similarly, the act of chewing passes from the grim crunching of the beetle, "plying his molars and swinging his forelegs like a sailor pulling a hawser," to Trygaeus' cheerful shout:

> Fall to it manfully,
> Grind with both your jaws, for there is no use, ye rogues,
> In having white teeth, except to chew with.[21]

After the negative images of voraciousness of the *Knights* Aristophanes seems to be working his way back toward the normal comic associations of food and feasting. One passage strongly recalls the *Knights*, however, as Polemos tosses the cities of Greece into his mortar, each in the guise of its characteristic food product, and prepares to pound them up into a hash, as the Sausage Seller was to make mincemeat of politics.[22]

Though the *Peace* may be lacking in real conflict, it is not lacking in movement; there is a palpable, resistless progress from war to peace, from the redolent gutters of the Piraeus to the sweetness of the countryside. This movement back toward the country is accented by the frequent repetition of the words, εἰς ἀγρόν, "to the field"; the phrase, or its close equivalent, recurs roughly a dozen times, beginning in the passage already quoted where Peace rises from the ground.[23] The theme gives a kind of dance rhythm to the play, and leads on a series of transformations; the chorus of farmers, who had entered dancing with irrespressible excitement, now prepare to return to the fields, marching, in a fine parody of an army, in ranks "close and fierce as a cake or a dinner party," their shovels and mattocks glinting in the sun.[24] In all the cities the sickle makers are celebrating and jeering at the armorers, who are tearing out their hair, a foreshadowing of the little scenes at the end, where Trygaeus well-nigh literally turns swords into ploughshares — the crest into a feather duster, the spear into a vine prop, the breastplate into a chamber pot, and so on.[25]

Less obvious, and also less easy to account for as deliberate, is the theme of pottery. When the war began, the storage jars began to strike against each other, and presently the chorus' "six-bushel jar" is smashed by the stone of the enemy. A little later Cratinus, famous for his toping, drops dead of a stroke when he sees a full cask of wine smashed by the Spartans.[26] The stone and broken pot are clear symbols of war; Peace herself, after Pylos, had approached the Athenians with a "full jar of truce," and in the end a grateful sickle manufacturer presents Trygaeus with sickles and casks, which now sell for three drachmas apiece, "for the fields." [27] The hostile stone that smashed the jar may have ended up on the rock pile under which Peace was buried; in any case, the bema where the warlike Hyperbolus holds forth is referred to, not very endearingly, as that "stone in the Pnyx." [28] These running images may not be so controllingly dramatic as those of other plays, but they assist and accompany the rhythm of the joyful dance, as the farmers escort Lady Harvest back to the field.[29]

Opora (Harvest) and her companion Theoria (Embassy) are figures which, like Demos in the *Knights*, waver tantalizingly between the abstractions which they represent and the attractions of the way they are represented. Peace is herself transcendent, and was probably represented by a statue; her two attendants, however, prefigure respectively the immanent aspects of private and public peace, or, more accurately, peace in the country and peace in the city. Such female figures form a regular part of an Aristophanean exodus, though not always with such explicitly allegorical significance. In the *Knights* Demos is given the *Spondai,* Truces; how many of them is not clear, though their meaning is. Dicaeopolis also appears in triumph with two girls, who, though they are praised for nothing but their physical charms, must by analogy be understood as symptoms, if not symbols, of peace.[30] Sometimes, indeed, these gay embodiments seem little more than gay bodies, naked at that; and the question of whether they were played in actual nudity by hetaerae or by actors costumed to represent them has raised a minor, but enthusiastic, philological controversy.[31]

Be that as it may, the association of Peace with sex is a natural one in the Old Comic tradition of fertility and fun, and Aristophanes develops it more broadly in the *Peace* than elsewhere, weaving in also, by pun and innuendo, images of country foods, appropriate to a bride who is herself the produce of the fields. When Hermes delivers Opora to Trygaeus, he says:

> Come how, on these conditions take Opora
> Unto yourself for wife; and in the fields
> Dwell with her, and raise up a brood of — grapes.[32]

And when Trygaeus wonders if he might get upset by making too free with Opora, who is, after all, food, Hermes replies, with a resounding impropriety, that he can cure himself with a dose of pennyroyal, for pennyroyal, besides being a common stomachic, had another use.[33] Here, of course, the poet builds essentially on a simple picture, such as the chorus' prayer "to live in peace, holding a girl and poking the coals," or "to sit by the fire with chick-peas, burning the beech log, and kissing the Thracian maid while your wife is bathing."[34] But by turning his images into each other, he achieves a metaphoric involvement, a unity of symbolic meaning which surpasses in poetic force such mere descriptions as those. Admittedly, much of the time Aristophanes is merely exploiting the wealth of Greek words which have secondary sexual meanings; what counts is the way in which both meanings are sustained in a delicate balance, neither being overpowered by the other. Figs, for instance, commonly stand as a metonym for *muliebria,* and "to grow fat" can be used of male sexual eagerness.[35] But is the following an erotic orgy, or a simple pastoral?

> And then, when the cicada sings
>   His sweet refrain,
> I love to scan my Lemnian vines,
> To see if they are ripening,
> For they put forth their shoot betimes;
> And I watch the cheat-fig swelling,
>   And then, when it's mature,
> I eat it, and I lay to, and I say,
>   "The season is a dear,"
> And I grind up thyme, and stew it,
>   And I grow fat all the summer.[36]

There is no need to add other examples; Aristophanes' treatment of the whole second half of the play builds a constantly shifting texture of double, triple, and multiple images, in which the pastoral world of figs, flowers, vineyards, and furrows is illuminated and brought to life by the warm gay imagery of sex, the peace which is love. The final songs are a simple fertility festival, and as Trygaeus leads Opora forth "to the fields," the chorus divides in two on either side of the bride, and shout antiphonally to each other:

> What shall we do to her?
> What shall we do to her?
> We'll gather a crop of her!
> We'll gather a crop of her! [37]

The word for the crop is *trygé,* and the bridegroom's name is Trygaeus. It is the Dionysian union of love-making and harvest-making.

The destiny of Peace's other attendant is equally erotic, but in very different terms. Theoria, Sacred Embassy, is handed over to the Council as mistress-general to them all. Since she represents peace in the city and in the government, this "wedding" takes place not in the guise of a fertility ritual but of a spectacular public festival, with all its hubbub; in fact, athletic games. Since no one can be trusted

to escort her to the Council, Trygaeus himself leads her toward the
prytaneis in the audience and presents her to them in a speech which
stands as a masterpiece of montage, a device used by other comic
poets, but seldom with such dexterity. The speech, which is unfortunately in two senses untranslatable, describes the Council's
future pleasures with Theoria as a dizzying series of athletics,
wrestling, boxing, pancratium, riding, and chariot racing.[38]

The lack of plot and conflict in the *Peace* contributes to its lyrical
flavor, so that its imagery tends to form a static blend, like iridescent
cloth. What movement there is, as said earlier, resembles dance
more than drama, a dance around the central figure, the great statue
of Peace. There are only two real scenes of action in the play, the
flight of Trygaeus and the raising of Peace from her deep rocky
pit. The raising of Peace illustrates once more, this time in action,
Aristophanes' gift for mingling grossness and delicacy. Peace herself
is conceived, naturally enough, as a beautiful and youthful goddess, yet she must be laboriously hauled up with shovels, crowbars,
and a block and tackle operated by all the farmers in Greece, while
Hermes and Trygaeus threaten malingerers and obstructionists with
blows. It involves something of the grotesque to lift an abstraction
with a block and tackle, yet it is an expression of deep, lyrical
earnestness, resembling the extravagance of Hotspur, who would
"dive down to the bottom of the sea, and draw up drowned honor
by the locks." If the structure is not precisely beast-man-god, it is
at least goddess-men-machine, and it illustrates well the manner
in which the lyrical and the grotesque may merge. In the *Peace*
such figures of language and action seem to take the place of a
plot, whereas in other plays the images move with it. The raising
of Peace is, on the one hand, action; on the other, it comes close
to static symbolism.

A degree of real dramatic conflict, however, rises between Hermes
on the one hand, and the chorus and Trygaeus on the other. Hermes
has been left behind by the gods to look after the kitchen ware and
to prevent Peace from being liberated. Hermes seems to have been

chosen for a reason; for the recovery of Peace is a theft, and Hermes is god of thieves. Trygaeus' first act is to bribe him with a piece of meat, which causes him to take a milder view of this visitation to Olympus.[39] But he will not permit the rescue of the goddess until he has been bribed again, this time with a gold cup, for Hermes is always "very merciful toward gold things."[40] Trygaeus tries first to joke him into acquiescence, and the chorus begs him in an ode, but he is adamant; it is only when Trygaeus tries harder-headed tactics that he begins to listen:

> Come, I beseech you, pity their appeal;
> They honor you more than they did before,
> For they are thieves more than they were before.[41]

The appeal to thievery and, even more, the promise to reveal the plot of the Sun and Moon against the gods win attention. The Sun and Moon are plotting to betray Greece to the Persians, so that all will sacrifice to the heavenly bodies instead of to the Olympians.[42] This happy invention savors of demagogic techniques in the Assembly and the frequent denunciations and calumnies of Cleon; it shows Trygaeus as a man accomplished in the art of *poneria*. He follows it with a promise to transfer all festivals hereafter from their rightful patrons and to celebrate the Panathenaea, Diipolia, Adonia, and even the Eleusinian Mysteries in honor of Hermes! [43] This is a bribe worth taking; the gold cup caps the climax, and Hermes agrees to help. Of course, once Peace is out of the ground, Trygaeus makes no mention of sacrificing to anyone but her, and Hermes is even rather casually dismissed later on.[44] The god of thieves and *poneria* has been outdone at his own game; but he remains an important motif, a token of Trygaeus' mastery at those same techniques of influencing affairs which made Dicaeopolis and the Sausage Seller into heroes of salvation. It is no wonder that Trygaeus can use the word *poneroi* of his friends, with all affection.[45]

Bellerophon's attempt to fly to heaven ended with his disastrous fall, and provided a traditional paradigm of vaulting ambition brought

low, a warning against trying to "climb to the stalls of heaven." [46]
Trygaeus' little daughter indeed warns him to take care, lest, having
fallen and lamed himself, he "provide a plot for Euripides and become a tragedy." [47] But comic heroes can do what tragic ones cannot. Trygaeus is the only figure in Greek literature who climbs the
heavens by his own effort, puts the gods in their places, and walks
home. The theme of humbling the gods, becomes, of course, a basic
one in the *Birds*, where its implications are far more profound. Here
it is played only lightly, but it serves to give Trygaeus that extra
dimension of implicit divinity which marks the early heroes of Aristophanes. Trygaeus gets the goddess Peace away from Zeus, and
leaves him a dung beetle in exchange. The elevation of the dung
beetle to the chariot of Zeus completes the grotesque circle of man-
beast-god, wherein humanity is redefined and reoriented. The transcendent aspect of the hero is not so much emphasized in this play
as is his humanity, for reasons given earlier; but enough is there
to make him a figure of salvation.

That the salvation was actually the work of Nicias did not bother
Aristophanes in the least; he preferred imagination to fact any time.
Indeed, the *Peace* stands in evidence against a pure escapist theory
of Aristophanean comedy: here is fantasy, in full sweep, but from
what does it escape? The peace was there, or all but there, already.
It is the joy of fantasy which prompts fantasy, and also the scope
which it gives for *poneria* and the grotesque. In his early years, at
least, Aristophanes kept away from any unnecessary responsibility
toward truth and fact. If this is clear from his treatment of Lamachus,
it is even clearer whenever he gives an account of how the war
started. In the *Acharnians* it had to do with the abduction of harlots
and Pericles' "Olympian" rage; in the *Peace* it turns out to be mostly
Phidias' fault, and Pericles was simply afraid of being involved in a
trial for embezzlement.[48] Let him who can extract historical relevance from these lighthearted jibes; factuality and consistency form
no part of Aristophanes' responsibility as a poet. Even Trygaeus
himself, the demonic apostle of peace, when told by Hermes that

the Athenian triremes, in retaliation for the Spartan invasions, had "eaten the figs of guiltless people," seems to forget who he is for a moment and cries: "And justly, too, for they cut down my fig tree, which I had planted and nurtured." The chorus of peace-loving farmers chimes in with similar words.[49] The poetry of Aristophanes reflects far more than it ever bothers to organize, regularly maintaining double perspectives on everything. Aristophanes was more consistent in his love of peace than in most things, but even here he could reflect also the sharp resentments of war, and the anger against the Spartans.[50] He can jeer at Cleonymus as well as at Lamachus, if not better.[51] And sometimes, as in the *Knights*, he seems to forget about peace almost entirely, staging a chorus of gallant young cavalry who boast of their military brilliance. The comic task was to reflect as many aspects of life as possible within an imaginative structure of personal salvation, to which for its own good the world in general then adapts itself. What was said within this scheme was far less important than its vitality, and the command of environment, indeed of all nature, which it dramatized. The grotesque emancipates the deepest sources of power to deal with the unintelligible, and to this basic comic framework the poet adds the dexterous shifts and verbal wonders wrought by *poneria*. This was his complex image of the world in the early plays, and it was still to reach its climax, before fading with the civilization which had bred it.

The *Acharnians*, *Knights*, and *Peace* are all political plays, more so than most of the others, but they are political in terms of a hero who overcomes, and sometimes completely transcends, society. If the *Peace* is the weakest of the three dramatically, yet in a way it summarizes the whole picture well, and its full, spontaneous lyricism gives it some of the quality of a hymn. It contains probably more sexual and scatalogical improprieties than any other play, yet its taste is sweet, and its sweetness does not return so fully ever again. Comedy was destined to include more somber reflections, and Aristophanes was to give fuller expression to his gift for such poignancy and melancholy as we find in the passage of the *Acharnians* on the old men in court, or in the *Peace*, where the soldier is shocked to find his name illegitimately posted on the service call.[52] But that time was still a few years off, and meanwhile the poet had been giving himself also to other, less political themes; it is now time to turn back to these as they unfold in the *Clouds* and the *Wasps*.

·IV·

THE WAR BETWEEN THE GENERATIONS

Clouds

IN 423 and 422 Aristophanes produced two plays on the themes of education and the contrast between the older and younger generations. The second, the *Wasps*, is a lighthearted extravaganza, one of the funniest of all the plays; the *Clouds*, on the other hand, presents many problems. Witty as it is in many places, and adorned with some of Aristophanes' finest lyricism, it is also apparently such a serious work that it is almost universally accepted as a manifesto of Aristophanes' educational beliefs, his hatred of sophistic teaching, and his belief in the old, conservative way; and indeed, as the play stands scarcely any other interpretation is possible. Yet, in the earlier plays it appears that Aristophanes had real affinities for the contemporary thought of the day, and for sophistic rhetoric especially, insofar as it provided the hero with tools to validate his rascality and impostorship; and these affinities are even clearer in the *Birds*. But the situation in the *Clouds* is very different, and while consistency is not to be required of Aristophanes, the reason for the change must be sought. Why should the introduction of new gods, or the escape from just debts, be considered a sin here, when precisely the same things are done with approbation in the *Birds*? [1] Why, in this instance, is the hero made to repent of his great effort, instead of triumphing? Repentance ill becomes a true comic hero, and in fact, Strepsiades has none of the heroic qualities which characterize other protagonists; he possesses a certain appealing charm, but lacks real *poneria* and the larger dimensions of the grotesque. He suggests somewhat the old men of New Comedy, who need admonishment, while the moralizing tone of the play in general has something of the ethos of Menander, in contrast to the supramoral heroism of Aristophanes.

Interpretation of the *Clouds* is seriously hampered by the fact that our version is not the original one. The performance at the City Dionysia in 423 was a failure; the reason for this may not be very significant, since we know of two masterpieces, at least, which gained only a second prize, the *Birds* and *Oedipus Rex*. Yet there must have been a reason, even if it was a poor one. One may easily believe that Cratinus' *Wine Bottle*, which got first, was an excellent piece by a popular and aging master, but it is less likely that Ameipsias' *Connus* deserved preference over Aristophanes. In any case, according to ancient tradition Aristophanes, who believed strongly in his play, revised it after some fashion with the intention of producing it again.[2] There is no evidence that a second production ever took place, and there has been some controversy as to whether the poet's revisions were sufficiently extensive to constitute a real second version such as the ancient commentators mention, or whether there were merely some lesser changes, notably in the parabasis.[3] The matter seems now to be put beyond any doubt by the discovery of a hitherto unnoticed scholium to *Clouds* 1115, in which Heliodorus refers his readers to his own commentary on "the first *Clouds*."[4] It appears therefore that both versions existed as late as the first century A.D., and that they differed sufficiently to justify two separate commentaries by a single scholiast.

Any critique of the *Clouds* must, therefore, take account to some degree of the problem of the first play. The effort to reconstruct its outlines cannot lead to any certain result because of the nature of the evidence available, but speculation may help to throw light on what Aristophanes intended by the surviving version, which is certainly unfinished. The parabasis alone, which mentions Cleon's death in its first part and in its second speaks of him as living, suffices to show that it is an ill-adjusted mingling of earlier and later passages. Such lack of consistency lends no humor, but only confusion, to a text. There is other evidence as well that the second edition never received final form.[5] For one thing, the ending is not very satisfactory, despite Strepsiades' table-turning on Socrates, with the line: "I tread on air and contemplate the sun."[6] Edifying as the burning of the Thinkery may be, from the point of view of comedy it is a depressing substitute for the more usual frolic; indeed, there is some reason to wonder whether it is even edifying.[7] True, it is, in a way, a typical "worsting of impostors" scene, but it does not represent a triumphant protagonist, but only a vengeful one. And in this case, there is good evidence, to which we shall return, that the burning scene was an addition in the later version, an addition which was difficult to accommodate satisfactorily to the play. All these facts prompt the serious question of how far it is justifiable to attempt an interpretation of a play which may not, as it was left, represent the poet's wishes in any very clear way.

Other scenes, especially in the latter half of the play, might similarly be questioned on grounds of comic taste and inspiration. Strepsiades' dispersal of his creditors fails to rouse the usual kind of approval, chiefly, no doubt, because Strepsiades never attains to any stature greater than he starts with, nor possesses any transcendent aura of personal or social salvation, but only the lineaments of a rustic fool. He has too little of Touchstone, and too much of William, to carry the banner of *poneria*. Indeed, *poneria* is precisely the art which he hoped to learn from Socrates, and failed; and while his son has mastered the real thing, Strepsiades' attempts to wield these devices are inept, not to say asinine. Now, a stupid attempt to be *poneros* has a special word in Modern Greek, *koutoponeria*, "fool's *poneria*," and it is not admired as is its true counterpart. It is, in fact, close to buffoonery, and Strepsiades in these two scenes is really a buffoon. We laugh at him more than with him, and our sympathy is deflected.

There are sundry scenes in Aristophanes where the hero responds as a buffoon when someone tries to teach him something, failing to get the point and perverting the actual words, only to use the whole lesson in his own fashion, in a later scene, against his teacher and to his own advantage. A good example comes in the *Wasps*, in the byplay over the fistfight between Ephoudion and Ascondas; [8] and a similar effect arises from the reuse of the "air-treading" line in the *Clouds* mentioned earlier. In such cases the buffoonery of an earlier scene engenders the *poneria* of a later one. But in the scenes between Strepsiades and his creditors the case is rather the reverse: Strepsiades, who had tried to learn *poneria* and failed, produces only buffoonery, a parody of what he wants. It is not that *koutoponeria* is never funny: the fumbling attempts of Euripides to be subtly clever in the *Thesmophoriazusae* are a triumph of comic art. But there the assumptions are different, for we are invited from the outset to laugh at Euripides, not with him. Here the familiar relish of an "impostor worsting" scene is lost through the pitiable stupidity of the hero, whose momentary victory in no way alters the fact that he is the victim of everybody, primarily of himself, throughout, at least until his moment of desperate retaliation. It might be said that Philocleon also fails to learn the elegant and lofty lessons of his son, and is in many ways his own victim. This is true, but it is also the way Philocleon wants it, and his intransigence is the opposite of Strepsiades' mixture of pliability and stolidness. Whatever he is, Philocleon is authentically himself; he will not learn, which is different from being unable to learn.

If the creditor scenes fall a little short of true gusto, the famous debate of the Just and Unjust Discourses shows real weaknesses of structure and purport. To begin with, their entrance seems to force an unmotivated exit by Socrates and Strepsiades, and the latter's re-entry at the end is equally puzzling; lack of dramaturgical finish is here obvious. The scene clearly replaces a different kind of scene, though we cannot say what. The content of the agon is also a somewhat uninspired invention. After an opening scene of mutual name-calling, which slightly recalls the *Knights*, the debate proper begins, presumably a struggle between the claims of the old and new kinds of education, but in fact in large part a discussion of sexual deportment. Other subjects do occur: the Just Discourse praises boys who are seen and not heard, the older musical modes, and resistance to raw weather; the Unjust counters with the advantages of warm baths and a ready tongue.[9] But it is surprising how persistently the theme of sex arises. The Unjust Discourse approves of adultery, and claims that through him it can be committed with impunity; the Just Discourse, ostensibly moralizing on the subject of boys' behavior toward male lovers, repeatedly bursts out in images of such pruriency that editorial abatement in school editions is driven to greater lengths than in the case of his openly unregenerate adversary. Here there is little plain, cheerful bawdry. Indeed, the Just Discourse talks a little like certain magazines which describe with enticing luridness the vices against which they purport to warn their readers. It must be noted that the motif of sex is elsewhere scarcely found in the *Clouds*, whose practical concerns are debts, law suits, barley, and horses. Sex is thematically irrelevant; yet it enters not with the merry irrelevance of certain unexpected dashes of invective — such as including in the joys of spring the fact that Morsimus' new play has been rejected [10] — but heavily and without wit, in the place where one might have expected a far more pointed display, or parody, of sophistic rhetoric, which is at most scantily deployed.

Such unaccustomed maladroitnesses in Aristophanes suggest that the second *Clouds* is unfinished in more than the parabasis and the lack of a few choral lines. One is tempted to believe that the poet's heart was not much in the revision, that he may have been compromising, putting new wine in old bottles, in the attempt to salvage a satisfactory play from what had been a grave disappointment to him. Anyway, he seems never to have bothered fitting its rough edges together. And if that is true, the apparent moral must be called in question. Did the first *Clouds* demonstrate that one should stick to the old gods, and pay just debts? If it did, it is perhaps no wonder that it failed, for as we have seen, the spirit of comedy is not really to be identified with the Just Discourse. It seems more probable that the first *Clouds* did nothing of the sort. We shall return to this problem later. First, it is important to examine the text as it stands, for its ideas and motifs, coinciding as they do to a degree with those of the *Wasps*, reveal a new and different range of poetic consciousness from that of the three plays already discussed, and foreshadow the great synthesis of the *Birds*. In the *Clouds* and *Wasps* the idea of transcendence, while not wholly absent, is far less central; the new dramaturgy is more complex, more intellectual, and it rests upon dialectic.

More than any other single feature, perhaps, the dialectic of the old versus the new in the *Clouds* accounts for Aristophanes' reputation as a conservative. Praise of the past, and especially of the generation of Marathon, was, of course, a commonplace of Old Comedy, and Aristophanes made use of it often. But the situation in the *Clouds* is somewhat more subtle. The action revolves around a series of paired antinomies which characterize, in their several ways, the division between the older and younger generations, the principal climax being, obviously, the scene of the two Discourses. Yet, though the end of the play emphatically asserts the rightness of the old, throughout the rest Aristophanes has shown singular skill in playing both ends of these antinomies, scarcely against the middle, but against each other, till both are attenuated and reduced to absurdity.

The *Wasps*, as will appear, is an even better example of this process, where the inversion of roles between father and son, comparable to that in the *Clouds*, is carried further into the realm of fantasy. But here, old Strepsiades going to school in place of his son presents the generational cleft in the light of a certain ambiguity, implying what is of course true, that the older and the younger are simply two aspects of the same substance, which is human nature.

The characteristics of the two are further complicated by the initial assumptions about the plot and characters. At the beginning the young Pheidippides is anything but an exponent of the new education; as the son of an aristocratic, Alcmaeonid mother, he is interested only in horse flesh, a respectable, though costly, pursuit for a young man, and one which recalls the valor, and harmless vanity, of the chorus of knights in the play of the preceding year. It is his father, the simple rustic, who wishes to enlist the help of philosophy and rhetoric in order to avoid paying the debts incurred by his luxurious son. Pheidippides' initial refusal to give up horses for higher education leads to Strepsiades' effort as a student, a sad failure; but the chorus, commenting on his matriculation, sings:

> Good luck to the man, for now being well
> Advanced in declining years,
> He colors his nature with young pursuits,
> And practices wisdom.[11]

These lines, which suggest the motif of rejuvenation familiar in other plays, are balanced by Strepsiades' remark to Pheidippides when the latter is finally induced to go to the Thinkery. The young man swears by Olympian Zeus that his father is mad:

> Streps.:   Listen to that, just listen! Olympian Zeus!
>   How silly, at your age, to believe in Zeus!
> Pheid.:   Well, what's funny about that?
> Streps.:   Oh, I was just thinking,
>   You're only a lad, and your mind's all out of date.[12]

In the course of the play, Pheidippides learns to be a regular "new" young man, full of all the new ideas and Attic salt, while Strepsiades learns, by suffering, to adhere to the principles of his own generation. Yet, despite that fact, the inversion of roles goes on. Imagistically, at least, Strepsiades appears briefly in the dashing role of a horse driver, as he flogs his creditor Amynias off the stage, calling him a "Samphoras," an excellent breed of horse, and telling him to clear away, "chariot wheels and all." [13] But if Strepsiades here momentarily steps into his son's equestrianism, the inversion reaches full circle in the scene which follows. In a quarrel about the relative virtues of Aeschylus and Euripides, Pheidippides has assailed his father with blows; he now proceeds to demonstrate, by Unjust Discourse, that he was quite justified in so doing, because, if parental chastisement is a sign of loving care, so is filial chastisement, and anyway, "old men are children twice over." [14] By skillful merging of action and images, Aristophanes has brought Pheidippides from a naïve youth with old-fashioned ideas to a man of the New Learning, with a firm, if unattractive, maturity. Correspondingly Strepsiades' wish for the New Learning has put him into the position of a child in his own house, wishing his son would go back to horses.[15] It is a kind of comic vicious circle, in which the old and the new imply and become each other. Perhaps the idea is reflected half-consciously in the poet's playing on the name for the last day of the month, when debts became due: it was called the "Old and New" day, and it threatens Strepsiades badly until his newly enlightened son proves that it simply does not exist.[16]

Similar ambiguities attend other paired antinomies which reflect the contrast between the older culture of Athens and the enlightenment, for instance the Olympian gods versus the "new gods," or the familiar theme of the country versus the city. The city is the natural home of novelty, troubles, and corruption; the country, a constant symbol of idyllic peace. Both, however, have to exist, and their uneasy union is symbolized by the rustic Strepsiades' marriage with the niece of Megacles "from the city":

> And when I married her, I lay beside her
> Smelling of wine lees, fig racks, fleece in plenty,
> But she of myrrh and saffron, and tongue kisses,
> Expenses, and gluttony.[17]

Like Dicaeopolis and Trygaeus, Strepsiades would like to return to the country; but unlike those heroes, he is not to achieve his wish, for he is bound in the dialectic of his marriage, which is the dialectic of the times. For this reason in the *Clouds* the motif of marriage has none of its usual joyous and positive meaning; it symbolizes here the dilemma of the war years, the confusion of social classes, and cultural irreconcilables.[18] Pheidippides is also trapped, between the education of his mother, who envisions him "driving a chariot in a great robe, like Megacles, to the Acropolis," and his father, who sees him "dressed in a leather jerkin, driving goats, like his father, out from Phelleus." [19] He yields at first to his mother, and drives horses; yet his father eventually re-educates him, though not to goat herding, but to the Unjust Discourse, the most urban of accomplishments. The symbols become reversed; by contrast with goat herding, the robe, horses, and chariot of Megacles seem citified indeed; by contrast with the Unjust Discourse, they seem innocently rural, for horses are, after all, raised in the country, while sophistic rhetoric flourished in law courts, elegant salons, and the lounges of the baths. The whole theme of country versus city is treated not simply as good versus evil, but as involving the inevitable conjunction of the two, with all its puzzlements. Aristophanes is not preaching a sermon on rusticity; he is reflecting the shape of the world around him. In the *Birds* the city-country theme will be even further developed in this way, until the contrast is lost in a larger vision of the world as a whole.

The chorus of clouds presents an even greater aspect of confusion. The clouds are the new deities of the philosophers, who deny even the existence of the Olympians. Their gifts to their devotees are of a singularly intellectual and urbane sort:

Soc.: These are the ones who provide us with wit, and with discourse, intellect also,
And with wondrous locution and circumlocution, inspection and firm apprehension;

and it is said that they nurture sophists, quack seers, doctors, dithyrambic humbugs and all good-for-nothings who sing their praises.[20] So far they sound like the true gods of the city sharpers. Yet their entrance is marked by one of the most melting pastoral lyrics in all

Aristophanes, in softly rolling dactyls, as they descend from Mt. Parnes toward the city in response to Socrates' invocation, which is equally full of fair images of land- and seascapes.[21]

Even more surprisingly, perhaps, these new natural deities, who, with *Dinos*, the Vortex, have supplanted all others, in the corresponding antistrophe celebrate Athens, and above all the famous cults of Athens, the Mysteries first, then the other temples and statues, the "fair-crowned sacrifices and banquets of the gods at all seasons," and finally the Great Dionysia.[22] Later, in the two songs which punctuate the parabasis, they call upon a number of gods, using all the appropriate epithets: Zeus, Poseidon, their father Aether, Helios, Delian Apollo, Artemis of Ephesus, Athena, and Dionysus.[23] It may be urged that the parabasis involves traditionally a partial abandonment of character by the chorus, and that therefore the patronesses of quackery can here celebrate the official gods, and also condemn such quacks as Cleon and the astronomer Meton. But the clouds do not wholly drop their character in the parabasis (nor for that matter does any chorus); they speak of having thundered and flashed dreadfully when Cleon was elected general, and of having talked with the Moon about the problems of the religious calendar.[24] Socrates certainly described them accurately when he said they took any shape they pleased, reflecting the things which they saw on earth.[25] They seem to sum up, in their irresponsible responsiveness, the blurring of apparently clear values, and the way things melt into other things.

The shiftingness of the clouds, however, goes even further, and it is dubious whether the last suggestion can account for their full change of character at the end of the play. After encouraging Strepsiades in his plan to become a master of sophistry, and, when that attempt fails, enticing him to make his son take his place, the clouds suddenly reveal themselves as deities of retribution, as it seems, visiting justice upon the foolish old man for having wanted to learn wicked practices. Trapped and beaten by his now uncontrollable son, he reproaches the clouds, and asks why they urged him on to his ruin.[26] Their reply recalls Herodotus' story of how the oracle at Branchidae once nearly tempted the Cumaeans to destruction:

> Thus always we devise, when we behold
> A man in love with wicked practices;
> Until we fling him into suffering,
> That he may learn to reverence the gods.[27]

The tone is that of tragedy, and one wonders what, if any, is the comic point. The situation is strongly reminiscent of the passage on the old men in court in the *Acharnians*, for if Strepsiades is ludicrous, he is also pathetic. The *Acharnians* passage, however, is a brief description, not weighty enough to upset the comic balance; here the whole play changes character, and turns toward an unmistakably serious, moral ending. The change is not wholly unmotivated, for the clouds have twice before prophesied the old man's repentance; [28] but the motivation seems insufficient, to say the least, and the ending remains an anomaly in Aristophanes.

Perhaps we are to understand, as one scholar maintains, that the clouds have intended all along to set Strepsiades straight; [29] this is, indeed, roughly what they say, but it is hard to see how the audience could ever have understood this early enough to prevent the feeling of having been deliberately misled. If Aristophanes was guilty of such misleading in the earlier version, the fact might account for its failure. It seems more likely, however, that the shift belongs to the revision and that it was never fully worked out so as to be motivated adequately in the earlier scenes.

But to return to the dialectic of the play, and the antinomies through which it evolves, the most important of all, perhaps, is the antinomy of nature and law, *physis* and *nomos*, the dichotomy which made itself felt, throughout the whole second half of the fifth century, between the nature of man and of the universe, and the conventions under which society is organized.[30] The widening horizon of Athens after the Persian wars brought about an increased consciousness of the variety of social and political customs, such as is reflected in Herodotus' sociological descriptions of Egypt, Thrace, or

Libya. The more *nomos*, custom-law, became a subject for thought and speculation, the less it appeared in the guise of an absolute structure, established by the gods, and the more it appeared in the relative light of a random, if inevitable, social growth. At the same time natural philosophy had begun to include theories of human nature which took account of the fact that man was a part of the natural, specifically animal, kingdom. All branches of thought were affected; history, politics, medicine, drama, and, perhaps above all, ethics were subjected to a rationalistic analysis which by the twenties threatened to disintegrate them altogether.

Stated in purely ethical terms, the question was: could one live within the restraints of law and society and still fulfill the needs of the human, individual nature, or psyche? The older thinkers, Protagoras and Democritus, had managed to evolve reasonably positive answers to this question. For Protagoras, as for Simonides, who wrote, "The city teaches the man," law and the polis were educative and progressive, not restrictive or damaging. Democritus developed an elegant moral calculus of pleasure and self-reverence whereby the psyche could be brought into harmony with the materialistic laws which governed the world.[31] But the balance was a fine one, and Protagoras himself was the first to claim, what Aristophanes attributes to Socrates, that he could make the weaker argument seem the better.[32] It was doubtless this all-important sophistic emphasis, especially by Gorgias, on the powers of speech and persuasion, and the consequent attenuation of any concept of "the truth," which did most in the late part of the century to breed the antimoral thinking of the younger sophists, and to widen the rift between *physis* and *nomos*. For Antiphon the two are hopelessly and fatally opposed, and law should be observed only when one cannot get away with disobeying it.[33] Antiphon did not, it is clear, make such a statement simply out of moral imbecility, but because he saw as the proper end of life the fulfillment of the integrated individual, whose "natural necessities," to use his own phrase, constitute "truth" for all individuals, a truth continually hampered by the obstacles of social law.[34] Viable or unviable, Antiphon's attitude was a logical conclusion, or seemed so for the time.

There is nothing new about noting the importance of the *nomos-physis* debate in the *Clouds*; the interesting thing is the way in which it is used. By writing a play whose central figure was to be the embodiment of contemporary philosophy, Aristophanes was practically compelled to bring this vital intellectual issue out into the open and treat it explicitly. As the play stands, moreover, it is a ringing attack on the exponents of *physis*. Socrates is presented as a natural philosopher, concerned with the "things of the air" (τὰ μετέωρα) and the things under the earth. The whole purport of the Unjust Discourse differs scarcely at all in its main point from the thought of Antiphon quoted above, even to the use of the phrase "natural necessities"; and his climax is that, when Pheidippides has learned his art, he may "use his nature, skip and laugh, consider nothing shameful." [35]

More explicit even is the scene where Pheidippides explains why it is just to beat one's father. Strepsiades says it is not lawful, but his son asserts that law is man-made, and why may it not be made by him as well as by the man who first "persuaded the men of old?" [36] Law is merely a matter of persuasion, whereas it is natural to beat one's father; witness the fighting cocks who do it all the time:

> And the other animals also,
> All of them fight with their fathers, and yet, wherein do they differ,
> They from us, except that they don't write any laws and decretals? [37]

Strepsiades suggests that if his son feels like a fighting cock, he may go and peck filth and sleep on a roosting perch; he is shortly to reject higher education. But the salient points of the new theory of human nature have been stated: man is an animal like others, except for writing laws; laws should be laughed at, anybody can make them; and what is important is to use one's nature, whose necessities are an inevitable part of the natural world.[38] It was perhaps a parodist's privilege to have loaded Antiphon's ethic with an overdose of shameless immorality; what is surprising is the exposure and rejection of the whole theory, for in other plays this same world of *physis* provides the motive power by which the heroic individual performs his miracles.

In earlier chapters the dilemma of the individual in the late fifth century has been described in various aspects: the political failure of Dicaeopolis, the Sausage Seller's doubt that he may not even be a man, Trygaeus shaking his fist at the sky and trying to climb ladders to heaven, all point to the helplessness felt by the individual before the events and circumstances of a world which was running away with the reins, and where the city-state, in its expansive imperialism and domestic complexity, was no longer responding to the needs of its constituents. The word used by philosophers for this helplessness, *amechania*, and their theories about the nature and meaning of the human psyche represent intellectual efforts to embrace and solve the problem.[39] Yet, as time went on the theory proliferated while the problem grew worse. As we have seen, Aristophanes could construct a comic hero in the image of this helplessness, and then, by a leap into chaos, send him off on a soul-saving fantasy wherein his selfhood is vindicated, and, as a by-product, society changed. These heroes do not, however, save themselves by any particular exercise of lawful behavior, restraint of obstreperous nature, or conformity to social custom. Quite the contrary, they "use their nature," fulfill their "natural necessities," "skip, laugh, and consider nothing shameful" except their enemies. They illustrate to the full, in fact, the liberation of *physis* from all inhibition, making laws unto themselves, to be enforced by quips, whips, and *poneria*. They do not, of course, exactly philosophize about it, but they all are gifted by nature with the Unjust Discourse, and use it freely along with their other talents. The question is, why did Aristophanes in the *Clouds* turn against what had been his authentic comic medium, expose it in a theoretical analysis, and then reject it in favor of traditional morality? He had certainly not outgrown the possibilities of heroic comedy in 423, for he continued to write it and to stage transcendent heroes, tentatively in the *Wasps*, emphatically in the *Peace* and *Birds*, and more delicately in the *Lysistrata*. And as for the immorality of not paying debts, the impiety of introducing new gods, the lubricity of speech, and the folly associated with cosmology, upper air imagery, and flying, all these become the heart and soul of his most splendid work. What happened in the *Clouds*?

Perhaps the safest thing to say is simply that Aristophanes is an inconsistent fellow, and leave it there. After all, the play did not gratify the audience's expectations of their new favorite, who had just won two successive firsts, perhaps because the formula was so different. Another possibility is that the theory of human nature which had liberated Dicaeopolis will not, when theoretically analyzed, bear moral scrutiny; it will do for parodic purposes, but if allowed to speak in its own person instead of through the mouth of a charming rogue — in short, if one stages the Unjust Discourse — it betrays itself instead of achieving salvation. If Aristophanes intended to show this, he did so at the expense of much of the comedy, in favor, perhaps, of a real moral purpose. Yet this wave of moralism, if Aristophanes really had it in 423, seems out of character, and certainly did not last long: in his very next work, which again deals with nature, education, and the rift between the old and new, no such point is made, but something nearer the opposite. What is in character for Aristophanes in the *Clouds* is the reversal of roles between father and son, the attempt to beat society through *poneria* (but not its failure), certain imagery, and, above all, the masterly caricature of modern learning which he labeled Socrates.

At this point it seems inevitable to digress at some length upon the subject of the earlier version. For the most part scholars have assumed that it was not essentially different in point from the second, and that it failed because it was too intellectually lofty and lacked the more popular elements of sex, politics, and revelry.[40] Certainly it might have failed for any of these reasons; but a better suggestion has been made, namely, that the first version was quite different, and that it failed because it was too sympathetic to the New Learning.[41] That the differences were considerable is evident from the Sixth Argument to the play, our only account of what Aristophanes did, and the scanty fragments of the first *Clouds* at least suggest the same. The Sixth Argument is quite specific, and deserves to be quoted in full:

> This play is the same as the former one. But it is revised in part, as if the poet intended to produce it a second time, but then for some reason did not do so. In general, emendation took place throughout almost every part. Some things were excised, other things were worked in, and there were alterations in arrangement [presumably of scenes] and in the interchange of the characters. The thoroughgoing parts of the revision were actually these: for example, the chorus' parabasis was changed, and the place where the Just Discourse speaks to the Unjust, and the last part where the study of Socrates is burned.

Certain minor difficulties of interpretation may be passed over; it is clear, at least, that there was a sedulous correction throughout, and three radical changes which affected the parabasis, the agon, and the finale.

The change in the parabasis needs no comment, for the first part, in Eupolidean meter, was clearly written after the death of Cleon and the production of Eupolis' *Maricas*, therefore after 422; also, it clashes in sense with the rest.[42] The remark about the agon has led some to believe that the whole debate of the Discourses belongs only to the second version, while others maintain quite the opposite, on the grounds that the play is unthinkable without it.[43] But the words of the Argument must mean something, and probably neither of the extreme interpretations is correct. The precise words are, "Where the Just Discourse speaks to the Unjust," and they imply that what was changed was the Just Discourse only, rather than both. Since this change is listed among the major ones, it seems likely that it was not a matter of correction or emendation, but of addition. The most logical conclusion is that it was an innovation of the second version to give the Unjust Logic an adversary, and that originally he held sway unopposed. In this case, the agon would have been conducted, as in the *Acharnians*, by a single character pleading, and no doubt winning, his cause; the character also may well have been Socrates himself, rather than a personification, for, as noted above, his exit before the present debate is meaningless and awkward.[44] The *Clouds* is, indeed, unthinkable without some representation of the sophistic rhetoric which is so central to its theme, while the Just Discourse, who presents his case at best lamely, for all his admired lyricism about the "plane tree whispering to the elm," is unsatisfying and quite dispensable.[45]

The third statement of the Argument, that there was a change in the finale, "where the study of Socrates is burned," must also mean that this feature was a new addition, for had it been merely altered, it would doubtless not have been included in the thoroughgoing revisions. How, then, did the play end? One can only speculate. With no Just Discourse and no burning of the Thinkery, it is at least not unlikely that there was no such full reversal as there is in the present version. The dramatic difficulty posed by the chorus' change of position has already been mentioned. It seems possible that Strepsiades, armed with sophistic *poneria*, scattered his creditors manfully, as he does in the second version, but without retribution falling on his head and without the vengeance upon Socrates. There is one difficulty with this suggestion, however, for the one fragment of the first *Clouds* which also stands in the second is the remark that "old men are children twice over." This line, which is part of Pheidippides' defense of father-beating, probably indicates that this scene was present also in the first version, in which case it is hard to see Strepsiades in the role of a triumphant comic hero, or the ending of the play as completely happy. But Strepsiades is not, in any case, a real hero, and the reversal of roles with his son is a basic point of structure, from the moment when he goes to school to Socrates. So the line might have occurred anywhere.

Without risking a detailed scenario, we may fairly presume that the first part was much as it stands, but that the agon was a single *epideixis*, or demonstration of the Unjust Discourse, probably by

Socrates; that Strepsiades beat his creditors but was beaten by Pheidippides, who then proceeded to demonstrate that he was acting
justly. Strepsiades might have complained, but in vain; the Unjust
Discourse would have been triumphant, and the reversal of roles
complete. Such an ending would have been chaos indeed, and perhaps not very satisfying; yet it would have dramatized the vicious
circle of *physis*, and structurally would have resembled the end of
the *Wasps*. The circle would not have been broken by a moral
peripety, but simply allowed to spin on, and the dialectic of law
versus nature would have been engulfed in another dialectic, that
of the double aspect of nature itself. If it was less successful than
the *Wasps*, this was perhaps precisely because it explicitly revealed
the secrets of *poneria* instead of exploiting them.

Whatever his real evaluation of contemporary thinking, Aristophanes knew a good deal about it, and there is no reason to believe
that his presentation of it in the first *Clouds* was any less trenchant
than in the second; the fact that it was all in the form of a parody
would make little difference if, as seems clear, there was no burning
of the Thinkery. Without the moral reversal at the end, the play
would stand as a monument to the power of sophistic doctrine, and
the suggestion mentioned earlier, that it was all too sympathetic to
the new education, may be the truth. If so, then it is possible to see
why the *Clouds* did not please the judges at the Dionysia of 423.
The years from about 430 B.C. on to the end of the century were
dangerous ones for the free-thinking philosophers; atheism and astronomy had become indictable offenses, and prosecutions were
numerous.[46] There was, it seems, something of a witch hunt, and
for Aristophanes to exercise his comic license to the extent of showing the victory of a Socrates who was not only an atheist and an
astronomer but a successful corrupter of youth as well could scarcely
have found favor with a public which was actually afraid, and
could condemn the real Socrates to death some years later. An audience could identify with a Dicaeopolis, perhaps even with a Sausage
Seller. There was no one in the *Clouds* with whom to identify, for

even Strepsiades is too involved with what was regarded as a public peril, while at the same time he lacks the intelligence to make clever use of it. His adventure releases nothing, and achieves no victory or salvation, and hence his *koutoponeria* seems evil. Also, his mistreatment by his son would have struck the audience as simultaneously well-deserved and shocking. All this is still true of the second version, but must have been even more true of the first, where, as suggested, the ending may have simply left the situation unresolved. If the play failed for these reasons, it is easy to see how Aristophanes would try to redress the moral balance by adding the burning scene, altering the character of the clouds, and inserting a figure to represent just logic and the old education. But the attempt did not really work. It is essential for the whole assumption of the play that the Unjust Discourse defeat all opponents; the clouds' change of character is unconvincing; and the burning of the Thinkery is not really a victory of law and order, but a jejune reprisal of nature, bruised and aroused. The poet seems to have recognized that he could not moralize his play without ruining it, and given up the attempt. The second version doubtless saw light only after his death, and was preserved in preference to the earlier one by the Byzantines, precisely because it seemed so moral.

All this is mere hypothesis, of course, but it may help to explain the play which we possess. In any case, the plot of the *Clouds*, even quite as it stands, shows Aristophanes experimenting with a new kind of dramatic formula, more involved than that of the simple heroic fantasy which sweeps the world before it. Here is fantasy, not a heroic one, but one which turns back on itself, producing not only the desired result, but its opposite as well. It may not have been his first use of this device. In the lost *Banqueters*, which also dealt with the old and new education, the father may have suffered a similar discomfiture at the hands of his sophistically trained son.[47] Aristophanes himself says that the *Clouds* is the sister comedy of the *Banqueters*, which may imply similarity of plot as well as of theme.[48] But the evidence is not at hand, and little can be said about the *Ban-*

queters except, as has been said, the interest of it must have lain in the bad son, not the good one.[49] But the fantasy with the unexpected yet somehow logical result was a form which continued to fascinate Aristophanes, and there may be some truth in the suggestion that the *Clouds* was designed to introduce a new kind of comedy which maintained plot interest up to the end.[50] On the other hand, in the *Knights* Aristophanes achieved this, as we have seen, by generously expanding the agonistic feature, and in the *Acharnians* the intermittent tension between Lamachus and the hero serves much the same purpose. It remained for the *Birds* to combine the one-directional heroic fantasy with the type which involves ironical results.

Spun as it is around intellectual antinomies and the parody of ideas, the *Clouds* depends less than other plays on the development and interplay of images. Yet some brilliant ones occur, the most important being, obviously, the cluster of air and cloud imagery, physically embodied in the chorus, and expansively developed by Socrates in the scene where he invokes their presence and praises their functions in the mixed terminology of science and hymn:

O lord and master, measureless Air, who hold the earth in suspension,
And gleaming Aether, and holy goddesses, clouds of the thunder and
 lightning,
Arise, appear to this man of thought, O mistresses lofty-suspended . . .
Come hither, O deeply honored clouds, and show this man demonstration;
Whether you now reside on the holy, snow-stricken peaks of Olympus,
Or in gardens of Ocean your father, you order the nymphs in sacred dances,
Or are drawing up from the mouths of the Nile its waters in golden ewers,
Or clinging round the Maeotic Lake or the snowy mountain of Mimas,
Give ear, receiving our sacrifice, and graciously hear our devotions.[51]

The language and form of address is that of prayer, yet there are woven into it the theories that the earth rests upon air, and that clouds cause thunder and lightning. The image of the divine clouds ordering the dances of the nymphs in the gardens of Ocean is juxtaposed with some scientific knowledge, in scarcely less poetic terms, of the vaporization of water. Throughout his exposition to his student Socrates maintains, in lofty tone, the ambiguity of the clouds both as goddesses, indeed the only goddesses, and as natural phenomena controlled "by necessity," that is physical laws.[52]

Meanwhile, Strepsiades sinks to the role of a mere *homolochos*, buffoon, interjecting comments which puncture, or reduce the master's words to his own level of comprehension. His version of the dual nature of the clouds is that clouds generally look like flying wool, while these have noses.[53] A good many of his comments have to do with his stomach, and he comprehends the scientific explanation of thunder only by analogy with the abdominal rumblings which follow overindulgence in Panathenaic soup.[54] This wedding of the astronomic with the gastronomic is typical both of Aristophanes in general, and of this particular play; one might compare, for instance, Socrates' explanation of the noise made by a gnat.[55] In the world of *physis* the necessities of the stomach do not differ radically from those of the upper air, any more than compressed air differs in essence from air at large; philosophy and cookery merge, and Strepsiades is driven "by necessity" to accept the clouds as goddesses, and to turn himself over to their instruction.[56]

Up-in-the-air imagery is too prevalent in the *Clouds* to require demonstration. If it takes the form here of a parody of Diogenes of Apollonia's theory of air, it remains, as elsewhere, almost a fixed symbol of vaporous nonsense, intellectual twaddle, delirium, and vertigo.[57] But it also has its own heroic madness, at times, and Socrates suspended in a basket bears a certain resemblance to Trygaeus on the dung beetle, just as his cosmological exegesis resembles Peithetaerus' account to the birds of the genesis of the world. The unity of imagistic structure in these passages illustrates precisely how close the hero is to the quack, the *alazon*. Indeed, Socrates is far nearer to being a hero than is Strepsiades, and if in the original version he suffered no retribution, he must have appeared much more so. Quackery is the hallmark of the hero, or one of his hallmarks, and Socrates has it, whereas Strepsiades barely learns the rudiments. Socrates is a master of *poneria*, in the specific sense of theft and graft. When there is no supper at the Thinkery, he solemnly sprinkles ashes on a table, bends a spit into a pair of compasses, and then most mathematically filches a coat from the palaestra next door, using the spit for a fish hook.[58] With equally adroit touch, he talks Strepsiades out of his cloak and shoes.[59] All this has about it something of the creative shamelessness which one expects of an Aristophanean protagonist. Also there is the matter of speech; Socrates knows and can teach the two Discourses, inspired by the clouds, whom he exalts, along with Chaos and the Tongue, into a kind of Unholy Trinity.[60] His pro-seminar consists entirely of instruction in rhythms, meters, and genders; [61] and what Strepsiades expects to become under his tutelage is described all in terms of specious talk, like the Hoopoe's description of Peithetaerus, only even longer:

> A bold, glib, impudent, reckless,
> Blackguardly contriver of fraud, a
> Deviser of words, pettifogger
> At law, a codex of statutes,
> A rattle, a rascal, a pitfall,
> A supple, sly, slippery impostor,
> A foul rogue, a twister, a torturesome
>   Chopper of logic.[62]

All these wonderful gifts come to Socrates from the clouds; why therefore is he not really a hero, in the sense that Peithetaerus is? It is perhaps because the real extra dimensions of animal and deity are lacking. His flying machine is a basket, not a beetle, let alone real wings; and the clouds, whatever their assumed divinity, and however they may reflect the shapes which they behold, do not reflect specifically the transcendent liberation of the individual. Or if they do, Socrates' liberation from restraints is already complete, a given quantity; it is not dramatized as a heroic effort. And Strepsiades' attempt to achieve it is a failure. Perhaps more important, all the clouds' lofty rumblings do not bring about any grand change, but only small thoughts, constantly struck off in diminutives, "thoughticals," "speechlets," characteristic of the piddling concerns of rhetoric and philosophy, here packaged as one.[63] The imagery of the clouds is broad and beautiful, but the diminutives which emerge keep undercutting the heroic aspect of Socrates' quackery, like an abundance of mice born of laboring mountains.

As for Strepsiades, his motivation is only to solve a problem in home economics. The vision of himself, quoted above, has its heroic aspects, since he commits himself without reservation to the art of being devilishly triumphant. Perhaps this passage, together with the scene where he becomes the horse driver of Amynias the banker, might suggest that in the first version he became more full of the true heroic fire. But this is very doubtful, and it is better to assume that Strepsiades was always what he is, an ignoramus, the sympathetic though foolish victim of his own devices. Indeed, one image seems to put him exactly where he belongs: an animal image, not one which represents the command of nature, but rather the opposite. This is the image of bugs and biting. In the prologue Strepsiades, worried about his son's horse-racing debts, is trying to sleep, but cannot because he is "*bitten* — by expenses, and mangers, and debts, on account of this here son." [64] He wishes for his life before marriage, when he "lay at random, unwashed, unkempt, full of honey, sheep, and olive cakes." [65] The image of bugs — though the expected bugs are displaced by expenses, mangers, and debts — representing as they do Strepsiades' distressed state, arrives at a climax in action when Strepsiades, at Socrates' direction, lies on the pallet trying to do original research and cannot think of a thing because the bedbugs are eating him alive.[66] A vivid word play has been developed into a scene, and the general effect is to create a theme of twisting and turning in discomfort, which accords well with the name Strepsiades.[67] This fellow is the victim of nature, the prey of generational progress, the toy of his son and the toy of the professor who, he hopes, is to save him from his son.

Socrates, however, remains one of Aristophanes' greatest creations, a magnificent impostor. Some scholars, shocked at what they consider a vicious misrepresentation, have reminded the world that Socrates never gave lessons or took money, was not interested in physics, and hated rhetoric in all its forms. Others have tried to demonstrate that it was not a misrepresentation, and that Socrates had much in common with his caricature.[68] There is some justice on both sides of this controversy: Socrates was surely the most creative ethical philosopher of his age, he did not give real lessons or take money, and his interest in physics was, at best, limited. But he was a man of his time, and, even as Plato presents him, one of the most dexterous, and at times slippery, practitioners of dialectic who has ever been heard of. Socrates was too well versed in sophistic thought to be wholly divorced from it.

It is less important, however, to trace the genuinely Socratic touches in the *Clouds*, than to recognize the composite image of the intellectual climate, under the name of Socrates. The poet might have called it by a different name, but Socrates' local pre-eminence entitled him to first consideration. The choice seems inevitable, not to say obvious, for an Athenian playwright dramatizing the cleft between the old and new modes of education. There could never have been any question of representing him seriously and accurately. Had there been, Aristophanes would scarcely have accredited him with practically all the intellectual accomplishments of the whole sophistic movement — plus the doctrines of Diogenes, which cannot be called sophistic. Rather, this was an inspired piece of poetic invention to gather together the Weaker Discourse of Protagoras, some of the rhetorical claims of Gorgias, the air physics of Diogenes, the linguistic studies of Prodicus, and the ethic of Antiphon, or some one of his predecessors, into one character. A dash of sheer crooked quackery was added and then the mixture was molded into an image of lofty, unscrupulous, and cloudy versatility — which itself suggests Hippias of Elis. The total brilliant imposture was staged under the name of the funniest-looking man in Athens, the fat and pug-nosed philosopher whose face was itself a comic mask.

The caricature of Socrates differs from that of Cleon in that it lacks hatred. Aristophanes' philosopher has a strange dignity, like Euripides in the *Thesmophoriazusae*, and he carries his role with a certain *grandezza*. Despite the nonsense, there is a kind of comic nobility about Socrates. Though the caricature does not emerge in heroic terms, it stands its ground, as bona fide humbug, with a world view of its own. The difficulty of accepting it as it stands, as a highly distinguished comic creation, is, of course, the *Apology* of Plato, where Socrates is made to include among his accusers the comic poets who say that he "treads on air, and scrutinizes the sun." [69] But the testimony of the *Symposium* far outweighs the passing remarks in the *Apology*; nor should it be assumed that Plato underwent some change of mind in later years.[70] In the *Apology* the speaker is merely trying to dispose of a general impression, created not only by Aristophanes, but by others too, though it seems evident from the fragments that no other poet went to such lengths in exploiting the philosophic front.[71] Had Plato really felt an enemy in Aristophanes, he certainly possessed the articulateness to say so clearly.

The *Clouds* is an unsatisfactory text, as we have it. Yet, if it lacks much of Aristophanes' familiar gift of freeing the spirit, it reflects vividly his apprehension of what it might be freed from. This much is probably true of both versions. For the moment, at least, the explicit recognition of the forces of which human *physis* consists may have necessitated a comedy which, albeit its author thought it his best, remains for us a somewhat sober experience, an analysis, a dialectic, rather than a poetic triumph. Even the first version may have had these faults, and therefore have struck the judges as no proper offering, "nothing to do with Dionysus," in its lack of pretty girls, "feasting, and fun." But Aristophanes was working toward something, his mind was deepening with the deepening shadows of his age. The dialectic kind of comedy, whereby dream defeats itself while achieving itself, was to produce two of his most beautiful, and hilarious, works.

Wasps

There is a great artistic difference between a play which is, formally and compositionally, a dilemma, and a play which is the formal and compositional dramatization of a dilemma. In the *Wasps* Aristophanes clearly achieved, by indirection, the victory which he missed in the frontal, and too explicit, *Clouds*. Not that the *Wasps* won a prize, for it seems it came in second. But the *Wasps* is a real comedy, pregnant with joy and vertiginous charm, and unburdened by the freight of apparent seriousness which makes the *Clouds* resemble a morality play. Indeed, if it were not for the *Clouds*, in its bowdlerized present state, it is a question how anyone would ever have made Aristophanes out to be the conservative savior of reason and religion which he is supposed to be. Refreshingly devoid of moralism, the *Wasps* is a testament of the Attic spirit, tough, witty, wicked, and full of a fiber worth bishoprics of small propriety.

Yet the theme is the same. "What is to be done with father?" is today comic commonplace. But Aristophanes was poet enough to conceive father as both impossible and inevitable, in fact, the father of all Greeks, perhaps the father of all humanity, fiery, perverse, obtuse, packed with humane integrity, and the devil to deal with. Philocleon is one of his greatest characters. He has an appeal derived from somewhere between Falstaff and the Bastard Faulconbridge, while his devotion to self-realization, in whatever unrealistic terms, has no little of the Quixotic spirit, to which his son Bdelycleon plays the sympathetic but dull ground bass of Sancho Panza. Philocleon is indeed the demos exiled by the empire, as the agon shows, and one feels distinctly sorry that his fantasy of kingly supremacy is shattered by his son's cold knowledge of facts. For in the *Wasps* the re-education of father proposes, not sophistic juggleries, but hard truth and the necessity of conformity. Philocleon, old Athenian wasp that he is, never quite grasps the point. Much cleverer than Strepsiades, he learns his lesson, but only in his own way, and he employs it ferociously, becoming ever more and more himself. A comic hero may suffer variously in his cause: Don Quixote dies of his fantasy, and Philocleon too is his own victim, in the end. But the point is different, for Aristophanes invites us to no tragic reflections. He simply spins us off into the endless circle of nature.

Once more, Aristophanes has constructed his play around the contrast between the older and younger generations, and the dialectic of nature versus convention; and once more, the roles of the generations appear reversed. The ethic which questioned the authority of custom-law and affirmed the necessity of fulfilling nature was ordinarily associated with the younger generation, while the old education aimed at instilling the values and behavior of tradition. But here, as in the beginning of the *Clouds*, it is the young man, Bdelycleon, who stands for propriety, comfort, and convention, in a way which foreshadows the fourth century, while his father is the image of natural, all too natural, man. Bdelycleon is anomalous in another way, too. Sons in comedy are not as a rule noted for their filial piety, but Bdelycleon is a good son, motivated wholly by the desire to take care of his father and keep him in peace and comfort.[1] He is the very opposite of the "enlightened" Pheidippides. His effort to divert the old man from his favorite occupation of jury duty and initiate him into the amenities of polite society represents a concern which may be considered natural, but natural under the old dispensation, with its immemorial commandment to honor the gods, parents, and strangers. Newer theories of nature, as we have seen, did not necessarily include such reverent observances. Indeed, the ambiguities involved in the concept of what is natural create, in great part, the meaning of the *Wasps*. For again here, as in the *Clouds*, the success of the plot effort is double-edged, producing an unexpected result; and the ending is quite unresolved.

The play begins on the level of simply satirizing the Athenian love of legal processes, and this theme remains a dominant one throughout the first two thirds of the play. Philocleon's devotion to this way of serving his country, and to drawing the daily three-obol fee, is so intense that it amounts to a mania. In one of Aristophanes' finest and most inflated pieces of exaggeration, the slave Xanthias describes his master's state as a "disease" and lists the symptoms, which are formidable indeed. He sleeps on the doorstep of the law court to avoid being late; three of his fingers are permanently stuck together from habitually holding a voting pebble; and to insure an abundant supply of these pebbles, he keeps a beach at home.[2] Before locking him up entirely, his son had tried everything to cure him, arguments, exorcism, incubation in the temple of Asclepius at Aegina; but even from Aegina he managed to get to court before dawn. The name Philocleon, together with its opposite Bdelycleon, perhaps does not indicate as much as its explicitness would suggest. Philocleon and all the old wasps of the chorus like Cleon because he fosters their conviction that they are the rulers of Athens by virtue of their office in the Heliastic court. But their affiliation with him ends there; in other respects they are old "Marathon fighters," crusty but sympathetic. And the meanings of the two names are not consistently followed out: Philocleon can speak of hoping to convict Cleon of theft, and Bdelycleon includes Cleon in the typical elegant symposium to which he wishes to escort his father.[3] Cleon's role in the play goes little beyond the fact that he encourages the old men's love of jury service and its attendant delusion of grandeur.

But there is something else besides to the "disease." These jurors, and in particular Philocleon, have no great concern with hearing both sides of a case, as the Heliastic oath required; their business, as they see it, is to convict, and to acquit anybody is actually liable to endanger their health.[4] Philocleon's fingernails always have wax under them from drawing the long line which indicates "guilty" on the wax tablet, and when a defendant beseeches him, he leans down to him and says, "You're boiling a stone."[5] Wrath is the spirit of their juridical procedure; they do not so much judge cases as catch victims. Philocleon, complaining of his confinement in tragic tones, says explicitly that he wants to go to the voting urns and "do some harm."[6] Cleon has summoned the jurors to come to court with three days' supply of rage, in order to try Laches for peculation in Sicily.[7] References to wrath and the atrabilious disposition of the jurors in general are too frequent to need illustration, and they suit, of course, the character of wasps. The "disease" includes a large element of pure *Schadenfreude*, which recalls Antiphon's complaint against legal actions, that they always did somebody "harm." [8] For these old jurors litigation is a sport, a game of getting the upper hand, with the cards well stacked in their favor.

Yet we have here something more than the scratchy-tempered, curmudgeonly type of old man well known to New Comedy. This type is often enough characterized as something contrary to nature, and in need of corrective admonishment. The old men of the *Wasps* are entirely within the scheme of nature and, in a way, represent it. True, Bdelycleon does not approve, and he tries to mend his father's ways, but the effort is a resounding failure, precisely because nature is intractable. And this is a good thing, from one point of view, for the anger and ferocity of the wasps is part of their virtue, as they themselves explain in the parabasis:

> We alone are justly named the denizens of Attica,
> We, the manliest tribe of all, the ones who in the battle line
> Once did most to save this city, when the wild barbarian came,
> Smoke erupting, fire a-brandishing, to raze the city whole,
> Eager thoughts bent violently on ravishing our nest of wasps.
> We, we came out on the double, charging forth with shield and spear.
> And we battled 'em and smote 'em with a vinegar sort of ire,
> Standing man by man; each one of us chewed his jaw off in his rage.
> And the arrows were so thick you could not even see the sky!
> Nevertheless, the gods were with us; so at eve, they turned and ran,
> For an owl, before we joined in battle, flew across our host.
> Then we chased 'em all like fishermen, and speared them in the pants,
> And they ran in all directions, nursing stings in cheek and brow.
> So it is among barbarians there is nothing anywhere
> Now regarded as more formidable than — an Attic wasp! [9]

The Attic wasp would be nothing without the sting with which he speared the Persians in their baggy breeches. There is, however, some designed ambiguity about the warlike ἐγκεντρίς, sting, and the judicial ἐγκεντρίς, voting stylus.[10] The end of the parabasis exploits the ambiguity nicely:

> Some however are among us sitting round, the merest drones,
> Prickless creatures, not a sting in 'em; they wait and gobble down
> All the tribute of our labor, and they haven't done a thing.

This, oh this it is which galls us, when an army-dodger comes
And he snaffles up our fees; but for his country's sake he shows
Not a spear shaft, not an oar haft, not a blister in his hands!
Hence, we are resolved, hereafter not a citizen shall receive
A three-obol fee, whoever he is, unless he's got a — quill.[11]

Whether as soldier or as juror, the wasp nature is the backbone of Athens, and the old men declare that their age is worth more than the ringleted debauchery of the young.[12] And there is more than mere self-conceit herein: they were the men who fought at Marathon, and whether it be sword or stylus, their sting is the badge of the heroic spirit.

The wasps are characterized, indeed, with no little appeal; they are more than a mere group of misled and bad-tempered dotards. They have their sweeter side. As they start off before dawn for their grim occupations at court, they go carrying torches and "twittering old-fashioned, honey-Sidonian-Phrynichus songs." [13] Versed in country things, they note the signs of coming rain, and offer to buy knuckle-bones for the lad who carries the lamp for them. They also cuff him, of course, and they refuse to buy him figs, but that is because they have so many expenses to pay out of their three obols.[14] They have their *poneria*, too, and recall such dashing youthful exploits as filching a kneading trough or someone's roasting spits, accomplishments to which Philocleon too lays claim.[15] Nowhere has Aristophanes exercised greater skill in characterization than in this parodos; the details seem to keep adding themselves spontaneously as in a Homeric simile, where the image develops for its own sake, momentarily oblivious of context. So here, the image of the old men is drawn *con amore*, in full but delicate contours, so that even their truculence takes on an amiable aspect. They fill out the portrait of their colleague Philocleon, and by contrast with them the realistic and well-disposed Bdelycleon is a saltless fellow. After the latter's exposé of the facts, of course, they change their tempers for the better, for it is the usual fate of a comic chorus to be won over by the results of the agon; from this point on their character is essentially suppressed.[16] Philocleon, on the other hand, though momentarily de-feated, is a man of finer mettle and does not give up so easily.

As said earlier, the *Wasps* has an action which is double-edged and seems to move simultaneously in two directions. The agon marks the intersection of the two, and there is one still moment at the center of the play where it seems as if Bdelycleon has won his case; the chorus grants his wisdom, and even Philocleon can think of no fur-ther argument in defense of the "mighty rule" of a juror.[17] This is the point at which, in a play of the shape of the *Acharnians*, the vic-torious hero would proceed to demonstrate and enjoy the fruits of his fantasy. But Bdelycleon is not the hero, and he has no fantasy. He has done no more than show that the jurors are being deceived and exploited by the demagogues, and his only further wish is to teach his father to live like a gentleman. Since his triumph is not a heroic one, nothing transcendent can follow it, and it is presently made clear, in any case, that he has not really won. The chorus, reflecting now that it is wise to hear always both sides of a case, feel "set straight"; they beg Philocleon to listen to reason and concur.[18] But Philocleon, though bankrupt of argument, does not concur: in a murderous parody of the love-sick Phaedra of Euripides, he cries:

> There is my love, there let me be,
> Where the herald cries, "Who has not voted?
> Let him stand up!"
> Then let me stand among the urns,
> Last of the voters! [19]

The verb he uses, which means "to be in love," has been used before of Philocleon's state.[20] Reason has not triumphed, for the passion is too mighty. Philocleon has himself described it in terms of the cravings of pregnant women.[21] Philocleon's illusions may have been shattered by the discourse of his son, but his passion remains im-pregnable. He must judge cases or die. Far from being jolted out of his fantasy, he has only altered its terms a little. Nature is not, after all, wholly unadaptable; it adapts in self-preservation. Philo-cleon, who had taken a sword and sworn to kill himself if he lost the debate, drops the sword, and adapts instead, accepting the suggestion that he hold court at home.[22]

A comic fantasy is a symbol of personal authenticity, and no true comic hero can afford to abandon it. If Cleon's patronage of the old jurors was in fact a deliberate and fraudulent design to produce delusions of grandeur, for Philocleon the delusion itself had become his personal mode of self-validation as the greatest and fiercest of the wasps. It is with relief that we hear his irrational declaration of loyalty to his fantasy. For him it had been a heroic fantasy, an exercise of his stinging and astringent spirit much to be preferred to "birds' milk"; he would rather "eat a little pot-boiled law suit than red mullet or eels." [23] There is, as he said, no "animal more happy, blessed, luxurious, or dread" than a judge, and he insists that his life is a rule, an empire.[24] In defense of the term he lists the satisfactions of a judge's occupation, and it is interesting to see what his "empire" consists of. Big men, four cubits tall, implore him for mercy; his victims put on wonderful shows, some telling stories or witticisms, some bringing their children to court to weep and whine for an acquittal; there is the pleasure of examining the young men for acceptance as ephebi, or forcing Oeagrus, the famous actor, to recite from Aeschylus before he can be released; and jurors may dispose of wills and heiresses as they choose, for they enjoy the almighty protection of Cleon and Theorus. Best of all is the three obols, and the flattery received at home from the members of one's household, who wish to get them away from him.

Every one of these great blessings amounts to nothing more than a gratification of the ego or the libido, or both, and the total adds up to a tremendously satisfied self. The administration of law puts the judge above the law, with a rule no less than that of Zeus:

> For if perchance we raise a rumpus,
> Each passer-by will say,
> "How the law court thunders,
>   O King Zeus!"
> And if I flash my lightning, rich
> Important men cry hush, and soil
>   Their breeches with fright.

> And you yourself, you especially fear me,
> Yes, by Demeter, you fear me, but I'll
> Be damned if I fear you.[25]

Comic fantasy regularly aspires to the position of a god, and defines that position in terms of personal satisfactions and freedom from the restraints of law and authority. It is the dream of nature, and Philocleon's conceit of himself as Zeus, flashing his lightning, is his answer to the helplessness of the individual. If he does not gain the full heroic victory of a Dicaeopolis or Peithetaerus, he nonetheless adheres to his principles, if they may be called that. When we see the last of him, he has not lost an inch of his self-assertiveness.

To this mighty dream of surpassing selfhood, Bdelycleon opposes what may be taken as the hard facts of Athenian political economy. Bdelycleon has been taking notes on his father's speech, but he never refutes, or for that matter directly confronts, a single one of his points. This is no wonder, of course, for facts and fantasy are not commensurate, and the word in question, "rule," means two different things to the two speakers. To Philocleon, as we have seen, "rule" means the self as Zeus; to Bdelycleon, it means the Athenian empire, with its thousand cities and yearly revenue of two thousand talents, ruled by venal demagogues who dole out three obols a day to the judges, and consume the real profits themselves. No one in this picture is exactly called Zeus, but it is interesting that it is the demagogue who "thunders" at the cities for tribute.[26] The equivocation on the word "rule" permits the most elegant dramatization of the dilemma, discussed in former chapters, of the individual psyche in the complex imperial society of late fifth-century Athens, the dilemma which induced Antiphon and other sophistic thinkers to reject, or all but reject, social institutions entirely. To return to the instance of the law, Antiphon regarded it as always doing somebody harm; Philocleon would agree, but his answer would be "Then be like Zeus and do all the harm you can." It is the answer of a battling, indeed waspish, spirit, but it achieves the comic fulfillment of the natural self. Bdelycleon's realistic appreciation of where rule really lies comes near to spoiling everything. For him, the answer would be, presumably, quietism, resignation, and the pursuit of private, harmless satisfactions. The elegant world of dinner parties and small talk into which he tries to bring his father anticipates, in a way, the retired conceptions of the good life which characterize the fourth century or the Hellenistic philosophies. "The world is impossible, let it be," is one kind of ethic, but not a very dynamic one, and certainly not one which accords with Philocleon's nature. He prefers to say, "Let us see who is more impossible, the world, or I."

Aristophanes' typical mingling of fantasy and realism seldom goes so far as to build a scene where the two meet in a dialectical confrontation; realism usually enters in unexpected thuds, flatly punctuating the high-spirited progress of the fantasy. In writing a scene like the agon of the *Wasps*, Aristophanes has again, as he did in the *Clouds*, approached an analytical exposure of his own comic art. The deflation of a heroic fantasy inverts the more usual procedure, and would defeat the comic end, did not the fantasy survive in altered form. But fortunately it does, and the dialectic of the agon is lost in a larger and subtler one. Though not a word is said in the agon about the *nomos-physis* antinomy, it is, as said earlier, clearly implied, with Philocleon's mirage representing the aspiration of individual nature, and his son's realism leading to, if not stating outright, acceptance of society and conformity to its conventions. Had Bdelycleon's humane and admirable educational effort succeeded, the play would probably have ended at something like half the usual length, and the moral would have resembled that of the present *Clouds*. Instead, one has the situation — rare in Aristophanean comedy — of reason and common sense defeating the chimeras of the hero, only to find that nothing has been achieved, or more precisely, that things are worse than before. Education, Bdelycleon finds, has its limits, and human incorrigibility has not. For the "disease," after all, is in essence only the affliction of the personal need for psychic fulfillment in Zeus-like supremacy, the disease of selfhood. As the chorus points out, ironically congratulating Bdelycleon on the "change" he has wrought in his father,

It is difficult to shift from the nature
Which one habitually has.[27]

In fact, all Bdelycleon's sane reasoning leads to one of the greatest and funniest scenes of pure nonsense in all literature, the trial of the dog. It has been thought that this scene was the genesis of the whole play, which owed its conception to the trial of the general Laches, three years before, on some kind of charges of peculation during his mission around Sicily.[28] Be that as it may, the chorus had been on its way to the trial of Laches in the parodos, and now they witness the trial of his canine counterpart, Labes (Snatcher), for seizure and total ingestation of a large Sicilian cheese. Philocleon is at this time established in his private law court for domestic cases, equipped with all the trappings of a court room, plus a rooster, a bowl of bean soup, and a conveniently placed chamber pot, and is drawing his pay from his son. (One wonders just what Bdelycleon has gained.) If extremes of laughter can ever be fatal, it is hard to see how the audience survived this apparition, with doubtless a real dog in the prisoner's box and the witness stand adorned with pots, pans, a brazier, a pestle, and a cheese grater ready to testify on the defendant's behalf. The name of the other dog, the plaintiff, is not given, but he comes from Cleon's deme, Kydathenaeon, and he is mentioned as a watchdog.[29]

But the charm of the scene goes far beyond the political satire. The language, parodying legal and rhetorical formulas, hovers with engaging elusiveness between human and animal contexts, while the judge on the bench relieves alternately his hunger and other needs. The charge is not so much the theft of the cheese as that Labes had failed to give any to the other dog, and the prosecution rises to a ringing denunciation whose imagistic confusion strikes off the spirit of the whole scene:

Do not acquit him, for he is by far
Of all dogs the lone-eatingest man,
Who sailed around the platter in a circle
And then gulped down the rind off the cities.[30]

One is somehow reminded of Shakespeare's "There is no more fearful wildfowl than your lion living." An admirable nonsense word assists the kaleidoscopic effect: Labes is said to have run off into a corner and there "katasicelized" the cheese.[31] The images of eating and gluttony as symbols of political corruption are akin, obviously, to the similar ones in the *Knights*, but this scene is infinitely gayer in its reliance on nonsense. The poetic tension is higher also, as is usually the case when Aristophanes begins inventing words in order to weld together the disparate elements in his scenic metaphor.

As the scene unfolds, the nonsense and ambiguity develop more and more. The prisoner takes the stand, but the poor fellow is struck dumb with confusion — like Thucydides, son of Melesias! — and cannot say a word for himself. Bdelycleon undertakes the defense for him, explaining that he is a good sheep dog and hunting dog, only a little uneducated, in that he never learned to play the lyre.[32] He summons the cheese grater to the witness stand, bidding it speak up in a loud voice; Philocleon claims it lies.[33] Finally, Labes' puppies come in, ascend the stand and beseech the court with whining and tears.[34] Throughout the whole trial there has been no question of impartiality on the part of the judge; he was set to condemn the prisoner the minute he looked at him, for he "smiled, showing his teeth, with intent to deceive." Here the verb to "smile showing the teeth" can also mean "make a clean sweep." [35] Remarking dryly that he too "never learned to play the lyre," Philocleon votes guilty. Since Philocleon is the sole juror, it is a crowning touch to have him cast his vote and then lean forward eagerly and ask for the results. But Bdelycleon has shifted the voting urns, Labes is acquitted, and Philocleon swoons.

Except for the unwilling acquittal, the trial scene marks, in one way, a further extension of Philocleon's fantasy. Relieved of colleagues, or even the necessity of leaving the house, his lonely eminence is now more than ever Zeus-like; he can exercise power and judgment while eating bean porridge, and the suppliants still beseech him for mercy. Yet, though he is no longer deceived by the demagogues, he is deceived by his son, and so, in another way, the end of the trial marks his second great reverse. He is now so downcast, indeed, that he agrees to let his son dress him and educate him for society. His heart is not in it, of course; but it is the dark night of the soul for him, and his fierce, fighting nature, momentarily subdued, has yet to be born anew, and to greater freedom.

It could be objected that the treatment of Philocleon so far deals with him too much as an individual, and not sufficiently with his representative and collective aspect. Indeed, he is not only himself, he is the Athenian demos as well, and bears clear resemblance, in his vanity and bad temper, to Demos in the *Knights*. When he describes Cleon's protection of the judges, he says he brushes the flies away from them, an image very similar to one in the *Knights* where Cleon "brushes the orators" away from Demos.[36] Throughout the agon Bdelycleon speaks to his father with a singular pronoun, but with the meaning of the common people at large, and the chorus, praising his filial devotion, call him a "lover of the demos"; finally Philocleon refers to himself explicitly as "the commonwealth." [37] From this point of view, Philocleon differs little if at all from his predecessor; but whereas Demos directly represents the sovereign people in the guise of an individual, Philocleon comes nearer to being the exact reverse, an individual in the guise of the sovereign people, a guise of which he is slowly divested, though he continues to be, in some sense, representative. Certainly he embodies, as shown earlier, the struggle of the individual for authenticity, and in this sense he stands almost in the position of the great comic heroes of the *Acharnians* and *Peace*, whereas Demos is not really even a central character. All in all, the character image of Philocleon fulfills nearly to perfection the playwright's dream of creating a character simultaneously individual and general, in short, symbolic.

The latter scenes of the play emphasize the individual side more than the earlier ones. Formerly, as a judge Philocleon had been part of society, not, as he thought, the main driving gear, but only a cog; still, a part. His son's struggle to open his eyes, divorce him from his calling, and bring him into line with the younger man's view of society leads by inevitable stages to his complete violation of all social boundaries in the play's final drunken orgy. Philocleon's drunkenness and his dismissal of all restraint has no little in common with Dicaeopolis' career, though it appears that different results ensue. There is the same breakthrough of untempered *physis*, raw human nature asserting itself in rude gestures before an appalled and conquered world.

The scene in which Bdelycleon dresses his father in fine city clothes and schools him in polite conversation is one of several in Aristophanes which depend on simple *homolochia*, buffoonery, for its effect. The essence of such scenes is to let the proponent express something of pretentious elegance or intellect, which the buffoon then reduces to his own limited scale with calculated bathos. The scene here recalls the schooling of Socrates, while Bdelycleon's comparison of the old man in his new clothes to a "boil dressed in garlic" foreshadows the uncomplimentary exchange between Peithetaerus and Euelpides when they first see each other dressed in feathers.[38] These scenes are not, as a rule, Aristophanes' best, and they may represent in part the kind of humor which he averred that he never stooped to present. But they often mark some kind of transformation, and that which the instructed character learns, or mislearns, as buffoon is regularly converted, or perverted, in a later scene to the higher purposes of *poneria* and comic victory. Here, the suggestions which Philocleon receives about elegant social discourse will serve later as a sauce to the slapstick, a newly acquired mode of adding insult to injury in the final apocalypse of unredeemed natural man.

Though the finale of the play has been thought inorganic, it could never be called ineffective.[39] The reason for thinking it inorganic is, of course, that it departs from the theme of Philocleon's love of litigation, hitherto central. But that is to misunderstand the larger design of the play, in which the love of litigation is no more than an important element. For the *Wasps* is not to be summarized, as so often is done, as a mere satire on Athenian litigation; it is much more, and it is hard to imagine a finale which would more aptly complete its meaning. During the rock fight which preceded the agon the chorus boasted that they would make Xanthias congratulate tortoises for their hard shells, and Xanthias now enters crying out these very words.[40] Philocleon, drunk and lordly, has battered him with his staff, insulted everyone at the symposium, and stolen the flute girl; now he is on his way home, hitting people. The company at dinner had been all the best known oligarchs, and Philocleon had been the most hubristic of them all. Most interesting is the language in which his misbehavior is described:

> As soon as he was well filled on good things,
> He jumped, he skipped, he farted, and he laughed,
> Just like a jackass stuffed with barley corn,
> And beat me with youthful vigor, shouting "Boy!" [41]

The words are surprisingly close to those of the Unjust Discourse to Pheidippides: "Use your nature, skip, laugh, consider nothing shameful." [42] Such skipping and laughing is the language of nature flouting law, the language of the New Learning, the new generation; Philocleon has broken through into the unlimited freedom for self-fulfillment promised by the ethics of pure *physis*; unfortunately, what is "natural" for Philocleon differs from what Bdelycleon had imagined was natural and appropriate for old men.[43] But this raises another matter; Philocleon is not so old as he was.

The motif of rejuvenation is very frequent in Aristophanes, and may originally have had some connection with spring vegetation rites. At the beginning of the play Philocleon was old enough to be described as toothless, though a little later he seems to have grown a new set of teeth.[44] Xanthias' report, that his beating was delivered "with youthful vigor," preludes one of the most astonishing rejuvenation scenes in all Aristophanes. It is of only minor consequence that Philocleon is not really rejuvenated, but only drunk: he feels young, and the imagery is there. As a matter of fact, rejuvenation had been implicit earlier in various passages where old and young had been contrasted. The lines of the chorus which declare that the old are better than the young are quite explicit: "From these remains must spring some youthful strength,"[45] which is a little like Gray's: "Even in our ashes live their wonted fires." The choristers urge Philocleon, when he is still imprisoned in the house, to recall the youthful vigor which he had on the occasion when he let himself down from a roof to steal somebody's roasting spits, and presently he does undertake to let himself down from his own roof.[46] Later, in suggesting examples of polished conversation, Bdelycleon says, "You must tell how Ephoudion fought the pancratium finely with Ascondas, though he was already old and gray."[47] A little later, he says, "Relate the manliest exploit of your youth"; and it is interesting to note that Philocleon's manliest exploit in his youth was again a theft, this time of the vine poles of one Ergasion. When Bdelycleon cannot accept this, and demands something "with youthful dash" in it, like a torch race or a hunt, Philocleon replies that he once "caught" the famous runner Phaÿllus by indicting him for libel and winning by two votes.[48]

All these earlier intimations now mature into the scene of Philocleon demonstrating his youthful manliness by stealing the flute girl, and beating up the neighborhood. As he staggers on stage the guest who follows him protesting, cries, "Tomorrow we will all have the law on you, even if you are very young," and is promptly beaten off with a flaming torch.[49] There follows then Philocleon's address to the flute girl, a singular piece of inspired lunacy which completes the image of rejuvenation:

> Now if you just won't be a naughty girl,
> When my son dies, I'll set you free, and take you
> All for myself, O little piggy-wig!
> As 'tis, I've not come into my estate,
> For I am young and most severely guarded.
> My dear son watches me, and he's a crusty
> And altogether hair-splitting mustard carver.
> So, he's afraid that I might be seduced,
> For I'm an only father . . . And here he comes
> Himself; he seems to be chasing you and me.
> Here, quick, stand here holding the torches so,
> So I can flout him in true youthful style.[50]

The youthful flouting consists of a threat of a black eye and a suggestive reminder of the story about Ephoudion and Ascondas, and how the older man knocked the younger down.[51]

It is hard to see anything inorganic about this scene, or understand why any editor should wish to omit it, if one considers it from the point of view of the imagery of rejuvenation, and the inversion of roles between father and son, which is so basic to the play.[52] Not only is Philocleon in the role of the wild and lawless youth, but Bdelycleon is thrust into the opposite role of a crusty old guardian, just "fallen out of his grave." [53] Moreover, nature has emerged with a vengeance, the very nature which Bdelycleon had tried to suppress. The wasp is, as Homer observed, "possessed of a warlike spirit"; [54] doubtless, as the flute girl's presence seems to indicate, it also takes some interest in mating. The wasp nature asserts itself, do what one will; and it is equally natural, from another point of view, for the son who began by mounting guard over his father to become in fact a guardian. At least as important for the unity of the play is the fact that this scene completes Philocleon's relation to the courts of law. Although he has repudiated his former love of jury service,[55] he is anything but finished with law suits. The bread girl whose wares he has ruined, the victim of assault and battery, and all the guests at the banquet have sworn to bring suit in the morning.[56] His attempts to put into practice his son's lessons in arbitration and settlement of cases without court action come out either in the form of sheer nonsense or thinly veiled threats of further mayhem. He is not an arbitrator by nature. Bdelycleon's magnanimous design has landed his father right back where he started, in the Heliastic court, only on the other side of the bar. And this result was anticipated by Philocleon himself, when his son says that they will get tipsy at the party:

> Philocl.: Drinking's no good; you know what comes of wine?
> Smashing in doors, and punching and throwing things,
> And afterwards shelling out cash with a hangover.[57]

That, at least, is how he was accustomed to drink when he was young.

This whole scene, far from being inorganic, is of great importance for the structure of the play. The futility of education and the incorrigibility of nature is the principle theme, and the finale completes it. Old has become young and young has become old, the judge without mercy has become the defendant who deserves none, but nature remains unchanged. Bdelycleon, the educator, has doubtless learned much, but Philocleon has not. In place of the fantasy of himself as a Zeus of the law, he now has the fantasy of utter freedom from law, which is not very different; and though he will certainly go to court in the morning to "shell out cash with a hangover," he will be found guilty, but impenitent, and not at all discouraged. Nature is a trap and a vicious circle, in which everything turns into its opposite, while remaining the same, and the chorus which closes the scene says so, more or less explicitly, amid ironical congratulations to Bdelycleon, as he carries his father bodily into the house.

The very final scene is no less well joined to the body of the play, though it may not seem so at first glance. Dramatically, it seems to exist to exhibit Philocleon once more, still unsubdued by his recent removal. Had the play ended with his being carried off, one might be tempted to imagine that he was, in fact, finally suppressed and brought into line. As it is, he closes the play in a transport of drunken self-satisfaction, dancing in the old-fashioned style from the days of Thespis, challenging all contemporary tragedians to dance as well, and howling derision at them.[58] Once more, also, the note of old versus new is sounded, though among the new tragedians Phrynichus is included rather surprisingly. Nor is Philocleon's natural force abated, though his eye may be dim: as usual, his conception of polite accomplishment shades off into the use of his fists, and as the son of Carcinus comes on to contend with him, he says he will destroy him with a "knuckle-dance." [59] Far from cured, Philocleon has merely a new disease, worse than the first, but with equally contentious, agonistic purport; according to Xanthias and Bdelycleon he is outright mad.[60] The threads are now all pulled together and the final dance begins, a whirling dance which seems to convey symbolically the underlying idea of the vicious circle where all things return upon themselves. Twice the three spinning sons of Carcinus are compared to tops, they twirl their feet, round and round, and move in a circle.[61] The motion is so compelling that the chorus itself is caught in it, and instead of marching out of the orchestra as usual, they dance away, whirling. It is the dance of the world's madness, the dizzying, infectious carousel of self-assertive, irrepressible nature, the great divine *Dinos*, Vortex, who has deposed Zeus and rules in his stead.[62]

The whirling dance, however, is not the first circle image in the play; it merely activates an implication which has been present from the first. The circle of nature is also a trap from which no one can escape. When the play begins Bdelycleon and the slaves, in order to keep the old man at home, have enclosed the whole house in a great net, "in a circle" all round.[63] The idea of circularity, especially in the context of trapping, seems to hover throughout the play. Philocleon urges the wasp chorus to surround his captors and sting them "in a circle"; [64] Bdelycleon, showing his father how the dicasts are caught by the demagogues, says:

And just consider, when you and all might revel in affluence, free as air,
How these same demagogues wheel you round, and cabin and coop you,
   I know not where.[65]

The dog Labes, in order to seize the cheese, first "sails round the platter in a circle." [66] Sometimes, the circle appears without specific reference to a trap, but only because it lurks compellingly in the texture, as when Bdelycleon, hearing his father climbing down from the roof, says, "A voice circles round me." [67] And all this circularity, culminating in the spinning dance which engulfs everyone, is a formal encompassing of the play's self-canceling progress, and a symbol of the changeless, and perhaps meaningless, gyration which surrounds the human process, with all its institutions, education, ethics, rational dialectics, and laws. The end of the play is unresolved — we do not know even the results of the dancing contest

— but the irresolution is part of the meaning; later on the idea of circularity will reappear, under different images, in the *Birds*.

It remains to examine more closely this play's remarkable protagonist in the light of what have been considered the features of an Aristophanean hero. In the *Clouds* the transcendent hero is virtually lacking; he returns, after a fashion, in the *Wasps*. More specifically, all his lineaments reappear, but in a dispersed and inconclusive way; not all center in Philocleon, who never arrives at full and absolute mastery of the world. There was good reason for this, if what was said above about circularity and self-cancellation be true. Aristophanes' response to life was deepening in perspective and complexity, and the heroic fantasy seemed now to be included within a world process, at once baffling and grand. He had not yet seen, as he would shortly, how the two could be combined. But meanwhile, the heroic vision was too important a part of his world (or of any Greek's world) to be left out entirely and for good; the problem of the individual had always to be faced, and it always led back to the heroic vision, which for Aristophanes was structured round the quality of *poneria* and the uneasy, but powerful, union of beast, man, and divinity which has here been defined as the grotesque.

Philocleon's *poneria* is amply demonstrated throughout, not least in the little scenes where he tries to escape from the house, disguising himself as smoke coming out of the chimney, and then as "No-man," riding like Odysseus from the Cyclops' cave on the underside of the ass.[68] The latter scene is one which also develops imagistically, to a degree, and comes around toward the grotesque. Bdelycleon compares his father to an ass's foal, a simile which grows into Xanthias' comparison of him, already quoted, to an "ass stuffed with barley," and the remark of Lysistratus at the symposium that he was like "an ass which had run off to the chaff heap." [69] Philocleon more or less becomes the ass, but not merely by making an ass of himself: for one of the words used for ass in this play is κλητήρ, signifying properly a process server, but used in slang for the braying donkey. This usage glances, of course, at the legal aspect of Philocleon, and process servers appear in abundance in the last scenes. The double meaning is doubtless also intended when the incensed bread girl gets Chaerephon to be her process server; poor Chaerephon seems to have been dragged mutely onto the stage for a moment for no other reason but to be "writ down an ass." [70] And it might just be noted, by way of observing how Aristophanes' mind works, that the ass imagery probably explains Philocleon's question to his son, "Have you fallen off your — tomb?" To fall off an ass was, by a misdivision of words in Greek, a way of saying also to go out of your mind. But in this line Philocleon is treating his son as an old man, and so invents this new phrase, carrying the same import of madness, but qualified more specifically as second childhood.[71]

But to return to the idea of the grotesque, an ass is not the only animal with whom Philocleon is imagistically identified: in the very opening lines of the play he is referred to as a "monster," and thereafter represented successively as a bee (twice), a jackdaw, a mouse, a sparrow, a weasel, perhaps an octopus, and a dog.[72] And of course he is always a wasp. The net itself suggests a trap for an animal, or fish, and Bdelycleon has to take care that he will not gnaw his way out.[73] The animals tend to be of the small, canny, and busy kind, except the dog, and they serve to characterize Philocleon from the point of view of *poneria* and persistence. But they also give him that kinship with the animal kingdom which is part of the heroic secret in comedy, and part of the heritage of *physis*. His kinship with the gods, on the other hand, is represented by the passage about thunder and Zeus discussed earlier. What is lacking is the merging of the two extra dimensions; the paradigmatic image of the grotesque is a man on a dung beetle arriving on Olympus, and Philocleon never achieves such cosmic unity. He is either a god or an animal, in addition to his humanity, but never all at once. As said above, the images are there, but dispersed, not welded into the true grotesque structure, for the *Wasps* is not a play of pure heroic achievement; it is a play of the framework which challenges and invites that achievement, and hence its pervasive ambiguity.

The dispersion of the grotesque images is further illustrated by their occurrence, in both the beginning and the end of the play, with little or no connection with Philocleon. The two dozing slaves have each had a dream; Xanthias tells his first:

> I dreamt an eagle,
> Very large, flew down to the market place,
> And snatching a brazen shield up in his talons
> Carried it far aloft into the heavens;
> Afterward it was dropped — by Cleonymus.[74]

Here the famous coward and glutton Cleonymus is given the full panoply of the grotesque; the passage has no relevance to the play, but it deploys the comic range, the wide horizon which Aristophanes commanded at its best. The other slave's dream lacks the divine overtones, but certainly develops the animal ones. Sosias dreamed that a flock of sheep, with cloaks and staves, were sitting in the Pnyx holding an assembly; and before these sheep a ravenous whale (Cleon) was making a speech in a voice like a pig being singed alive; the whale is also weighing and dividing beef fat (with a pun on δημός, "fat," and δῆμος, "people"), while Theorus sits by having the head of a crow, which then by punning mispronunciation turns into the head of a flatterer.[75] The satire here undergoes a kind of baroque elaboration, very characteristic of Aristophanes, but does not quite answer to the present definition of the grotesque.

But the poet is not finished with Cleon; in the parabasis he describes him again in one of the most majestic invectives ever devised, with loving care, for an enemy. In fact, it was so good, it could not be surpassed; it could only be repeated, and Aristophanes repeated it word for word in the *Peace* the next year. Here the demonic element is not lacking: Cleon is a "jag-toothed beast, from whose eyes flash the most awesome gleams of a Cynna [a prostitute, apparently] and round whose head flicker a hundred heads of doomed flatterers; he has the voice of a death-mothering torrent, the stench of a seal," and a couple of other attributes too coarse to mention but suitably added for a climax.[76] The chief sources of this fascinating conglomerate have long been duly recognized: the hydra and the demon Typhoeus of the *Theogony*. The word "jag-toothed" is regularly used in Homer for a wild boar. This is grotesque in the full sense; yet scarcely heroic, be it noted, for the immortal elements are of the darker sort, the monsters and spooks cast into hell by Zeus. Yet the total image is akin to the heroic world; it is the sort of thing which heroes assail, a fabulous abomination, worthy of the expressive nightmares of Aubrey Beardsley, and fit, as James Thurber might say, to frighten an octopus to death.

Finally, at the very end of the play comes a rather charming touch of the grotesque, but again with no heroic overtones and no real connection with the play's meaning. It deserves mention because it shows how naturally Aristophanes' mind moved into this pattern, even when he had no particular need for it. In the dancing match the three sons of the tragic poet Carcinus come dancing in. Carcinus means crab, and his three sons were notoriously small and spindly. The poet treats them to a series of animal and other comparisons — spiders, vinegar cruets, wrens, tops — but crab and shrimp are the natural choices.[77] Presently these children of the sea are joined by their father, Carcinus himself, and the chorus greets him with the epithets of Poseidon, "Lord and father, Regent of ocean, pleased with his potent offspring." [78] As said, the image relates little, if at all, to the rest of the drama, and certainly the last thing Aristophanes would want is to treat the Carcinus family as heroic. It is only a motif, like the slave's dream at the beginning, and like the line where Xanthias, meaning simply that he is sleepy, joins god and animal in the metaphor, "cow-herding Sabazius," the Thracian Dionysus.[79] These motifs float rootlessly and whimsically, as if left adrift when the heroic core vanished, and Philocleon's position verges toward, but never quite grasps, the transcendent power to gather them round himself.

The real hero was to return; he returns the next year in Trygaeus, and in Peithetaerus he acquires a new and finer guise in an even wider horizon of comic insight. But meanwhile the *Wasps* represents a stage in Aristophanes' development which is simultaneously satisfying in itself, and a promise of greater things to come. The world of comedy is the world of *physis*, and any comedy which rejects that world, as the present *Clouds* seems to do, defeats itself. In the *Wasps*, Aristophanes plunged to a greater depth into the analysis of his own comic world, and valiantly faced the infinite ambiguities and incorrigibilities of the concept "nature," emerging with a play tender and delicate in its unblinking clarity. Though there is little that could be called "intellectual material" in the text itself, the *Wasps* rests soundly upon familiarity with the intellectual and spiritual conflicts of the day, the moral dialectics of nature versus law, and nature versus education. But these dialectics have now found a poetic language, and a truly representative action, by virtue of which their outlines are clothed in a becoming comic garb; and this poetic texture further allows the opposing antinomies of the intellect to be absorbed into the broader image of the encircling trap of nature. It all goes far deeper than a satire on litigation, which is only a springboard; it is a kind of counterpiece to the *Clouds*, and the irresolution of the end is a token of dramatic honesty far superior to the weak moralizing of the finale of its predecessor. The end was to be resolved at least once more in the poet's career, but in the *Wasps* as yet there was no way to defeat the circle and evade the trap. If this makes it sound too serious, and almost tragic, be it said that the concerns of tragedy and comedy do not radically differ. But there is nothing tragic or sad about the *Wasps*; it is one of Aristophanes' wittiest texts, poetically rich, and spun around one of his most appealing characters. And if the circle seems to be inexorable, and a trap, it should be remembered that it is also a gay and whirling dance.

,V,

THE ANATOMY OF NOTHINGNESS

Birds

THE *Birds* is, as a rule, regarded as the most mysterious of the comedies. Interpreters who seek the essence of the plays in current political or social situations have found in the *Birds* some cause for embarrassment. It is not a "peace" play exactly, and it is not a play against Cleon, who was now dead; Euripides, for an exception, is not even mentioned in it; Socrates has a brief stanza, but no more. One commentator has seen in it a political allegory having to do with Alcibiades and the Sicilian expedition, but his theory turns the *Birds* into a cryptographic political treatise so intricate that no one could possibly have detected the meaning even in its own time. Who would suspect from watching a performance that the birds were the Athenians, the gods the Spartans, and the hero a cross between Alcibiades and Gorgias of Leontini? [1] Other interpreters, more realistic, but inclined, perhaps, to settle for too little, have regarded it as a flight of purest fancy having little to do with anything.[2] But poetry cannot be quite so lacking in relevance to experience, though the *Birds* is indeed a flight of fancy. A third group, favoring an Aristophanes who is more a moral reformer than a political one, sees the play as a condemnation of the Athenian vices of gullibility, fickleness, waywardness, and superstition. Perhaps; but then it must be asked why the hero Peithetaerus, whose operations can scarcely be called supremely moral, is so marvelously successful, even to ascending the throne of the whole world; and the answer has to be that after the end of the play the gods struck him down, and of course everybody knew that that was going to happen.[3] This is to pull a rabbit, and not a very pleasing rabbit, out of a very old hat. One tries in vain to imagine, after the triumphant riotings of the last scene, the thoughtful Athenians turning homeward, spiritually admonished, and murmuring, "Ah, that Peithetaerus is headed for a bad fall! Good old Aristophanes has straightened us out again."

Yet for all these differences of interpretation, the *Birds* is also regarded as the poet's masterpiece, and a glance at the scenario may suggest the reason, or one of the reasons. Two aging Athenians, Peithetaerus and Euelpides, disgusted with the life in Athens, its tumult of business, war, debts, and litigation, have decided to consult the birds about a better place to live. Guided by a crow and a jackdaw which they have bought, they seek the Hoopoe, who was once Tereus, King of Daulis, and husband of the Athenian princess Procne. This first stage of the search introduces the theme of a pristine world, far away and long ago, under the rule of Tereus and Procne, who here, their crimes forgotten, represent not only the carefree world of pastoral bliss but also a further range of knowledge, "all that men know, and all that birds know." [4] The next theme is more hardheaded, however, and concerns the world of empire. The two Athenians make a compact with the birds, and convince them that they, the birds, are the original gods, who have been cheated of their rights by the Olympians. They proceed to build a new city in the air, Cloud-cuckoo-land, and intercept the smoke of sacrifices rising to heaven, thus bringing the gods into parley. Zeus capitulates and yields to the now winged Peithetaerus his scepter and the Princess Basileia, and therewith complete supremacy. Thus outlined, the play appears like an escapist manifesto, the utopian dream of a new and perfect city where men can live as freely and happily as birds. The utopian theme is certainly there, but so too is the theme of power, and close scrutiny of the way the two work together, and of the motifs through which they develop, reveals beneath the broad laughter a striking poetic intuition, laced with deep and wistful irony.

The *Birds* is strangely free of political concerns; there are the usual topical allusions, indeed, but they are passing ones, and there is no consistent reference to any specific issue or issues of the city, as there is in the five preceding plays. In the *Birds* comedy seems to detach itself, to a degree, in search of a broader and more symbolic scheme; and though the old form persists, it becomes more free of the immediate topicalities on which it once relied so heavily. In this freedom from parochial concern lies one of the play's chief claims to supremacy: its scene is the world, not merely Athens. Moreover, it has a greater dramatic unity than any of the comedies so far, a unity unbroken even by the parabasis. Normally the parabasis of the chorus marks an interruption in the progress of the play, as the chorus comes forward, and, speaking as much in the poet's person as in character, addresses the audience about matters quite outside the drama. There is no such breaking of the illusion in the *Birds*; rather the parabasis abets the illusion, with its famous parody on cosmogonic poetry explaining how the world was created by birds, the original gods. The demands of dramaturgy have triumphed in the *Birds* over the need for certain traditional components, and the result is a play of singularly sustained dramatic force.

But what is dramatized? The earlier plays of Aristophanes regularly mingle their fantasy and satire in such a way that the satiric element provides a clue to the meaning of the fantasy. Out of the satire on the war party rises the great individualist Dicaeopolis with his fantastic peace; out of the satire on interminable litigation rises the fantasy of the *Wasps*, the dream of personal power blending into the inescapable vortex of nature. With the element of a satiric nucleus apparently lacking in the *Birds*, one is left with the fantasy itself, to discover its relevance as best one may from an analysis of its structure and motifs.

The hero himself is clear. He is not Alcibiades or Gorgias, or anyone else, though Gorgias, as we shall see, may have some relevance to the meaning of the play. The hero is simply the man of heroic *poneria* par excellence; more properly, he becomes that in much the same way Dicaeopolis did. Like Dicaeopolis, he represents the individual fugitive from an increasingly impossible society, and he also reaches the point where he is suddenly inundated by a vision of supremacy, which he immediately implements with all his resources. He is the grandest and most successful of all Aristophanes' heroes. Even before he becomes inspired, the germ of his *poneria* is implicit in his name: Peithetaerus, "Companion-persuader" (if that is the right form), certainly implies the suspicious powers of rhetoric and guile. His companion's name, Euelpides, "McHopeful," suggests naïveté, if not exactly innocence. One might justifiably regard these two, perhaps, as two familiar aspects of Athenian character, cleverness and gullibility, but in fact these possibilities are not dramatically exploited, for Euelpides is not duped. Rather he acts as the principal foil to Peithetaerus' boundless vision until he is no longer necessary, partaking of the fantasy and eventually disappearing into it.

Up to the point where Peithetaerus gets his great idea, Euelpides does more of the talking; he has his eye more firmly on the object than does the visionary Peithetaerus. It is Euelpides who discusses with the Hoopoe the possible whereabouts of a city which will be free of the faults of Athens; Peithetaerus during this scene is the aloof, brooding mastermind whose thoughts have not yet come to fullness. But from the point where the mastermind suddenly springs into action and begins erecting its gigantic fantasy of a bird city in the air, the objectivity and realism of Euelpides take the form of earthy comments characteristic of the role of buffoon, and swing into a poised and familiar dramatic relation to Peithetaerus' inspired leadership. Euelpides contributes little or nothing to the structure of the fantasy, but his practical remarks throughout the agon fall with sudden dull thuds in the interstices of Peithetaerus' airy verbiage. This is familiar comic technique — to blow up a large balloon and then burst it — and Aristophanes makes use of it often, but it is a major principle in the *Birds*. Not only in the scenes with Euelpides, but roughly everywhere, lyrical fancy and vaporous superstructures of wit and sophistry alternate with a trudging realism which, for all it may bring us back to earth in a sense, never really wins the day; the fantasy goes on with tireless rhythm, unperturbed by the dragging weights of what is usually called reality. If the process were reversed, if soaring fancy foundered on ineluctable fact, one might discover a common-sense view, and the *Birds* might be taken as similar to Brueghel's "Fall of Icarus," where a winged man has just fallen out of the sky into the sea, his legs still visible, but nobody takes notice; the ship sails on, and the peasant goes on driving his furrow. Here is just the opposite: the balloon never quite bursts; it just loses a little air and then shoots higher. References to everyday familiarities only feed the fantasy, through Peithetaerus' genius for turning everything to advantage. Here *poneria* achieves its most developed sense, in that the self-advantage which it pursues is identified with nothing less than the restructuring of the world itself, and challenges the authority of Zeus, the god of things as they are. Euelpides' part is to embody the solid facts which dissolve before the skilled language of the demiurgic man of words.

All this is nonsense, of course, but in the sense of nonsense poetry, which, at its best, regularly juxtaposes real and imaginary things or words in such a way as to exploit the real in favor of the imaginary. In reading Edward Lear's "Pobble Who Has No Toes" we may doubt the existence of Pobbles, but not of toes; yet, in the long poem which tells how this Pobble lost his toes despite his mother's warning to take care of them, toes make the Pobble as clothes make the man. Their solid factuality does not detract at all from the imaginary Pobble's reality. And in the lovely Pogo lyric

> How pierceful grows the hazy yon!
> How myrtle petal thou!
> For spring hath sprung the cyclotron —
> How high browse thou, brown cow?[5]

171

the sudden apearance of the cyclotron is a bit of a shock; yet, the cyclotron is carried along somehow in the pastoral air, and the song pursues its serene and gentle way.

The observation that the *Birds* is nonsense may not seem to be either very helpful, or very different from the interpretation previously rejected, that it is a flight of purest fancy, signifying nothing. But the answer may be that a work may signify nothing in one of two senses, for "nothing" is a metaphysical term. The word may mean "absence of anything," and thus be quite negative; but it may also have the more positive meaning of the articulable conception "nothing," or "nothingness," and in this second meaning it is as useful to thought and criticism as zero is to a mathematician. By the hypostasis of language "nothing" becomes something to which we give a name, and about which we may invent a whole series of predicates which signify, no doubt, nothing, but which may be the rightful language of absurdity.[6] In any case, when we speak this language, we play with words and give them a primacy over their meanings which inverts our usual sense of reality. The *Birds* plays with language in a way far beyond any of the other comedies, and the sense of reality undergoes considerable change by consequence. If the word play "Katagela" in the *Acharnians* creates a city with metaphoric existence in Sicily, the *Birds*, which is one vast, finely woven texture of word plays, creates the absurd and wonderful metaphor of Utopia, Nowhere, the ideal city of Nephelococcygia. One of the ways to say in Greek "You are talking nonsense," is οὐδὲν λέγεις, "you talk nothing." If we take that "nothing" in the second sense, it becomes clear what Aristophanes is about; for the nothing that people talk is the reality which they possess. The word is all, it creates consciousness, and its enormous vitality stubbornly resists fact. A word becomes image or metaphor, and the image or metaphor lives in the mind, independent of reason and far more compelling. Philocleon suffered from an ineradicable image of himself, but Peithetaerus' imagery includes also a world appropriate to himself, and he manufactures it. Images and metaphors are dream substance and make dream worlds, and every world is an absurdity, a verbal nothing. All this is beyond satire, as handled in the *Birds*; it is a poetic weft comically adumbrating the world in which we live, the world where there can be no tragic reversal or recognition, the world of *poneria* and the self, where the persuasive and manipulable word is king.

To interpret so may seem to do historical violence, by introducing modern ideas of relativism, subjectivism, and the question of the relation between reality and language. But such ideas are by no means exclusively modern. Probably around the third quarter of the fifth century B.C. Gorgias composed a book called "On Non-being," or "Concerning Nature," in which, according to Sextus Empiricus, he maintained three propositions: first, that nothing exists; second, that if anything exists it is not intellectively graspable; and third, that even if it is intellectively graspable, it is incommunicable.[7] The last of these is the most relevant to the *Birds*, and is really the source of the other two; for Gorgias believed that speech, and speech alone, is what is communicated, and that speech does not correspond to reality. His mode of reasoning may not be wholly flawless, but there can be no doubt that he is facing the epistemological problem of communication:

> For if the real things, which have external existence, are visible and audible, and commonly perceptible by the senses, and of these things the visible ones are grasped by vision, the audible ones by hearing, and there is no interchange, how then can these be communicated to another person? For the instrument by which we communicate is speech, and speech is not "existent real things"; therefore it is not real things which we communicate to our neighbors, but speech, which is different from existent objects. And so, just as the visible cannot become the audible and the reverse, so too, since reality exists externally, it could not become our speech.[8]

It has been said by a number of scholars that Gorgias is here doing no more than displaying his ingenuity with words, in a playful refutation of Eleatic metaphysics. Even if this view were correct, the treatise "On Non-being" would be not merely an argument, but also an object lesson on the power of speech. But it has been recently demonstrated that this theory of communication and reality is wholly consistent with the rest of the work of Gorgias, and in particular with his theory of *peitho* (persuasion), and *apaté* (deception, illusion) as the psychic and aesthetic basis of the rhetorical art.[9] Certainly relativism and subjectivism were nothing new in the late fifth century, after Protagoras and even Democritus.[10] Gorgias simply pressed matters further, in denying all knowable connection between being, or reality, and the communicative medium of language, and in asserting that language is the controlling factor in the life of the psyche. As it has been well stated: " 'Reality' for him [Gorgias] lies in the human psyche and its malleability and susceptibility to the effects of verbal coruscation. Thus his rhetoric, though concerned primarily with a technique of verbal elaboration, rests ultimately upon a psychology of literary experience. These two, psyche and *logos*, lie both within the realm of tangible experience and become for Gorgias the new reality." [11]

If such views were indeed characteristic of Gorgias, whose influence was great, one must assume an intellectual climate in which subjectivism, relativism, and the priority of speech to reality were familiar if not always approved theories; theories which, in fact, one finds Plato later retrospectively combating. But in the fifth century, in at least some intellectual quarters, the persuasive "deception" of speech created the *doxa*, or private opinion, upon which people acted, in a world where ultimate or final truth was undiscoverable.[12] Speech assists and directs the "subjective restructuring of the world," and thus occupies a position of power analogous to, if not identifiable with, divinity itself.[13] And it is precisely such a psychology which underlies the *Birds* of Aristophanes. The airy empire of the birds is created out of words by that demiurge of persuasion, Peithetaerus, in a vast "subjective restructuring of the world" which is both lyrical and ironic. Peithetaerus knows his Gorgias, and though Gorgias undoubtedly felt that the rightful ends of rhetorical persuasion were good, for the comic hero no such scruple need exist: *peitho* and *apaté* are the most serviceable modes of *poneria*, in that they build their own reality and lead on to the boundless.[14]

One cannot begin to analyze in full the way this underlying idea is worked out in the *Birds*, but a few examples will serve to illustrate, for essentially everything contributes toward it, even the parabasis, as pointed out earlier. The play begins with a dramatized metaphor. The two Athenians, turning their backs on troubled Athens, are going to visit the birds. Euelpides makes sure we get the joke, because going to the birds is like going to the crows, which is Greek for going to the dogs:

> Isn't it dreadful, here we are, we two,
> Ready and willing to go to the crows,
> And cannot find the road? [15]

Or, as it has been translated with succinct felicity: "Two of us for the birds, and we can't even find the road!" [16] The metaphor in hand may be no more than simple slang, but to stage two characters who pace out the actual steps of "going to the birds" has the unmistakable effect of putting language itself in the controlling position.[17] Once evoked, the phrase plots the poetic course of the play through a preposterous series of verbal pyrotechnics whose iridescent web of innuendoes gradually reveals the poet's gay but profound reflection upon his world.

The image goes deeper than the slang phrase. Peithetaerus and Euelpides leave their world to go to the birds, which is going to the crows on the one hand; but it is also a return to nature. At first they seek another city, better than Athens, but when none can be found, Euelpides asks what life is like among the birds:

Hoopoe: Not a bad way to spend your time.
    First of all, here we live without a purse.
Euelp.: Then you get rid of a great deal of life's hugger-mugger.
Hoopoe: We feed in gardens on white sesame,
    On poppy seed and mint and myrtle berries.
Euelp.: You live the life of newlyweds! [18]

This passage is double-edged, for it points to two aspects of the life of nature, *physis*. The remark about the purse reminds us that one of the reasons why the two men left Athens was their desire not to have to pay debts.[19] Further, one is reminded of Strepsiades in the

Clouds, where nonpayment of debt is regarded as natural enough if you can get away with it; and one can get away with it with the help of Unjust Discourse, whose basic principle is the φύσεως ἀνάγκαι, the necessities of nature.[20] Nature is here again invoked, after the late sophistic fashion, as an antimoral force, and one which in the human creature does not naturally acquiesce to law, let alone create it. To escape *nomos* and to arrive at the fulfillment of *physis* becomes therefore a natural desideratum. On the other hand, the Hoopoe's description of the life of birds is the first of a series of marvelous pastorales exalting the innocence of nature and the sweetness of birdsong, which reaches up toward the harmony of the gods themselves. And yet, both views go somehow together, for the gods are indeed above morality, in that state of divine supremacy toward which, as said often before, the comic hero also strives, yet without renouncing his humanity, his "necessities of nature." As we have seen, in the *Wasps* Aristophanes studied nature as a trap, a vicious circle coming always round upon itself. But in the *Birds* nature's innate antinomies are drawn with a clearer sense of the unity of all natural phenomena. And if the outcome involves, as it does in the *Wasps*, some unexpected turns, yet the presence of a true comic hero, Peithetaerus, who can include multitudes of inconsistencies, keeps the fantasy triumphantly afloat to the last, so that the vicious circle itself becomes a victory.

Nowhere has Aristophanes given fuller expression to the comic dream, and in no way could he have reached more subtly into the psychology of his contemporary audience. To return to nature is to evade, or better, to transcend law, and most of the advantages of Nephelococcygia amount, as we shall see, to a happy lawlessness. Yet such is scarcely the moral. Half the charm of the *Birds* lies in its paradox, in its exploitation of the ambiguities of the *nomos-physis* debate. Not only is nature a term of ambiguous value; there are further equivocations and puns on *nomos*, which with one accentuation, can mean either "law" or "song," and then with a different one, "pasture," or the haunts of birds.[21] Peithetaerus and Euelpides cannot live in Athens, with its laws, bailiffs, and bother; they will seek songs and pastures, the lawless *nomos* which is *physis*, the life of nature, fit for birds and gods. And this, incidentally, is the reason why the *Birds* does not arise from any specific issue in the city, as the other plays do; the city itself is the issue, or pretext, for the fantasy, and there is no need to satirize a part when the whole is dismissed and transformed.

The scene with the Hoopoe thematically introduces the ambiguities which are to be developed dramatically in the remainder. The climax of the scene, and also the first inkling of the circularity which is to characterize the play, is the sudden formulation of the Great Idea by which the comic hero comes into being. Naturally, it is all done with words, and the Great Idea is simply a pun. Peithetaerus has been gazing at the sky, which is occasionally referred to in poetry as *polos*, meaning pole or celestial sphere; and it occurs to him that one need only colonize and fortify this *polos* for it to become a *polis*, a city.[22] No true Greek could live without a city, even if he was returning to nature. And nothing could be simpler: in a world where words control facts, the sky can become a city as easily as *polos* becomes *polis*. But now also the whole basic self-contradiction of the fantasy begins to reveal itself. From the point of view of birds and the countryside, the life of nature is the life of carefree innocence; from the point of view of the city, the unit of human society, it is the law of the talon, the sophistic doctrine of "nature's necessities," and the right of the stronger to rule the weaker. The two things merge weirdly, as Peithetaerus' plan takes shape. The birds, he explains, should stop fluttering around aimlessly and settle down; they should, in fact, build a city, and if they build it in the air, they can rule men like locusts, and starve the gods into submission with "Melian hunger."[23] The reference to the brutal siege of Melos provides a stark example of "nature's" grimmer side. They can even impose customs fees, and refuse to enfranchise the sacrificial smoke unless the gods pay tribute.[24] The happy innocence of the birds, the vision of redemption, is undergoing a change. And yet it is not that Peithetaerus is corrupting nature by imposing civilization upon it. Nature, in its two aspects as described above, is simply asserting itself, with something of the circularity observed in the *Wasps*; it has its own dialectic of opposites. Men can join the birds, and grow wings. But the birds, once informed of their destiny, are happy to "settle down" and build a city like men.

Immediately upon the formulation of the plan follows the summoning of the birds, and the pure pastoral notes re-enter. In a lovely *aubade* the Hoopoe rouses his mate the nightingale:

> Consort mine, come rise from sleep,
> Scatter strains of holy song
> From divine lips, wailing Itys
> Yours and mine, for whom we weep.
> As your quivering throat is shaken
> By your sacred melodies,
> Purely through the leafy bindweed
> Goes the echo to Zeus' dwelling,
> Where the golden-haired Apollo,
> Listening, answers your lamenting,
> Plucks his ivory lyre, and stations
> Dances of the gods, and onward
> Through the immortal mouths, harmonious
> Flows the singing of the Blest.[25]

The nightingale is actually a flute girl, and to the obbligato of her music, the Hoopoe calls to all the birds, wild olive nibblers, arbutus peckers, and gnat snappers, all the birds from mountain, marsh, or seashore, to come to listen to the new plan. Nonsense words, representing birdcalls, become real words: for example, ἰτὼ ἰτὼ becomes ἴτω, "come," and the chorus alters its bird cry τιτιτίγξ into τιτιτίνα λόγον, where the τι syllable becomes the interrogative "what?" [26] The effect is extraordinary, creating as it does a confusion between the human and the ornithological realms soon to merge. Nor does Aristophanes ignore the possibilities for lampoon. Some of the birds which muster to this pastoral invocation bear surprising resemblances to certain Athenians: the profligate Callias, badly plucked; the luckless Cleonymus, who enters as a great turkey gobbler, and surprises

Peithetaerus by not having yet thrown away his crest.[27] It is an old joke, apparently, to invent birds out of words, like the "yellow-bellied turntail" or the "bronze-throated angelus." By an obvious but workable pun on κηρύλος, "kingfisher," and κείρω, to cut, Aristophanes brings in a bird who is Sporgilus, a popular Athenian barber, as if he were, instead of a pipit, a snippit.[28] And so on, until there is a formidable chorus of birds who proceed to attack their ancient enemy, Man — an odd inversion indeed, especially since no eagles or other really fierce birds are even mentioned.

As prelude to the agon, a strange scene follows. The two heroes protect themselves by seizing spits and donning armor made of pots and saucers. Where they get them is a question — from the Hoopoe's kitchen? — but we soon find out why they choose this defense. It is all an elaborate charade, the first part of which is unfortunately lost on us: "Take up a pot," says Peithetaerus, "and the owl will not come near us." [29] We do not know why an owl would not approach a pot, but it is perhaps a reference to a children's game; there was a dance called "owl" and a children's game which involved putting a pot over the head.[30] In any case, it is a saying, and the dramatic enactment of sayings, such as this, or "going to the crows," lies close to the heart of the *Birds*. The rest is clearer: as they stand on guard with their ceramic armor, Euelpides asks, "If we fall in this battle, where shall we be buried?" "In the Potters' Quarter," says Peithetaerus, referring to the famous Ceramicus cemetery, "at public expense, and we'll tell the generals that we died fighting at Orneae." [31] The last remark adds the crowning touch: Orneae, besides being a pun on *orneon*, "bird," was a little town between Sicyon and Corinth which two years before had been besieged by the Athenians for one day; the occupying enemy, however, escaped during the night and abandoned the town, so that nobody was killed at Orneae, because there had been no battle. The absurdity is further underscored by Peithetaerus' saying "We will *tell* the generals we died."

The whole scene, with its sharply pointed self-contradictions, suggests that the theme of the *Birds* is absurdity itself, and that the substance of reality is words, words, words. Everything in the *Birds* turns round upon itself and comes to nothing, except the deified human bird Peithetaerus, the embodiment of grotesquerie and *poneria*, that "close-counseled rogue," as the Hoopoe calls him, "all sophism, swindle, smoothness, and subtlety." [32] These terms all characterize the slick persuasive rhetoric which had become the new higher education, and Peithetaerus' use of it is a clear example of what was said earlier about Gorgias' theory of speech versus reality. The view that language makes everyone's world what it is stands in anticipation of all nominalist and existential philosophy, at whose heart lie the basic concepts of nothingness and absurdity; and in such a framework a comic hero might well, by talking lively, persuade the high Athenian command that he had been killed in a battle which never took place.

The verbal impositions continue in cohorts and legions, as Peithetaerus persuades the birds that he has come to do them good. With fine demagoguery, he cries that he feels great pain for their plight, for they were once kings, indeed the real gods, the original rulers of the world, and he is prepared to prove it.[33] The crested lark, for instance, existed before the earth was made; the proof is that when the lark's father died she had no place to bury him, so she buried him in her own head. All this, which Peithetaerus lays at Aesop's door, is a kind of free romance on the epithet of the lark, ἐπιτυμβίδιος, a word of doubtful significance which could mean either "with a crest on top" or "with a tomb on top"! The ordinary rooster was commonly nicknamed the Persian bird, because his upright comb was thought to resemble the upright tiara of the Persian kings; *ergo*, the rooster originally ruled the Persians. And everybody still obeys him, for when a rooster crows, everyone gets up and goes to work. In similar plausible ways the kite and the cuckoo are proved to be kings. Also in the old days no one swore by the gods, but by the birds; this is proved by the fact that whenever the soothsayer Lampon swears to his own dubious prophecies, he swears "by the goose," which makes the goose a god.[34] This is a clear sophistic inversion, for Lampon's oath by the goose, somewhat like Socrates' "by the dog," was chosen precisely because the goose is not a god and therefore one may swear by it falsely without risk. Such reasoning may not be quite Gorgian rhetoric, but it is just as specious, and even more successful.

The birds are convinced. Men can do nothing without birds — at least, without augury — and birds can do everything for men, much better than the gods. They can even increase the length of men's lives, because of an old wives' tale in Hesiod that a squawking crow lives through five (or nine) generations of men.[35] Hereafter, instead of sacrificing simply to Aphrodite, Poseidon, and Heracles, men will sacrifice first to lovebirds, ducks, and voracious cormorants.[36] The birds rise to the occasion; they hail Peithetaerus as a savior, and agree to build the city.[37] Peithetaerus goes to be fitted to a pair of wings by the Hoopoe.

The accession of wings marks the first stage of Peithetaerus' conquest of nature; the familiar grotesque complex of beast-man-god will be completed when Zeus surrenders to the triumphing hero. But first he must enter nature and become one with it:

Peith.: How shall I and this fellow
Live without wings among you winged ones?
Hoopoe: Quite well.
Peith.: Look here, there is some sort of tale
In Aesop's fables, that a fox once made
Common cause with an eagle, and regretted it.
Hoopoe: Don't be afraid, for there's a little root
Which you shall eat, and presently grow wings.[38]

The birds know the secret, magical roots which will bridge the gap between man and the organic world at large. Peithetaerus is already a fox in cleverness, but more is needed. He must have wings, and wings are a complex symbol in the play. Images of flying, as well as of all up-in-the-air imagery, are very frequent in Aristophanes, and, as noted often, are regularly associated with high-flown rhetoric and other forms of nonsense.[39] Peithetaerus must have the proper equipment to build and govern a city of windy nothingness. But wings also signify, as will appear in later passages, freedom from restraint of all sort, and therefore they mark the liberation of the hero from the common lot of humanity. Wings are to Peithetaerus what the thirty-year-old wine was to Dicaeopolis, or the dung beetle to Trygaeus; the token of natural liberty and individual sufficiency to manipulate and control the world.

The merging of bird and man had been adumbrated comically, but delicately, in sundry images of the opening scenes: Euelpides explains that he and his friend have "flown away from Athens with both feet," and the Hoopoe, before his entrance, calls from within as to a doorkeeper, "Open the woods, that I may issue forth." [40] It should be noted, too, that even before their conversion by Peithetaerus, the birds have learned to speak Greek, they have "oaths and compacts," and sufficient military organization to speak of "leading on the right wing." [41] There is a steady progress toward fulfillment of the grotesque dramatic image, "human bird," or "winged man," with the idea of deity always overhanging it, so that it need hardly be said that the controlling image of the *Birds* is flying. Indeed, Aristophanes has practiced a singular poetic economy in deriving from wings or winged objects all but some peripheral and casual images. Throughout the play numberless variations are played on the motif, whether it be as nonsense, or lawless freedom, or the sheer lyrical joy of flight, that childlike, but irrepressible human dream. And toward the end, the themes of flying and of speech are drawn simply and naturally together when words themselves are identified as wings.[42] The winged Peithetaerus, struggling with the gods themselves for supreme power, is the most majestic of Aristophanes' grotesque figures, the comic hero come to fullness.

And now the chorus launches into the great parabasis, which, as said before, does not break the illusion, but furthers it. In fact, it is the heart of the illusion, the supreme joke, the triumphant lyrical image of nothingness. And despite the fact that it is a garbled parody on practically everybody who ever had committed cosmogonic speculation, especially Hesiod, Empedocles, and the Orphics, it is also high-flown poetry, full of mocking and graceful solemnity. The cosmogonic content itself, and the identification of the birds with all the phenomena of life, from the labors of the various seasons to love-making which knows no season, give it a suprapolitical, universal breadth wholly in accord with the rest of the play. After a second tender invocation to the nightingale the chorus begins:

Come, you who by nature are dwellers in darkness, mankind, like the leaves' generations,
Feeble of force, creations of clay, ye marrowless, shadowy species,
Wingless and miserable things of a day, humanity dreamlike and mortal,
Give ear and attend to us who continue forever, to us who are deathless,
And ageless, to us who dwell in the aether and counsel unperishing counsel,
That you may hear all, true doctrine and science, from us about heavenly matters,
Of the nature of birds, and the birth of the gods, of rivers and Darkness and Chaos,
And then, in full wisdom hereafter, for me, tell Prodicus go to the devil!
There was Chaos at first, and Night, black Darkness, and vast, vast Tartarus; neither
Earth nor the air nor the heaven was yet; but in Darkness' measureless bosom
The black-winged Night gave birth to the first aboriginal thing, a wind egg,
Out of which, as the circle of seasons came round, rose Love, the desired, his shoulders
Glistening and bright with his golden wings, like winds in hastening eddies.
And mingling with pinioned Chaos he, in the gloom, amid Tartarus' vastness,
Hatched out this brood of ourselves, and then first brought us forth to the daylight.[43]

Two things here call for preliminary notice: one, the mention of "heavenly matters" ($\tau\grave{\alpha}$ $\mu\varepsilon\tau\acute{\varepsilon}\omega\rho\alpha$), which is tantamount to nonsense; cosmology, climatology, explanations of clouds and winds and rain, all this was heavily and cheerfully derided in the *Clouds*, and in the *Peace*. The birds are now kindly offering to give a full scientific explanation of taradiddle. They parody science and religion, affirming the great zero, nonsense. The other point is the mention of Prodicus the sophist. The chorus' remark treats him as a writer on cosmology, about which he did apparently write a book.[44] But he was most famous for his study of language, especially of semantics, and for hair-splitting distinctions of shades of meaning.[45] He is an appropriate foil, therefore, to an account of creation which depends upon deflected meanings of words, an apt symbol of the windy, wordy philosophical imposture at which the birds are about to outdo him.

But the main image of this passage is the egg of dark-winged Night, and it is an image of pure nothingness, which focuses succinctly and meaningfully the series of strongly accented epithets by which the birds characterize the human scene: "obscure of life," "like leaves," "feeble," "frail shadow shapes," "ephemeral," "dreamlike." Rogers translates the words ὑπηνέμιον ᾠὸν as simply "egg conceived of the wind," oddly enough, and the point is obscured. For this is not a quite regular egg, it is a wind egg, an unfertilized egg which will not, of course, hatch.[46] It is perhaps only to be expected that the chorus, who had promised to give a scientific explanation of airy nothings, begin by deriving the gods and all existence from an egg incapable of hatching. Here is the central image of absurdity, dream, illusion, concentrating in a word all the other images of nothingness; the world itself is a contradiction in terms, a big joke, a hoax. Yet out of this egg of nothing comes winged Love, the generative principle, who by an odd union with the neuter Chaos creates the birds, clearly his kin because of the wings and the efficacy of tasty birds as love presents. And now these birds rule the world and set the seasons in motion in an illusory but lovely dance, promising everything good that mortals enjoy: health, wealth, life, peace, youth, laughter, dances, festivals, and — birds' milk! [47] They conclude, "You will be exhausted by all these blessings," a final, delicate contradiction in terms, with just a touch of wistfulness amid the mockery.[48] Happiness and birds' milk, "exhausted with blessings" — it is all nothing.

The remaining parts of the parabasis which follow the anapaests present in clear, dialectical terms the dual aspect of nature first sketched in the scene with the Hoopoe. The strophe and antistrophe, beginning with an invocation of the Woodland Muse and punctuated by the *tiotinx* birdcalls, celebrate in pastoral style the beauty of bird song. The music subdues the earth, inspiring its poets, then rises to heaven and quite overwhelms the gods:

> Muse of the thicket,
> *tio tio tio tio tio tio tiotinx*
> Dappled, with whom I perch
> In the vales and the heights of the hills,
> *tio tio tio tiotinx*
> On a leafy-locked ash,
> *tio tio tio tiotinx*
> From a trilling throat showing forth to Pan
> Sacred strains of melody,
> And solemn chorales to the Mountain Mother,
> *toto toto toto to to tinx*
> Whence, like a bee, old Phrynichus culled
> A harvest of our ambrosial music
> To feed his own sweet songs,
> *tio tio tiotinx.*

> Such music the swans,
> *tio tio tio tio tio tio tiotinx*
> Weaving their mingled cry
> With wing beats called on Apollo
> *tio tio tio tiotinx*
> Settling on banks of the Hebrus river,
> *tio tio tio tiotinx*
> And the call went up through ethereal cloud;
> The mottled tribes of beasts all cringed,
> And windless sky subdued the sea,
> *toto toto toto to to totinx*
> And all Olympus echoed, and wonder
> Seized the gods, the Olympian Graces
> And Muses joined the song.
> *tio tio tiotinx.*[49]

Here a majestic, pervasive harmony arises from the peaceful trills and twitterings of the thicket.

In contrast, the intervening trochaic passages celebrate the practical advantages of living with the birds. In the first place, the birds have a totally different moral system from men. Everything which is against the law among men is allowable among the birds: beating one's father, for instance, is quite respectable among the birds, because young cocks do it. A runaway, *branded* slave becomes a *speckled* francolin; and a foreigner can gain the rights of citizenship by breeding his own ancestors, because the word for grandfather and hedge sparrow is the same.[50] By such puns on words, or plays on the real or supposed habits of birds, the chorus disposes entirely of human social mores. In the corresponding passage they dispose of personal mores as well; if one is winged, one can satisfy, without concern for others, nature's most basic needs, for food, sex, and the like — here, specifically, adultery.[51] Now the basic image is no longer music or harmony, but wings, the givers of freedom. Winged nature is above the law. This is *physis* versus *nomos* with a vengeance, a vision of godlike freedom from moral restraints, much as the lyrical stanzas had revealed the godlike eloquence and beauty of nature. Aristophanes ties the two aspects together with the single word *nomos*, which in the strophe means "melody," and in the trochaic passage, "law," [52] The law crumbles, the melody triumphs. But the argument is scarcely, if at all, different from that of the Unjust Discourse of the *Clouds*, whose veneered talk, as he intimates, will enable Pheidippides to commit adultery with impunity, like Zeus, to beat his father, and in general "use his nature." [53] Slick talk is the native medium of *poneria*, and the birds mingle the most refined ingenuities of language with their innocent twitter, dethroning law and exalting themselves, in a divinely happy scheme devised as the only answer to the nothingness of the wind-egg world.

If the parabasis of the *Birds* is unusual in that instead of being a digression it contains the heart of the play, the remaining scenes bear out the feeling that Aristophanes was peculiarly concerned in this work with inner structural unity. In two earlier plays Aristophanes had introduced "impostors," stereotypes of city enterprise, who after one fashion or another try to upset the hero's new scheme. The *Birds*, however, has an extraordinary number of these, and they wish rather to share in the new scheme. They are arranged in two groups. The first consists of priests, oracle mongers, spies, and decree sellers; [54] the second, more specifically connected with the plot, introduces fools and delinquents from the earth in search of wings. Between the two groups comes the so-called second parabasis (again a mixture of charming pastoralism and nonsense), two messengers' speeches of parallel import, and the scene where the goddess Iris is apprehended for trespassing on the air. The elaborate symmetry of these scenes and the sustained movement of the plot are unusual.[55] Within their framework the contradictions and word play continue to develop the theme of the absurd and impossible. The second parabasis states this theme clearly when the birds pass a decree issuing large rewards to anyone who will slay Diagoras of Melos, who was probably dead already, or one of the Pisistratid tyrants, who certainly were.[56]

After the first parabasis the scene is presumably in the air, and the new city must first of all be named and dedicated. In a play whose keynote is the formative power of words, it is not surprising that the naming of the city should receive considerable emphasis. It must be a large, grand name, and it must be appropriate to the nature and purpose of the city. At the Hoopoe's suggestion Peithetaerus derives a name from their present ambience of clouds and the regions of the middle air, "something really vacuous," and arrives at Nephelococcygia, Cloud-cuckoo-land.[57] Its suitability is immediately recognized: "This must be," says Euelpides, "the place where Theogenes and Aeschines keep all their wealth" [58] — again, the theme of nothingness, for the poverty of Theogenes and Aeschines was well known. Peithetaerus then makes some reference to the plain of Phlegra, "where the gods overcame the Titans in a boasting contest." [59] Unfortunately, the text is not quite sound here, so we do not know exactly what Peithetaerus said, but clearly Nephelococcygia is compared somehow to the Phlegraean plain because it is an appropriate place for an imposters' boasting match. The remark glances also, of course, at the myth of the succession of the gods; as the Olympians outdid the Titans in boasting and swaggering, so now they are in their turn to be outdone by the birds in the same art, for power is his who can pull off the most gigantic bluff. The new city is the rightful home of *poneria* and *alazoneia,* and it will most effectively live up to its name. Peithetaerus proceeds to dedicate it to "the new gods," a phrase which keeps recurring, as if to emphasize the unholy sacrilege of the whole scheme. The introduction of new gods, apparently an actionable offense in Athens in these years, and one of which various philosophers were convicted, is apparently condemned in the *Clouds,* but here it is quite blandly carried out; it is the supreme touch, the towering height of comic villainy and impudence, and the logical conclusion of Aristophanes' conception of comic heroism.[60]

And now the quacks begin to arrive. If it be asked why they are not welcome in the city of quackery, the answer is, as said at the outset, "*My* quackery is a form of noble *élan vital*; *yours* is insufferable humbug." After all, the gods owe their supremacy to the art of brag. Whenever the comic hero seems to be a humble fellow, his irony is simply a veil for his supreme *alazoneia.* But Peithetaerus has little or no irony in his approach. He simply ejects the priest who is offering the sacrificial prayers because he is inviting too many of the new gods — that is, birds — to the feast; the victim is nothing but "chin and horns," or as we would say, skin and bones, and the invocation is accordingly changed from summoning "the blessed ones" to "No, just one of them."[61] So the sacrifice comes to nothing save the successful perpetration of another fraud, this time at the expense of the new gods themselves.

The next quack, however, is a startling exception to the comic rule. As Peithetaerus takes over the ritual himself, he is interrupted by a poet, a ragged bohemian, who enters singing an ode in honor of the new city. Indeed, he says that he has been composing in honor of Nephelococcygia "for a long time," though it is only now in the process of being founded — a nice reminder of the general theme of nonexistence.[62] The verses which he sings are an unpromising jumble of phrases from Pindar, with bits of Homer thrown in, but, though they verge on sheer nonsense, they manage to convey quite explicitly, in their lofty style, that the poet is badly in need of a new coat, especially since it is cold up in the air. (No one else feels cold, incidentally; the poet is suffering from the frigidity of his own verses). The oddity is that Peithetaerus gives him not only the coat, but a tunic as well, instead of driving him off. The poet is the only quack who gains anything, and there must be a reason for it. "We must help the poet," says Peithetaerus — he even calls him a wise poet — "because he will make trouble for us if we don't." [63] The poet is a man of words, and though the words be mumbo-jumbo, or perhaps even because they are, he must not be disappointed. Sense and meaning may come another day, but the word is the controlling force for now; the poet must be helped, or the whole structure will fall. So he gets his coat, and departs, singing some lines which, one feels, though hair-raising, are not altogether out of place:

Celebrate, O golden-throned, the shivering and quivering;
To the snow-smitten plains of much passage I have come a battle cry! [64]

Nephelococcygia can do with a poet laureate of this caliber, and his reward is just.

The other imposters, however, fare less well. The oracle monger is beaten off with his own book of oracles, and the spy and the decree seller are similarly disposed of. The scene with Meton, famous astronomer and engineer, has a fine touch of characteristic nonsense. Meton has come with his instruments to survey the air and cut it up into acres. One would like to see the instruments, which he identifies as "yardsticks of air." Their significance, at any rate, comes clear enough as Meton explains their use:

Met.:   First now, the shape of the air is, all in all,
           Just like a damper. Hence I, placing here
           My yardstick, and setting on the top of it
           The crooked compass — get it?
Peith.:   No, I don't get it.
Met.:   Laying my stick straight, I will measure so
           That out will come a circle with four corners,
           Market place in the middle, and the streets
           Straight into the center. [65]

One might expect that Nephelococcygia would naturally be laid out so, in the shape of a perfectly four-cornered circle, and that Meton could take his place beside the poet. But one must not look for consistency. Meton escapes just before the birds set upon him.

And now the transformations begun in the first half of the play are fully carried out. A messenger reports to Peithetaerus that the birds have fortified the air with a wall a hundred fathoms long, and wide enough to accommodate Theogenes' and Proxenides' vaunted but nonexistent chariots.[66] The birds have done this, not with the aid of brickmakers, stonemasons, or carpenters, but with their own "hands." Thirty thousand cranes brought the foundation stones, since cranes were popularly supposed to swallow stones for ballast; river birds and marsh fowl supplied the water and clay for bricks, which were then carried to position by ducks, "with their clothes tucked up"; woodpeckers naturally took care of the carpentry.[67] "I was amazed," says the messenger; "In truth, it sounds like lies," says Peithetaerus.[68] But it is only the imagery working itself out. The birds were to settle down, and they have done so, through a series of saucy puns, perverted proverbs, and common superstitions. Bird imagery blends into human imagery with dizzying effect, until it is not surprising to hear that the frontiers are patrolled by cavalry squadrons of hawks armed with bows.[69]

But the transformation of the birds into a cooperative and organized society is matched and balanced by the transformation of men into birds. A second messenger arrives from the earth and relates how men down there have all gone bird-mad. First thing upon arising in the morning, they flutter off to pasture ($\nu o\mu\acute{o}\nu$), with a pun of course on *nomos*, law and litigation; thereafter they alight on the *biblia*, which seems to mean either bookstalls, or papyrus reeds, and they peck away with their bills at legislation.[70] The image from the prologue, of Athenians chirping all day over law suits, is here rounded into a metamorphosis. We next hear of a whole list of Athenians who have been appropriately renamed after various kinds of birds, for the most unflattering reasons.[71] Finally it is reported that more than a thousand human beings are on their way to Nephelococcygia to acquire wings — and "talon-shaped habits." [72] The last phrase suggests birds of prey, sharp dealers, and brings us back to the themes of *poneria*, lawlessness, and power, the other aspect of nature, where the stronger rules the weaker. Peithetaerus' plan has worked out to a perfect equation. A simple, but boldly sustained manipulation of language has turned birds into men and men into birds, all to enormous advantage, especially of Peithetaerus himself.

Between the two messengers' reports, Aristophanes keeps the plot in motion by inserting a scene in which Iris is intercepted on a mission to the earth, and arrested for violation of the borders of "another people's city and Chaos." [73] Iris had been on her way to remind men of an important sacrifice to the gods, but Nephelococcygia was founded precisely to interrupt and reap the benefits of such observances. Peithetaerus tells her that the only gods now worshiped by men are the birds, and the Olympians are to obey their betters; shocked, Iris comes out with some Aeschylean expostulations on divine vengeance:

> O fool, fool! Stir not the awesome hearts
> Of gods, lest Justice with the spade of Zeus
> O'erturn your tribe deracinate and entire,
> And dark fume round your flesh and blanketing halls
> Blast you down flashing with Licymnian bolts! [74]

"Oh, shut up," says Peithetaerus, and proceeds in his turn to threaten Zeus with — a pun: the giant Porphyrion had once staggered the throne of Zeus, and now, if Zeus causes trouble, Peithetaerus will send against him six hundred "porphyrions," a kind of water bird, "dressed in leopard skins!" [75] The scene amply motivates the later one where the gods' embassy and capitulation form the exodus of the play. The theme of empire is further lightly accented in the comparison of Iris, as she comes sailing in, to the Athenian state dispatch galleys, Paralos and Salaminia, with implications of sea power and all that Peithetaerus had originally fled from. [76] It is a fine touch, too, rather like the birds' decree of reward to anyone

191

who slays a Pisistratid, when Peithetaerus tells Iris that, despite her immortality, she should by rights be executed for trespassing:

Peith.:   Do you know, caught like this,
          In justice if you got what you deserve,
          You would have died the death of all Irises?
Iris: But I'm immortal.
Peith.:   All the same, you'd have died.[77]

In the end, however, she is let off with a threat less dire, and more appropriate to her attractions, and sent back to Olympus to tell the news to Zeus.

The second set of impostors, mortals who want to be given wings, develops dramatically the metaphoric identity of speech and flying. None of the three wing-seekers gets any wings, though they all get fast talk. The chorus had told Peithetaerus to be sure to give each one the wings appropriate to his nature, and this, in a way, is what happens.[78] The first is a young man who hates his father and wants to beat him up — in fact, strangle him and have the property; he has heard that this is customary and respectable among the birds.[79] Here Aristophanes demolishes one fable with another. If young cocks are said to fight their fathers, it was also said that young storks piously carry their aged parents around on their wings.[80] Once more, as in the *Wasps*, one feels the two-sided force of nature: if the war between the generations is natural, so too is filial piety. Nature is not to be pinned into corners, and neither is Peithetaerus. The father-beater is crestfallen, but Peithetaerus gives him a wing — perhaps a helmet? — and a spur, doubtless a spear, and tells him to consider that he has the crest of a fighting cock, the father-beating bird, and sends him off to do garrison duty in Thrace where there is always fighting.

Next comes Cinesias, the dithyrambic poet, a favorite butt of Aristophanes. He gets no wings either, but one suspects that he does not need them. Plagiarizing Anacreon, he sings:

I fly to Olympus on light wings,
I flit now on one way of song, now on another.[81]

He wants to be a nightingale, so that he may fly up in the air and gather new "airy-whirled, snow-driven preludes," for the whole art of the dithyrambist, as he says, dangles from thence.[82] He starts to give samples, but is firmly suppressed. Peithetaerus meets this request for wings with an equivocation on the word πτεροδόνητος, "wing-driven." What Peithetaerus does to him is not quite clear from the text, but the construction put upon "wing-driven" is not what Cinesias had expected, nor as conducive to poetic inspiration.[83] But the dithyrambist's language is perhaps enough; he is all "up in the air" anyway, as he says, "nearing his body to the north wind, and cutting the harborless furrow of the ether."

The third and last wing-seeker is a sycophant, or informer; in this scene the secret is explicitly told. He wants wings so that he can indict an islander and summon him to a suit, then fly to Athens, where the case must be tried, and by getting there ahead of the defendant, make him lose by default. The scene turns on two verbal plays, the first of which is almost a statement of the theme of the *Birds*. "I will give you wings by talking," says Peithetaerus, and then proceeds to explain that everyone is winged by words, as when a father says, "So-and-so has talked my son into a flutter about horse-racing," or "My son is all up in the air and has flown off his wits over tragedy." [84] Under the spell of words, he says, the mind floats in mid-air (μετεωρίζεται), and a man is raised up (ἐπαίρεται).[85] Peithetaerus offers to fledge the informer with noble speeches and turn him to an honorable profession, but the informer is unwilling to disgrace a long line of sycophants by such an act, and insists on being winged. So Peithetaerus "wings" him with a second word play — namely the two lashes, or "wings," as they were called, of a special kind of double-thonged whip from Corcyra. Thus impelled, the informer literally takes to flight.[86] The scene is a fine one throughout, but its chief interest lies in the passages about speech as a source of wings. Here the whole underlying assumption of the play rises simply and naturally to the surface, in verbalizings which summarize the Aristophanean gestalt of lunacy and language, the nothingness of things and the power of the word. The entire play is a house of words, its structure now complete and confessed. It only remains for the gods, figures that usually betoken to the Greek mind the ultimate realities, to bow down before Peithetaerus' irresistible fabrication.

Before the gods enter, however, the chorus sings a brief ode. Traditionally, toward the end of an Old Comedy the chorus injects a passage of pure, irrelevant, personal abuse. In the *Birds* this element is expanded, like so much else, to include four stanzas, the first two together, and the second pair separated by the embassy scene.[87] More important than the expansion, however, is the fact that each of the four stanzas describes a strange and fearful phenomenon, in the form of a parody of reports of distant geographical wonders. The mode somehow is suitable to Nephelococcygia, the greatest of geographical wonders, and once more, in its tone of legend and thaumaturgy, contributes to the unity of the play instead of breaking it, as was more usual with such passages. The subject matter is irrelevant enough, but the form somehow accords with the whole. The Shadow Feet, a mythical people having one foot in the shape of an umbrella which they use for a sunshade while sleeping, the rhetoricians Gorgias and Philippus, that "tongue-and-stomach brood" who dwell by the Klepsydra, Pisander the oligarch, Socrates, the highwayman Orestes, and Chaerephon, all appear mixed up together, and bathed in the weird glow of the remote and fabulous. The poetic effect is strikingly vivid, as well as hilarious.

But the best is Cleonymus, the fat and gluttonous informer, who lost his shield on the field of battle. Cleonymus appears in all the early plays, never in person, but often in strange guises. (Sometimes he is doubled for by one Cleisthenes, who resembles Cleonymus in most respects, but lacks his military distinction.) In the *Acharnians* we meet an oriental bird three times the size of Cleonymus, and its name is Humbug. In the *Knights* we see the rich men who entertain Cleonymus humbly beseeching him to come out of the meal tub and take pity on the table; also a new and stringent law about military draft is said to bite Cleonymus in the shield strap. In the *Clouds* the very sight of Cleonymus causes the clouds to take the shape of frightened deer, and later Socrates, expounding the mysteries of grammatical gender, explains that Cleonymus, like a feeding trough oddly enough, might more properly have a feminine ending, since the word for "trough" is feminine. In the *Wasps* a slave makes a riddle: "What kind of animal throws away its shield in earth and sky and sea?" The answer is "Cleonymus." In the *Peace* Cleonymus has more shield trouble, which culminates in the scene where his son sings the famous epigram of Archilochus. The image is inexhaustible. But the greatest triumph, the final metamorphosis, comes in the *Birds*. The chorus sings:

> Many the strange unlikely things
> > Portentous we in our flights have seen:
> Far away and well removed
> From the land of the brave, there grows a tree,
> > The Cleonymus tree,
> Useful in nothing that it yields,
> But wondrous big and cowardly.
> And every spring it blossoms green
> With figments, fraud, and flattery;
> In winter most deciduously
> > It leaves — shields.[88]

Cleonymus has at last reached mythic stature, in the form of a great and cowardly tree, one of the finest comic images in Aristophanes, and one which combines all his lyrical, grotesque, and satiric gifts in a superb multiple perspective of true surrealistic caliber.

In the final scene Prometheus enters hiding under a parasol so that Zeus will not see him. He has come to betray the plight of the gods, and to advise Peithetaerus how to deliver the *coup de grâce*. The gods are so starved for sacrifices that the barbarian gods are threatening civil war; now is the time to force Zeus to yield the scepter and the princess, Basileia. An embassy is coming from Zeus, and Peithetaerus is not to make peace until Zeus agrees to these terms. Yet even here the touch of self-contradiction is not forgotten;

for when Peithetaerus says, "Yes, you have always hated the gods," Prometheus answers, "I'm a perfect Timon," so that the Titan's allegiance to the human cause is bewilderingly figured under the image of utter misanthropy.[89]

When the embassy comes, consisting of Poseidon, Heracles, and a barbarian god who speaks all but unintelligible Thracian, the master mind of Peithetaerus prevails with easy skill.[90] Here all kinds of *poneria* — bribery, legal acuity, and smooth diplomacy — combine with the exploitation of speech and nonsense. Heracles is won over by an invitation to the promising dinner which Peithetaerus is preparing, and bullies the barbarian god into yielding the scepter of Zeus. Poseidon warns Heracles that he is selling his own inheritance, but Peithetaerus says that Heracles, as a bastard, has no inheritance; to prove it, he invokes a law of Solon, which, though properly in effect only in Athens, has somehow crept into the constitution of Olympus. "Your own Uncle Poseidon here would be the first to dispute any such legacy," says Peithetaerus, adroitly dividing the embassy against itself.[91] But the final stroke is simply a verbal trick. Heracles is prepared to yield Basileia along with the scepter, but Poseidon again objects, and the barbarian god has the deciding vote. What he says is half gibberish, but it sounds as if he says, "Give her to the birds."

> Pos.: By Zeus, no! He does not say give her over,
> He's only twittering the way swallows do.
> Peith.: Precisely. He says, "Give her to the swallows."[92]

Poseidon gives up, the birds are victorious, and presently Basileia is delivered to Peithetaerus for the wedding ceremony.

The final scene presents the most astounding victory in Aristophanes, perhaps in all comedy. Peithetaerus enters in an apotheosis, as tyrant, himself gleaming like a star, his bride shining brighter than the sun; incense coils around him in the breeze, and in his hand he wields Zeus's own thunderbolt, here signalized by the epithet "winged," for obvious reasons.[93] Zeus has been relieved of his command, and the point is driven home by the epithalamion of the chorus, which celebrates, ironically enough, the former marriage of Zeus with Hera:

> Once did the Fates unite the grand
> Lord of the gods, of towering throne,
> With Hera, queen of Olympus,
> In such a hymeneal.[94]

In that wedding the charioteer was "golden-winged Eros," who, as we know from the parabasis, bred before all other creatures the race of birds, by a union with "Winged Chaos." [95] Now that wings have come into their own again, they wave festively around the new bridal pair, and Basileia holds her husband's wing as he dances her off to everlasting bliss.[96]

Basileia is perhaps the most complex, yet most natural, of Aristophanes' apocalyptic personifications. Early in the play the chorus had spoken of recovering their lost monarchy ($\beta \alpha \sigma \iota \lambda \epsilon \iota \alpha$), and now it appears to them, but with a different accent by which it is transformed into a bridal figure of plenty and salvation, in fact a princess ($\beta \alpha \sigma \iota \lambda \epsilon \iota \alpha$).[97] But there is more to the lady as well. Prometheus had described her as "a very pretty girl, who looks after the thunderbolts of Zeus, and all his other possessions — wise counsel, good government, self-restraint, shipyards, libel, court recorders, and three-obol fees." [98] Among Zeus's possessions are some singularly Athenian items, especially shipyards and three-obol fees; and everyone knew that the custodian of Zeus's thunderbolts was Athena. A producer might well be tempted to stage Basileia in helmet and aegis.

One is now reminded of several earlier remarks which motivate this interpretation; the Hoopoe, on hearing the name Nephelococcygia, cried out "A shining city! Who will the tutelary deity be? For whom shall we weave the robe?" He refers, of course, to the robe presented to Athena at the Panathenaea; even the epithet "shining" is one always used of Athens.[99] One recalls also that the new city was to have a Pelargicon, a by-form, chosen for its resemblance to *pelargos*, "stork," for the sacred precinct Pelasgicon in Athens.[100] Moreover, the priest, in offering the dedicatory prayers for the city, had prayed for health and safety for the Nephelococcygians, "both themselves and the Chians," according to a formula in Athens, by which the Chians, in recognition of their services, were traditionally included in public prayers for the Athenians themselves.[101] Nephelococcygia is also showing strongly democratic tendencies; at least, the birds which Peithetaerus is roasting in the last scene have been guilty of an attempt at oligarchic revolution, and the popular element has voted to knock them on the head.[102] Apparently the city of perfect peace in the sky is not wholly free from some familiar forms of political dissent, and Peithetaerus, who wanted to get out of Athens because it was so full of business, politics, and debts, has succeeded, by the elaborate process of the plot, in re-creating Athens all over again, the only difference being that now he is on top instead of on the bottom.[103] Nephelococcygia is the imperial city to end imperial cities, and it has starved out the gods themselves as the Athenians starved out Melos. The great plan has come full circle, and the comic hero triumphs over the world by a dissociative circularity, by making it into a world which a comic hero can triumph over, a world where words are absolute, where the absurd, impossible hatching of a wind egg has long since licensed any and every impossibility as the rightful mode for fulfilling the logic of absurdity.

The equations of the *Birds* cancel out. In order to evade the imperial metropolis, the imperial metropolis must be rebuilt; in order to achieve reality, reality must be denied existence; in order to find meaning, language must be handed over to its most limitless ambiguities; the return to nature, with its songs and pastures, becomes a return to the city, with its laws and conventions. But what does it all mean? Is it that the *Birds* is meaningless and without relevance apart from its fine artistry? Hardly so; but it is about meaninglessness, the circle of inscrutable nature again, the absurdity which calls for the heroic act of individual freedom and self-transformation. Meaning is a word, and it requires a hero to give the word meaning. In the *Clouds* and in the *Wasps* Aristophanes dealt in various ways with the problems of nature, law, and education, but in both plays he abandoned temporarily the heroic figure of transcendent fantasy, save insofar as Philocleon may be said to approach it. The result was drama bifurcated by dialectic, and ending in ironic unresolved images of nature as insurmountable. In the *Birds* the hero returns, grotesque and grand, a bird-man-god who commands all and unites all in himself, and so resolves the ambiguities of nature and the world. But the tool is language, and the underlying secret is the acquiescence to the view that meaning is a created structure, a heroic achievement. The hero gives what meaning he will to the words of which he builds his empire, and by such masterful transvaluations, the world from which he fled becomes the world which he commands. The terms may be nonsense, but they effect the self-authentication which is indispensable to heroic experience. The *Birds* is the crown of Aristophanes' works in that it unites the unilinear heroic fantasy of the "polis" plays with the intellectual dilemmas of the "education" plays, in a mysterious and shimmering comedy whose range and import are unequaled, save, perhaps, by the somber and wholly different *Frogs*.

The *Frogs*, as will appear, is in some way the opposite of the *Birds*; it is a quest for meaning beyond mere words, a deeply concerned effort to penetrate to the heart of a world on the verge of disappearance. Profound and beautiful as it is, however, it has not quite the visionary breadth and encompassing totality of the *Birds*, nor has it the detachment and creative freedom which arise from the full heroic acceptance of nothingness. When the world begins to appear meaningless, as well it might have to the mature Aristophanes in 414, one may be free, if one is Aristophanes, to dramatize its nonsense with an irony so detached and yet so imaginative that the product is something like a myth; a myth gives a view of the whole world, and so does the *Birds*. Its detachment and involvement are mingled in an equal suspension which Aristophanes never repeated; and hence it is at once the gayest and the saddest of the plays. Neither a reform play, a political play, nor an escape play, the *Birds* is about nothingness — and therefore everything.

ꞏVIꞏ

THE WAR BETWEEN THE SEXES

Lysistrata

THE *Birds*, with its detachment and its view of Athens under the guise of a kind of comic whole, was a performance which could not be repeated. One could always return to the parts, however, and in the plays of 411 Aristophanes returns to more confined issues for the sources of fantasy. But "one cannot cross the same river twice": Athens had changed, and Aristophanes had changed. The theme is familiar: peace, conceived not negatively as the mere absence of war, but as a set of concrete images, focusing in this case around the central image of sex. But the mood is far different from that of the *Acharnians* or the *Peace*, which celebrated the confident and essentially victorious city of the twenties, when the polis, and especially this particular polis, was its own rounded world, and, despite its increasing imperialism, its alienation of the individual, and its tendency toward bureaucratic atrophy, a structure to take pride in, as the natural social order. In 411 there was little of this feeling left. After the terrible defeat in Sicily Athens' pride was that of the lion at bay, and her faith in the democracy which had voted the expedition was so shaken that a board of ten Probouloi, Commissioners of Public Safety, had been appointed as an emergency substitute for the Council of 500. In the earlier plays of Aristophanes the city had been blandly subsumed as an integral, given fact. The outspoken criticism of policies, politicians, and officials had been a symptom of basic confidence in the democratic scheme, whether or not one believes that that criticism was offered with serious intent. In the *Lysistrata* a passing jibe at Pisander and an even milder one at the general Eucrates pretty well total up the political references involving names; one of the Probouloi, indeed, is an important character, but there is no recognizable indication as to which one he is. Part of this reticence is doubtless due to a circumstantial limitation of comic license, for the appointment of the Probouloi was, in fact, the first step toward the oligarchic revolution which took place a few months after the play was performed. But it is in part attributable also to the broader view of things which characterizes Aristophanes' later work; if the full-blown symbolism of the *Birds* could not be repeated, neither could it be totally forgotten, and in his later plays, except for the heart-felt curses on Cleophon in the *Frogs*, the political aspect expresses itself very seldom in personal attack, and more in general figures and actions which respond symbolically to the state of the city.

The clearest examples of this method, as will be seen, are the figures of Dionysus, Aeschylus, and Euripides in the *Frogs*. Lysistrata too belongs with them, in that she is, so to speak, a collective, representing not only women in general, but also a historical and political view of Athens, and perhaps even something of the Panhellenic ideal. But she is far from being pure allegory, for she is also an individual whose personality is strikingly clear, and like the earlier protagonists of Aristophanes she possesses a heroic decisiveness which at once isolates her and permits her to subdue society to her ends. She does not, however, transcend society; she transforms it by restoring peace, while she herself stays within it. For this reason, perhaps, there is little or nothing of the motif of apotheosis. Lysistrata is not, in fact, a grotesque figure, in the sense in which the word has been used in this book, for she does not possess the animal and divine dimensions — except, perhaps, in a different sense and one which befits the nature of her fantastic effort.[1] One might be tempted to assert some metaphoric identity between Lysistrata and Reconciliation, the divinity whom she presents to the embattled parties at the end; but if that were so, she should dominate the finale, as Peithetaerus and Trygaeus do; instead, the finale is wholly choral, and Lysistrata fades away into the general rejoicing. Lysistrata is a woman, with a woman's purpose and a woman's methods, and when her purpose is accomplished, she retires with becoming modesty, presumably into the arms of her own husband. It is sometimes stated that she is masculine in temper and manner, and as evidence the Spartan's remark about "Lysistratus" is adduced.[2] This is a serious mistake, however; the whole point of the action lies in femininity and the desirable charms which Lysistrata and her accomplices withhold. She is without question strong-minded, but whoever considers that quality a strictly masculine one is in error, not to say danger. It is clear from the beginning, where Calonice tells her that frowning does not become her, to the end, where the leaders of all Greece are "caught by her love-charm," that Lysistrata is young and pretty.[3] The role can be played properly only by an actress of singular grace and charm.

As often, Aristophanes' mind is overfertile in the invention of fantastic devices, which quite overwhelm literal consistency. Lysistrata's basic plan, for women to refuse intercourse with their husbands until peace is made, is based on the sound and ancient observation that Aphrodite subdues every creature, even Zeus, with the exception, of course, of her three virgin sisters, Athena, Artemis, and Hestia.[4] Actually, the plan involves a practical dilemma: the thing which is troubling Lysistrata and her friends is precisely the fact that their husbands are never at home, but always at war, so that there is no sex anyway — not even with an adulterer.[5] But practical dilemmas never obstruct a comic plot, and often they further it. What Aristophanes wants is the confrontation of the symbols of war and peace as embodied in the two sexes, on the theory that the bosom is mightier than the sword. As the Spartan woman puts it:

> When Menelaus cast an eye upon
> Bare Helen's apples, he threw down his sword.[6]

Accordingly, the men are to be enticed out of their wits by seeing their wives parading beautifully but untouchably about the house, adorned by every cosmetic wile known to woman, but maddeningly chaste.[7] We are not told how, with the men away, this is to happen; and as a matter of fact, it does not happen. What happens is rather the opposite; the women secure their position by seizing the Acropolis and barricading themselves within, where they are anon besieged by the men. This might seem clashingly inconsistent with the plan as stated; yet in the symbolic terms of drama it finds justification in that it fulfills the given situation of the plot, that the act of war has supplanted the act of love. Certainly it motivates with skill the fighting parodos and the agon which follows.

The proposed tactics of enticement and refusal at home, which could scarcely have been presented en masse, are carried out only in the scene between Myrrhine and Cinesias. The major effort occurs at the Acropolis, in the struggle between the mocking women and the helpless warmongers who curse, threaten, and appeal, but all in vain. And yet the two schemes are not wholly divorced from each other. As Lysistrata follows her friends into the Propylaea, she swears that

> The men will come with neither fire nor threats
> Such as to make us open up these gates
> Again, save on the conditions we have said.[8]

In view of what had been said, it is hardly farfetched to see in the gates of the citadel an analogue to the gates of love; and it should not be forgotten that the Acropolis was the shrine of virgin Athena, goddess of war, indeed, but one of the three who resist Aphrodite. Athena and her rock thus become a complex motif, embodying generally the women's position; and it becomes a question, later in the play, whether they can maintain that position with Athena-like restraint, or whether they will prove weaker than the men and yield to their own desires. Somehow, the total symbol of the Acropolis is felicitously expressive of feminine sexual attitudes.[9]

The other two goddesses who resist Aphrodite are not without notice in the play. As the Proboulos orders his archers to arrest Lysi-strata, and one starts to do so, she swears by Artemis that he will get the worst of it. Her oath must be a little more than casually chosen, for three of her followers similarly threaten the other three archers, invoking, in turn, Pandrosos, Phosphorus, and Tauropolus. Phosphorus and Tauropolus are certainly epithets of Artemis; whether or not Pandrosos is also, as has been suggested, is perhaps not crucial, for it could be equally appropriate to invoke the virgin heroine Pan-drosos, daughter of Cecrops, whose precinct lay near the north edge of the Acropolis.[10] The point is inviolable chastity. As for the third goddess, Hestia, she is not in fact mentioned, but as little more than the personification of the home and the sacred hearth, her presence, or at least her meaning, makes itself felt throughout the play in the abundant images of domestic life, especially the domestic life of women. Hestia, the sanctity of the hearth as the center of the home, is really more important to the *Lysistrata* than either Athena or Artemis; even Aphrodite is in alliance with her, for the nonce, for the chief antinomy to war in the play is not simply sex, but domes-ticity, including sex. Aristophanes had dramatized the war between the generations in the *Wasps* and *Clouds*; he dramatizes here the war between the sexes, the male painted in its extremest colors of belligerence, bull-headedness, and the will to victory, the female with equal extremity identified with security, harmony, and the centripetal life of the home. Both, of course, are characterized by comically exaggerated carnal drives, and this in the end unites them. But the women's action unfolds through two simultaneous efforts: first, to recover Aphrodite, as Trygaeus struggled to recover Peace; and second, to recover Hestia, domestic integrity, for which pur-pose Aphrodite must be temporarily sequestered behind the ram-parts of virgin goddesses.

This statement may appear like an overrational explanation of comic incongruence and farce. But it consists, at least, with the feminine inconsistencies revealed in the characters, and it explains why in the symbolic world of comedy love and peace can be recovered by means of warlike hostilities. More important, it offers a clue to why the *Lysistrata*, despite its evident bawdry and the coarseness of numerous episodes, possesses a delicacy of charm very difficult to convey in translation, but pervasively felt in the Greek. Far from being a pornographic orgy, as is often supposed, the play is a celebration of the life-giving properties of love, a fertility rite, not a witches' sabbath.[11] Aristophanes was, of course, quite capable of writing uninhibitedly about any kind of sexual practice, and did so in many a play; but in this one, despite passing references to adultery and other makeshifts, he wrote about marriage, the marriage of men and women, and, in the end, the marriage of Athens and Sparta.

The play abounds in images of home life. When the women do not appear at Lysistrata's summons, Calonice explains why:

> They'll come; it's hard for women to get out.
> One of us, you know, is fussing with her husband,
> One's waking the hired man, one's tucking in
> The baby, one's bathing, another feeding him.[12]

Lysistrata herself is a part of this existence, or had been. She had been a good wife, and she makes it clear that her present revolt has been thrust upon her only after long-suffering and patience:

We bore as we could your earlier war, a long time bravely enduring,
Because of our patient restraint, in the face of whatever you menfolk were doing.
Anyway, you didn't let us complain, however little you pleased us;
But we were aware of your antics throughout, and often at home in our houses,
We'd hear of the miserable mess that you'd made of a really imperative business;
And then in our sorrow, but smiling in any case (indoor creatures!), we'd ask you:
"Well, what was decided today about peace, to write on a public inscription,
In the people's assembly?" And what do you think my husband said? He said, "Shut up!
What's that to you?" So I shut up.[13]

Here, the note of war, entering and damaging domestic harmony, leads on to even wintrier images of husbands and sons sent to the campaigns, while the young girl sits at home, losing her bloom, and becoming a day-dreaming spinster.[14] The cessation of the life of the home somewhat recalls the frozen stoppage throughout the earth described in the Babylonian poem where the goddess Inanna descends into the underworld: "The ox goes not to the plough, the maiden lies on her side." Of all the so-called "peace" plays, the *Lysistrata* has the saddest and tenderest imagery, for it is drawn not from the proliferations of a gigantic and preposterous metaphor, but simply and directly from life, the life of Athenian women who tend their families, and girls who fetch water from the fountain houses, "jostled by slaves, in the crowd and noise and rattle of pots," [15] the girls whom the city reared "in luxuriant pride," each taking her part in the festivals and liturgies, as an *arrhephoros*, a mill girl for the sacred meal, a Brauronian "bear," a stately basket bearer at the Panathenaea.[16]

The image of the young girl unmarried and hopeless is balanced and countered by the image of the baby quoted earlier. As loud and vigorous proof of regenerate life, and the natural opposite of the imagery of war, a baby is a domestic focal point, and as such he appears in the scene between Cinesias and Myrrhine. Even here, where the action comes close to the traditional strip tease of burlesque, the symbol of the household is present, and the quarrel between the male and the female takes the well-known familial form of each parent telling the child it is the other's fault.[17] Again, in the scene where Lysistrata is having trouble with her troops, the basic antinomy of the play involves at least an imaginary baby. One of the women claims that she is pregnant and must go home to avoid giving birth on the sacred Acropolis. Yesterday she had not been pregnant, but today she tells her leader, showing her distended belly, that she is having a "male child"; male indeed, for the bulge turns out to be a helmet, in fact Athena's own helmet.[18] It is, one might say, the image of the nonbaby, the "hollow, brass thing" of war, at once the cause of the trouble, and the symbol of the city's total plight.

More important than the baby, however, is the image of wool. Cinesias accuses Myrrhine of neglecting her household:

> Myrrh.:   I care little for that.
> Cines.:   You care little as well for your yarn, all pulled
>   Apart by the chickens?
> Myrrh.:   That's right, by Zeus.[19]

From earliest times the spinning and weaving of wool marks the good wife; "lanam fecit" says an early Roman tombstone, and no more need be said. It is true, Cinesias has not come primarily out of concern for the wool, and he passes immediately to the "rites of Aphrodite" which Myrrhine has also been neglecting.[20] This juxtaposition of the two, marking the balance of woman's married life, has also occurred before, in the scene where the women are trying to desert the cause:

> Woman: I have a lot of Milesian wool at home,
>   All being chomped up by the moths.
> Lysis.:   Moths, eh?
>   Come back here!
> Woman: By the two goddesses, I'll come back
>   Immediately! Just let me spread it on the bed —
> Lysis.:   Don't spread anything.[21]

And with similar sexual innuendo, the next woman protests that she must peel the hackles off some flax from Amorgos.[22]

These are, of course, mere pretexts, for the women's real motives do not differ from that of the girl whom Lysistrata pulled back by the hair as she was headed on sparrow-back for the brothel of Orsilochus.[23] But the neglected wool, or flax, keeps before us the image of the wasted home nonetheless. If Eros has suffered from the war, it is part of Lysistrata's therapy that wool shall suffer too, and she is no longer ready to submit as she did formerly, when her husband told her to leave public matters alone, and "spin her thread, or get a whack in the face." [24] All this finds its positive converse in the agon, where the heroine argues with the Proboulos. The Proboulos demands to know how Lysistrata proposes to solve the tangled problems of the city, and she replies in a magnificent simile, the reverse of Demosthenes' image in the *Knights* of politics as hash:

Why, in the way that we loosen our wool, when it gets all tangled; we take it
And picking out single threads with our spindles, we lead them this way or
    that way,
Just so too we will loosen this war from the mess that it's in, if you let us.[25]

And she continues the analogue for nearly twenty lines more, concluding that when the yarn is washed clean — of dirty politicians — she will make "a big skein and weave from it a cloak for the people." [26] The Proboulos is naturally not impressed by this vision of the body politic wrapped in the homespun cloak of peace and harmony. Yet, as the action moves on the image achieves dramatic form when the chorus of old women coaxingly make up to the chorus of old men, and help them put on their cloaks, which they had thrown off in their rage.[27] It is the turning point of the play, for the Spartan herald has just entered to offer peace.

The running imagery of domestic life is not, perhaps, the first thing which attracts attention in the *Lysistrata*, nor is it, perhaps, meant to be. But it is there, however implicitly, throughout the texture, to emerge with clear and tender simplicity in Lysistrata's two last speeches:

Now purify yourselves
That we women may entertain you all
In the citadel, on what our stores afford.
And there you will exchange good faith, and oaths,
And afterward, take each of you his own
Wife, and depart.

And later: "Let husband stand by wife,/And wife by husband." [28] It is the cluster of domestic images which constitutes the heart of the play, the real antitype of war, the warm, woolly cloak versus the hollow, brass helmet. And it is surely this undercurrent which gives the rampant bawdry of the play its charm. Aristophanes has offered a whole vision, not a half. Sex is not viewed through any distorting lenses of unreal glamour or inhibited wish, but directly and realistically in the context of that institution which G. B. Shaw said combined the maximum of temptation with the maximum of opportunity. Nor is domestic life romanticized, as in the Menandrian world of stereotyped lovers ending up in a stereotype of happy union. Aristophanes' family picture includes a full measure of humdrum homeliness, bickerings, and ear-boxing. But the keynote is love. "Yes, I love my husband," says Myrrhine, "but he does not want to be loved by me," [29] an odd thing to say when Cinesias is on his knees begging for her return. All that she means is that her husband, merely by being male, stands with the belligerents as a violator of the total vision, peace-love-home. If he will not settle for the whole, he can do without the part.

But if domesticity and marriage form a delicate inner symbolism of the play which determines the character of its denouement, the more evident imagery throughout presents, by contrast, a cheerful and compelling indelicacy. The chief controlling image of the play's action is, of course, the phallus. Whatever be the answer to the controversy over whether or not comic actors wore a leather phallus, it is hard to see how it is dispensable in this particular play.[30] Old Comedy dealt so freely in what we call obscenity, that one wonders why such antics do not strike us as simply jejune and immature. Part of the answer may be in the fact that there is never any question of "daring," that lurid word which today sells so many mildly suggestive novels and movies. The adolescent, or the novelist who writes to appeal to the adolescent mentality, tries to show how far he dares to go in transgressing taboos. But the Old Comic poet did not have to dare to smash taboos; he was supposed to smash them, and his challenge lay in trying to discover how ingeniously he could smash them. For there were taboos, of course, and the place to smash them was the comic stage. There were in Greek, for instance, proper and improper words for the reproductive organs. The proper words occur with reasonable frequency from Homer to Aristotle, and quite frequently in the scholiasts of comedy, but they never occur in comedy; they would have been as out of place there as the improper words would have been in Homer. The absence of the element of daring, therefore, threw the poet totally onto his own competitive genius, whether for subtle innuendo or gargantuan breadth, and Aristophanes is a master of both. Nor was there any limit as to how far one could go; the *Lysistrata* is one of the best examples of the comic power of putting shame to shame by the sheer limitlessness of its freedom. Yet all the licentiousness of its speech and action does not contradict the motifs of domesticity, or even contrast with them, for as yet marrying and burning had not been thought of as opposites; they all fit together in the harmonious lyrical tension of Aristophanes' work at its best. Titania with the ass's head of Bottom in her lap gives something of the perspective.

If the play as a whole, then, tends to show that it is love that makes the world go round, it is certainly lust that makes the plot move forward. The phallus motif moves in a steady crescendo from the moment Lysistrata proposes to her horrified colleagues that they abstain from it, until peace is made. Climaxing the high seriousness of her prelude, the word she uses for it, one of the improper ones, strikes with satisfying dissonance across the texture hitherto decorated by only a few innuendoes.[31] It is a case of verbal slapstick, to be developed visually in the second part of the play, where the frustrated men try vainly to conceal the evidence of their plight. There are few scenes better calculated to illustrate the unholy joy of *poneria* than this, where the weaker sex have gained the upper hand by a device inherent in their desirability, and the sacred walls of Athena's Acropolis are lined with winning faces laughing sweetly at the group of priapean ambassadors below. The Myrrhine-Cinesias scene needs little comment.[32]

Throughout all this there are some word plays which reflect the contemporary political atmosphere, and draw it mockingly into the comic fantasy. In 411 many feared that political dissension would lead to the establishment of a tyranny, probably by Alcibiades. And in the battle of words between the old men and old women which takes the place of the parabasis the old men assert that conspirators have put the women up to their revolt, as a first step toward tyranny. But it is not the tyranny of Alcibiades or any other current candidate that they mention; they "smell the tyranny of Hippias." [33] Hippias provides a pun on a well-known mode of sexual intercourse.[34] To frustrate the attempt, they will do as the tyrannicide Aristogiton, and carry a sword hidden in a myrtle bough, probably also a *double-entendre*.[35] In any case, the idea of the concealed weapon recurs at the entrance of the Spartan herald, whose all-too-obvious condition is such that the Proboulos accuses him of hiding a spear under his cloak.[36] Unlike Aristogiton's sword, the weapon cannot be concealed; it is the weapon of peace, anyway, and the women's "tyranny" continues to a successful conclusion.

So Aphrodite wins the day, and the wiles by which she wins it are, as Euripides would say, "worthy of woman." [37] *Peitho*, Persuasion, is her handmaiden, and her arts include more than rhetoric;[38] in this play *Peitho* is, as in Homer, the attendant of Aphrodite and specifically so named. Lysistrata herself, as said earlier, possesses a sort of high seriousness; she is comic only because of the nature of her plan. Her companions have none of her heroic qualities, and are won over only with difficulty; for the most part the younger ones are characterized by the two qualities then commonly attributed — in comedy, at least — to women, lust and bibulousness. Myrrhine in particular represents bibulousness;[39] the Boeotian girl is, like Boeotia, luxuriantly attractive, and the Corinthian, naturally, is an out-and-out harlot.[40] Only the Spartan girl, Lampito, shares Lysistrata's high-mindedness to a degree, and it is by her help that the plan is adopted; the reason for this is obviously political, for Sparta herself was always more ready than her allies to make peace, and furthermore, the finale of the play presents a visionary kind of Cimonian alliance between the two great powers. But one should beware of taking Lampito as a sign of pro-Spartan tendencies in Aristophanes, or as any kind of real propagandistic figure. She is a counterpart to Lysistrata, necessary to bring the Spartan women around to the plan, and she does little more except provide some fun with her broad Laconian dialect, and her healthy, strapping figure. For the rest, the women make no bones about admitting and practicing their little foibles:

Lysis.:   O Calonice, my heart's all on fire!
           I suffer horribly because of us
           Women, and how among men we are constantly
           Called wretches —
Calon.:   Well, and so we are, by Zeus.[41]

But it does not matter. They have *Peitho*, and they use it; nor is it the first time in Aristophanes that this almighty medium has assisted frank human frailty to change the world. *Poneria* is a sweet and healthy tonic.

There is little need to emphasize the obvious relation of the play, whose prime action is the rediscovery of the lost fertility symbol, to the underlying Dionysian ritual. That aspect is undeniable. But it leads to much more. It has been asserted, perhaps rightly, that the antiphonal songs of the two choruses (a phenomenon unique in this play) are modeled on traditional singing contests between groups representing summer and winter, life and death.[42] As we have them, they form a contest between fire and water, also, and the matter is handled, for all its slapstick, with some subtlety. As the old men trudge up to the gates of the Acropolis with battering rams and fire pots, they recall their defeat of Cleomenes and the victorious trophy at Marathon.[43] Nothing is made of the fact that they are about to burn their own citadel, but there is more than a hint therein of the self-ruination of the war policy. The women souse them from above with water, and shout jeeringly that they can warm themselves at their own fire.[44] Their mockery includes images of life and death also: they call the old men "things of the grave," and cry that their cold drenching is a "nuptial lustration," and that they are watering the old men so that they will blossom.[45] The old men, soaked, and blinded by their smoke, are in a sorry plight; but the old women are transforming them, and gradually their rage is quenched.

When the Spartan herald and the Proboulos begin to capitulate, the two choruses also begin to make up. The symbolism of helping the men on with their cloaks has already been described. Even more pointed is the little passage where one takes a gnat out of an old man's eye. The gnat, he says, had been biting him for a long time in the eye — "digging wells in it," in fact — and he is grumblingly appreciative of the old woman's help, which is followed by a kiss.[46] Somehow, the biting gnat completes the imagery of the fire and smoke of the parodos, for, say the men, "the smoke bites the eyes like a mad dog." [47] A common colloquialism seems to underlie both passages: in the *Acharnians* Dicaeopolis refers to his own fury under the figure of eyes stinging with soap, and the verb used is "bite." [48] To be "bitten in the eye" is to be enraged, and when the women have removed the gnat, there is no further conflict between the choruses. What happens to them at the end is not wholly clear, but apparently they retire, to reappear as the chorus of Laconians and the chorus of Athenians whose songs end the play. They have indeed blossomed, both of them, from decrepit choruses of the warring sexes into full-bodied images of a rejuvenated and unified Hellas, invoking "Tranquillity, whom the goddess Cypris created." [49]

Something rather similar happens between Lysistrata and the Proboulos whom she winds around her finger. First, with wonderful impudence, she forces him into the passive role of a woman, tossing him her wimple and basket, and telling him to keep quiet, tuck up his skirts and spin; "war shall be women's concern." [50] Later, she and two others dress him up as a corpse laid out for burial:

> Lys.: What's the matter with you? Why don't you go die?
> There's plenty of space there; go buy a coffin,
> I myself will knead you a honey cake,
> Here, take these and crown yourself! . . .
> Charon is calling,
> You're keeping him from sailing! [51]

The indignant Proboulos stamps off saying he will show himself to his colleagues just as he is, in tomb clothes. But death is not to win; "sweet-spirited Love and Cyprus-born Aphrodite have breathed desire on breast and thigh," as Lysistrata had prayed.[52] When we see the Proboulos again, his decrepitude has been enlivened by the same desperate tension as everyone else, and he marches off once more, this time to treat for peace and show his colleagues something quite different.[53]

It is usual, and quite justified, to see in the *Lysistrata* a strong infusion of Panhellenic feeling; the idea was in the air, and was soon to be expressed eloquently by Gorgias in his Olympic oration.[54] But it is surely a mistake to try to discover any outline of real policy in this tenderly ribald fantasy of reconciliation. It is true that Lysistrata, as she rebukes the two parties, reminds them of their former cooperation, and the chorus of Spartans too later recalls the combined effort at Artemisium and Thermopylae.[55] But the Panhellenic idea remained a vision in the mind of retired thinkers, and, since the only real Panhellenic effort within historical memory had been the Persian wars, these thinkers often propounded a war against the Great King as the means to Panhellenic unity.[56] Of this there is no trace in Aristophanes, though Persia was at the time assisting the Spartans in her devious way. Lysistrata does, indeed, refer to the Spartans' help in expelling the Pisistratids, and to Cimon's expedition to help Sparta in the Messenian revolt; one might, therefore, try to see the play as a recommendation to return to the old Cimonian policy of Sparta and Athens as the "yokefellows" of Greece. But such practical suggestions are alien to comedy in the first place, and in the second, a re-establishment of the world of Cimon was about as unthinkable in 411 as anything one could imagine; rather, there was shortly to be a coup by the pro-Spartan faction. Lysistrata is only picking two rather rare examples of Athenian and Spartan mutual help, and it is noticeable that she does not go on to say that the Spartans, after repelling the tyrant, tried to overthrow the democracy at Athens, or that Cimon's help in the Messenian War was rudely rebuffed, the "yokefellow" policy discredited, and Cimon ostracized.

Finally, it may be wondered whether the Athenians, fond as they were of politics, could have been expected to be turning practical measures over in their minds during the final scene of this play, while Reconciliation, gloriously nude, brings the respective emissaries back to friendship, leading the reluctant ones by their phalluses. One is more certain that they were rocked by the impertinent bawdry, and touched by the wistful remembrance of earlier, and better, times. As for Panhellenism there was always the feeling that Greeks ought to stick together, and yet there was almost always a war between Greeks; in the midst of the latter Aristophanes has reflected the former, which, as was usually the case with Panhellenism, comes closer to reverie than to political program.

It is true that the Spartans are handled very gently in the play. Lampito is distinctly attractive and sympathetic, as Lysistrata's chief ally; and it is the Spartan chorus which closes the play with a meltingly lovely hymn, reminiscent of Alcman, in honor of Sparta:

> Where choruses of the gods sing on,
>   With treading of feet,
> And girls, like fillies, along Eurotas,
> Leap with quick feet whirling,
> With hair flung out like playing Bacchants,
>   With thyrsus high,
> And the daughter of Leda, fair and pure,
>   Leads on as choral queen.[57]

But this is vision, and the image of Helen comes as a natural reflex in this play on the compelling power of Aphrodite. There is nothing here to put Aristophanes into the oligarchic camp, or, for that matter, any camp. Everyone is handled gently in the *Lysistrata*; even in the places where the chorus as a rule sings scurrilous lyrics against private persons, they disclaim all such intention, and sing instead some droll and innocent songs, based, no doubt, on folk poetry, in the form of mock invitations to partake of nonexistent wealth and dinners.[58] One must not turn all this into a prescription for public health, or reduce to a set of specifics the gay and haunting images which flash across the poet's lens. The weddings in the *Lysistrata*, both of the sexes and of Athens and Sparta, are weddings of eternal youth in Paradise; and Paradise, though it may be in the future, we know is in the past.

Thesmophoriazusae

The *Thesmophoriazusae* is perhaps the lighest play in the Aristophanic corpus. Produced in the same year as the *Lysistrata*, or perhaps in the following one, it stand as a kind of companion piece thereto, in that it also is constructed around the struggle between the sexes.[1] More properly it might be said that it is a struggle between the supposed misogynist Euripides and the irate women whose faults he has repeatedly exposed in his plays; yet the theme of men versus women in general forms the burden of the parabasis, and this basic antipathy is felt throughout, not least in the impact of such epicene figures as Cleisthenes and the poet Agathon (as here represented), who seem to bridge the gap. On the other hand, the treatment of the sexes in this play could hardly be more different from what it is in the *Lysistrata*. The *Lysistrata*, as said earlier, has the rhythm of a fertility rite, the old Dionysiac invocation of the roots of life as such sounding clearly through a rich poetic texture of sexual and domestic imagery. In this respect it only carries to greater extremes an element which appears often in Aristophanes, usually in the form of actual or implicit rejuvenation, or the marriage of the hero with a goddess. But all this is conspicuously absent from the *Thesmophoriazusae*; there is no trace of a rejuvenation, no "marriage," unless one counts the hasty interchange between the Scythian and the dancing girl at the end — in short, little of the theme of fertility or life. Sexual imagery there is, in plenty, but it is almost exclusively homosexual, and its use here does not appear to betoken the exercise of cheerful lust, as it sometimes does in Aristophanes.[2] Nor is the poet using it as a simple target for derisive scurrility, as is even more frequently the case. In this, as in so many other matters, Aristophanes shows no preternatural love of consistency. But in this play homosexual imagery has an important symbolic role, associated, however, justly or unjustly, with the literary and intellectual temper of the times; for light and flippant as it is, the *Thesmophoriazusae* in various ways anticipates the *Frogs* in its use of tragedy as an index of the state of the world.

It may seem unreasonable to call any one play of Aristophanes "flippant" in distinction to the others. All that is meant, however, is that the *Thesmophoriazusae*, though one of the cleverest and funniest of the plays, at no point reflects any strong, general human feeling; it appeals to no widely acknowledged or intuited concern of either individual or society at large. For its humor it depends almost entirely on parody of Euripides; but unlike the *Frogs*, where similar parodies prevail, the *Thesmophoriazusae* asserts without sorrow the bankruptcy of contemporary tragedy. Euripides is laughed at, but not condemned, as he is in the *Frogs*. As was long since noted by Gilbert Murray, he ought to have felt complimented rather than chagrined by being made fun of at such length and with such masterly skill.[3] For parody does not, ordinarily, aim to destroy its original, and the greatest poets from Homer on have sustained numberless parodies without a mortal wound. And so here, the parody is without venom, and the plot, or fantasy, is without reference to very much beyond its own inconsequential proposition: How would old Euripides, with all his supposed subtlety, extricate himself if the women, by solemn vote at the Thesmophoria, should condemn him to death? The art of tragedy is shown to be on the wane, but any deeper implications that might have been involved in that fact are saved for the *Frogs*.

It is obvious that whenever a figure who is to be lampooned stands at the center of the plot, there can be no heroic fantasy which takes wing and soars off to a happy conclusion. Such a situation, as already observed in an earlier chapter, avails in the version of the *Clouds* which we have, where the fall of Socrates results from the collapse of the dream structure of his disappointed disciple, and the consequent loss of that transcendent joy which rounds off the heroic plays. In the *Thesmophoriazusae* there is an analogous problem, but it is better solved. The poet achieves a happy, or in any case a genuinely funny, ending, not because the fantasy works, for a Euripidean fantasy must not be allowed to win, but because it is abandoned in favor of earthier tactics. The play is a well-fashioned one, exhibiting the steadily rising suspense and unity of structure which in particular mark Aristophanes' later work. This he achieves in part by deferring and protracting the *agon*, in part by limiting the choral parts to mere hymns such as might form part of the Thesmophoria, with little trace of the irrelevant invectives, personal or political, which enliven earlier plays. Whatever may be gained by such tightness, there is also a distinct loss, and one which clearly foretells the fading of the Old Comedy; it is very questionable whether a well-carpentered plot is to be preferred to the exuberant poetic farrago of comic awareness which flourished in the twenties, and achieved at least once, in the *Birds*, dramatic unity without loss of textural wealth. But be that as it may, personal satire here falls only on characters who are actually staged in the play, while political references are confined to some rather footless remarks in the parabasis about Cleophon, the defeated general Charminus, and "the councilor who last year made over his office to another." [4] The rest is farce, parody, and the dexterous deflation of Euripidean dramaturgy.

Euripides himself, if not quite such a masterpiece as Socrates, is yet a wonderful caricature, the same in essence as he is in the *Acharnians* and *Frogs*, though his role is different. In the *Acharnians* his rags and rhetoric are indispensable to Dicaeopolis' success as a hero; in the *Frogs* he is rejected as a poisonous leaven in society. Here he enters quite for his own sake, a rather morose, even pathetic, figure, compounded of magniloquent twaddle and abysmally inept expedients. Like Socrates, he believes wholeheartedly in his own humbug, but unlike him, he is a dreadful failure, and his very helplessness robs the caricature of any suggestion of threat. In the end all his stratagems are scuttled, and he is forced to capitulate and mend his ways toward womankind. Nothing could be farther from the pattern of the comic hero, or a better example of the flex-ibility of Aristophanes' comic materials. The *poneria* which can achieve triumph and transformation in the hands of one character can serve merely to sprawl another as the victim of his own devices.

At the very outset much is made of Euripides' cleverness. The mystified Mnesilochus, if the "Kinsman" is properly so named, wants to know where they are going; Euripides will not tell him because presently he will see for himself, and one cannot hear what one sees, nor, conversely, see what one hears. Mnesilochus is more impressed than enlightened:

> Mn.: How's that you say? My, you speak cleverly!
> You say that I am not either to hear or see?
> Eur.: The nature of the two are quite distinct.
> Mn.: Nature of neither hearing nor seeing?
> Eur.: Verily.
> Mn.: Distinct, eh?
> Eur.: They were separated thus:
> When ether first divided elements
> And in itself bore moving animals,
> Wherewith to see, it first contrived the eye,
> Mimic of the sun's wheel, and then for hearing
> It bored the hollow funnel of the ear.
> Mn.: So, through the funnel I shan't hear nor see?
> By Zeus, I'm gratified to learn all that.
> What a great thing is learned intercourse!
> Eur.: You may learn many such things from me.[5]

Throughout the play there are numerous other references to his great subtlety in shifts and intrigues.[6] The only one which works, however, is the last one, which differs in quality from all the others, and is not, in fact, very subtle: Mnesilochus, apprehended and under guard by a Scythian archer, is finally rescued by Euripides, who manages to divert the archer's attention by means of a pretty dancing girl. This is, as will be seen, imagistically a reversal of the play's tenor, and there is perhaps a final twist of irony in the great misogynist's being forced to fall back at last on the services of the female.

His other stratagems all serve as illustrations of the play's main theme, the decline of tragedy. Be it said once more, Aristophanes' real and positive beliefs about any of the issues which he raises are almost impossible to determine. We have no way of knowing whether or not Aristophanes really regarded Euripides as the destroyer of his art. Even in the *Frogs*, where Euripides serves as a symbol for the ruinous present, and is identified with every form of public or private corruption and decay, the image is so distorted and the caricature so much the comedian's invention, that to take it literally comes close to humorless pedantry. The seriousness of the *Frogs* and the lightheartedness of the *Thesmophoriazusae* alike find their meaning in a realm wider than the poet's real, considered opinion of Euripides: that realm of reflected human life created by poetic knowledge, whose particulars, however specific they may seem, are always general. Euripides is the eternal spoof artist, the long-haired hoax, made funnier than usual by the addition of the name and a few of the idiosyncrasies, of a great living tragedian. Between such fully achieved artistic universals and what are sometimes called "stock characters" there is a great and important difference, and if any traditional "mask" of the Learned Doctor underlies the Aristophanic Euripides — or Socrates — it has assuredly developed a great deal from its stock-in-trade origins.[7]

Confronted by the doom threatened by the angry women, Euripides proposes to dress up someone as a woman and send him to the Thesmophoria to plead his case. On the one hand, this is a theatrical technique: Euripides will stage a character to save himself. On the other hand, it introduces the idea of transvestitism, a basic motif insofar as all the main characters sooner or later dress as women. The connection between the two is presently made clear when the poet Agathon emerges from his house, in female clothes, and prepares to compose a tragedy. When Mnesilochus, with broad mockery, asks him what he is up to, Agathon explains:

> The man who is a poet should behave
> In keeping with the dramas he must write;

Hence, if he writes a drama about women,
His body must participate in their ways.[8]

Such a theory of artistic composition, akin to homeopathy in medicine, seems to have been current; something similar occurs in the *Frogs* where Aeschylus explains that large words, "the size of Parnassus or Lycabettus," are necessary to express large thoughts, "even as heroes wear grander clothes than we." [9] In the theory as developed here, however, the dress and appearance of the poet actually determine the nature of his writing; hence the handsome Phrynichus wrote handsomely, the luxurious Ibycus, Anacreon, and Alcaeus wrote in soft and mellow veins. "And besides," says Agathon, "it is uncultured for a poet to be countrified and hairy." [10] Certainly Agathon is no such matter; his female garments suit him so well that Euripides has chosen him to be his advocate before the women, an honor which Agathon prudently declines. But the effeminacy of his person is matched by the effeminacy of his art: his delicate, involved music is compared to "ants' tracks," and his chorus is hailed by Mnesilochus as a kind of aphrodisiac.[11]

Agathon is the apt symbol of the emasculated art of new tragedy, invented by Euripides and rounded out into full decadence by his successors. Hairiness, from Homer on, is the token of virility, and is mentioned as such in the *Lysistrata*, as well as elsewhere.[12] Mnesilochus here is clearly a bushy fellow, and even Euripides has a beard. But Agathon's house is full of razors, not to mention the hair nets, girdles, and brassières with which Mnesilochus is later fitted out.[13] The whole scene resembles, of course, the one in the *Acharnians* where Dicaeopolis borrows tragic equipment from Euripides. But there the emphasis lay on Euripidean rhetoric and *poneria*, as powerful assets to the comic hero in his great effort. Here the emphasis is quite different; and the picture of tragic poetry, gelded and hairless, in woman's clothes, and singing soprano, points to weakness, not power, and paves the way for the later scenes where Euripides' own art fails to convince.[14]

It is not that Agathon lacks rhetoric. His servant's description of his creative processes recalls a passage in the *Knights* which satirizes, apparently, the overuse of figures drawn from manual trades by demagogic orators: "The fair-versed Agathon prepares," says the servant,

> To lay the keel, the beginning of a play.
> He bends the new felloes of verse
> Some lines he turns on a lathe, some glues,
> He fashions maxims, he coins new names,
> Pours wax in his mold, and models his clay,
> And casts in bronze.[15]

"And swishes," adds Mnesilochus, and the fanfaronade collapses. This rhetoric is only vaporous claptrap. It is also frigid; Agathon must compose out of doors because his stanzas get so stiff in the winter that he cannot manipulate them until they have been in the sun for a while.[16] All this is a picture of Agathon, of course, not of Euripides, and it seems to have been developed so fully both for its own sake and as a motif. It has little further connection with the plot, for after Agathon's refusal it is Mnesilochus who offers to play the advocate. But the image of unmanned and ineffectual theatrical-ism spreads as Euripides shaves and singes his long-suffering relative for the part he is to play. If the phallus was the primary dramatic image of the *Lysistrata*, it is certainly its absence which is controlling in the *Thesmophoriazusae*.[17]

Mnesilochus turns out to be more notable for loyalty than for aptitude; his speech for the defense, consisting of a long account of hair-raising female crimes which Euripides might have exposed and did not, leads to his arrest and recognition as a man. Mnesilochus now becomes somewhat more than the traditional buffoon, although in the first scenes his replies to Euripides and Agathon announce him as merely such. After he assumes his disguise he becomes the impostor who reveals the truth despite himself, and his dogged, useless attempts to play tragic female roles even after he is known for a man suggest, somehow, the spirit of comedy itself in the act of cutting tragedy down to size. He tries hard to play the roles imposed by tragedy, even as he tries to conceal his phallus, but in vain; his rough, comic masculinity keeps tearing through the texture, leaving the tragic scheme in tatters. In these respects, too, he resembles Strepsiades, who likewise tried, in defiance of his nature, to adapt himself to ideas beyond his scope.

Thus, it appears that comedy and tragedy — that is, contemporary tragedy — are both vaguely adumbrated under the guise of the two sexes. Comedy is virile, like Mnesilochus, and essentially truthful; tragedy is at best a hermaphroditic affair, evolving contrived but fragile structures of illusion, and simultaneously allying itself with the female and betraying it. Such an alignment perhaps explains the character of the women in this play, in contrast to the *Lysistrata*. In the *Lysistrata* the women, though liberally sprinkled with little naughtinesses, are distinctly charming and sympathetic; their cause is love, home, and harmony, and their leader is a lady of stature. In the *Thesmophoriazusae* many of the same faults appear, such as tippling and love affairs, but they are rather more heavily underlined. And the real objection to Euripides is that because of his revelations, the women cannot get away with anything any more.[18] Weaving a chaplet, or the least touch of illness, is taken as a sign of some illicit attachment, and even pilfering bits of flour, oil, or wine is no longer possible around husbands made suspicious by Euripides.[19] Also, because he once wrote, "A young wife is a tyrant to an old husband," older men will no longer marry young girls — an interesting touch, since it exactly reverses a passage in the *Lysistrata* where such marriages are deplored.[20] There is quite a bit said or suggested about supposititious children, whereby fecundity itself is involved in the general air of falsehood.[21] Their great friend and proxenus is Cleisthenes, the beardless effeminate informer whose role in the play is to inform against Mnesilochus. Though according to the plot they are struggling against Euripides, they are involved in the same set of motifs as he is, and nothing is ever said to indicate that he is wrong about them. These women are scarcely the warm wives and mothers of the *Lysistrata*, but rather a pack of vengeful furies; and as for supposititious children, the one which Mnesilochus seizes for hostage and threatens to slay — in fact, does slay — turns out to be a dressed-up wine skin.[22]

The parabasis should have been the place for the women to show their positive and beneficial side, and they attempt to do so; but Aristophanes seems to have found the task difficult. The comparison of the bad performances of specific men with the virtues implied in ordinary women's names is feeble, either as argument or humor, and the poet, perhaps realizing the fact, cut the parabasis short. Somehow in the *Thesmophoriazusae* femininity, whether real or assumed, is under a somewhat morbid cloud; by contrast, there is something genuinely refreshing about the masculinity of Mnesilochus, however coarse, and of the Scythian archer, whose main male attribute plays an unblushing role in the solution of the play.

The scenes after the parabasis in which Mnesilochus tries to escape from his captors by re-enacting various Euripidean roles contain some of Aristophanes' finest comic imagination. Mnesilochus had made Euripides swear to rescue him if difficulty arose, and he had made sure that it was his heart and not his tongue which swore.[23] Captured and surrounded, he tries to summon Euripides by cutting SOS messages on votive tablets, as Palamedes had done on oar blades, and flinging them about.[24] But the role of the astute Palamedes hardly suits the simple Mnesilochus, in woman's clothes at that, and when no rescue appears, he reverts to female parts, and plays Helen. This works better, and presently Euripides arrives as Menelaus, prepared to retrieve his truant wife from Egypt. As they play out the recognition scene some magnificent confusions arise. The woman guard tries to make it clear that Mnesilochus is not really Helen, but is sufficiently drawn into the fiction to believe that "Menelaus" has just arrived by sea and is still a little seasick, while Euripides finds himself making some replies which are appropriate to the guard's information and not at all to his drama.[25] But when Menelaus-Euripides tries to free "Helen," the fiction breaks down completely, and Euripides is driven off. The Scythian policeman arrives now and ties Mnesilochus to a plank, which suggests a new role, Andromeda. Once more Euripides enters, this time as Perseus, with much the same result: the Scythian is prepared to believe that "Perseus" is in love with the captive, but fails to see Mnesilochus as the fair Andromeda exposed to a sea monster.[26] The Scythian is well armed, and Euripides gives up. He makes terms for himself with the women by promising to speak better of them in future, and gets Mnesilochus off by the aforementioned trick with the dancing girl.

Much of the humor of these scenes lies in the absurd relation which is implied between drama and actuality. The art of the drama might be described as a technique of imposing a fiction, or mythic shape, upon reality and thus altering it, or creating it anew in the mind. No one, however, expects a dramatist literally to turn chickens into chimpanzees, which is roughly what Euripides is trying to do here. His fantasies rear themselves up grandly, gain a confused half-credence, and then plop earthward, as fiction shatters on fact. The drama of Euripides is not, it appears, sufficiently compelling to alter reality of this sort; and it is the more ironical, for the trouble which Mnesilochus is in is the direct outcome of Euripides' original "stage-craft" in dressing him up as a woman. It is as if the tragedian were trying to supersede one dramatic fiction by erecting another, till the whole coil of illusion blows away like so much smoke. When he surrenders, he implicitly concedes his failure as myth-maker, and the ruse with the dancing girl has little in itself to do with the art of drama. And yet, in another way it does, for in order to carry it off, Euripides must himself in the end dress as a woman, the pan-deress Artemisia, and acquiesce in the feeble scheme of drama which Aristophanes has laid at his door, in images of transvestitism, emas-culation, and humbug.

When one considers the transformations wrought by comic al-chemy in the *Birds*, it may seem rather invidious of Aristophanes not to let Euripides turn Mnesilochus into Helen or Andromeda. But for one thing, comedy does turn chickens into chimpanzees most

triumphantly, and, what is more, it makes a great difference as to
who is doing the turning. The century which saw the rise of the
first ontological relativism invited poets to deal in a new and conscious way with the problem of reality, and we have already seen
how, in the *Birds*, Aristophanes made poetic capital out of some of
the ideas in Gorgias' "Treatise on Non-being." But there was nothing to compel him to tolerate such nonsense from anyone else. In
the *Frogs* he was soon to flout Euripides with his own line, "Who
knows if life be death or death be life?" and at the same time build
much of the play around that very idea, by making Dionysus pass
through the heroic death journey which ends in the discovery of
true life. The glib eloquence of Telephus is a scandal — until Dicaeopolis uses it; and even then, Euripides gets no thanks. And so
too here, Euripides' dramaturgy is represented as a series of antic
and imbecilic toyings with the ineluctable facts of reality, and once
more, Gorgias seems to be in the background. The speech of Euripides quoted above, distinguishing between the objects of sight and
hearing, is almost a quotation from the book "On Non-being," and
the passage goes on to demonstrate the difference between thought
and reality by saying that one may conceive of chariots running on
the sea, though the actual phenomenon is unheard-of.[27] For Gorgias,
all this leads to the conclusion that reality is not objective, but subjective, created and controlled by speech, a notion which was of
great use to Aristophanes when he wanted to put wings on Peithetaerus and build a city in the air. But now matters lie differently.
The Scythian and the plank are solidly, grimly real, and for Euripides to try to obviate such clear facts by tricky talk and poetic fancy
is simply another example of the fellow's unconscionable, fatuous
drivel. The answer to the Scythian is not a pretended tragic heroine, but a real comic strumpet, and the sexual act which ends the
play brings down in a final crash the cloud lands of transvestite poesy.

The *Thesmophoriazusae* can hardly be called a real satire, for as
usual Aristophanes' visionary powers have tempted him too far
from the verities of the case. But the satire which adheres to them

too closely becomes soon dated, while a grandly conceived monstrosity lives on in its own world of representative structures of experience. It is parody, not satire, which creates the monstrous Euripides of this play; the image is inflated, not deflated, for parody in a way adds dimensions to its object. Even if Euripides' art is deflated at the end, the image is not reduced, for ineptitude had been one of its basic premises. He is certainly one of Aristophanes' most successful inventions, and one of the most lightly conceived. In a few years he was to be brought out again, much the same in essence, but in a far different role which required the emphasis to fall on the knave rather than on the fool.

·VII·

DEATH AND LIFE

Frogs

Earlier it was said that the *Peace* was the last play to be written wholly within the scheme of the polis, and certainly no play afterwards deals quite so confidently with Athens as a given quantity, whose details may be exalted or derided, but whose essence is never examined. After the broad vista of the *Birds*, with its searching irony, the plays of 411, as we have observed, once more narrowed the scheme of comedy to the familiar themes of peace and poetry, but with a difference. These themes serve now as modes by which the poet is trying to evoke the essence of the city, the meaning of its history and the condition of its culture. A new note of earnestness has entered, almost imperceptible as yet, but destined to grow stronger, while the earlier visions of heroic transcendence have all but vanished. The whole tone is quieter and more wary: though the *Lysistrata* ends with peace restored, its closing choruses are decorously reserved compared with the licentious rumpus of fertility rites in the *Peace*; while the hilarious parodies and insouciant argument of the *Thesmophoriazusae* are dampened by the imagery of emasculation, the symbol of the decline of tragic art. The poet has returned to Athens from Nephelococcygia, but he approaches her with some loss of high spirits, almost with trepidation.

But Aristophanes was still young; if the plays of 411 show a decline in spirits, they show none, certainly, in versatility or invention.

Six years later the versatility and invention were still with him, but anything even resembling high spirits had vanished totally, giving place to something close to despair. Produced at the Lenaea of 405 B.C., six months after Arginusae and six before Aegospotami, the *Frogs* testifies poignantly to Aristophanes', and doubtless all intelligent Athenians', intimations of the city's impending doom. The play is unique for a number of reasons, not least because it marks a return to civic immediacy, and contains in itself almost all the real evidence to support any theory of Aristophanes as a serious political adviser. At least, it is difficult to dismiss, as one may the parabasis of the *Acharnians*, the deep undercurrent of political concern which runs through the *Frogs*, whether it be expressed in the omnipresent death imagery or in seemingly specific passages of admonition, such as the parabasis, where for once in his life the poet appears to speak without a comic mask. One may, perhaps, say simply that the terrifying claims of the year 405 drove his mind to face "realities," and turn away from the heroic fantasies of transcendence and the poetry of metaphysical nonsense. There would be some truth in this, though it might seem to entail the converse, which is erroneous, that the earlier plays involved no grasp of reality, and that the vision of heroic transcendence was something which a poet should outgrow. The *Frogs*, though it differs from all the earlier work, does not reverse or cancel it, nor does one serious quasi-prescriptive parabasis make a poet a reformer or a doctrinaire.

The fantasy of the *Frogs* does not, indeed, involve any individual's victory over society, but the reason is not that Aristophanes had become a "realist." For a hero to transcend society, not only must there be heroic vision, there must also be a society to transcend; but by 405 the repressive machinery by which the demagogues led, or misled, the people, the machinery which touched off the revolts of such heroes as Dicaeopolis or Peithetaerus, was no longer in quite such good working order. The execution of the victorious generals of Arginusae betokened — in fact, almost symbolized — the lack, or rejection, of all leadership in the Athens of Cleophon, while the enfranchisement of the slaves who fought in the battle added one more motley element to an already distracted civic body. The boundaries of society itself had crumbled, no longer providing limits for a hero to defy and transcend. Athens herself, threatened both from within and from without as never before in her history, had become the underdog whose salvation was of concern. Yet, Aristophanes is still the poet of transcendent fantasies, albeit he is watching with more than the corner of his eye the shadow of things to come. The fantasy of the *Frogs*, though a somber one, is a full poetic structure, a transformation, not a mirror image, of reality, and one which, in its dark but tender adumbration of the future, can justifiably take its place beside Sophocles' reflections in the *Oedipus at Colonus*, where Athens, already virtually fallen, is envisioned in a phoenixlike apotheosis.

In external form as well, the *Frogs* is unique; indeed, it has often been thought formally defective, but its apparent lack of unity is almost certainly part of the meaning.[1] In the *Knights* and the *Thesmophoriazusae* Aristophanes had extended the agonistic element, so that the tension carried throughout the play. Here the agon, seven hundred lines long, is simply saved for the second half which it all but entirely fills, while whatever revelry there is, usually a feature of the finale, is to be found only in the parodos of the chorus. The group of genre scenes, including the lesser agon between Xanthias and Dionysus, do not, as in other plays, serve to illustrate the results of a new order, but rather form steps along the way to its achievement; for in the *Frogs* no new order is established until the very end. The parabasis also is somewhat strange, consisting as it does of only two lyrics and two epirrhemes, without the anapaests of a parabasis proper. On the other hand, the parodos is interrupted by a passage of anapaests, where the leader of the initiates warns the profane away from the sacred procession.[2] Half gay, half serious, these lines bear a suspicious resemblance to a regular parabasis, though instead of breaking the illusion they form a part of it, somewhat as does the parabasis of the *Birds*. Aristophanes has not only rearranged the usual order of the parts, he has even mixed them up, with extraordinary suppleness and freedom.

The result is a feeling of inversion, which accords well with the purport of the drama, for the *Frogs*, though it is often referred to as the last Old Comedy, is not really a comedy at all, but a tragedy in comic form, the first of a dramatic kind of which Mozart's *Don Giovanni* is perhaps the greatest example. The *Frogs* is tragic, not merely because it reflects the grim world of 405 B.C., but also because the quest of Dionysus, comic enough at the outset, does not achieve its expected, or even a comic, result, but continues to the end, where the resurrection of Aeschylus involves, as we shall see, some very dark implications. Dionysus' descent into hell is in every way the opposite of Trygaeus' flight to heaven, and the vision which results from it is correspondingly grave. It is not without meaning, certainly, that Dionysus is wearing the cothurnus, the boot of tragedy, as he sets forth.[3]

The *Frogs* is by no means the first or only play built around a mission to the underworld in search of deceased worthies. In the *Demoi* of 412 Eupolis had resurrected a number of dead statesmen in order to set things right in Athens, and a few years later Aristophanes in the *Gerytades* appears to have done something similar, with an eye to recovering the poetry of the past.[4] There is one fragment of Pherecrates in which Aeschylus, clearly in Hades, makes a boastful speech, and another in which a kind of Utopia in Hades is described.[5] The theme is, in fact, related to that of Utopia, which was a favorite one with all the comic poets. Both Utopia and death are regions of the boundless, and though death is enclosed in a ring of darkness, it is nonetheless, as the ultimate receptacle of all good things, a kind of land of the heart's desire. In thinking of it, especially in anticipation of one's own death, it has not been customary to dwell upon the evils which also have found their way there, or to anticipate association with the damned. Death is, on this view, the land of departed goodness, and the comic convention of praising the past made it natural on occasion to stage the spirits of the great men of old amid the shadows of infernal landscapes.

It is doubtful, however, that either Eupolis or Pherecrates treated the journey into Hades in anything like the manner of Aristophanes. In the *Frogs* Hades is not only a Utopia; it also emerges as the land of truth, so to speak, the place where true values and true knowledge abide. When Dionysus has chosen Aeschylus rather than Euripides, the chorus sings,

> Happy is the man who possesses
> Precise intelligence,

as though the god's choice had marked his arrival at something lastingly true.[6] And of course it does: Dionysus had gone to Hades to recover the recently dead Euripides, the poet of the world of the present, but had become wiser during the journey and returned instead with the poet of Athens' early greatness. This action completes the explicit critique of tragedy which runs throughout the play; it also completes Dionysus' search for himself, which is equally, if not more, important.

It has recently been shown, in answer to attacks on the unity of the *Frogs*, that the play is carefully built around the development of Dionysus, who represents, in a complex way, the community of Athens, disjointed at first, but slowly reachieving civic coherence through a journey into the unknown.[7] The communal problem is only thinly masked as a poetic problem, for the two went hand in hand, with Euripides embodying the divisive and centrifugal forces of relativism, irresponsible rhetoric, and in general the new education, while Aeschylus stands for the staunch beliefs and public solidarity of the days of Marathon. The symbolic role of the two poets cannot be denied; what is rare is for Aristophanes to stage, in all seriousness, a character who represents, not the aspiring little individual, not the antisocial *poneros*, but the collective selfhood of Athens, a selfhood all but lost to its own identity and seeking to

recover it by a spiritual journey into Hell. It is part of the immemorial heroic tradition for the questing individual to seek authenticity by a confrontation with death; by the loneliness of his search
the hero does what all must do, and thus becomes Everyman. But
Everyman is the universal individual. It is seldom that the heroic
death journey can be conceived in terms of a community, for the
community is, properly speaking, that which continues and outlives
the individual. Yet that is what Dionysus is, Athenian culture incarnate, so to speak, undertaking the soul's far journey after self-
knowledge and true identity. The club and lion skin of Heracles are
therefore not so wholly ludicrous as they at first appear, but make
a kind of ironical disguise suggestive of an ulterior truth. In any
case, the implications are highly complex, for somehow the question
of communal continuity has been crossed with the myth of heroic
self-search to make of Dionysus a character who bears a singularly
heavy burden of meaning.

Dionysus' journey to Hades was not invented by Aristophanes.
The story is told that the god, having established his cult throughout
the known world, descended into the underworld in order to redeem
not Euripides, but his mother Semele, whom he then brought to
Olympus.[8] Although the myth does not stand in any early author,
Pindar seems to know of it, and it is likely that it is older than Aristophanes.[9] It seems possible, at least, that the idea for the play had
its origin in this story, for several of the details correspond. It is said
that the god did not know the way to Hades, and had to ask it of a
certain Prosymnus;[10] in Aristophanes, this aspect of the journey has
become the prologue with Heracles, whom Dionysus consults about

> havens, bakeries,
> Brothels, rest areas, detours, fountains, roads,
> Towns, buildings, hotesses of inns with fewest
> Bedbugs.[11]

Usually Dionysus is said to have descended through the Bottomless
Lake of Lerna. Another version has it that he went down through a
great chasm at Troezen; this place, according to Plutarch, was called

the Place of Forgetfulness.[12] The name may possibly account for the Plain of Lethe which Charon lists among the places whither his skiff is about to sail.[13] In any event, it seems clear that the scenario of the *Frogs* is built upon the legend of Dionysus' quest for his mother, and that the themes of life, death, and immortality, so prevalent in the play, have their roots in this apocalyptic myth of resurrection and apotheosis.

Mythic tradition may also account for certain other details, and even for the chorus of the play, consisting as it does of the redeemed souls of the Eleusinian initiates. Once more, it is hard to say how early the story was invented, but Dionysus is said to have been initiated into the Mysteries before he went down to Hades, and so too was Heracles.[14] One of the benefits promised by the Mysteries was some kind of return from the nether darkness. The two brothers of the prologue are, therefore, the only two gods who had ever been initiated into the Mysteries, and Heracles had been initiated as a mortal, before he was taken up into Olympus. As for Dionysus, it is a tormented question to what extent, if at all, he was associated with the Mysteries of Demeter; [15] but he was surely by the middle of the fifth century identified with the Eleusinian Iacchus, the divine personification of the exultant, mystic procession.[16] The point need not be labored; but Dionysus appears in the play not only as the god of the theater, but also as a deity affiliated, if only by initiation, with the Eleusinian Mysteries, and therefore with one of the greatest of Athenian cults and the only one which dealt specifically with the eschatological fortunes of the soul. The chorus of Mystae which greets Dionysus in Hades is a collective representation of an Athens redeemed beyond the grave, and if the god does not recognize himself in the invocation of Iacchus, he nonetheless is moved to join in the dancing and singing.[17] This whole aspect of the play could be regarded as a montage upon the initiation of Dionysus, who, like any initiate, is in search of his own and his city's salvation; the old myth is transposed into a comic mode, yet retains its basic meaning.

But the montage is a multiple one. The principal scene of the

play is, of course, the agon between Euripides and Aeschylus, so
that the dramatic contests of the City Dionysia are also adumbrated.
B. B. Rogers long ago noted that the boat fare which Charon collects
is not one obol, the usual charge for conveyance across the Styx, but
two, which is the entrance fee for the theater.[18] The *Frogs* thus becomes a play within a play, the first known example in Western
literature of that haunting device which was to become a total theatrical method with Pirandello. The mode is apt for artistic self-
scrutiny, for thus the poet holds the mirror, not up to life, but up to
another mirror, as it were, thus producing an infinite regress of implication. One is not sure whether he is saying that the world is a
stage or that the stage is the world, and this ambiguity is carried out
in the more searching one of life and death. Since the demise of
Euripides and Sophocles the price of a theater ticket has become the
price of entering the realm of the dead, and there alone can a "fruitful," "generative" poet be found. Only on the initiates in Hades
do the sun and gay light shine.[19]

Imagery drawn from the theater is ubiquitous throughout, and
nothing could be more subtle than the way in which the question
of Dionysus' identity is developed through the critique of dramatic
poetry; for if the second half of the play explicitly (though not
necessarily too scientifically) explores the nature of tragedy, the first
half weighs the nature of comedy.[20] As patron of both arts Dionysus
may appropriately seek to know himself by knowing them. The very
opening lines of the play set the tone of self-conscious artistry:

> Xan.:   Shall I say one of the usual things, master,
>   The sort of thing the audience always laughs at?

Bantering the audience was a frequent part of Old Comedy, but
this jibe leads to something more. Dionysus' reply indicates a certain
discrimination about kinds of humor, and he forbids certain jokes
which, he says, make him feel a year older — the very opposite of
the rejuvenation motif so frequently observed in comedy.[21] Before
a dozen lines have passed, however, two of the prohibited jests — dull

vulgarities, fit only for Aristophanes' rivals — are trundled out, and something very like a third occurs somewhat later.[22] Clearly the art of comedy is out of hand, if its own deity has so little control of it; and presently, as he arrives at Heracles' door, the question of what he is up to arises quite directly.

Whatever was said earlier about the possible appropriateness of some of Dionysus' equipment, the combination of club, lion skin, tragic buskin, and a woman's robe is a strangely assorted one, and the astonishment of Heracles is understandable enough. Piling as it does male, female, and animal disguises on the person of a god, the costume may fairly be described as grotesque;[23] almost as if to complete the hybrid picture, the god is several times referred to as a "man." But the grotesquerie has a different significance from that of Peithetaerus: Dionysus is a hybrid whose multiple guises indicate not the possession of secret and magical keys, but rather uncertainty as to who he is. It is as if the theater were enacting all its repertoire at once in a self-burlesque. Yet this farrago, which cannot choose but be hilarious, is composed of things which hint at tragic and heroic seriousness; even the woman's robe is no exception. For though by the fifth century Dionysus was often represented as an effeminate youth, the female dress ($\kappa\rho\kappa\omega\tau\delta s$) can hardly fail to recall specifically its counterpart in the dress of Agathon in the *Thesmophoriazusae*, and the symbolism thereof, noted earlier.[24] Aristophanes has costumed his main character admirably to his purpose: in the light of the deaths of Sophocles and Euripides, comedy puts on the buskin of high seriousness and the club and lion skin of heroic self-search, and undertakes the quest to recover poetic and political virility. Perhaps for this reason the word which Dionysus chooses for the kind of poet he wants is $\gamma\delta\nu\iota\mu\sigma s$, literally "fruitful," "generative," a word expressive of natural, healthy fertility.[25] Dionysus thinks that Euripides is such a poet, but his view changes once his own real identity is established in Hades.

The question of identity is dramatized with full comic effect in the middle scenes of the play. Since these scenes have been carefully analyzed of late, be it said but briefly that Dionysus, though he has

claimed that he could "play Ercles rarely," does not in fact live up
to the fiercer part of his costume when faced with characters whom
Heracles mistreated on his trip into Hell. Aeacus, still seething over
the rape of Cerberus, bursts out in a thunderous salvo of threats,
and the terrified god promptly induces Xanthias to exchange his
burden of luggage for the club and lion skin.[26] The process is
quickly reversed, however, when a maid enters with an invitation
for Heracles to dinner, complete with roast ox, cake, and dancing
girls.[27] But as Dionysus-Heracles is about to enjoy these pleasures,
he is assailed by the hostess of an inn whose goods Heracles formerly
had devoured without paying. The costumes are changed again,
so that when Aeacus returns with bailiffs and constables, it is Xanthias the slave whom he points out as the thief of Cerberus. The
theatrical imagery is never forgotten: a shift of costumes is a shift
of roles, and therefore a shifting of responsibility. But in the ordeal
which follows the ground too shifts a little. Xanthias maintains his
role of Heracles, but denies the charges against him, and offers his
"slave" for torture to prove his innocence. Dionysus, cornered, tells
his real name, and to settle the dispute, it is agreed that whichever
cannot feel the blows of a whip is the real god. The question is now
not which is Heracles, but which is a god and which the slave.[28] The
elimination of the Heracles disguise brings Dionysus one step
further toward his true self, but the ordeal is inconclusive, and
Aeacus refers the matter to Pluto and Persephone, by whom it is
promptly settled offstage during the parabasis.

The repeated interchanges of slave and free man, or at least slave
and god, glance at the manumission of the slaves who fought at
Arginusae. Xanthias had not fought, but he shows some of the
stamina necessary for putting himself on an equal basis with the
free. Loaded with bundles, he cries to Dionysus:

> What a wretch am I! Why didn't I fight at sea?
> Then I'd have given you something to howl about.[29]

In turning the tables on Dionysus he shows some genuine *poneria*,
though it is less the *poneria* of the comic hero, than of the clever

slave of New Comedy.³⁰ His general superiority to his master is
made clear throughout the first part of the play, especially in the
recurrence of words meaning "noble" or "gentleman." For lack of
a porter Xanthias agrees to go on carrying the bundles; "You are
noble and a gentleman," says Dionysus by way of thanks. Aeacus
likewise finds Xanthias a man of proper breeding.³¹ When the truth
comes out, however, it is Dionysus who Aeacus has decided is the
true gentleman; but Xanthias quickly undercuts his judgment with
the remark "What else should he be but a gentleman, who knows
nothing but drinking and lechery?" ³²

The question of free men versus slaves becomes explicit in the
famous parabasis, sometimes thought to be one of the clearest examples of political programming in Aristophanes; deeply felt as the
passage is, there is no program, but only a yearning for a real Athens
and real Athenians. Aristophanes writes in a prescriptive mode, appropriate to the role of comic "educator":

> So I say it's villainous that those who fought one fight at sea
> All are now reborn Plataeans, slaves no longer, masters, free;
> Yet, I can't say this was badly done, but rather to be classed
> With the most intelligent resolutions that you've ever passed.
> Others though, your brothers, men who manned your fleet,
>   their fathers too,
> Wisely banish wrath, forgive one fault, and take them back to you!
> Let all men be kept our kinsmen, citizens, enfranchised free,
> One condition still availing — tug an oar and fight at sea! ³³

These lines urging, as they seem to do, common sense and a general
amnesty for those involved in the revolution of 411, are echoed in
the corresponding epirrheme by words of more general import. In a
fine image comparing citizens, new and old, with the currency of
Athens, now badly debased, Aristophanes calls upon the city to
make use of its good citizens, and he pours out all the words implying civic righteousness — καλὸς κἀγαθός, εὐγενής, σώφρων, δίκαιος,
χρηστός — to describe the men "reared in gymnasiums, dances, and
music." But the supply of these is low, and when later Aeschylus
asks if Athens employs her good citizens, Dionysus must reply that

she does not, but rather employs the wicked perforce, for lack of better.[34] It appears thus from the parabasis that parallel with the search for a great poet runs the search for the good citizen, and that these two searches are in no way distinct from Dionysus' search for his true selfhood; they constitute in great part its meaning, as is clear from much of the great agon. But throughout the multiple changes of role, in the first part of the play it seems unlikely that the quest will be fulfilled, and Dionysus' final reply to Aeschylus about good citizens is not very encouraging.

The confusion between slave and free reaches a rather weird climax in the intermediate scene just after the parabasis. It is now clear who Dionysus is, and that Xanthias is the slave; but so too, it turns out, is Aeacus himself, and the two compare notes on the low satisfactions of slavery — privately cursing the master, spying on his secrets and telling them abroad, and so on. All these little joys constitute a special world, presided over by a new and unfamiliar aspect of Zeus himself: Xanthias speaks of "brother Zeus," and, "Zeus who is our fellow whipping post." [35] Even the Eleusinian aspect is included: Aeacus so delights in slavish knavery that it seems to initiate him into "Final Revelation," and he uses the verb denoting the last stage of the Mysteries.[36] To each his own; the true levels are emerging. The recognition of Dionysus by Pluto could scarcely have made good comic material; instead, Aristophanes stages the parallel unmasking of Xanthias, but to keep the unlikelihood of it all alive, he turns Aeacus too into a slave. And not only Aeacus, the divine judge of the dead, but also Zeus has been transformed into a slave, to complete the inverted image of a society where nothing is any longer what it is supposed to be. The scene forms a skillful transition between the role-changing of the first part of the play and the slow discovery of the true poet in the second.

The shifting of roles between Dionysus and Xanthias, however, is only part of a larger scheme, deeply basic to the play. It was said above that the god is in search of something lastingly true; but before he approaches it he is driven through phase upon phase of seeming and changeability, of which his own transformations are a reflection. The scene with Empusa is like a motif:

Xanth.: By Zeus, I see a monster, very big!
Dion.: What sort?
Xanth.: Dreadful. It turns all kinds of things,
Sometimes a cow, sometimes a mule, sometimes
A beautiful woman.
Dion.: Where is she? Let me at her!
Xanth.: It's not a woman any more, but hound.
Dion.: Ah, it's Empusa!
Xanth.: Yes, and her whole face
Is alight with fire.
Dion.: And has she one brass foot?
Xanth.: Yes, by Poseidon, and the other — dung! [37]

Faced with this shifty apparition, Dionysus in terror forbids his servant to address him either as Heracles or by his right name, thus rejecting identity altogether.[38] Well may he do so in a world where good citizens languish in exile, while slaves overnight turn into "Plataeans and masters." [39] The chorus ironically praises, later, the kind of adaptability which keeps a man out of trouble:

This is the way of a man of brains
And shrewdness, one who has been around:
To turn himself forever about,
To whatever side is the fortunate side,
Rather than stand like a painted picture,
With only one device. To shift
To the cozier berth is the way of the man
Who is bright and, by nature, Theramenes.[40]

Theramenes had already become, justly or unjustly, a byword for self-interested fence-jumping, and had perhaps also earned his famous nickname, cothurnus, the boot which fits either foot; if so, there is doubtless yet a further significance in that part of Dionysus' costume. He is god not only of roles, but of shifting roles, in a monstrous Empusa-world where nothing is stable, and everything turns into something else; even comedy is turning into tragedy.

In the latter half of the play the theme of changeability deepens and begins to involve the whole question of relativism. We have seen in the *Birds* a lofty extravaganza upon the relative or subjective nature of reality, and the demiurgic power of speech; indeed, much of the earlier work of Aristophanes showed a tendency to exploit this sophistic theory, while overtly condemning it with mock-moral zeal. But the *Frogs* is different. Here, instead of contenting himself with the language of absurdity and the salvation of private reality, Aristophanes seems to be trying to plunge deeper, to get beyond the veils of speech, and arrive at something more absolute. Speech is no longer the touchstone of personal power over the world; it has become the symbol of individual deception, disintegration of reality, and social decay. Euripides appears as the embodiment of talk, both trivial and shifty, a quibbling immoralist concerned on the one hand with verbal exactitude, and on the other with morally ruinous equivocation. The role is no new one for him, of course, but there is a contrast between the negative function it fulfills here and that which it served in the *Acharnians*, where the rhetoric of Euripides provided the tool for a heroic success. Here, it seems, Euripides is to blame for all the ills of society:

Aesch.: What next? You taught them to practice babble and insubordinate mouthing!
         The result of your teaching was empty gymnasia, thin buttocks worn to a frazzle,
         As the boys went yammering on and on; and the men of the fleet you persuaded
         To answer their officers back! But I, in the old days, when I was living,
         They knew no more than to shout for a loaf, and call "heave-ho, my hearties!" [41]

And not only has he corrupted the fleet; on account of his plays, which presented procurers, childbirths in temples, incestuous siblings, and people "saying life isn't life," the whole city is "full of undersecretaries, political buffoons, and deceivers." [42] This is no mean accomplishment for a dramatic poet, to be personally responsible for the demagogues and bureaucracy. But it is all because, unlike Aeschylus, he had made all the characters in his plays *talk*:

Eurip.: Well then, from the very first I wasted no opportunity, not I!
         With me the women talked, no less the slave talked, and the master
         Talked, and the young girl talked, the old woman talked . . .
Aesch.:   You should have been murdered.[43]

Once more, it is worth noting how Aristophanes slips back and forth between the context of the theater and real life. Euripides' characters talk glibly and so do the Athenians; the poet, however, is not represented as reflecting society but impelling it, according to the conventional view of antiquity that the poet educates the people, and it is his task to improve his fellow citizens.[44] Euripides' prize pupil, however, is Theramenes, the slippery politician mentioned earlier by the chorus as more remarkable for versatility and self-preservation than for steadfastness of principle.[45] And the result of all his teaching is a world of vain and garrulous argument, limitless questioning, insubordination, and pusillanimous suspicion.

In contrast with all this talk is the silence of Aeschylus. Upon his first entrance Aeschylus disdains to speak at all in reply to the vituperations of his rival.[46] Euripides accuses him of putting on airs, just as he did in his tragedies; indeed, the first fault that Euripides finds with Aeschylus is that his characters did not talk enough:

Eur.: Well, first he'd sit one character down, all muffled up in mourning,
       Achilles, say, or Niobe, not even their faces showing —
       A poor excuse for tragedy — and never a grunt or murmur.
Dion.: That's true by Zeus!
Eur.:   The chorus, though, would pile up strings of lyric,
       Four odes straight off without a break; and they just sat in silence.[47]

Half the play went by before anyone but the chorus said anything, and then out would come twelve words, the size of bulls, which nobody could understand.[48] However adroit the satire, we are bound to prefer Aeschylus' long silence and twelve big words to the prattle of Euripides not only by the final outcome, but also by the prayers uttered by the two poets before the contest begins. Aeschylus, an Eleusinian by birth, prays solemnly:

> Demeter, you who nurtured up my mind
> Let me be worthy of your Mysteries.[49]

It should be remembered that the climactic vision of the Mysteries was protected by a vow of silence, a secrecy so strict that to this day we know nothing of the *epopteia*. Euripides, however, prays to his own private gods, a "new coinage," as Dionysus says, recalling the imagery of the parabasis, where the new, worthless citizens are compared to the debased currency of the war years: [50]

> Ether, my fodder, and axle of the tongue,
> Intelligence, and nostrils of keen scent,
> Let me refute what words I meet withal.[51]

Though the language of both poets is subjected to the most scorching parody, "horse-crested and plank-sized" words versus "splinters and filings," at root it is the contest between the axle of the tongue and the holy silence of Demeter, the contrived ambiguities of speech versus that which is always true.

Near the end of the agon the matter is treated more explicitly, and also in darker colors. Dionysus is weighing individual lines in a scale. This scene, itself a parody of an epic *psychostasis*, or weighing of lives to see which will die and which will live, has somewhat deathly overtones, and the image of death supplants that of silence. Euripides offers a line from his *Antigone*:

> Eur.: Persuasion has no shrine other than speech.
> Aesch.: Alone of gods Death has no love for gifts.
> Dion.: Let go, let go; again, he's heavier.
> He threw in Death, a very weighty ill.
> Eur.: But I threw in Persuasion, a fine word.
> Dion.: Persuasion's light and empty, and makes no sense.[52]

Persuasion, *Peitho*, is explicitly rejected; the mainspring of the *Birds* and of so many other plays, the comic touchstone, the almighty word, is swept away by death. A few lines later Aeschylus does it again; he outweighs a huge mace with two corpses.[53] Comedy yields to tragedy, and the kaleidoscopic multiplicity of speech yields to the single, ineluctable fact of death.

It had always been Aristophanes' way to revel in the multifarious-
ness of things. The hero's will to the boundless carried with it the
power to transform everything to advantage, and all these self-interested transformations lie close to the heart of comic poetry. The
comic hero identifies with the boundless, becoming what he will
in it, untroubled by considerations of consistency. The tragic hero's
relation with the boundless differs somewhat; he confronts it, or
enters it, but rather than identifying with it, he extracts something
from it, a single truth. And it is this which Dionysus is doing in the
Frogs. He seeks to extract from the boundless world of death the
true poet, and to do so he must penetrate and pass beyond the infinite shiftingness and changeability of the phenomenal world, transcend the Many and find the One. Euripides is found to be the
dramatist of words, and his buskin is that of Theramenes; he is the
poet of the Many. Dionysus was intent on bringing him back, but
he himself lacked true identity, and had to keep changing costumes.
In the lyrical competition Aeschylus again drives home the all too
diverse nature of his opponent's poetry, and damns it as meretricious;
he himself derived his lyrics from the "fair source for a fair purpose,"
presumably meaning Homer, but Euripides got his from all kinds
of sources indiscriminately:

> Aesch.:   He draws his songs from everything, from harlots,
>   Meletus' drinking catches, Carian flutings,
>   Dirges, and dance music.[54]

His very variety is against him, and Aeschylus proceeds to give a
sample of Euripidean lyric, which he compares to the versatility of
the courtesan Cyrene, famous for no less than twelve different modes
of sexual intercourse.[55] Cyrene climaxes Aeschylus' strictures upon
Euripides' plays about sexual problems, as Theramenes climaxes
the charges of glib speech and political instability; but both represent
the variety which is devoid of a central core, the diversity which is
the opposite of truth.

When Dionysus finally chooses Aeschylus, he disposes of Euripides with three of his own equivocations. The first of these states clearly the lubricity of speech:

Eur.:   Remember now the gods by whom you swore
         To bring me home again! Choose now your own.
Dion.:   "My tongue swore"; and my choice is Aeschylus.[56]

The famous line from the *Hippolytus*, "My tongue swore but not my heart," [57] liberates Dionysus, and the poet of verbal equivocation is caught in his own trap. In the second equivocation moral relativism destroys itself:

Eur.:   Can you look me in the face, having wrought such shame?
Dion.:   What's shame, unless it seem so to the audience? [58]

The parody here serves a double purpose. Euripides had written, "What is shame, unless it seem so to the person who commits it?" [59] Dionysus not only makes use of Euripides' own dismissal of exterior or objective moral standards, but in substituting "the audience" he reinvokes the theatrical imagery of the play, with its tone of conscious dramatic self-criticism, and implies that the audience will not think it a shame at all to leave Euripides in Hell. The third equivocation will be taken up later.

But to answer the multiformity of language with the uniformity of silence, or perhaps of death, is scarcely to resolve the poetic or political problem. There is another and more positive alternative to the deceptiveness of speech, and that is music. But it must be true music; that of Euripides will not do, of course. When Aeschylus is about to give his parody of Euripidean lyric, he sets aside the lyre, calling instead for an accompaniment of castanets, the instrument of dancing girls and treated elsewhere in a comic fragment as typical of mere noise.[60] The art of Euripides, composed of "debates, and twists, and turns," leads to chaos, and is attractive principally to "highwaymen, cutpurses, parricides, and housebreakers." [61] True music is explicitly contrasted by the chorus with the quibblings of philosophy:

> Go, cast off music, poetry,
>> And sit with Socrates and gas!
> Leave the great art of tragedy
>> And be — an ass!
>
> Go, plunge in solemn argument,
>> And spend a worthless afternoon
> In quibble, quiddity and cant,
>> And be — a goon! [62]

True music, the great art of tragedy, was what Dionysus went to Hades to rescue, "that the city might be saved and present her choruses." [63] True music reflects and encourages cultural cohesiveness; it includes, by implication in the symbolic scheme, both a public and a private moral force which penetrates and illuminates society.

Ironically, this ethical theory of music seems to have been first formulated by the sophist Damon, the pupil of Prodicus, much admired by Socrates and Plato; but it is by no means untypical of Aristophanes to assume and exploit a principle which he would not tolerate if theoretically expounded. Yet there is reason herein, for theoretical formulation from one point of view embarrasses the intuition of music's cultural power; analysis is a kind of talk, and by its basic definition it dissolves the economy of symbols and confounds their effect. In any case, Aristophanes is dealing not in theory but example, and he has staged the cultural cohesiveness of Athens, not only in the symbolic figure of Aeschylus, but also in the chorus of Mystae with their lovely hymns of mingled revelry and reverence. As suggested above, the Eleusinian aspects of the *Frogs* indicate an Athens redeemed from time, suffering, and error, albeit on the other side of the veil. The music of the Mystae is emphasized: "Thereafter, the breath of flutes will surround you," says Heracles to Dionysus; and presently, after the Empusa episode, the flutes are heard. [64]

The Mystae are unusually friendly for a comic chorus, which has a tendency to enter in warlike mood; but this is inevitable in view of their character as spirits of harmony and gentle piety. [65] Like the chorus of birds, they sing in pastoral images, invoking the gods, celebrating the beauties of nature. But there is no irony here; nature is purified in the simplicities of singing, play, and sacred dance:

> Go forward now, each manfully,
>> On to the flowering folds
>>> Of the meadows,
> Dancing and mocking, playing and jesting:
>> Our feast was full enough!

> But come, that you may worthily
>> Exalt the goddess of salvation,
> Chanting aloud to her who promises
>> To save this land forever.[66]

The invocation of Kore as goddess of salvation obviously strikes the central theme of the play, and is echoed by the prayer to Demeter to "preserve her own chorus, to play and dance all day in safety." [67] In these prayers one hears the twinge of real anxiety for the city, perhaps a specific reference to the suspension of the Eleusinian processions because of the besieging Spartans. But these songs are also part of the music of a sound and healthy city, a city of men "nourished in palaestras, choral dances, and music." [68] It is a mystical music in every sense, as the chorus all but states, calling upon the "Muse of the sacred chorus," and referring to the rites of Demeter and of the Muses by the same word, *orgia*, connoting secret enactments or mysteries.[69] True music and the redeeming Mysteries are one, and the coryphaeus, acting as hierophant in the parabasis-like passage which interrupts the lyrics of the parodos, specifically excludes from the ceremonies not only malefactors against the city, but also "whoever has never seen the *orgia* of the noble Muses, nor danced, nor been initiated into the mysteries of the tongue of bull-eating Cratinus." [70]

Not the least musical element in the play is the little extra chorus of frogs. What they are doing in the play, and why they should give it its title, are questions not easy to answer. Charon, however, speaks of them in something of the way that Heracles speaks of the beautiful light and the flute music of the Mystae:

Charon: Will you stop babbling and brace your feet
                And row with zeal?

Dion.:   And how ever should I,
          Unskilled, unoceaned, and unsalamised,
          How should I row?

Charon: Easily. You will hear songs,
          Most lovely, if you once lay to.

Dion.:   What sort?

Charon: Wonderful. Swan-frogs.[71]

Swans are sacred to Apollo, and for some reason have always been thought of as possessed of the power of song, albeit only at the hour of death.[72] These ghostly swan-frogs have something of the magical hybrid about them, and their compelling rhythm has its effect on Dionysus; they are, after all, his own frogs:

> Offspring of lakes and fountains we,
>   Sing we the cry that rings in concord
> With hymns, my clear-voiced song,
>   *Koax koax,*
>   The song that once we shouted aloud
>   Round Dionysus, son of Zeus,
>   In Limnae, when on the Feast of Pots
>   The drunken-headed rout of the people
>   Came to my sacred precinct,
>   *Brekekekex, koax.*[73]

Dionysus finds rowing painful and the song monotonous. A strange interchange follows:

Dion.:   I'm getting a pain in the tail, *koax.*
          That, I suppose, means nothing to you.

Frogs: *Brekekekex-koax-koax.*

Dion.:   To hell with you and your *koax!*
          There's nothing to you but *koax!*

Frogs: Of course, O Busybody!
          For I am loved by the Muses of the lovely lyre,
          By horned Pan who plays the vocal reed pipe,
          And Apollo the harper, too, takes joy in me.[74]

Do Apollo, the Muses, and Pan particularly love monotonous music? Perhaps we have here no more than a frog's-eye view of aesthetics, but the song does not, at least, suffer from the indiscriminate and slatternly multiformity of Euripides.

Moreover, these frogs are associated with the spring festival of Dionysus in Limnae, the Anthesteria, not with strange deities like Ether or the axle of the tongue. They are genuine Athenian frogs, and above all, they teach Dionysus to row, whereas the sailors brought up on Euripides are good only at talking back to their officers.[75] The rhythm of the frogs is the rhythm of the victorious Athenian fleets, and Dionysus learns it despite himself, to the sorrow of his blistered hands and backside.[76] He begs them to stop, but the frogs croak on and on, urging each other to sing, as the Mystae also do, until the god takes up the song himself and finally shouts them down. The episode is one of Aristophanes' most graceful and droll inspirations, and though it may seem at first to have little connection with the rest of the play, it is in fact closely bound to it by the theme of music, true and false, and it forms a legitimate part of the quest for the "generative" poet and the sound citizen. With their animal grumpings and unchanging refrain, they balance grotesquely the sublime invocations of the immortal Mystae, and the verb which they use of their own singing ($\iota\alpha\chi\acute{\epsilon}\omega$) is that which was used to describe the religious shouting of the initiates in procession, and personified and worshiped as the god Iacchus.[77]

Interspersed with the imagery of music, run occasional images of light and darkness, corresponding vaguely to salvation and damnation. The Hell of Mud, described by Heracles, where sinners (including admirers of Morsimus) wallow, and the "darkness and filth" reported by Xanthias are probably not derived specifically from anything in Eleusinian ritual, though they may be Orphic.[78] The light, however, is certainly Eleusinian, for it is at first simply the light of the torch procession, described in advance by Heracles and presented on stage in the parodos.[79] Iacchus is invoked as the "dawn star of the nightly initiation," holding a torch, and the whole meadow gleams with the flare.[80] At the end of the parodos the light of the actual torches begins to blend into the supernal joyous light of that other sun which shines "only on the initiates who have kept their lives holy." [81] The lines are reminiscent of Pindar's descriptions of the afterlife of the blest, and presumably represent the kind of bright future promised by the Mysteries to the initiates. [82]

The Eleusinian torch is the lamp of redemption, and it has cultural implications within the play, as well as personal, eschatological ones. Aeschylus, as we have observed, is closely associated with the cluster of Eleusinian images and themes throughout. He is even addressed by the same epithet as Iacchus and Kore. [83] As he finishes his first denunciation of Euripides, describing the social corruption resulting from the unhappy poet's work, he adds:

> Now, all through a lack of manly training,
> There is no one left who can lift a torch. [84]

The image is there, though this torch may be not an Eleusinian one, specifically; Dionysus, agreeing, takes it as a Panathenaic one:

> By Zeus, there isn't! I almost withered
> With laughing, at the Panathenaea,
> When some slow fellow ran, all bent over,
> Pale-skinned and fat, lagging behind,
> And fussing along; and the potters that stood
> At the gates all whacked him,
> Belly and buttock and flank and rib,
> Till what with the flats of their palms, well smacked,
>   With a bit of a fart,
> He blew out his lamp and escaped. [85]

Panathenaic or Eleusinian, the torch is a property of a city festival, a token of its cultural integrity, and Euripides' man blows it out. Aeschylus, however, as he returns "to the light" to save the city, is escorted by the sacred lamps of the Mystae to music of his own composing. [86] The true light and the true music join at the end in the vision of salvation.

Before attempting to penetrate the meaning of that vision, and the selection of Aeschylus as its minister, it may be well to re-emphasize the symbolic nature of the two poets as presented. The agon is often taken for essentially serious literary criticism, but if the foregoing analysis of the imagery is in any sense correct, it is clear that the whole literary level is ancillary to a larger design, in which the survival of Athens forms the core. Poets are, as a rule, representative of their times, and it was logical to let Aeschylus speak for the glorious Athenian past, and Euripides for the contemporary decay. To cast the conflict in the form of a literary debate was a scheme which offered infinite opportunity for parody and caricature. The Euripides here presented, however, is much the same straw figure that appeared in the *Acharnians* and *Thesmophoriazusae*, and the Aeschylus who thunders about in images of storms and wild beasts is only his antitype, carefully contrived to knock him down.[87] Caricature, to be effective, must include some truth, and doubtless there is some truth in these, but it can hardly be called serious literary criticism to let these two inventions sneer at each other for seven hundred lines, or to equate the art of Aeschylus with obscurity and bombast, and that of Euripides with the harlot Cyrene. It is sometimes said, also, that Aristophanes is quite impartial in his distribution of the blows exchanged by the two tragedians, but this is not really true; Euripides lands a few adroit punches, but the cards are stacked in Aeschylus' favor from the very first, when Dionysus addresses him as "Most-honored Aeschylus," the epithet of Iacchus, and says in the next line, "wicked [*poneros*] Euripides."[88] The agon is constructed in five parts, devoted respectively to the criticism of plots and purpose, prologues, lyrics, poetic "weight," and practical advice. In all five Aeschylus is the second speaker, with the advantage of the climactic last word. No real concern is felt for the justice of either's claims: it is not true that Aeschylus always wrote about wars and Euripides always wrote about sex; Aeschylus' choruses are seldom really obscure, and Euripides' seldom, if ever, trivial; and one scholar, at least, has shown that the trick of "ruining prologues with one small oil flask" can be used, not only on Aeschylus, but even on the immaculate style of Sophocles himself.[89] Parody exists for fun's sake, and there is plenty of fun here.

But if serious literary criticism is lacking, especially in regard to the actual details discussed, that does not mean that there is no serious level in the agon. It is, literally, a life-and-death struggle, dramatized in terms of literature. Whatever be the case for the poet as pedagogue, Aristophanes has, by association, made his two poets into composite symbols, each of a condition or state of affairs in the Athenian commonwealth, one spelling life and the other death. We have seen, in the first part of the agon, how Aeschylus' grand and martial themes bred a generation of soldiers with the virile virtues of Patrocluses and Teucers, while the domestic intrigues of Euripides were responsible for the bureaucrats and Theramenes. The next section, on prologues, has the fewest symbolic overtones, if any. But by the end of the battle of the lyrics Euripides has been neatly packaged up with Cyrene, and associated with infinite variability and lack of authenticity. With the weighing of lines the colors really darken as the grim reality of death sweeps away *Peitho*, and the delusiveness of speech. At this point the fact that Dionysus says that he is unable to decide between the two does not mean that Aristophanes cannot; it is simply that the tension must be maintained through the last part of the agon, the contest in practical advice, where all the cards are finally laid on the table, and the full tragedy of the situation is delicately but firmly made clear. Aeschylus is, of course, chosen; but what does that mean?

To a poet of the Old Comedy all things were possible, and we are therefore perhaps at liberty to think that Aristophanes, in resurrecting Aeschylus, is simply bringing back the good old days with as gay a disregard for the facts of life as when Dicaeopolis made his private treaty with Sparta. But the atmosphere of the *Frogs* is against this view; a real fear for the city is felt throughout, implicit in the various references, at once proud and anxious, to the recent sea fight off Arginusae; [90] explicit in such remarks as the city lying "in the arms of the waves," or Dionysus' statement that he came to Hades "in order that the city might be saved and present her choruses." [91] Moreover, as said earlier the shape of the plot follows a tragic rather than a comic scheme, in that Dionysus does not seek to identify himself with the boundless, but to extract the truth from it, while the prime comic vehicle, speech, is clearly rejected in the person of Euripides. These facts, together with the air of gravity imposed by the ever present Eleusinian theme and a chorus of not very comic Mystae, prompt the suspicion that the choice of Aeschylus and his return to life are not so brightly cheerful as they might seem.

Dionysus puts the problem clearly in the line just quoted; he then asks two questions, one very specific, the second general. A degree of ambiguity hovers over the answers of the two poets, and one could make the case that from the practical point of view Euripides' replies are at least as helpful as those of Aeschylus. Asked for his opinion of Alcibiades, Euripides states in three crisp, epigrammatic lines the perfectly clear opinion that Alcibiades is a self-interested traitor.[92] His advice for the ultimate safety of the city comes clad in a heavy robe of nonsense, but it could be interpreted as embracing a sane idea, indeed much the same idea as is suggested in the parabasis, that salvation lies in placing the city in the hands of the better citizens. At least this is what he says when, at Dionysus' request, he stops talking about "winging Cleocritus with Cinesias," and devising sharp sophistic figures of speech, and states clearly:

> If we distrust the citizens whom now
> We trust, and those whom we do not employ
> Employ again, perhaps we might be saved.
> For if in our present ways we fare ill, why
> Might not salvation lie in the reverse?[93]

In summary, then, Euripides recommends expelling Alcibiades (which had already been done), and turning the government over to the better citizens, whoever they may have been (which the chorus also recommends); he seems to be quite on the side of the angels. One might well expect him to win on these grounds. Instead, partly perhaps just because he has answered in apparently practical terms, and therefore has answered for the world of the present, Dionysus hails him as Palamedes, the type of clever speaker, and turns to Aeschylus.

The answers of Aeschylus are very different. Whether or not Euripides' counsels may be considered feasible, his rival's seem at a considerable remove from practicality. About Alcibiades he says:

> Best if the city rear no lion's whelp,
> But if it rear one, it must serve his ways.[94]

Are we to conclude that Aeschylus favored the recall of Alcibiades? Since the real Aeschylus could never have had any thoughts at all about Alcibiades, Aristophanes is quite free to make his character say what he pleases. Yet it is unlikely that he would put into the mouth of the archpoet of Athenian democracy a statement in favor of "serving the ways" of this flagrant would-be tyrant, while attributing the opposite view to the somewhat antidemocratic Euripides. Aristophanes has something else in mind, something which could hardly be stated outright. There can be little doubt that the image of the lion's whelp, as some have observed, comes from the famous chorus of the *Agamemnon*:

> Once in his home a man raised up
> A lion's whelp, at life's beginning
> Udderless nurseling, gentle and mild
> To the children, a sport for elders . . .
> In time he showed his nature, sprung
> From his forebears; paying his fosterers thanks,
> Unbidden he makes his feast
> In reckless sheep slaughter.[95]

This lion cub is usually taken to stand for Helen, who came at first as a delight to the Trojans, and then caused their destruction; more likely it is Paris, whom the oracle bade Hecuba not to rear when he was born.[96] In either case, however, the meaning is the same: destruction wrought from within. The Trojans "served the ways" of the lion cub with well-known results, and Aeschylus is darkly indicating that the city has nursed its own doom. Whether Aristophanes actually thought Alcibiades responsible is immaterial; the analogy between him and Paris provided a way to put this indirect prophecy into the mouth of Aeschylus.

In response to the question of how to secure the city's safety, Aeschylus is at first unwilling to say anything until he gets back to earth. Dionysus, however, presses him, using a formula of prayer to the dead, and is answered with these words:

> When they shall think the enemy's land their own,
> And their own land the enemy's, ships their resource,
> And their resources mere resourcelessness.[97]

To complete the sentence, we must understand that the Athenians will be saved only when they do these things; but what is Aeschylus saying? His first stipulation is nothing more than a restatement of the policy of Pericles, now dead for twenty-five years, that the Athenians should allow the enemy their will of Attica, while they themselves harry the Peloponnesian coasts.[98] Whatever the merits of this policy in 431, in 405 it was somewhat outmoded, to say the least. The sole surviving fleet could not be spared to harry the Peloponnesus, since it was needed to keep the Pontic grain route open against the Spartan-Persian coalition; as for letting the Spartans have their will of Attica, they had had it with little or no question since the fortification of Decelea in 413. If Aeschylus is proposing to resurrect Periclean policy, he must first resurrect Periclean Athens. As for the statement about the ships as resource, it is a clear reference to the Battle of Salamis, when the Athenians, led by Themistocles, literally abandoned all their resources except their ships. Once more, this policy, so salutary in 480, could not strike anyone as very practical in 405; from the literal point of view, Euripides' advice is much better.

But Aristophanes is not dealing with literal facts and policies, for all the apparent immediate concern with politics in this play. The quest was for the truth about Athens, her culture and her corporate selfhood, and it is perhaps no wonder that Aeschylus hesitates to speak. When he invokes the two great leaders of the imperial democracy, both long since in their graves, and says that only by their counsels will Athens be saved, he has told the truth, and a very sad truth. The great days are over; the city will not be saved; it must serve the ways of the lion's whelp.[99] Dionysus has come for the truth, and now he has it. His reply is a problem: "Yes," he says, "but only the judge will swallow that." It is impossible to take this line, as is usually done, as a reference to the embezzlement of public revenue by the judiciary; [100] by the judge he must mean himself, and by "swallow" he must mean "believe." [101] Aeschylus has spoken the truth, but no one will believe it except Dionysus, the god who has taken upon himself the responsible journey into Hades; for truth is known only when it is experienced.

So the resurrection of Aeschylus is really a paradox. Like the *Frogs* as a whole, it is far less cheerful than it seems. Though it follows externally the comic design in achieving the impossible, the lack of revelry, the gravity of the issue, and the sorrowful tone betray the underlying lament. Aeschylus departs for the upper world to the solemn roll of dactylic hexameters, the rhythm of heroic and oracular poetry; the effect is funereal.[102] The familiar comic theme of rejuvenation, though not totally absent, has been supplanted for the most part by the theme of resurrection; but the indispensable condition for resurrection is death. Whatever the Mysteries promised by way of immortality, it does not seem that they envisioned so simple a return from the grave as this of Aeschylus. To resurrect the poet in this sense, and in the terms used, comes close to confessing that he is gone forever.

And yet, though that threnodic tone is distinctly audible, it is not the whole truth, for the paradox goes further. What seems to be a settled dialectic of true and false, steadfast and variable, "generative" and sterile, is all seen through the veil of an inclusive ambiguity, created by a number of passages which invert, or even break down, the distinction between life and death. The third equivocation which Dionysus turns back upon its author at the end is the line: "Who knows if life be death or death be life?" [103] Earlier in the play Aeschylus had included this famous remark in the list of Euripides' sins, presumably as a piece of philosophic twaddle; but it nonetheless summarizes one of the most poignant motifs of the play. The whole quest is paradoxical — to journey into death to find a life-giving poet, and to find the vivifying cultural principle in a voice which had been silent for fifty years. The scene with the corpse at the beginning sets the tone. He wants two drachmas to carry the luggage to Hades. Dionysus offers nine obols, and the corpse replies: "I'll get out of my grave first." [104] This scene might pass for a bit of macabre but merry nonsense, save that it agrees with so much else. The lower world and the upper, specifically Athens, are deliberately confused: the light that shines on the Mystae is like the light that shines in the upper world; [105] Theseus is responsible for the two-obol payment in Hell; [106] the better element in the infernal population is as scarce as it is in Athens; [107] most pointedly, the chorus refers to the living as "the upper dead." [108] Here as elsewhere, Aristophanes seems to feel and exploit the force of the corrosive and paradoxical questioning that characterized the new intellectualism; distinctions once clear are no longer clear, and reality totters. When Dionysus quotes Euripides' line, he adds another, of almost nihilistic mockery, which seems to imply, "Who knows if anything be anything?" He might be just making fun of Euripides, but in fact, how does one know? The age of philosophy had arrived.

> For we alone possess the sun
> And joyous light,

sing the Mystae.[109] Amid all the shifting sands, a rallying point is perhaps to be found in the Eleusinian theme. The Mysteries seem to bridge the gap between the two worlds, so that the distinction, if there is any, no longer matters. But within the play, the Eleusinian theme has gained, as we have seen, the added significance of public and cultural, as well as personal, redemption. In this respect, the Mysteries connect with the view of tragedy (and comedy) characteristic of the play: the city must be safe *and stage choruses*. Poetry, too, has her mysteries, and the *orgia* of the Muses, the Bacchic rites

of "bull-eating Cratinus," and the *teletai* of Dionysus are all celebrated by the chorus as holy rituals, somehow analogous to the
Mysteries of Demeter herself. Perhaps it is simply that poetry, in
particular the dramatic poetry of Athens, is the public symptom of
what the Mysteries revealed in secret, the inviolable life of the spirit.
In any case, on true poetry the sun does not cease to shine, as
Aeschylus said:

> Aesch.: I didn't want to stage a contest here.
> The fight between us isn't fair.
> Dion.: Why not?
> Aesch.: Because my poetry did not die with me,
> His did; he has it handy to declaim.[110]

With nineteen plays extant against Aeschylus' seven, the ghost of
Euripides may now console himself a little for this unkind cut; but
in 405 he had to play the role assigned him. In Aeschylus Aristophanes found a figure through whom he could say, "Athens is
falling; her meaning is immortal."

·VIII·

DISCOURSE OF FANTASY

ALTHOUGH the art of Aristophanes is generally recognized as a compound of the fantastic and the realistic, interpreters have on the whole based their views on the realistic and satiric element, and dismissed, or better subsumed, the fantastic aspect as simply the mode appropriate to comedy, the vehicle by which the satirical message is conveyed. By this approach the poet's point becomes an essentially critical one, with reformative overtones, and the plays turn into explicit commentaries on the daily social and political life of Athens. Such commentary is, of course, present, but if the whole play exists to serve this part, then poetry is being put to a practical use from which its nature recoils. Indeed, the degree of recoil is measured by the difficulty, as we have seen, of discovering any consistency of practical intention in any play among the true Old Comedies of Aristophanes. Poetry, one feels, never exists for such a purpose, even when it claims to. It was the convention of Roman satire to avow a reformative end, but the result of all Juvenal's *saeva indignatio* is a picture of the Roman underworld which exists for its own lurid sake, an enticingly evil image which the true reformer could have better done without. Bertolt Brecht has often asserted the didacticism of his plays, and even called them parables; yet his poetic force and his use of legends and paradigmatic characters have given these plays a relevance beyond the evils which they criticize. It is the business of a poet, says Aristotle, to make myths, and it is the mytho-

259

poeic factor in Aristophanes which is the controlling one.[1] The comic fantasy, which becomes a myth of its own times, is at once the source and the final end of Aristophanean art, and by its powerful impulse all the satire, all the sharp realistic images, all the wit and slapstick, are carried along as the spokes of a wheel are carried by the rotation of the rim. To interpret thus is not to deprive Aristophanes of his relevance or "seriousness" as an artist, but to insist that his relevance is of the larger, rather than the smaller, variety.

Fantasy may be regarded as a kind of harmless, and perhaps aimless, free-wheeling of the mind, by which it entertains an assortment of mirages, signifying nothing save perhaps the vague desires of a pipe dream. Viewed so, fantasy is as amorphous and insubstantial as smoke, and where there is smoke of this kind, one suspects, there may not be very much fire. But nothing so vapid is the case with Aristophanes. An Aristophanean fantasy is a structure, an elaborate and powerful one; as such, it evokes response from the mind's most basic function, which is to transform the chaotic spate of sense experience into an order of intelligible classes. To say that the classes are intelligible only because they are created by the mind for that purpose is, of course, simple nominalism; but after what has been seen of the power of words to affect reality in the *Birds*, and elsewhere, one may be confident that nominalism and Old Comedy have their points in common. When things become what they are called, rather than being called what they are, one has — though the *Frogs* may be something of an exception — the Aristophanean view; the true nominalist also believes that the thingness of a thing is in its name, not in its essence. Hence the demiurgic property of the Aristophanean pun: the *polos* literally becomes a *polis*; *nomos*, "law," and *nomos*, "melody," merge into each other, to form a symbol of the new dispensation of Nephelococcygia. The mind at first forms classes and gives them names; the names then further aid and abet the process through their own propensity for connotation, combination, and ambiguity. By this process, which might be called "treading on air," the intelligible world is extended to astonishing imaginative heights which could never be meaningful were it not for the fact that the verbal, poetic extension of reality is parallel to, and part of, the mind's formation of reality for itself. We may leave aside the extreme relativistic possibility that every mind forms only its own reality, which is therefore incommunicable — though this may have been the view of Gorgias — and assume that poetic structures are, by whatever way, communicative.

A fantasy, then, is a structure, an imaginatively erected reality akin in a way to the mind's erection of intelligible order. The medium is not always so highly verbal as it is in the *Birds*, though words always are important. There are numerous kinds of fantasy, and Aristophanes, in the extant plays at least, indulges in very little repetition. Each of the three "peace" plays has its distinctive fantasy: in the *Acharnians*, of an individual peace treaty in the form of a sack of wine, which is efficacious though the rest of the world is at war; in the *Peace*, of a flight to Olympus to recover the lost goddess; in the *Lysistrata*, of a *coup d'état* more fanciful in the fifth century B.C. than in the days of lady senators. But whatever the madness may be, a city in the sky or the trial of a dog, it is regularly the product of what is called, in Existential terms, a "boundary situation," where an individual's engagement in an action has brought him to the point where he must decide between a yea or a nay of grave import. Hitherto, some evasion of consequences or implications may have been possible; now there is only the absolute choice whereby one is to decide whether or not he is the man his actions have shown him to be. If he chooses yea, he accepts his responsibility, or "guilt," as it is sometimes called; if nay, he denies his responsibility and therewith his authenticity as a person.

In the opening chapter it was stated that the structure of this moral crux was the same for both tragedy and comedy; and indeed, the purest example is Oedipus, who, confronted by the choice of pursuing his quest or renouncing it, as Jocasta begs him to, unhesitatingly chooses yea, and becomes his true self. In tragedy the choice is ineluctable, though it is not always presented with such clarity as in *Oedipus*; there is never a third alternative. But herein comedy differs, and its difference responds to the helpless wish of the spirit writhing before an ineluctable choice; comedy invents a third alternative, and rides happily off on it. It is the release from ineluctable choice which gives Aristophanean comedy its initial free impulse, its heroic altitude, and its ability, noted earlier, to dissociate from moral or any other consistency. As Robert Frost once wrote, "Me for the hills where I don't have to choose." The comic alternative also involves the affirmation of *poneria*, the device, shift, or gimmick that will win, transform the world, and cure it of its intractability. Above all, it is the evasion of limit, and as such, it necessitates the creation of a new reality.

These statements are true, in varying degrees, of all the plays, though certainly not all comic alternatives are worked out in the same way; neither are all equally successful, for much depends on whether the protagonist is a real hero of *poneria*, like Peithetaerus, or a bungler, like Euripides in the *Thesmophoriazusae*. Sometimes, even, as in the *Clouds* and *Wasps*, we have a success balanced by a failure. The terms of these boundary situations vary considerably, some being more real than others. The debts of Strepsiades, the threat to Euripides' life, and Philocleon's love of jury duty cannot be regarded in quite the same light as the issue of the war, or the real "to be or not to be" question which confronted Athens in 405. But the content does not matter greatly; what matters is that the hero comes to the point where he feels called upon to act or be lost in the face of what seems like a hopeless situation. And act he does. The individual's rejection of society, such as is implied in the *Birds*, could be dramatized tragically into a play like the *Philoctetes*; or one could imagine Dicaeopolis' rejection of war developed tragically into a conscientious-objector play. In the tragic view these dilemmas could not be solved. Comedy goes between the horns.

Put so, it sounds again as if comedy were mere escapism. Yet like all poetry comedy reframes experience and orders reality as it sees it. In a way the sense of nothingness and absurdity so prevalent in the *Birds* is a major premise in all the plays. It becomes the function of poetry, therefore, to impose upon absurdity an order accommodated to the situation's need, and the process of doing so becomes the discourse of the fantasy. One may see the basic figure of this discourse as a kind of syllogism, or pseudosyllogism, of which the two premises state the boundary situation, and the conclusion, the comic alternative. Thus in the *Acharnians* we have: (a) disgust with war, (b) inability to stop the war; conclusion, make a private peace. In what we call real life this is impossible, but we are invited not to be bigoted about reality. In the *Birds* the syllogism would run: (a) Athens is bad; (b) no place is better; conclusion, build No-place and live there. Such licensed toying with reality is most clearly marked in the *Birds*, as the negative phrase "no place" is capitalized into the positive and satisfying "No-place," whose nothingness is constantly echoed in the contradictions of word play and wind egg. Again, in the *Wasps*: (a) constant litigation ruins home life; (b) you cannot keep an Athenian out of a courtroom; conclusion, bring the courtroom home. Here, the results are rather different from what is expected, for a variety of reasons, but chiefly because, as pointed out earlier, the fantasy is not the original creation of the hero, Philocleon, but of his son. The great scheme of salvation, therefore, is not in this play simply activated and brought to success by the hero; rather it is foisted upon him, up to the point where, under its influence, he bursts out of all limits in the drunken last scene, and, so to speak, runs away with the ball. The first perversion of reality has yielded to a second one, this time Philocleon's own.

As observed in earlier chapters, the fantasies which involve an unexpected turn carry a more ironical meaning than those in which the hero triumphs in unilinear course. These plots more or less invert the heroic idea, and show the hero either totally reduced, as in the *Thesmophoriazusae*; repentant and distracted, as in the *Clouds*; or asserting himself at best in a fugitive and momentary victory, as in the *Wasps*. The *Frogs* is a special case, of course; the heroic aspect, centered in Dionysus, follows the classical pattern of the death journey, but the return of Aeschylus reverses the original tenor of the quest and turns the whole into a funeral oration. In these plays the mingling of fantasy and realism is a different one; in varying degrees the hard facts crumble the fantastic effort. And yet even here, it is fantasy which gives the play its character, the hard facts serving, despite themselves, to limn the brilliance of the imaginative flight; the language is still the language of heroic absurdity.

The other comedies follow a more direct course, with the hero plunging between the dilemma's horns straight on toward the fabrication of a new reality. And it *is* a new reality, because the conclusion of the pseudosyllogism adds another dimension to the usual ones of experience. One may logically divide all things that exist into the class A and the class Not-A, and truthfully assert that there is nothing outside these two classes. But with equal logic, though of a different kind, one may posit a certain class which is neither A nor Not-A, but something else, and this must exist in another dimension. If asked what dimension, one may only answer, the dimension of realizable metaphor, which is, in simple fact, the dimension in which all true drama takes place. What is on the stage before us is never a mirror of life, but a metaphor of life, realized through the media of impersonation, dialogue, scene, or whatever. It is the metaphor which constitutes the reality of the play; it is metaphor which disturbs the sense of ordinary reality and erects a new one. This function of metaphor may, of course, be exploited as a singularly self-conscious form of theatricalism, as it was by Pirandello. But all drama, tragic or comic, depends essentially on representing the world under an altered guise, in relation to which the limits of actual experience may be felt in a variety of ways, and sometimes scarcely at all. Aristophanic comedy plays a particularly bold and free hand, realizing metaphors which are so extreme as to be surrealistic. To say, "This man soars above us," is to use a metaphor. To dramatize men turning birds is to realize a metaphor of supremacy by means of the "other-dimensional" logic of fantasy. To say, "Athenian poetry will never die," is simple metaphor; to bring back Aeschylus from the dead is to dramatize the full poignancy of a wishful, retrospective dream.

Now to call this kind of thing surrealistic may seem to be presuming on terms, or even juggling them inexcusably. But the juggling and presumption, if such they be, may prove suggestive if one compares certain practices of the surrealists with what happens in Aristophanes, bearing in mind that the extralogical dimension of fantasy is the mainspring of Aristophanes' poetic power. Such fantasies look, quite of themselves, to something of deep human relevance, and are neither irresponsible childishness, nor mere sugar designed to coat and make palatable an allegoric or satiric pill.

Giuseppe Verdi once wrote, "It may be a good thing to imitate reality; it is better to invent it." By this remark he surely meant to call attention to the integrity of a dramatic work of art as determined by its own inner rules, apart from the content, historical or whatever, which it uses. The reality of any work of art lies in its form, in the artist's ability to discern and fulfill the emotional logic proposed by his original conception. Hence all art commits distortion, even when it least seems to. The apparently flawless body of the Velázquez Venus is attributable to the fact that she is conceived in terms of her elongated reclining posture. If she got up and tried to walk, we would discover that the disparity in the size of her hips had made her quite lame. It is the invented reality which works. Perhaps for this reason, that most inventive, though controversial painter, Dali, has long since eschewed the term surrealism, and called his work simply realism.[2] One may at first wonder by what right he does so, in view of his double heads, his deserts adorned with limp watches, and his marsupial centaurs with gaping, open bellies. Is it realistic to support eyelids on crutches, to protract the human head into a long lump of dough, to raise the epidermis of a grand piano, or to make three young women imitate the gestures of a schooner? The answer is obviously yes, if we are willing to create our own reality. Few of us have peered under the epidermis of a grand piano, or observed three women imitating the gestures of a schooner; above all, when we need to know what time it is, we rejoice that our watches do not go suddenly limp. But in the painting called "The Persistence of Memory" the three limp watches against the background of an utterly glassy and luminous sea add no little to the magic, as suggestive symbols of the stoppage of time in the moment of ineradicable memory.[3] And the "Family of Marsupial Centaurs" is a tender and exalted bacchanal of domesticity and fecundity, austerely structured in four triangles with a common apex. These, together with others far too numerous to mention, are inventions, inventions which indicate, if they do not actually embody, a different kind of reality, a reality born of imagination and brought to intelligible form through inner, other-dimensional logic. For the most part, they are quite serious extensions of experience, seldom satiric, and very often based on dream states and free association, which are among the deepest, and most inscrutable, sources of the poetic impulse.

Above all, perhaps, they illustrate the mind's subconscious transforming power. In one haunting work called "Nostalgic Echo" the outline of a keyhole in a wooden chest becomes successively, as it recedes through the planes of the picture, a girl skipping rope, a bell ringing in a tower, and a dim figure in the far background. Though there is nothing humorous about this painting, it differs formally very little from the successive changes of the imagery of coals or feathers in the *Acharnians*, or from Peithetaerus' smooth and logical transitions from a fugitive, to a bird, to a god. These developments are not particularly surrealistic; but other formally comparable ones distinctly are. For instance, in the treatment of scene: a Dalinian landscape is often a most ambiguous affair, as witness the "Impression of Africa," where faces fade in and out of nowhere, and distinctions of sea, sky, and earth are by no means clear. With this we might compare the middle scene of the *Peace*: Trygaeus has flown to heaven to find Peace; he finds, however, that she is buried in a deep pit, apparently in the ground. A chorus of farmers from all the cities in Greece now help to pull her out. We are bound to ask, where are we? If we are still up in heaven, whence the earthy pit and whence the farmers, who did not accompany Trygaeus on his flight; if we are now back on earth, why does Trygaeus have to descend to earth again later, this time, naturally enough, walking through the air? It will not make sense except by its own logic, which in this case is governed by the regular nonsensical Aristophanean associations with "up in the air" imagery.[4] The scene is a special landscape in the absolute elsewhere, especially designed to accommodate the achievement of Trygaeus, and it works perfectly.

Now it might be claimed that some, at least, of the inventions of Dali are monstrosities; indeed, one painting is entitled "The Invention of the Monsters." But these monstrosities, though sometimes focusing some of the darker states of the psyche, are no more monstrous than the hair-raising and side-splitting image of Cleon in the *Wasps*, the Megarian girls transformed into pigs, the Socrates of the *Clouds*, or Dicaeopolis in the rags of Telephus with his head on a chopping block explaining that the Peloponnesian War was caused by the abduction of a couple of loose ladies. Monstrosity is precisely the point: monstrosity and lyric have in common a self-enclosed structure, whereby both communicate as organism and entity, rather than through discourse and comment; and both have much in common with the grotesque, not only in its usual usage, but also in the specifically classical sense adopted above.

In his brilliant essay on the source of laughter Baudelaire distinguished between the significantly comic and the absolutely comic. The significantly comic is the mode of satire and caricature, parody and wit, and all forms of humor which arise from direct relevance to practical experience. They make fun of something, or signify that something is laughable. In contrast, the absolutely comic is an invention, a creation, which bears no direct relevance to anything else, does not comment on anything, but merely is. The classical Aristophanic grotesque, such as Trygaeus on the dung beetle, Peithetaerus with wings, or the demiurgic Sausage Seller, are forms of the absolutely comic, and so are inventions such as the town of Katagela. Where the significantly comic is reductive, and its laughter is that of deprecation, the absolutely comic is creative, and its laughter is that of joy. It provides the inclusive vision which dwarfs all else to its own greater glory.

Baudelaire's distinction is similar to that of Aristotle between lampoon and true comedy, but he has carried it further, and his insight is of great importance in understanding Aristophanes. For though Aristophanes abounds in the significantly comic, it is his creations of the absolutely comic which give his art its main impetus and distinction. The hybrid grotesquerie of his heroes, and of numerous other images, is the stuff of the absolutely comic, and it is, perhaps, this aspect of his genius which prompted the ancient critics to find such grace, *charis*, in his work. The bird-men, the market place of Dicaeopolis, the block and tackle that hauls up Peace, all the basic fantasies in fact, are expressions of joy, whatever else they may be, things comic in themselves to which the other elements in the plays are subordinated. Even the most directly satiric elements, like the ubiquitous Cleonymus, though significantly comic to begin with, tend in the direction of the absolute and its chief touchstone, the grotesque; after many transformations Cleonymus becomes a wonderful mythic tree of fat and fraud, deciduously shedding its shields in the winter months.

Such poetry is in the mode of nonsense, and the structure of nonsense does not point out the absurdity of something; it presents an image of absurdity itself. In Dali's phrase, it systematizes confusion, and discredits the world of reality. Its rules are its own, and though its content comes, as it must, from our everyday experience, the poem follows its own structural rules and achieves a new reality as the monstrous, lyrical, absolutely comic. The whole process is identical with Huizinga's view of play, as a magic circle within which a different reality exists by virtue of strict adherence to the given rules.[5] Within the circle seriously upheld assumptions, like the names which children give themselves in a game or the impersonations in a ritual, transform experience and enact a different, but more fully knowable world. The assumptions may be nonsense, but they create order. For nonsense is a kind of specially designed order. Thus, one may suggest a scale of comic techniques, all basic to Aristophanes: satire, wit, humor, nonsense. Satire denounces the world, wit penetrates it, humor accepts it, but nonsense transforms it. And it is the transforming function which distinguishes an art from a skill.

Nonsense is, therefore, the language of the absolutely comic, of monstrosity, and of the grotesque. The structural comparison made earlier between monstrosity and lyric suggests that nonsense might also be the language of lyric as well. It appears that what we call lyric differs from grotesquerie essentially only in possessing a content which we do not find laughable. Yet even that distinction can break down on occasion, in the poetry of Gertrude Stein, for example, and certainly in Aristophanes — witness, again, the Cleonymus tree, which has the charm of a tree for all its Cleonymosity, or the song of the frogs:

> Sing we on, if ever on sunny
> Days we hopped through the galingale
> And river weed, with melodious ploppings,
> Happy in song, or fleeing the rain,
> Sang our chorus, wet and wavering,
> Down in the depths, with bubbles a-popping,
> *Brekekekex, koax, koax.*[6]

Such delicate doggerel does not invite classification; it can be fairly called both lyrical and grotesque, and grotesque in strictest sense, if it be remembered that these are frogs who have died and are immortal, "swan-frogs" sacred to Apollo, the Muses, and Dionysus, and, as seen in the last chapter, somehow symbolic of Athenian salvation. For an inquiry into the nature of comic poetry, such a passage has the importance of a paradigm. The fullness of Aristophanes' genius seems concentrated in it.

But to return to the matter of fantasy and transformation: what the fantasy transforms is necessarily the familiar, for no mythical monster, however farfetched, can be made except by imaginative recombination of known elements. This fact leads to a constant interplay of juxtaposed incongruities as the fantasy proceeds, picking up well-known bits of everyday experience and sweeping them into the general vortex; as each enters, one feels the jar of realism, as if one had suddenly run into a post. Sometimes these firm realities are completely transformed, like the Laurian owls in the *Birds*, where the distinction between a live owl and a silver coin is felicitously demolished by a metaphor.[7] At other times the realistic elements are left raw, so to speak, to produce a bumpiness in the texture, comic by virtue of incongruity, no doubt, but also poetic by virtue of juxtaposing two kinds of reality indispensable to the third reality, the poetic whole. Of this kind are the coarse and earthy interruptions of Euelpides as Peithetaerus develops his plan, or his notice of the fact that the nightingale's attractions are not exclusively musical. Here also belong the stolid replies of the Scythian policeman as Euripides tries to persuade him that Mnesilochus is really Andromeda; here belong the informers, oracle mongers, and other impostors who enter the heroic fantasy direct from the streets of Athens; here belong the bedbugs which nearly devour Strepsiades, together with certain unmentionable evidences of fear, outbursts of irrelevant abuse, Philocleon's chick-peas and chamber pot, and the blister which develops on Dionysus' posterior as he rows to the lilting rhythm of the frogs. Herein lies much of the delight, and perhaps one reason why the obscenities of Aristophanes, however broad, are so seldom offensive: they are an integral part of the "play with reality," the enormous, limitless game which the comic hero is playing. Once in a while, as with the old men in court in the *Acharnians*, these realisms strike a grim note, but for the most part their effect is pure hilarity, as when, in singing the joys of spring, the poet includes, along with the delight of swallows' song, the fact that two unlucky tragic poets have had their plays rejected, and invites the divine Muse to spit upon them generously, and come celebrate with him.[8]

Such juxtapositions, serious or comic, have a kind of analogue in the juxtapositions of fanciful and photographic in some of Dali's works. One painting is entitled, "Portrait of the Back of My Wife Contemplating Architectural Form." In the foreground Mrs. Dali sits, nude, and painted with the most direct representationalism; in the distance the outline of her form has become a fantastic palace of finely articulated arches, domes, and staircases. Beside her an uprooted dandelion puff comments on the transitoriness of all flesh, while a classic marble head follows her gaze toward the formal, architectural apotheosis of loving fancy. In another, rather haunting work attractively entitled "The Weaning of Furniture Nutrition," some perfectly recognizable boats are drawn up on a beach beside a woman with a large window in her back and some very oddly behaved pieces of furniture becoming other things. These are serious, even rather sombre works. But Dali can also be wonderfully humorous; one example is "Average Atmospherocephalic Bureaucrat in the Act of Milking a Cranial Harp." The title betrays the satire. The bureaucrat's head is produced in all directions in a cloudy, amorphous mass, from which a harplike shape depends with udderlike strings more liable to milking than to music. Below, the bureaucrat's left leg appears, almost photographically painted, and adorned by a dull garter upholding an unimaginative man's sock. Though Aristophanes' Demos is a more engaging figure, one feels that he has similar atmospherocephalic qualities, and is equally gartered to the earth. But in point of pure method, Peithetaerus' wings and the "wings" of the double Corcyrean whip are a fully comparable confrontation of the imaginative with the impact of familiarity.

One further example from Dali exhibits a truly Aristophanean delicacy and absurdity. This is the portrait of Harpo Marx. Harpo is represented quite in his own person, seated at his harp in a desert, and around him, listening, stand three giraffes, their necks wildly aflame. It is impossible not to feel the appropriateness of these fiery giraffes, more of whom are marching away on the horizon.[9] It is less easy to analyze them, but the effect of mingled tenderness and hilarity, of real and more than real, is entirely in the spirit of Aristophanes, and approaches some of his lyrical and grotesque visions of human creatures framed and magnified by subhuman and superhuman attributes. The transformation is before us, along with the thing transformed, and reality shimmers off into a new structure.

Another transforming mode is the double image. Even a common pun is a double image, and so in a way is parody. Aristophanes builds so much on puns and parodies that it would be impossible, not to say unnecessary, to analyze these aspects of the comic art; they have been extensively studied since antiquity, when the scholiasts devoted themselves to the dreary labor of explaining puns and parodies which, without their efforts, we would never have understood. Be it said here only that whereas a pun nearly always involves some kind of double imagery, some are very simple, while others have something akin to the lyrical, in possessing an added element which gives them a different structure and function. To use an illustration from the *Wasps*, described earlier: there is a simple double image pun in the slave's dream of Theorus: he dreamt that Theorus, a famous sycophant, had the head of a crow (κόραξ); this word is then mispronounced to mean "flatterer" (κόλαξ), and the implication is little more than that the flatterer Theorus may go to the crows, Greek for going to the dogs.[10] Such a simple, perhaps feeble, drollery is indeed a double image, but it differs in kind from the city of Katagela, which is not only a double image of a Sicilian city and a verb of derisive mockery, but, as said earlier, a sort of invention, a birth, a new poetic reality. One might illustrate the difference in another way. In the matter of exaggeration, for instance, one may exaggerate simply, or one may compound the felony with elements from spheres outside the immediate thing exaggerated. Paul Bunyan's hot-cake griddle was so big that it had to be greased by a number of men skating over it with sides of bacon strapped to their shoes. A large griddle indeed! But what can we say to that great tree in the forest, which was so tall it took five men a week to see the top? This is more than exaggeration: it is a disturbing speculation on the nature of time and space.

Double imagery is a tour de force, a kind of trick; but it is a trick which hints at hidden, inner realities not always expressible otherwise. Its kinship with some of the methods of surrealism is clear from such a painting as Dali's *Spain*. Spain is represented as an apparently headless woman leaning on a chest of drawers in an autumnal landscape. As one looks at it, various elements in the landscape — furrows, people, a pair of knights tilting — slowly re-form themselves into the woman's head and shoulders, and the head is deeply tragic in poise and expression. One would not wish to paraphrase the meaning, but clearly the same meaning could scarcely have been gained without the trick. Double imagery is a singularly delicate and light-touch method — though in the case of Aristophanes what it touches may not always be delicate. Again, it would be diffi-cult to state exactly why, in his training years, Dali persisted in seeing a Gothic Madonna as a pair of scales; or why for a time he saw telephones as lobsters and lobsters as telephones; or precisely what aesthetic significance he found in poising a pair of raw pork chops on his wife's bare shoulders. Yet such insights are akin to some of Aristophanes' most basic impulses as a poet, involving, as they do, the juxtapositions and implied identities of disparate things in the light of ulterior, if inexpressible, realities.

All this is, of course, the realization of metaphor, and Dali has called his own method of achieving it "paranoiac." He is using the term in a somewhat special sense, to indicate the mind's ability to fabricate reality out of images. He once wrote: "The double image may be extended, continuing the paranoiac advance, and then the presence of another dominant idea is enough to make a third image appear, and so on, until there is a number of images, limited only by the mind's degree of paranoiac capacity." [11] This statement aptly summarizes the way in which an Aristophanean fantasy proceeds — between the horns of a logical dilemma, along a new coordinate, and into the fecund irrealism of an invented world, where images breed images to the mind's capacity. If "paranoiac" seems an extreme word for it, still it is clearly a form of madness, and like paranoia it involves the hero's magnificent delusion of a triumphant self.

Limitless in its intention, it can make use of everything with which it comes into contact. Such was the almost infinite sensuous and intellectual responsiveness of Aristophanes that the fantasy's ravenous hunger is fed to overflowing with constant images of all that the world contains, sometimes in clearly limned singleness, like the whispering elm, the shrewd Athenian corpse, the thieving slave girl; sometimes in great heaps and piles, like the bustle in the wartime shipyards, the rollicking lists of foods, the occupations of bird-mad Athenians, or the iridescent images of countryside and sea. "I hate simplicity in all its forms," said Dali. There is certainly nothing simple about the art of Aristophanes.

If this whole view of the poet has any validity, we are bound to ask, finally, what its significance may be. Is Aristophanes merely leading us all into a paranoiac state by dramatizing the dreams of lunacy? Or does this elaborate effort have a higher purpose? We have repeatedly dismissed the idea that these extravaganzas conceal allegories implying political or moral reform. We must now confront the possibility that they are wish-fulfilling, purgative indulgences of the spirit's desire to defy law and transgress taboo. This is a popular theory today which owes its existence partly to the Aristotelian theory of catharsis, and partly to the Freudian doctrine of inhibition and sublimation. By this approach Aristophanean comedy would turn out to be, both in actual effect and subconscious purpose, a release, a discharge of certain drives of the libido, or ego, not otherwise to be satisfied amid the repressing society which surrounds it. Like the Roman Saturnalia, or the Medieval Season of Misrule, it would give the dog his day, and permit the safe renewal, for another year, of moral sanctions and custom-law.

There is something to be said for this view, but it does not provide a wholly satisfactory interpretation of Aristophanes. In the first place, like moral interpretations, it implies practicality of purpose and effect in the form of a psychotherapeutic purge, and there is no evidence for supposing comedy to have reduced the incidence of adultery, violence, or whatever by vicarious satisfaction. The taboo-smashing seems to have been enjoyable, but the cathartic function may be overestimated, especially for a society so open as that of late-fifth-century Athens, though it may have been efficacious for one reared under the ecclesiastical constraints of the Middle Ages. But more important, the cathartic view explains at most some of the content and not the form of Aristophanic comedy. There is an obvious relish in seeing a creditor get flogged instead of paid; we sympathize with illicit liaisons on the stage which might offend us in real life; violence, improper language, and naked girls abound in Aristophanes. But mere vicarious satisfaction can be effected by a peep show, pornography, or the least artful of cartoons as well as, if not better than, by a developed work of art. The purgation theory misses the wholeness of Aristophanes, and therefore, in its partiality, misinterprets to a degree even the part upon which it is based.

There is, for instance, the matter of slapstick; in a way slapstick is one of the simplest and most basic ways of discharging suppressed desires. We do not know how much unwritten roughhousing took place in the actual performances of Aristophanes, but there are some scenes, usually beating scenes, which are quite clearly slapstick and little else: Strepsiades' creditors, the sycophant in the *Birds*, the burning of the Thinkery. These are ordinary, simple slapstick, and convey the usual sort of satisfaction. But there is also what one might call the "higher slapstick," which satisfies not just a suppressed desire, but something more like an intuition for the true nature of things. To illustrate: it is funny when anybody gets hit by a custard pie, though it is funnier if an alderman gets hit with a custard pie; but it is funniest of all when everybody gets hit with custard pie, from the offending wretch who caused the trouble, to the most innocent bystander, and especially the policeman who is trying to restore order. There is a superb example of this by Laurel and Hardy from the great period of slapstick movies. The timing and development are flawless, and not a pie, of the several thousand that are thrown, misses its mark, or some mark. By the end — though the scene does not seem to end, but to continue toward a glorious eternity — the total *mise en scène*, an everyday street corner, is draped, inundated, and festooned with the squashy viscosity of custard and cream; men, women, buildings, dogs, and automobiles are transfigured in a perfect apocalypse of pie. The feeling which overtakes the spectator of this rapturous scene is more than a vicarious satisfaction of individual desire; it is a feeling of sublime peace, of an access of knowledge which is true, of a revelation of the essence of things. Custard pie has become a way of life, and the world has been transformed by it. As always with a fully drawn monstrosity, that which is imaged is Absurdity itself. One well-thrown custard pie is a happy impiety; but if there are enough pies, the boundless swings into view, and the yearning which is satisfied is too deep and humane ever to be purged from the human psyche. It is the heroic longing, fulfilling its own metaphor of order, its own order, sprouting wings and deposing Zeus.

Now it is precisely this higher slapstick which Aristophanes is up to. There are no pies, to be sure, but there are other equally effective ways of achieving the purpose. For one of the secrets of good slapstick is its elaboration; sometimes this can be done by mere quantity, at other times a fiendishly careful and scientific preparation of the event brings off a sense of great accomplishment. Harpo Marx, for instance, on going to bed, punctiliously sets his alarm clock, puts a sledge hammer on the floor beside his bed, and goes to sleep. Eight hours later the alarm rings, Harpo takes the hammer, smashes the clock, and goes back to sleep. The delight here is in the elaboration of the act of smashing the clock. One might compare the scene in the *Acharnians* where, instead of simply driving off the informer with a whip, Dicaeopolis has him carefully packed up in a crate, upside down, and shipped off to Boeotia. An added pleasure lies in the fact that the informer who has come to denounce contraband has himself been turned into an illegal commodity, quite properly sold in the free market of the hero. This scene is the higher slapstick, in that it effects a transformation.

Another fine scene comes in the *Frogs*, where the weighing of lines of poetry in a scale involves a contrived, not to say labored, transformation of verses into Aeschylean logs and Euripidean twigs. The scene itself, as a burlesque of the Homeric *psychostasis*, somehow epitomizes the play's weighing of the meaning of life and death, as Athens herself teeters in the fateful balances. If the scene is not strictly slapstick in our sense, it is a physical rendering of the absurd for its own sake, and looks to a meaning more poetic than purgative. Of the same kind is the hoisting of Peace with the block and tackle. And yet, no individual scene illustrates the point so well as any of the total conceptions. Each of Aristophanes' invented worlds is a kind of higher slapstick, a gigantically elaborated violation of the apparent way things are, in favor of the malleable absurdity of the comic hero's remolding of them — or, as Dali would put it, "the tender, extravagant and solitary paranoiac-critical camembert of time and space," the word camembert here being Dali's private symbol for the ductile quality of reality.[12]

But in dealing with so individual an artist as Aristophanes, words like slapstick, or surrealism, do not absolutely fit; they can at best suggest the objects and methods of his art, and perhaps liberate criticism from subsuming its motives under some partial rubric, such as political satire, moral reform, or psychic purgation. Comic poetry is too large for that. There is only one answer to the question of what end this comic poetry serves: it serves the same end as all poetry, as Dr. Johnson said, "to expand the sensibilities." But that is an evasive answer, and one might well counter with, "which sensibilities?" With his infinite range of awareness and expressiveness, there are few sensibilities that Aristophanes does not reach, but peculiarly fundamental seems to be his transforming power, his ability to shift reality, unmake it and remake it before our eyes. Such tamperings are always the business of poets, who serve our quest for reality by offering metaphors of it, extensions of knowability, constructs of the spirit in its wholeness.

The pleasure of tragedy, according to Aristotle, consists in its ability to present us with an action as a structured whole, like Robert Frost's "shapes against chaos," for this gratifies the spirit's wish for wholeness, symmetry, and form. Aristophanic comedy does likewise, and if the whole seems to be a different one, it is nonetheless a product of the characteristically Greek conception of a hero, the human individual who aspires to a godlike supremacy without losing his humanity. Since we have here the comic version of a hero, his structural essence lies, as said, in that combination of animal, human, and divine attributes which seem to have been the classical origins of the grotesque, a hybrid magic, providing a certain range of spirit, with some special keys to nature and a degree of power over it. In addition, the comic hero's determining genius lies in *poneria*, the crafty and unrestrained, self-admiring pursuit of boundless life and power, a quality which he exercises in the erection of a fantastic structure of the impossible and the absurd. Absurdity and structure, being mutually contradictory, of course, meet only in the mode of what we call nonsense; but once the structure is built, it becomes a bastion against the chaos of unknowable nature, and at the same time, a natural and humane triumph. For human nature is both order and chaos at once, and the comic hero embodies both its logic and its passionate illogic. The comic hero fulfills his quest for wholeness by developing his nature into a grotesquerie capable of matching and including the corresponding shapes of absurdity, from Persian ambassadors and dung beetles to wings and Zeus. Only thus can he defeat confusion and assert life. To return to the modern Greek shadow plays, the lowly Karaghiozes and his counterego Alexander the Great are really one and the same on the deepest level of the hero's self. He is Aristotle's low character who masters all, and he does it by a wishful, even better, a willful tampering with reality.

Yet the hero's action is no common or small wish or will-fulfill-ment. The sense of human dignity runs high in Aristophanes, and he does not just invent substitute worlds where any petty psyche can revel in irrealism. Like the imagery in *Oedipus Rex*, of outer sight which is blindness and inner sight which is true, the upsetting of visible reality in Aristophanes implies another reality, a truth beyond the truth, so to speak, which is, in fact, the spirit's formulation of the way things are. This is a transfiguring function, and a metaphysical one. In the service of such a vision, it is right and truthful to pervert what meets the eye, to lavish every metaphorical resource on the effort to meet absurdity on its own terms, and to outdo it. Such poetry captures a psychic state not to purge it, but to exalt it; for the perception of absurdity, and the heroic realization that it must be manipulated to the greater clarity of the spirit, are among the truest actions which the spirit can perform. If the manipulations — the private peace treaties, the cities in the sky, the revivals from the dead — seem like nothing more than helpless dreams, we should recall that dreams are perfectly real experiences, and to dramatize them in poetry is to produce a structure of self-knowledge. This is not to say that any dreamer of a poet can truthfully create a dream world. But a poet of Aristophanes' sensitive and detailed knowledge of this life has a right, in his realism about this world, to create the reality of others.

To conclude, Aristophanes' comedy is the last ancient hymn to the spirit's victory over absurdity in its own terms; it presents no less of a triumph over external and apparent reality than does the revealing exaltation which follows upon the tragic hero's moment of final knowledge. All heroism discredits reality in favor of a vision involving divinity and the self. This vision is a counterimage of the things which are, and it is always the ardent self which contrives it. Heroes often seem self-centered, even selfish. But be it by the simplicity of tragic self-sacrifice or the complexities of comic "selfmanship," the search is to find a truth which is viable. Truth of this kind is a "made" commodity, and cannot tolerate what is merely found or given; it needs heroism. The heroic nonsense of Aristophanes, whether by a delicate metaphor, a lame and obvious pun, or a resounding obscenity, strives to catch a counterimage, which then becomes the real. The Socrates, Cleon, and Euripides of Aristophanes are very much his own magnificent monsters and bugbears. But for him they are, like Nephelococcygia, the truth beyond the truth, not because they possess any factual being, but because they are the way they have to be in the created world of comic knowability. They are stuff of the absolutely comic, self-existent lyrics of broad laughter, absurdities designed to appall Absurdity's own self. This could be done only by the poet whose loving concern for, and penetration of, the world could make a myth of it, the myth of the individual's smallness and greatness, hilarious but heroic; the poet who, with high-hearted and shameless innocence, could commend his poetry to posterity:

> Keep my verses in your closet with the apples,
> So that all year long your clothes may smell of — wit.

APPENDIX

KARAGHIOZES AND ARISTOPHANIC COMEDY

The most accessible general accounts of the Karaghiozes shadow theater are to be found in Giulio Caïmi, *Karaghiozi, ou la comédie grecque dans l'âme du théâtre d'ombres* (Athens, 1935), or, for readers of modern Greek, Sotiris Spatharis, *Apomnemonevmata* (Athens, 1960). Less detailed, but informative, is Louis Roussel, *Karagheuz, ou un théâtre d'ombres à Athènes* (Athens, 1921), and Olive Blackham, *Shadow Puppets*, (New York, 1960), pp. 59 f. Among Greek scholars there is nothing new in the feeling that there are deep similarities between the comedies of Aristophanes and those of the Greek shadow theater; see, for example, G. Caïmi in Νέα Ἑστία, 45 (1949): 377 f. Whether these similarities are fortuitous or rest upon some historical connection is a question which it is probably impossible to answer with any certainty. Nothing like real evidence for a historical connection exists. Indirectly, however, one may infer that some kind of popular comic tradition underlay the development of Karaghiozes in Greece; and for this the evidence is slight, but plausible. But first be it noted that the question before us, namely Karaghiozes' resemblance to an Aristophanic hero and other points of similarity between the shadow theater and Old Comedy, is distinct from the problem of the origin of shadow theater as a form, or the question of whether or not there was a real historical Karaghiozes, and of what nationality he was.

The distinction has not always been kept. Some scholars, such as Costas Biris ('Ο Καραγκιόζης, Έλληνικὸ Λαικὸ Θέατρο, Athens, 1952), have tried to prove that shadow drama existed in antiquity, and indeed formed the central revelation of the Eleusinian Mysteries; but even if that could be established as fact, it would not prove that any such character as Karaghiozes existed in it. Others, such as Caïmi, assume, but do not demonstrate, a vague continuity from ancient times, while still others, usually themselves Karaghiozes players, believe that the original, historical Karaghiozes, despite his Turkish name, was really a Greek. All such theories confuse the situation, and the last mentioned is badly embarrassed by the fact that the Karaghiozes theater was unknown in Greece until it was introduced into the Piraeus by Barbayannis Vrachalis from Constantinople in 1860. (This is the usual date, but R. Dostálová-Jenistová gives it as 1852; see *Probleme der Neugriechischen Literatur*, 4 [1959]: 185 f. Biris speaks as if Epirote Karaghiozes players were known in Greece earlier, but does not support his statement with any evidence; see C. Biris, 'Η Βαβυλωνία τοῦ Δ. Κ. Βυζαντίου, Athens, 1948, pp. 17 f.) But the origin of shadow plays is irrelevant here. No doubt, if Karaghiozes himself could be shown to have been originally a Greek invention, or even a real Greek who somehow acquired a Turkish name, that knowledge might help to explain his resemblance to Dicaeopolis and others. But the attempts to show this are clearly strained and chauvinistic efforts of Greeks who feel a strong possessiveness about their barefoot hero. It is far safer to assume what the evidence and the tradition suggest, that Karaghiozes, whether real or fictional, was originally a Turk, named Karagöz, meaning "Black eyes," and that he came to Greece about 1860. The first question then is, why and how did this Turk, scarcely a generation after the War of Liberation, become a naturalized Greek, and at that, one who symbolizes and embodies the Greek spirit struggling heroically, though deviously, for survival under the Turkish domination? The second question, even more important, is, what determined the peculiar Greek form he took, which is very different from his Turkish original, and strangely reminiscent of Old Comedy?

Something is known about the process of his development in Greece. The performances introduced by Vrachalis appear at first to have adhered essentially to the Turkish pattern, although his Karaghiozes figure was already of the Greek type (see Spatharis, *Apomnemonevmata*, p. 160). The Turkish pattern involved a few basic figures: Karagöz, the common man; Haçivad, learned and shrewd; Zeibék, the nobleman; a lady of high rank and other women, a drunkard, an opium eater, and a fool. The plays included songs, social lampoon, and philosophical or moralizing dialogue; the plots, though sometimes erotic, turned mostly on scapegrace attempts by Karagöz and Haçivad to get money from the other characters. (For accounts in English, see Sabri Esat Siyavusgil, *Karagöz*, Istanbul, 1961; Metin And, "Dances of Anatolian Turkey," *Dance Perspectives*, 3 [1959]:36 f.) The change to the characteristic Greek form is associated chiefly with the name of Demetrius Sardounis, commonly called Mimaros, who in the early and middle nineties began to divest the shadow theater of its obscenities, at least in good part, and to introduce heroic legends into the repertoire. He also created the figures of Sior Dionysios, Barba-Georgos, and others, thus instituting the basic series of characters which form the *thiasos*, or company, of the classic Karaghiozes player. Further changes and additions were made by many others, including the famous Antonios Mollas, whose career is generally considered to mark the golden age of Karaghiozes.

The classic *thiasos* came to be very large indeed, including as many as a thousand figures (see Spatharis, *Apomnemonevmata*, p. 180), of which, however, the core consists of Karaghiozes and Chatziavates (the only two from the original Turkish version) and ten or twelve others whose natures, dress, dialects, and songs represent the various types and, above all, districts of Greece. Besides these contemporary figures there are the historical heroes of the Greek Revolution, such as Kolokotronis, Katsandonis, Athanasios Diakos.

Occasionally also there is an ancient hero, the most popular being Alexander the Great, who according to medieval Greek folklore never died; in the Karaghiozes theater, he slays a dragon while singing the litany, in a manner which shows that he got mixed up somewhere with St. George. The comic and heroic elements are sometimes kept separate, sometimes mingled in an unlikely, but strangely effective union. The classic repertoire includes literally hundreds of comedies and historical-legend plays, the theme common to both being the survival of the Greek people, sometimes dramatized in episodes from the War of Independence, sometimes in the ingenious cleverness which Karaghiozes shows in outwitting the Turkish lords.

It is the latter aspect which is of concern here. The Turkish Karagöz is clever, and a poor man, though not destitute. The Greek Karaghiozes has become an utter tatterdemalion, dwelling in sordid poverty in a hovel with his wife and three children, strongly disinclined toward honest labor, but superbly gifted at stealing and other methods of living by one's wits. This quality, *poneria*, is his chief characteristic; but to it is added a kind of half-innocent madness, an antic humor as difficult as Hamlet's to assign wholly either to irony or sincerity. The combination makes him inevitably appealing, despite his repulsive appearance. With peculiarly Greek volatility he becomes many different things by sudden and surprising turns, a thief, a bully, a boaster, a fantastic, a patriot, a theorist, an adventurer, a philosopher, a lout. His inner versatility is matched by the wide variety of roles which he is made to play in the repertoire — a repertoire which is still growing, so that some of Karaghiozes' most recent exploits have been as an astronaut. Though smaller than most of the other figures, he regularly gets the better of them all, and even when he does not, but ends by getting pommeled, he is unsubdued. He is also immortal: at the end of one play he is blown to bits by a cannon, but returns immediately. He is regularly hunchbacked, barefoot, bald, with an enormous monstrosity of a nose; and for more effective gesticulations, one arm is longer than the other. The quality of his humor ranges from the most stinging satire to such quasi-lyrical flights of half-pathetic nonsense as his decision, developed in an elaborate soliloquy, to avoid starvation by eating himself to death on Turkish paste.

It is almost superfluous to point out the resemblance to the complex of guile, fantasy, satire, lyric, and nonsense which Aristophanes spun into his comic heroes. Above all, the image of the little self, oppressed but resilient, is crucial to both Karaghiozes and the Aristophanic hero, as survival symbols, both national and individual. Yet, besides the general outline of the character, there are other similarities between Karaghiozes plays and Old Comedy, little details or comic ploys; and while some are no doubt common property, others suggest a real connection. For example: in one play Karaghiozes proposes to make a living by running a refrigerator on the sun; compare Strepsiades' plan to catch the moon, *Clouds* 749 f. In another play it is his task to beat off pretenders to the heroine's hand; compare the expulsion of "impostors" in *Acharnians* and *Birds*. Karaghiozes often forgets his own name, or gives it as "Penelope"; compare the nonsense names given by Peithetaerus and Euelpides, *Birds* 65 f. Karaghiozes sometimes appears suddenly in a strange new costume, and is jeered at by Chatziavates; compare *Birds* 804 f, *Frogs* 42 f. Karaghiozes' son lisps in the ancient fashion (πατέλα for πατέρα); compare *Wasps* 44 f. When the Bey's daughter tells Karaghiozes she loves him, he is afraid to answer for fear his mother might scold him, for he is not yet of age, being only 45; compare *Wasps* 1354 f (also Margites and his wife). Knocking on a door with explosive comic effect forms a major motif in Karaghiozes plays; compare *Frogs* 37 f, *Birds* 55 f. Karaghiozes sometimes demands a passport of Chatziavates for passing his house; compare *Birds* 1213 f. When the lovers are receiving the blessing and prayers of the bride's father, Karaghiozes intersperses them with mocking parodies; compare *Birds* 864 f (and H. Kleinknecht, "Die Gebetsparodie in der Antike," *Tübingen Beitrag.*, 28 [1937]: 27 f). Reeling off lists of foods is dear to both forms; the relation between

Karaghiozes and Chatziavates has a great deal in common with that between Philocleon and Bdelycleon; both forms on occasion involve a comic hero with heroes and worthies of old; comic exploitation of dialects is basic to Karaghiozes theater, and occurs also in four extant plays of Aristophanes.

These are, of course, mere details, though suggestive ones. The real point lies in the central character, with his *poneria, anaideia,* and *alazoneia,* his mingling of fantastic nonsense and satire, and his large capacity for wish fulfillment and transcendent victory. The question is, how did this character, such a far cry from his Turkish namesake and so like his ancient forebears, come about? How did Mimaros and other Karaghiozes players, for the most part all but illiterate and certainly not versed in Aristophanic comedy, shape such a character? It could scarcely have been out of nothing, and the only plausible answer is that there was some kind of comic popular tradition in Greece in the light of which Karagöz became Karaghiozes; a tradition which preserved, after some fashion, a formalized image of Greek Comic Man, with roots deep in the psychology of the people, and extending, however deviously, back to antiquity. It is difficult to trace this tradition because popular entertainments seldom survive in written form.

With the fall of Constantinople cultural activity in Greece proper underwent a sudden and all but total eclipse, to survive for the next four hundred years in thin and obscure streams of tradition. Before that event, however, we know of dramatic and quasi-dramatic celebrations of a popular sort, especially connected with New Year's and Epiphany. These performances, which involved buffoonery and transvestitism as well as the acting out of roles, have been referred in origin, no doubt correctly, to vintage festivals, ultimately pagan and Dionysiac, which the Church could not suppress and was therefore driven to adapt. (For a convenient account, see Vénétia Cottas, *Le Théâtre à Byzance,* Paris, 1931, chap. 1.) Other such survivals of fertility rites are well known in Greece today, and have even been adduced as evidence for the origins of Old Comedy

APPENDIX

(see G. Megas, Ἑλληνικαὶ Ἑορταὶ, Athens, 1957, pp. 101 f; cf. F. Cornford, *Origins of Attic Comedy*, pp. 62 f). Although nothing like the character of Karaghiozes occurs in these representations, they may be taken as possible contributing factors in his formulation for two reasons: first, they contain an inherent sense of communal survival; and second, with at least some of them there came to be associated in late Byzantine times a heroic element foreshadowing that which figures in the Greek Karaghiozes. This was the singing of ἀπελατικά, technically hymns celebrating the Emperor's triumphs; yet the name is derived from ἀπελάτης, which means ἁρματωλός, or κλέφτης, a "brigand," of the type who later, as irregulars in the War for Independence, came to represent more than all others the heroic individualism of the Greek people. Not much is known about these songs, but one may assume that they represent some early stage of the klephtic tradition. There was also a dance called "Vlach," a mountaineer's dance, from the Vlachoi, a mountain people of northern Greece. (Cf. Cottas, *Le Théâtre à Byzance*, pp. 22 f.) In the Karaghiozes plays, Barba-Georgos is a Vlach, and very proud of his dancing.

All this proves nothing, but it suggests the continuity of a natively Greek festival spirit, involving rudimentary dramatic presentation of communal significance, combined with clowning and the singing of heroic exploits. And herein may perhaps be found some of the inspiration for the mixed comic-heroic product which Mimaros, who worked much in northern Greece, made of the shadow theater. In any case, it would be hard to overestimate the importance of the klephtic tradition in the shaping of the Greek Karaghiozes play. Barba-Georgos, we know, was the creation of Mimaros, and originally a real man. But he represents the vigorous Roumeliote peasantry, the men who, though laughed at in Athens for their broad accent and fustanella, after they had distinguished themselves in the Greco-Turkish war of 1886 as the first Evzones became the Royal Guard and made the kilt the national costume of Greece. (See C. Biris, "Ἡ Λεβεντιὰ τῆς Ῥούμελης," *Problemata der Neugriechischen*

Literatur, 4 [1959]: 209 f.) The entry of the heroic, national element into the shadow theater has been reasonably associated with the sudden prominence of these Roumeliotes, among whom the klephtic spirit was most strong.

But to return to Karaghiozes. Costas Biris, Ὁ Καραγκιόζης, Athens, 1952, pp. 10 f, asserts that Karaghiozes is the direct descendant of the clever slave of Old Comedy, adducing such characters as Xanthias in the *Frogs* or Carion in the *Plutus*. Curiously enough, for Biris this slave is an all but omnipresent stereotype in Aristophanes, despite the fact that only in the above-named plays and in the *Knights* does a slave have any prominence. Now the clever slave, who belongs really to New Comedy, and Karaghiozes have something to do with each other, insofar as both are underdogs who must win by trickery. But the connection with Aristophanes is complicated by the fact that Karaghiozes is not a slave, but a symbol of freedom of spirit; cf. Γ. Τσαρούχη, "Σκόρπιες Σκέψεις γιὰ τὸν Καραγκιόζη," Ἐπιθεώρηση Τέχνης, 9 (1959): 122, on Karaghiozes as a new embodiment of Antigone and Electra, and the remark: "ἀπ᾽ ὅλο τὸ τύπο τοῦ Καραγκιόζη βγαίνει μιὰ ἀναρχικὴ ἐλευθερία" ("An anarchical freedom issues from every aspect of Karaghiozes.") Furthermore, Aristophanic slaves are not, as a rule, victorious or symbolic of survival; it is the hero who plays that role, and Karaghiozes resembles the hero more than he does the clever slave. And herein may lie some inkling of how the Greek Karaghiozes came about. When the gradual change from Old Comedy to New took place, the triumphant hero of fantasy yielded to the clever slave as the central comic figure, and the comic pattern thus created became the standard for all subsequent Western comedy from Plautus and Terence to Goldoni. The creation of the Greek Karaghiozes out of the Turkish seems to be a kind of reversal of the process, as if, for special reasons, the clever slave in turn yielded to the hero of fantasy. We can only guess at how this happened. Although Greece proper lost contact with the Western tradition after the Turkish invasion, in the Ionian islands, and especially in Crete, the Venetians maintained their theater and their literature, which influenced Greek poets. Thus the *Fortunatus* of the Cretan Marcos Phoscolos (1669) is a Greek comedy entirely in the Italian manner, and containing all the familiar masks of the Roman tradition, including clever slaves, lovers, a greedy widow, bad-tempered old men, a boastful soldier, and a quack doctor. Greek literature in the seventeenth century flourished in Crete until the island fell to the Turks; after that, partly because of the refugees who fled there, the center shifted to the Ionian islands, and especially Zante, the place where the heroic spirit of the Revolution first found literary expression in the poems of Solomos. Here in the eighteenth century one may observe something natively Greek rediscovering itself, after its cross-fertilization with Italian culture.

Zante is unique in having possessed the only known popular Greek theater, if such it can be called, before the shadow theater. During the *Apokrea*, or Carnival season, working and country classes presented improvised plays called *omilies* (ὁμιλίες) on themes from a fixed or partly fixed repertoire, out of doors and without scenery. The origin of these plays is unknown, though it seems clear that they developed under Venetian influence. (On *omilies* in general, see Γλυκερία Πρωτοπαπᾶ-Μπουμπουλίδου, Τὸ θέατρον ἐν Ζακύνθῳ, Athens, 1958, pp. 19 f.) They were developed plays, in contrast to the ritual miming and mummery of the vintage festivals, on themes for the most part romantic, derived from fairy tales, but spiced with parody and satire on contemporary customs and types, especially lawyers. The great monuments of Cretan poetry, *Erophile*, *Erotocritos*, and the *Sacrifice of Abraham* could also be presented as *omilies*. There can be little doubt that the *commedia dell' arte* played a part in the formulation of these performances, but the themes were Greek; and it is of the greatest importance to our inquiry that we hear of an *omilia* on the subject of the hero Athanasios Diakos (Κ. Πορφύρη, "Τὸ Ζακύνθικο Λαϊκὸ Θέατρο," Ἐπιθεώρηση Τέχνης, 2 [1955]: 145 f). His martyrdom forms one of the classics of the Karaghiozes theater, to which it was introduced by Theodorellos, a pupil of Mimaros, but only after 1900; it seems likely that such national subjects existed earlier in the Zacynthian *omilia*.

The *omilies* were influential also in the literary drama of Zante. Though originally unwritten, they began to be put into written verse by poets unfortunately unknown; some texts have been collected, and at least three have been published (see Marietta Minotou, " Ὁμιλίες," *Ionios Anthologia*, 8 (1934):139 f). Probably the most famous literary text from Zante before Solomos is the Χάσης of Demetrius Gouzeli (1774–1843), and this play has been called one long *omilia*. Though Gouzeli was well trained in Italian and translated Tasso, the Χάσης is a genuine Greek work, with a hero who is the eternal boaster with enough good luck on his side to keep him successful. But if this character, drawn essentially from Greek life rather than Italian tradition, suggests the kind of swashbuckling, swindling *alazoneia* which we are seeking, it is even more clearly to be found in the work of an almost unknown Zacynthian poet, Savoias Rousmelis (ca. 1700–1772). This is *The Quack Doctors* (Κωμῳδία τῶν Ψευτογιατρῶν), a satire on the Κομπογιαννῖται, a quite real group of wandering physicians from Jannina, who practiced their unconscionable deceptions on community after community, remaining in each only so long as their fraud went undetected, and thereafter escaping. The play is unfortunately unpublished as yet, but a full description may be found in Πρωτοπαπᾶ, pp. 69 f. See also Λ. Χ. Ζώη, Αἱ Μοῦσαι, ΛΑ´ fsc. 723 (June 1, 1923), pp. 1 f.

There is little or no romanticism here, and the play is free from the stock masks, for even these quack doctors are drawn from life. The structure is purely episodic, like an *omilia*, the language racy, and at times lyrical. The satire is very broad, verging on the fantastic, yet with close observation of reality. One may perhaps see something akin to the local types of the Karaghiozes *thiasos* in Rousmelis' exploitation of the local faults in the Ionian islands — the traditional naïveté of the Zacynthians, the envy of the Corcyreans, the *poneria* of the Cephalonians. An even fuller use of Greek local types and dialects for comic ends, and one very like that in the Karaghiozes theater, is to be found in Dem. Byzantios' play *Babylonia* (1836), whose whole theme is precisely the exploitation of the character, speech, and costume of the various parts of Greece. This work, written by a patriot of the War for Independence, clearly is a reflection of the new national consciousness. (I cannot help feeling that Biris' statement, in his edition, that Byzantios was influenced by early Karaghiozes players, is unsupported by evidence of Karaghiozes in Greece so early. Rather both phenomena reflect the same reawakening of national feeling, and the influence is, if anything, the other way around.) But some rudiments of the feeling exist already in Rousmelis' much earlier play (1745). Above all, there is relevance in the supreme character who in the end outwits the doctors themselves, and collects their gains. This is the hunchback Vittoros, a poor man who lives by *poneria*; he follows the doctors, observing them carefully, until the moment when, by a bold and simple coup, he can rob them. If Vittoros is not Karaghiozes, he has at least something of his physical and moral shape, and he wins all the sympathy. He offers perhaps a token of the comic model in the popular mind to which the Greek Karaghiozes was drawn. (A Roman ceramic head, fifth century A.D., excavated from the Athenian agora, with close counterparts in the Cerameicus museum, so closely resembles the regular type of Karaghiozes that one is tempted to believe that the physical aspects of this kind of comic character never died out. Homer's Thersites is very similar.)

To conclude, therefore: it seems reasonable to ascribe the similarities between Karaghiozes and Old Comedy to a revival, rather than a survival, of a certain, peculiarly Greek, kind of comic spirit. One thing is clear, that the Greek form of Karaghiozes derives in very great part from the War of Independence, and we must assume that this event, and the subsequent struggles of Greece to attain full national integrity in Europe, provided the necessary focus for the formulation of the hero. His forebears include much more than the Turkish Karagöz, who may well have been, as H. Reich (*Der Mimus*, Berlin, 1903, pp. 614 f) long ago stated, a survival from the Byzantine mime, transformed like many a Western counterpart into a strolling player after the fall of the Hippodrome, to become in turn a court entertainer under the Ottomans. The native tenacity of Greek tradition, especially in northern Greece, which kept certain, originally Dionysiac, festivals in observance; the heroic songs and legends of unsubduable mountaineers, which may, in the form of the ἀπελατικά, have become part of these festivals; the klephtic tradition proper — all these kept alive parts and aspects of antiquity, however scattered and transformed, under the Turkish yoke. Meanwhile in the parts of Greece occupied by the more sympathetic Venetians the Western comic tradition flourished, in a late Italian form combining elements derived from *commedia dell'arte*, Roman mime, Roman comedy, and ultimately New Comedy, and from this source the "clever slave" mask returned to Greece. But the growing national consciousness in the eighteenth century, which ultimately produced the revolution, was reflected in an increasingly national kind of theater, in the *omilies*, in the work of Rousmelis, Gouzeli, and later in Byzantios, and the "clever slave" also became slowly transformed. When the revolution came, Greece was ready to express herself in a "national," dramatic character. Karaghiozes provided the raw material, and the Greek players did the rest; the clever slave became the heroic symbol of the national struggle, and gathered around himself the diverse but spiritually unified aspects of his country, from Alexander the Great to the tavern bully, Stavrakas.

It would seem, therefore, that in the Greek tradition of *poneria* there can be many phases. The heroic one, which comes to embrace the idea of both individual authenticity and communal survival, occurs at times of deep national concern and self-consciousness. The Athens of Aristophanes and the Greece of Capodistria and Mavrocordato were indeed very different places, but over both there loomed many threats and challenges. A nation moiled in its final struggle and a nation re-creating itself from ruins may well both experience much the same communal awareness, personal need, and general defiance which is incarnate in Karaghiozes and Aristophanes' protagonists. The clever slave, like the *Graeculus esuriens*, is typical of ages when the heroic spirit is asleep, dead, or unnecessary; and indeed the heroic spirit is hard to find in Greece, in any powerful national form, between the fall of Athens and the War for Independence, though its traces are preserved in the Acritic ballads and other scattered remains. But certainly it awoke with a vengeance in 1821, breeding a proud roster of epic and tragic names; and shortly thereafter, even as ancient heroic tragedy was echoed and complemented by the Old Comedy, there came the comic hero again, no longer a clever slave, but the essence of his people, and incorrigibly himself. True, he came from Turkey and had a Turkish name, but Greece can borrow anything because she can assimilate and transform anything; and the grounds for transformation were already there. As one Greek writer puts it: "The triumph of Karaghiozes over his enemies indicates the unsubduable force, thanks to which alone Hellenism was not buried under slavery." (N. Sot. Chrestides, "Τί εἶνε ὁ Καραγκιόζης," in the collected shadow plays of Constantine Ganios, I, p. 2, Athens, no date).

NOTES

INDEX

TITLES FREQUENTLY CITED

AJP	American Journal of Philology
Cornford	F. Cornford, Origin of Attic Comedy, London, 1914
CP	Classical Philology
CQ	Classical Quarterly
CR	Classical Review
Croiset	M. Croiset, Aristophanes and the Political Parties at Athens, translated by J. Loeb, London, 1909
CW	Classical Weekly
Diehl	E. Diehl, Anthologia Lyrica Graeca, Leipzig, 1925
DK, Vorsokr.	H. Diels and W. Kranz, Die Fragmente der Vorsokratiker, 9th ed., 1959
Ehrenberg	V. Ehrenberg, The People of Aristophanes, Cambridge, Mass., 1951
HSCP	Harvard Studies in Classical Philology
Mazon, Essai	P. Mazon, Essai sur la composition des comédies d'Aristophane, Paris, 1904
Murphy, "Rhetoric"	C. T. Murphy, "Aristophanes and the Art of Rhetoric," HSCP 49 (1938), pp. 69 f
Murray	G. Murray, Aristophanes, Oxford, 1933
Mus. Helv.	Museum Helveticum
Newiger	H. J. Newiger, "Metapher und Allegorie. Studien zu Aristophanes," Zetemata 16, Munich, 1957
NGA	Nachrichten der Akademie in Göttingen
RE	Pauly-Wissowa, Real-Encyclopädie der klassischen Altertumswissenschaft
Reinhardt	K. Reinhardt, "Aristophanes und Athen," in Werken und Formen, Bonn, 1948, pp. 285 f
Rhein. Mus.	Rheinisches Museum für Philologie
Rogers	B. B. Rogers, Aristophanes' Comedies, London, 1902–1916
Russo	C. Russo, Aristofane, Gli Acarnesi, Bari, 1953
SB Berlin	Sitzungsberichte der Königlichen Akademie der Wissenschaften, Berlin
SB Vienna	Sitzungsberichte der Königlichen Akademie der Wissenschaften, Vienna
Süss, "Inkongruenzen"	W. Süss, "Scheinbare und wirkliche Inkongruenzen in den Dramen des Aristophanes," Rheinisches Museum, 97 (1954); 115–159, 229–254, 289–316
Van Leeuwen	J. van Leeuwen, Aristophanis Comoediae, Leipzig, 1896–1909
Wilam., "Wespen"	U. von Wilamowitz-Moellendorff, "Über die Wespen des Aristophanes," SB Berlin, 1911, pp. 460 f, 504 f

Fragments of Aristophanes are cited from the edition of F. W. Hall and W. M. Geldart, Oxford, 1900–1901; of others from the edition of J. M. Edmonds, The Fragments of Attic Comedy, Leiden, 1957–1961.

NOTES

I. Criticism and Old Comedy

1. For collections of the ancient writers on comedy, see F. Dübner, *Scholia Graeca in Aristophanem* (Paris, 1877), pp. xiii f; G. Kaibel, *Comicorum Graecorum Fragmenta* (Berlin, 1899), pp. 1 f; R. Cantarella, *Aristofane. Le Commedie* (Milan, 1948), I (*Prolegomena*), 14 f.

2. R. Cantarella, "Das Werk des Aristophanes," *Altertum*, 3 (1957): 212.

3. Aristotle, *Poetics* 1451b; *Eth. Nic.* 1128a22 f. Cf. A. Plebe, "La teoria del comico da Aristotele a Plutarco," *Pubblicazzioni della Facoltà di Lettere e Filosofia* (Turin, 1952), esp. p. 21, n. 77.

4. Horace, *Sat.* I, 4, 1 f.

5. Plutarch, *Moralia* 853 f; see also Lucian, *Piscator* 25, *Bis Accusatus* 33.

6. Quintilian, *Inst. Or.* X, 1, 65. Few scholars have taken much account of this view of comic language, but see Cantarella, "Das Werk," p. 209; see also the remark of the Anon., *De Comoedia* VI, 28 (Cantarella), about Cratinus: ποιητικώτατος καὶ κατασκευάζων εἰς τὸν Αἰσχύλου χαρακτῆρα; see also, note 5 of Chap. II.

7. Anon., *De Sublim.* 40, 2.

8. An elaborate reconstruction of a presumed Aristotelian theory of comic catharsis is offered by A. Plebe, "La teoria del comico"; for the chief source of the theory, the *Tractatus Coislinianus*, see Cantarella, I, 33 f, and its brilliant application to the language of Aristophanes in W. J. M. Starkie, *The Acharnians of Aristophanes* (London, 1909), pp. xxxviii f.

9. Cf. *Schol. ad Dion. Thrac.*, Cantarella, I, 28; Anon., *De Comoed.* XVI, *ibid.*, pp. 38 f; S. H. Butcher, *Aristotle's Theory of Poetry and Fine Art* (London, 1932), p. 218.

10. J. Tzetzes, Στίχοι περὶ διαφορᾶς ποιητῶν, 69 f, in Cantarella I, 49; cf. the Anon., *De Comoed.* XVI, 51 (Cantarella), to the effect that comedy is συστατικὴ τοῦ βίου.

11. But now see G. Else, *Aristotle's Poetics* (Cambridge, Mass. 1957), esp. pp. 414–447, for a new appraisal of Aristotle's meaning, particularly as regards *Hamartia* and *Katharsis*.

12. For the general inadequacy of ancient literary criticism, in all areas except rhetoric, see G. Kennedy, *The Art of Persuasion in Greece* (Princeton, 1963), p. 8.

13. T. Zielinski, *Die Gliederung der altattischen Komödie* (Leipzig, 1885); P. Mazon, *Essai sur la composition des comédies d' Aristophane* (Paris, 1904); T. Gelzer, *Der epirrhematische Agon bei Aristophanes* (Munich, 1960).

14. A. Couat, *Aristophane et l'ancienne comédie attique* (Paris, 1889; 3rd ed., 1902); cf. H. Müller-Strübung, *Aristophanes und die historische Kritik* (Leipzig, 1873), esp. p. 105.

15. M. Croiset, *Aristophane et les parties politiques à Athènes* (Paris, 1906; English trans., J. Loeb, London, 1909). Cf. now also, B. Bilinski, *La Lutte des idées dans les comédies d' Aristophane* (Warsaw, 1957); this book has not been available to me.

16. W. M. Hugill, *Panhellenism in Aristophanes* (Chicago, 1936), developing some ideas proposed by U. von Wilamovitz-Moellendorff, *Lysistrata* (Berlin, 1927); V. Paronzini, "L'ideale politica di Aristofane," *Dioniso*, 11 (1948): 26 f.

17. G. Murray, *Aristophanes* (Oxford, 1933).

18. A. W. Gomme, "Aristophanes and Politics," *CR*, 52 (1938): 97 f.

19. G. Perrotta, "Aristofane," *Maia*, 5 (1952): 1 f. This article shows the need for a more critical insight into comic poetry as poetry; the author, for all his warmth and eloquence, reverses himself on the subject within five pages, when he says, p. 23, that not everything in Aristophanes is poetry (he excludes the "lazzi triviali," and "insipide freddure"); and then, p. 28: "Aristofane è quasi sempre poeta." Perrotta is doubtless telling the truth when he says that Aristophanes' art is "la figlia di gioia," but this phrase does more to commend than to explain her.

20. C. Russo, *Aristofane, Gli Acarnesi* (Bari, 1953); see esp. pp. 117, 131. Russo maintains that comedy is anti-heroic, a view which will be, I hope, refuted in these pages.

21. W. Jaeger, *Paideia*, 2nd ed., trans. G. Highet (New York, 1945), I, 367, 369, 358.

22. Cf. Northrup Frye, *Anatomy of Criticism* (Princeton, 1957), pp. 89 f, on commentary and allegory.

23. H. Newiger, "Metapher und Allegorie," *Zetemata* 16 (Munich, 1957).

24. K. Reinhardt, "Aristophanes und Athen," *Von Werken und Formen* (Bonn, 1948), pp. 285–310; see esp. 292 f, 305 f.

25. Cf. Perrotta, "Aristofane," pp. 14 f; Cantarella, "Das Werk," pp. 206, 208 f, 210; O. Seel, *Aristophanes* (Stuttgart, 1960).

26. See Gomme, "Aristophanes and Politics," who tends in this direction; more extreme is E. Capps, "Comedy" in *Greek Literature, A Series of Lectures Delivered at Columbia University* (New York, 1912), pp. 138 f; also, W. Süss, "Die Technik der Aristophanischen Komödie," *Neue Jahrbücher für das klassische Altertum*, 25 (1910): 400 f. G. Kaibel, *RE*, *s.v.* "Aristophanes," rightly doubts that comedy ever had any practical effect.

27. For example, V. Ehrenberg, *The People of Aristophanes* (Cambridge, Mass., 1951), p. 9. Ehrenberg's particular form of "middle ground" is quite proper for his purpose, however, and leads to an admirable general view, quoted below.

28. For example, M. Platnauer, *Oxford Classical Dictionary, s.v.* "Aristophanes."

29. On the multiple origins of Old Comedy, see below, n. 41. It should be observed, however, that it was precisely the feeling that Aristophanic plots were unified which prompted Cornford's theory of comic origins. Both sides of the argument have been exaggerated in the criticism of the plays themselves. Old Comedy is a farrago, certainly, but it also has a coherence of its own, discernible through a literary, if not through an anthropological approach. See D. Parker, *Aristophanes, The Acharnians* (Ann Arbor, 1961), introduction, 1 f, for an excellent defense of the coherence of the play, usually criticised as particularly disunified.

30. Cf. Platnauer, *OCD, s.v.* "Aristophanes."

31. The plot outline given here is substantially that which Cornford believed was the outline of the Old and New Year ritual from which, in his view, Old Comedy arose; see below, note 41. For a general critique, see Sir A. W. Pickard-Cambridge, *Dithyramb, Tragedy, and Comedy* (1st ed., Oxford, 1927), pp. 329 f (omitted in the revised second edition by T. B. L. Webster).

32. Zielinski's distinctions about what is and is not an *agon* may be set aside here; cf. the protest against his "starre dogmatik," W. Süss, "Scheinbare und wirkliche Inkongruenzen in den Dramen des Aristophanes," *Rhein. Mus.*, 97 (1954): 250; also Mazon, *Essai*; and Pickard-Cambridge, *Dithyramb*, pp. 298 f. The epirrhematic agon is indeed absent from *Acharnians*, *Peace*, and *Thesmophoriazusae*, as Gelzer says, but the agonistic element is there. Whatever the importance of the agon for the origins of comedy, in the developed art of Aristophanes the varieties of its form seem to justify the use of the term to designate the chief agonistic element, the main struggle of the plot, in contrast to the more celebratory parts of the play.

33. For example, *Wasps* 1075 f, *Lysis.* 1150 f; cf. *Frogs* 1039 f.

34. Gomme, "Aristophanes and Politics," pp. 99 f.

35. Cf. C. T. Murphy, "Aristophanes and the Art of Rhetoric," *HSCP* 49 (1938), pp. 69 f; G. Pianko, "La musica nelle commedie di Aristofane," *Eos*, 47 (1954): 23 f.

36. Cratinus, Frag. 307.

37. R. E. Wycherley, "Aristophanes and Euripides," *Greece and Rome*, 15 (1946): 98 f; cf. G. Murray, *Aristophanes* (Oxford, 1933), pp. 106 f.

38. Ehrenberg, pp. 365 f.

39. Plato [?] Frag. 14 (Diehl). It seems evident that more is to be inferred about Plato's attitude toward Aristophanes from the full-dress portrait

in the *Symposium* than from the passing remarks in the *Apology*; cf. U. von Wilamowitz-Moellendorff, *Platon*, ed. B. Snell (3rd ed., Berlin, 1948), p. 282.

40. See, for example, Demetrius, *On Style* III, 150, 153, 161; *Greek Anthology*, IX, 186. Often, however, the word seems to mean simply "wit," for example, Anon., *De Comoed.* XVI (Cantarella).

41. The generally prevalent view is that of Pickard-Cambridge, *Dithyramb*, pp. 225 f, that Old Comedy is a combination of an Attic "animal" *komos*, containing set elements of parodos, agon, and parabasis, with scenes derived from Dorian farces. Now, however, see Lennart Breitholtz, *Die dorische Farce im griechischen Mutterland vor dem 5 Jahrhundert. Hypothese oder Realität?* (Stockholm, 1960), demonstrating the lack of evidence for Dorian farce in Greece proper early enough to influence Attic comedy; cf. T. B. L. Webster's review in *Gnomon*, 33 (1961): 452 f. Other recent theories and variants: H. Herter, *Vom dionysischen Tanz zum komischen Spiel* (Iserlohn, Germ., 1947) (finds origin in ithyphallic songs, following Aristotle, *Poetics* 1449a); D. L. Drew and D. S. Crawford, "Greek Comedy's Ancestry," *Bulletin of the Faculty of Arts, Cairo*, 14 (1952): 69 f (origin in a marriage rite); M. Pohlenz, "Die Entstehung der attische Komödie," *NGA*, no. 2 (1949), pp. 31 f (opposing Herter and reaffirming multiple origins); P. Mazon, "La Farce dans Aristophane, et les origines de la comédie en Grèce," *Revue d'histoire du théâtre* (1951), pp. 7 f (the two halves of an Old Comedy correspond to two different types of original farce); see also remarks in T. B. L. Webster, "The Costume of the Actors in Aristophanic Comedy," *CQ*, 49 (1955): 94 f. The theory of Francis Cornford, *The Origin of Attic Comedy* (London, 1914), that both tragedy and comedy originated in a vegetation rite involving Old and New Year Spirits, has few adherents among scholars. The theory is certainly exaggerated and only feebly supported by ancient evidence, if at all. Yet its emphasis on a consistent plot pattern, discernible in at least a number of plays, and on the motif of rejuvenation, which occurs in many, commands attention, and suggests that some kind of ritual fertility drama may have played a part in the growth of Attic comedy. For a more favorable estimate than Pickard-Cambridge's, see T. B. L. Webster's comments in the second revised edition of *Dithyramb, Tragedy and Comedy*, (Oxford, 1962), pp. 192 f.

42. J. Huizinga, *Homo Ludens* (English translation, London, 1949); C. Baudelaire, "On the Essence of Laughter" in *The Mirror of Art, Critical Studies by Baudelaire* (Doubleday Anchor Books, New York, 1956), pp. 131 f.

43. See Russo.

44. The most recent discussion of the problem, first raised in the last century by J. Fallmerayer, is to be found in Romilly Jenkins, *Byzantium and Byzantinism; Lectures in Memory of Louise Taft Semple* (University of Cin-

cinnati, 1963); see also G. Finlay, *History of Greece from Its Conquest by the Crusaders to Its Conquest by the Turks* (London, 1851), chap. I.

45. For example, the pioneer work of J. C. Lawson, *Modern Greek Folklore and Ancient Greek Religion* (Cambridge, 1910); in comparative oral epic, see the various studies of J. A. Notopoulos; also the remark of K. J. Dover in M. Platnauer, *Fifty Years of Classical Scholarship* (Oxford, 1954), p. 100; K. Romaios, Οἱ Κόκκυγες τρεῖς τοῦ Ἀριστοφάνους, *Athena*, 59 (1955): 73 f; G. P. Anagnostopoulos, "Γλωσσικὰ Ἀνάλεκτα I," *Athena*, 36 (1924): 1 f, an extended effort to isolate popular speech in Aristophanes by comparison with modern Greek vernacular.

46. *Wasps* 20 f; cf. *Carmina Popularia* 10 (Diehl, II, 196); also Cratinus, Frags. 85 f; Crates, Frag. 29; the riddles of Cleobulus and Cleobulina, Diehl, I, 264.

47. Athenaeus, XIV, 648 f (Gulick's translation), *Carm. Pop.* 13; cf. also 12 and 14. Food is a favorite motif generally in the popular and iambic traditions, for example, Semonides 8, 10, 13 (Diehl), and Alcman 49 and 56.

48. For example, *Knights* 1166 f; *Eccl.* 1169 f; *Ach.* 545 f; Frag. 320.

49. *Scolia Anon.* 21 (Diehl, II, 187).

50. *Ach.* 532 f; cf. Timocreon, 5 (Diehl, II, 122).

51. Cf. *Ach.* 260 f; *Carm. Pop.* 47, 48.

52. *Carm. Pop.* 1, 2, 32; cf. *Peace* 796 f. Aristophanes' use of swallow imagery closely resembles the χελιδονίσματα in its association of swallows with both spring and nonsensical chatter; cf. *Thesm.* 1; *Birds* 1417, 1681; Frag. 601; *Frogs* 93. It seems to have been a popular conception, cf. E. Fraenkel, ed. Aeschylus, *Agamemnon* (Oxford, 1950), *ad v.* 1050.

II. *Comic Heroism*

1. *Ach.* 377 f.

2. If Aristotle did evolve a theory of comic catharsis, it is doubtful if it had much application to Old Comedy, which seems to have been for him a phase in the teleological development toward the New; cf. Chap. I, notes 3 and 8.

3. Plato, *Gorgias* 482b4.

4. W. Whitman, *Song of Myself.* Cf. the remarks of K. Reinhardt on the constant "Widersprüchlichkeit" of the comic hero, "Aristophanes und Athen," pp. 298 f.

5. Anon., *De Comoed.* XVI, 63 (Cantarella).

6. *Ach.* 1037 f.

7. Aristotle, *Eth. Nic.* 1108a25.

8. *Clouds* 449 f; the verb εἰρωνεύεσθαι occurs in *Birds* 1211, and εἰρωνικῶς in *Wasps* 174, in both cases implying a questionable hidden intention. For a study of the fifth-century meaning of the word, and its close similarity to the meaning of *alazon*, see R. Stark, "Sokratisches in der Vögeln," *Rhein. Mus.*,

96 (1953): 77 f. The term βωμολόχος also comes close to the meaning of ἀλαζών, *Knights* 1358 f, where it gains threatening overtones.

9. Aristotle, *Rhet.* III, 18, 1419b8.

10. *Il.* IX, 443.

11. *Il.* III, 202.

12. *Od.* 13, 291 f.

13. For example, *Il.* I, 149, IV, 339; *Od.* 2, 88; 8, 548; cf. Sophocles, *Antig.* 1037, 1047, 1061; *Oed. R.* 388.

14. *Knights* 178 f; on the identification of the two slaves, see below, Chap. III, "Knights," n. 10.

15. *Knights* 336 f.

16. *Wasps* 192; cf. Calypso's use of ἀλιτρός, *Od.* 5, 182, to mean "clever" rather than, as usual, "sinful."

17. *Clouds* 1065 f.

18. *Birds* 430 f, Rogers' trans. Cf. Murphy, "Rhetoric," p. 92.

19. On *poneria* in Greece today and how children are trained to it, see Ernestine Friedl, *Vasilika, A Village in Modern Greece* (New York, 1962), esp. pp. 78 f. I am indebted to J. A. Notopoulos for this reference.

20. *Od.* 18, 281 f. See C. H. Whitman, *Homer and the Heroic Tradition* (Cambridge, Mass., 1958), p. 303, for what seems to be the more essential meaning of this scene.

21. *H. Hermes* 13 f. With these epithets, cf. also those applied to the Cercopes in Suidas.

22. *Ibid.* 31; cf. Dicaeopolis' address to the eel, *Ach.* 885 f.

23. *Ibid.* 54 f.

24. *Ibid.* 156; cf. *Il.* I, 149.

25. *Ibid.* 171 f.

26. *Ibid.* 265 f.

27. *Wasps* 354 f, 1200 f.

28. *Il.* VI, 234 f.

29. Hesiod, *Theog.* 535 f; *Erga* 47 f.

30. Paus. IV, 15, 5; cf. his escape from the Keadas pit with the aid of a fox, IV, 18, 6–7. I am indebted to M. Ostwald for pointing out these stories to me.

31. See *Ox. Pap.* XXII, 2309 (Lobel); for the reconstructions, see H. Langerbeck, "Margites," *HSCP* 63 (1958), pp. 33 f; M. Forderer, *Zum homerischen Margites* (Amsterdam, 1960), known to me only in review by W. Ludwig, *Gnomon*, 33 (1961): 448 f. See also K. Latte in *Gnomon*, 27 (1955): 492, and J. A. Davison in *CR*, N.S. 6 (1956): 13; 8 (1958): 13 f. Forderer and Davison deny that the papyrus is part of the Homeric *Margites*, Davison asserting that it belongs to a later poem on the same theme, perhaps by Pigres of Halicarnassus; cf. Suidas, *s.v.* "Pigres." Lobel, Latte, and Langerbeck accept the papyrus as part of the *Margites*, probably rightly.

32. *Schol. ad Aeschin. In Ctesiph.* 160; see T. W. Allen, *Homeri Opera*, V (Oxford, 1952), 152 f, for *testimonia*.

33. Forderer, *Zum homerischen Margites*, and Langerbeck, "Margites," respectively. I cannot extract so much from the meager remains, least of all Langerbeck's elaborate theory, rightly criticized by Ludwig in the review of Forderer, pp. 449 f.

34. *Poetics* 1448b.

35. *Poetics* 1449a. On the formal relations between iambus and comedy, see W. Jaeger, *Paideia*, 2nd ed., I, 361 f.

36. Arch., Frag. 1 (Diehl).

37. Frags. 18, 77. One might add the phallic exaggeration of Frag. 102.

38. Frag. 79. Cf. Katherine Lever, *The Art of Greek Comedy* (London, 1956), p. 4. Cf. also Alcaeus, Frag. 39; such a mood could be considered appropriate to lyric as well as iambic, as often in Aristophanic passages of invective.

39. *Ach.* 1156 f.

40. Frag. 64.

41. *Peace* 1270 f.

42. One would like to know more about Cratinus' *Archilochi*.

43. See N. M. Kondoleou, "Νέαι ἐπιγραφαὶ περὶ τοῦ Ἀρχιλόχου ἐκ Πάρου," Ἀρχαιολογικὴ Ἐφημερίς, 1952, pp. 32 f; also Werner Peek, "Neues von Archilochos," *Philologus*, 99 (1955): 4 f.

44. *Erga* 371; cf. 375.

45. On Tisias and Corax, see Sext. Emp., *Adv. Math.* II, 96 f.

46. *Poetics* 1448a16; 1449a31.

47. *Das Groteske in Malerei und Dichtung* (Munich, 1960). The grotesque has also been studied in Aristophanes by H. Steiger in *Philologus*, 89 (1934): 161 f, 275 f, 416 f. Although Steiger recognizes the relations between the grotesque and fantasy and transformation, his conception seems to involve too much the ideas of simple exaggeration and satire rather than extradimensionality.

48. *Ibid.*, 136 f.

49. Vitruv., *De Architectura* VII, 5, 3–4, quoted by Kayser, p. 14; Horace, *Ars Poetica* 1 f.

50. *Ecl.* VI, 48.

51. *Frogs* 930 f., cf. *Birds* 800; for fragments of a sculptured horse-cock, and references to painted ones on vases, see G. Dickins, *Catalog of the Acropolis Museum*, (Cambridge, England, 1912–21) no. 597.

52. See Pickard-Cambridge, *Dithyramb* (2nd ed.), 151 f, and plates VII–IX.

53. *Bacchae* 920 f.

54. *Hymn to Dion.* 13 f.

55. *Il.* II, 270.

56. *Il.* II, 213; cf. *Margites*, reconstructed from Plato, *Alcib.* 2, 147b.

57. *Ach.* 578 f.

58. Cf. above, n. 9.

59. Cf. *Il.* I, 163 f, 231 f, and *Il.* II, 225 f; see Whitman, *Homer and the Heroic Tradition*, p. 161.

60. *Od.* 9, 369 f.

61. For example, the scene between Peithetaerus and the oracle monger in *Birds*, 974 f. The practice seems to have been frequent, cf. Plato, *Phaedrus* 236 c.

62. *Od.* 9, 357 f.

63. *Birds* 1583 f.

64. Cf. Cornford, pp. 20 f, on the "new Zeus" motif. Plutus will not fit here, for he was always a god; and it is confusing to introduce, as Cornford does, the new Zeus (Dinos) of the *Clouds,* since he does not coincide with the hero. Cornford's argument is, of course, aimed in a different direction.

65. The threat to the self runs throughout the *nomos-physis* debate, and finds its most pointed statement in the work of Antiphon. But it is implicit earlier in the very formulation of the idea of the psyche, and especially in the ethical and political fragments of Democritus. Although E. A. Havelock is doubtless right in saying that Democritus was incapable of thinking of the individual as such, in our terms (*The Liberal Temper in Greek Politics,* New Haven, 1957, p. 130), he was certainly approaching it in such declarations of moral responsibility as Frags. B 170, 171, 173, 174, in DK, *Vorsokr.,* II, 178 f. For a full exploration of Democritus' sense of human helplessness, and possible cures for it arising from natural adaptability and skillful manipulation, see C. P. Segal, "Reason, Emotion, and Society in the Sophists and Democritus" (unpubl. diss., Harvard, 1961). See also the brief but telling remarks of Ehrenberg, p. 358.

66. *Oed. R.* 1076 f.

67. Aesch., *Septem* 689 f.

68. Epicharmus, Frag. 276 (Kaibel).

69. *The Greeks and Their Gods* (Boston, 1955), 113 f.

III. *City and Individual*

ACHARNIANS

1. The two themes are neatly combined in *Thesmophoriazusae.* The monologue type is not necessarily a parody of tragedy; see Russo, p. 149.

2. Pindar, *Pyth.* VIII, 22. On "grand" compounds, see Demetrius, *On Style* II, 92; cf. Peithetaerus, Lysistrata (a real name, however), Philocleon, etc. See C. Bailey, "Who played Dicaeopolis?" *Greek Poetry and Life* (Oxford, 1936), for the theory that "Dicaeopolis" indicates "Aeginetan," that is, Aristophanes himself, who played the role.

3. *Ach.* 6. The allusion is unexplained. Van Leeuwen, *Acharnenses*

(Leiden, 1901), *ad loc.*, and Starkie, *Acharnians of Aristophanes* (cf. Excursus I), followed by A. Rostagni, "I Babilonesi," *Rivista di Filologia*, 53 (1925): 486 f, believe it refers to a scene in Aristophanes' own *Babylonians*, produced in 426, and hence is a self-compliment. Such a scene, perhaps of actual vomiting, is not so unlikely as Croiset thought (43 f) in view of *Ach.* 585 f, and Ben Jonson's *Poetaster*. For theories that Cleon was actually prosecuted, see Croiset, pp. 52 f; U. von Wilamowitz-Moellendorff, "Über die Wespen des Aristophanes," *SB Berlin*, 1911, p. 462; G. Busolt, *Griechische Geschichte* (Gotha, 1885–97), III pt. 2, 994, n. 6.

4. Amphitheus is obscure. Van Leeuwen follows H. Müller-Strübung (*Aristophanes und die historische Kritik*, pp. 697 f) in believing him to be the brother of Callias, Hermogenes, who claimed descent from the gods on both sides and had strong Spartan affiliations. (Cf. Xen., *Hell.* VI, 3, 6; *Symp.* 3, 14; 4, 48; *Mem.* II, 10; Plato, *Cratyl.* 384c). Starkie, *ad loc.*, is noncommittal. Russo, p. 150, tries to find in him a figure of more general significance, representing the rural democracy, with Eleusinian affiliations connecting him with the soil.

5. *Ach.* 111–122.
6. Twice, *Ach.* 59, 123.
7. *Ach.* 163 f.
8. *Ach.* 128.
9. *Ach.* 167 f.
10. *Ach.* 195 f.
11. *Ach.* 985.
12. *Thesm.* 67 f; cf. 80.
13. *Clouds* 607 f; cf. *Birds* 992 f.
14. *Ach.* 1002, 1234.
15. *Ach.* 133.
16. The existence of an agon in the *Acharnians* was denied by Zielinski, *Gliederung*, pp. 52 f, on grounds of meter and the lack of a truly symmetrical antagonist. This argument is unnecessarily rigid, and is rightly answered by Russo, pp. 178 f; see also Mazon, *Essai*, pp. 173 f, distinguishing between the double and single agon, and Pohlenz, p. 40.
17. Cf. *Frogs* 892.
18. See Chap. I, note 35.
19. *Ach.* 634. Plato's summary description of a sophist, *Soph.* 268c8, comes close to describing the hero of Old Comedy as well.
20. *Ach.* 429.
21. *Ach.* 300 f. Why, if the Acharnians oppose peace, they hate the leader of the war policy is unclear. One may assume a reference to the *Knights*, already planned and perhaps partly written, or simply that Aristophanes wanted to get Cleon into the picture. He is seldom bothered, especially in passages of invective, by considerations of consistency or relevance.
22. *Ach.* 333.

23. *Ach.* 180 f.

24. *Ach.* 416, 447, 444.

25. *Ach.* 445, 451 f.

26. *Ach.* 484 f.

27. *Ach.* 490 f; earlier at 391 the chorus has attributed the wiles of Sisyphus to Dicaeopolis.

28. *Ach.* 523. Note the different interpretation of the cause of the decree in *Peace* 605 f.

29. Cratinus, Frags. 37–48 (the *Dionysalexandros*); also Frags. 240, 241. Yet it must have been upon this speech that Croiset, pp. 57 f, based his theory that the *Acharnians* was directed chiefly against Pericles. On parodies of Herodotus in Aristophanes, see G. Perrotta, "Erodoto parodiato da Aristofane," *Rendiconti del Istituto Lombardo delle Scientie e Lettere*, 59 (1926): pp. 205 f; Russo, p. 151.

30. See Starkie, *Acharnians*, Excursus VI; and Murphy, "Rhetoric," p. 104.

31. Thuc. V, 19, 24.

32. *Ach.* 269 f. Most editors have seen this point. For a recent canvassing of the problem, see Russo, p. 177, n. 35.

33. *Ach.* 589. Rogers suggests "the Great Boastard."

34. *Ach.* 593 f. The compounds in 603 and 605 seem to be made partly of personal names.

35. *Frogs* 919 f; cf. 966, 1056 f.

36. *Ach.* 600 f; cf. 65–72.

37. *Ach.* 676 f.

38. It is quite clear in *Wasps* 1365; perhaps also in *Lysis.* 600 f.

39. See Rogers, *ad loc.*

40. *Ach.* 609, 613. Ἀνθράκυλλος, Reiske's conjecture for Δράκυλλος *codd.* All the other names are significant.

41. *Ach.* 321.

42. *Ach.* 336, 348.

43. *Ach.* 350 f.

44. *Ach.* 883; cf. Aesch., Frag. 174.

45. *Ach.* 665 f.

46. *Ach.* 575.

47. *Ach.* 965.

48. *Ach.* 1074; cf. 970, 988.

49. *Ach.* 1105 f.

50. *Ach.* 1182 f.

51. *Ach.* 230 f.

52. *Ach.* 979 f.

53. *Ach.* 1178.

54. By D. Page, in *Wiener Studien*, 69 (1956): 116 f; cf. Starkie, *ad loc.* The passage is defended by W. Süss, "Inkongruenzen," pp. 126 f. While dif-

fering from Page's opinion about this passage, I wish to express admiration for the other textual suggestions offered in this brilliant article.

55. *Ach.* 1174 f.
56. For example, *Birds* 1372 f, 1004 f; *Ach.* 485.
57. *Ach.* 606.
58. *Ach.* 620 f.
59. *Ach.* 33 f.
60. *Ach.* 816 f.
61. *Ach.* 784 f.
62. *Ach.* 836 f.
63. *Ach.* 929 f.
64. *Ach.* 966.
65. *Ach.* 1018 f.
66. *Ach.* 1062.
67. *Ach.* 1008 f, 1037 f.
68. *Ach.* 1090 f.
69. *Ach.* 626 f.

KNIGHTS

1. C. A. Behr, "Old Comedy and the Free State" (unpubl. diss., Harvard, 1960); summary in *HSCP* 65 (1961), pp. 345 f. However, see also Croiset, p. 50, to the effect that εἰσαγγελία before the Council was precisely for cases *not* strictly defined by law.

2. For the view that Callistratus was actually the one indicted, see S. Srebrny, "De Aristophanis origine peregrina," *Charisteria Sinko* (Warsaw, 1951), pp. 320 f; the more likely view, that it was Aristophanes himself, is upheld by V. Steffen, "De Aristophane a Cleone in ius vocato," *Eos*, 47.1 (1954): 7 f; cf. C. Bailey, "Who Played Dicaeopolis?" *Greek Poetry and Life* (Oxford, 1936), p. 232. The whole problem is confused by the tradition that Aristophanes was also accused of foreign birth; see Schol. *ad Ach.* 378, and the various *Vitae*. Van Leeuwen, "De Aristophane Peregrino," *Mnem.*, N.S., 16 (1888): 263 f, and *Wasps, Proleg.*, pp. xii and xxiii, believes he was actually exiled, and hence produced under others' names; Srebrny, that he was attacked for ξενία by Cleon after the *Knights*, on the grounds of Aeginetan origin, but got off by "playing the ape a little" (cf. *Wasps* 1284 and Schol. *ad loc.*); similarly, Croiset, pp. 89 f; Steffen, p. 17, is skeptical about any Aeginetan connections, and rejects the whole story of the γραφὴ ξενίας, and emends Schol. *ad Ach.* 378 by writing *αἰξωνείας = βλασφημίας for ξενίας, and identifies the two suits as one, after the *Babylonians*. This emendation is more than dubious, since * αἰξωνεία is unattested, and αἰξωνεύομαι is almost certainly a comic coinage. Aristophanes' connection with Aegina, whatever its nature, is clear from *Ach.* 652 f, and it may well have provided Cleon with a legal quibble whereby he could retaliate for the *Knights*. The charge

would have been serious and difficult to answer, and Aristophanes may have been forced to "play the ape," and extricate himself by jestingly quoting *Od.* 1, 215 f.

3. See T. A. Dorey, "Aristophanes and Cleon," *Greece and Rome,* 2nd series, 3 (1956): 132 f. Cf. Perrotta, *Aristofane,* p. 4.

4. Cf. Croiset, p. 83; K. J. Dover, in Platnauer, *Fifty Years,* p. 102.

5. Croiset, p. 73; Ehrenberg, pp. 49 f.

6. *Knights* 507 f.

7. *Knights* 580, 1121.

8. For example, Cratinus, Frags. 160 f, 238, 239; Telecleides, Frag. 1; Eupolis, *Demoi,* Frags. 90 f, 276 f; Pherecrates, Frags. 10, 130.

9. Croiset, pp. 86 f.

10. There seems to me no reasonable doubt that the two slaves are Nicias and Demosthenes, though never so named in the text; neither is the Paphlagonian ever called Cleon, whose name occurs in the play only once, and then in a context which does not connect him with the figure on the stage (*Kn.* 976). But see K. J. Dover, "Aristophanes' *Knights* 11–20," *CR,* IX.3 (1959): 196 f; also Croiset, p. 77.

11. So Reinhardt, pp. 298 f, seems to include Demos as an example of the comic hero with all his contradictions, because he is simultaneously a small farmer and the sovereign people of Athens. This is not really a contradiction, however, and Newiger's account is more satisfactory; see below, note 12.

12. Newiger. For other studies of personified abstractions, see L. Deubner, "Personificationen abstracter Begriffe," Roscher, *Lexikon,* III, 2068 f; T. B. L. Webster, "Interplay of Greek Art and Literature," Inaugural Lecture, London, 1949; Katherine Lever, "Poetic Metaphor and Dramatic Allegory in Aristophanes," *CW,* 46 (1953): 220 f.

13. *Kn.* 41 f; the personification of Demos may have been common coin, since it was done also by Eupolis (see Frags. 213, 321); but these may be also the plagiarisms mentioned in *Clouds* 553 f.

14. See Eup. Frags. 90–131, and Edmonds' reconstruction of the play, Vol. I, 978 f; cf. D. Page, *Greek Literary Papyri* (Loeb Classical Library, Cambridge, Mass., and London, 1950), I, 202 f.

15. Reinhardt, p. 289. Cf. *Kn.* 776, where Cleon boasts that he has cared for no individual provided he could please Demos; the line strongly emphasizes the paradox, for Demos is both individual and collective, as Newiger says.

16. *Kn.* 147.

17. *Kn.* 152 f; cf. 193 f.

18. *Kn.* 178 f.

19. *Kn.* 180 f.

20. *Kn.* 903.

21. Pherecr: Anon., *De Comoed.* VI, 8 (Cantarella); Edmonds, I, 207.

Eupolis: Platonius, Περὶ διαφορᾶς χαρακτήρων, 15 (Cantarella); Edmonds, I, 313.

22. Cf. M. Pohlenz, "Aristophanes Ritter," *NGA*, 1952, pp. 113 f.

23. Cf. *Ach.* 6; *Kn.* 402 f, 833 f, 996; see above n. 3, and Chap. III, "Acharnians," n. 3.

24. *Kn.* 324 f.

25. *Kn.* 275 f.

26. *Kn.* 430 f.

27. *Kn.* 756 f.

28. *Kn.* 830.

29. *Kn.* 511, 692, 919 f; cf. 637 f.

30. *Kn.* 801 f, 864 f.

31. *Kn.* 984; cf. *Peace* 228 f, 259.

32. Cf. Thuc. III, 36, 5; V, 16, 1.

33. *Kn.* 248, 416; κυνοκέφαλλος; cf. 1017 f.

34. *Kn.* 74 f.

35. *Kn.* 19.

36. *Kn.* 46 f.

37. *Kn.* 188 f., 414.

38. *Kn.* 128 f, 181, 293, 297, 410, 500.

39. *Kn.* 213 f.

40. *Kn.* 278 f.

41. *Kn.* 353 f. On eating alone, cf. *Wasps*, 923.

42. *Kn.* 490 f.

43. *Kn.* 642 f; 676 f.

44. *Kn.* 706 f *passim*.

45. *Kn.* 715 f.

46. *Kn.* 824 f, 954, 1007.

47. *Kn.* 814 f; Athens, it seems, "lunches" on the Piraeus, ἀριστώσῃ!

48. *Kn.* 1004.

49. *Kn.* 1135 f, 1147 f.

50. *Kn.* 1229 f. The Scholia list three plays of Euripides of which this is supposed to be a parody, but H. Steiger, *Groteske*, pp. 173 f, rightly points out that the clearest resemblance is to *Oedipus Rex*, perhaps performed the previous year. Cf. B. Knox, "The Date of the *Oedipus Tyrannus* of Sophocles," *AJP*, 77 (1956): 133 f.

51. *Kn.* 1325.

52. F. Fergusson, *The Idea of a Theater* (Princeton, 1949), Appendix.

53. *Kn.* 1184 f.

54. Cf. the regular opposition of *logos* to *ergon* in Thucydides; the concept of *logos* in Gorgias, and its association with *apaté* (see T. Rosenmeyer, "Gorgias, Aeschylus and *Apate*," *AJP*, 76 (1955): 225 f.

55. *Kn.* 216; cf. *Ach.* 447, *Peace* 534.

56. *Kn.* 634 f.

57. *Kn.* 782, 352; with the latter, cf. *Ach.* 380.

58. *Kn.* 342 f.

59. *Kn.* 720; cf. below, Chap. V. A small example of how poetic language acts upon itself may be observed in *Kn.* 841 and 847 f, where the metaphoric use of λαβή seems to prompt the fantasy on the shield handles.

60. *Kn.* 61, 1011 f, and Van Leeuwen *ad loc.*, 1086 f; cf. Thuc. II, 21, *Birds* 978.

61. *Kn.* 1017–1034; on the designation of demagogues as "watchdogs of the people," see Starkie on *Wasps* 895 (*The Wasps of Aristophanes*, London and New York, 1897).

62. *Kn.* 1037–1049.

63. *Kn.* 1067 f.

64. *Kn.* 1080 f.

65. *Kn.* 1092 f; cf. 199.

66. *Kn.* 836 f.

67. *Kn.* 985 f; perhaps suggested to Aristophanes by Cratinus' Δωροῖ συκοπέδιλε, quoted in 529, and itself an excellent example of the practice under discussion.

68. *Kn.* 595 f.

69. *Kn.* 1300 f. The whole passage has been attributed to Eupolis (Schol. *ad loc.*, cf. Eup. Frag. 78; also, Frags. 52, 213), but there is little to suggest Eupolis, so far as we know him, in this fantasia. Perhaps *Kn.* 1288 f (= Eup. Frag. 454) were his. Pohlenz, "Aristophanes Ritter," pp. 120 f, strongly supports Aristophanes' authorship.

70. For example, *Lys.* 591 f.

71. *Kn.* 197 f.

72. Eup. Frag. 78; cf. n. 69 above.

73. Platonius, Περὶ διαφ. χαρακτ. 15 (Cantarella).

74. *Kn.* 684 f.

75. See Pohlenz, "Aristophanes Ritter," pp. 124 f. Pohlenz notes the divine implications of 1322 and 1336 f.

76. Cf. *Kn.* 148 f.

77. Cf. Pindar, *Pyth.* III, 108 f.

78. *Kn.* 1336 f.

PEACE

1. Wilam., "Wespen," p. 465; cf., for example, Rogers, *Peace*, pp. xv f; G. Murray, *Ancient Greek Literature* (London, 1897), p. 285 (Murray offers a kindlier view later, *Aristophanes*, p. 57).

2. Thuc. V, 17, 2. The effort to date the play to 419/8 on the basis of line 990 is surely wrong; see Rogers, *Peace*, p. xv.

3. *Peace* 473.

4. *Peace* 918 f; cf. 190.

5. *Peace* 54 f.

6. *Peace* 154 f.

7. *Peace* 182 f.

8. *Peace* 131 f.

9. *Peace* 722; the line parodies Eur. *Beller.* Frag. 314 (Nauck).

10. *Peace* 42.

11. *Peace* 456.

12. *Peace* 25 f.

13. *Peace* 827 f. Cf. below, Chap. V. Cf. also Socrates in the *Clouds*, who must suspend himself in a basket in order to study "the things of the air."

14. Cf. *Peace* 54 f, 75 f, 90, 95, 114 f, for associations of madness and flying.

15. *Peace* 166 f. A kind of intermediate stage, a cheerful stench, one might say, comes at 335 from the chorus. There is perhaps a subtle association of dung and war in 151, where ἡμερῶν τριῶν is the regular phrase for soldiers' rations; cf. 312, and *Ach.* 197; it is transformed in 716 to a "three-days' soup" of Theoria.

16. *Peace* 530 f.

17. *Peace* 860 f, 868.

18. *Peace* 1078.

19. *Peace* 758.

20. *Peace* 1, 1357; cf. 1314, 869.

21. *Peace* 33 f, 1307 f.

22. *Peace* 242 f; cf. *Kn.* 213 f.

23. *Peace* 536; the motiflike significance of the phrase may justify the text reading against the scholiast's ἐς ἱπνόν; other occurrences: 552, 563, 569, 585, (632, ἐκ τῶν ἀγρῶν), 707, 866, 1202, 1249, 1318, 1329.

24. *Peace* 564 f.

25. *Peace* 544 f; cf. 1210 f. As in the *Ach.* vineyards symbolize peace, and are strictly opposed to "crests," "Gorgons," etc.: cf. 307, 394 f, 474, 557, 561, 596 f, 1159–1174.

26. *Peace* 613, 631 f, 700 f. Cratinus was probably not really dead; cf. Schol. *ad Ach.* 521, Lucian, *Macrob.* 25, and Rogers, *ad loc.*

27. *Peace* 665 f, 1202 f.

28. *Peace* 680 f.

29. *Peace* 1316 f.

30. *Kn.* 1389 f; *Ach.* 1198 f; cf. Basileia (*Birds*), Diallagé (*Lysistrata*). The flute girl of the *Wasps* and the dancing girl of the *Thesmophoriazusae* play similar dramatic, though less symbolic roles.

31. In favor of nudity are Wilamowitz, *Lysistrata*, pp. 186 f; and Alphonse Willem, *Aristophane*, III, 381 f. Actual nudity is denied, for a number of complicated reasons, by Russo, p. 195; a simpler, and seemingly conclusive reason is given by K. Holzinger, "Erklärung umstrittender Stellen des Aristo-

phanes," *SB Vienna*, 208.5 (1928): 34–60 — at the time of the dramatic festivals it is simply too cold.

32. *Peace* 706 f.

33. *Peace* 712; cf. *Lys.* 89.

34. *Peace* 439 f, 1136 f.

35. For example, *Peace* 1349 f, to go no further.

36. *Peace* 1159 f.

37. *Peace* 1336 f.

38. *Peace* 886 f. For this kind of virtuosity, compare Plato Comicus, Frag. 174; Pherecrates, Frags. 144b, 145.

39. *Peace* 192.

40. *Peace* 423 f.

41. *Peace* 400 f.

42. *Peace* 406 f.

43. *Peace* 418 f.

44. *Peace* 924.

45. *Peace* 1309.

46. Pindar, *Isthm.* VII, 44 f.

47. *Peace* 146 f.

48. *Peace* 605 f. On the whole tormented question of Phidias' trial, which has nothing to do with the interpretation of the play, see O. Lendle, "Philochorus über den Prozess des Phidias," *Hermes*, 83 (1955): 284 f, dating the trial in 432; see also H. Bloch, review of Jacoby, *Commentary on the Historians of Athens*, in *Gnomon*, 31 (1959): 494 f.

49. *Peace* 626 f.

50. For example, *Peace* 244, 623.

51. *Peace* 673 f; 1298 f.

52. *Peace* 1179 f. Cf. Van Leeuwen's remarks, *Pax*, p. iv.

IV. *The War between the Generations*

CLOUDS

1. Cf. T. Gelzer, "Aristophanes und sein Sokrates," *Mus. Helv.*, 13 (1956): 90 f, on the moral analogies between Strepsiades and Peithetaerus.

2. See esp. *Argumenta* 5, 6, 7; *Scholia, passim*. Cf. Frags. 378 f.

3. The second version is denied by Van Leeuwen, *Nubes*, pp. ix, xvi, and 6, n. 2, who states that only the parabasis was changed; cf. also H. van Daele, *Aristophane*, I, 155 f. Most scholars accept the second edition, for example, U. von Wilamowitz, "Der chor der Wolken des Aristophanes," *SB Berlin* (1921): 738 f; Süss, "Inkongruenzen," p. 124; Merry, *Aristophanes, The Clouds* (Oxford, 1880), p. ix; I. Bekker, *Aristophanis Nubes* (London, 1826), pp. 134 f; Murray, pp. 85 f; Starkie, *Clouds*, p. li.

4. See D. Holwerda, "De novo priorum Aristophanis Nubium indicio," *Mnemosyne*, XI (1958): 32 f; the scholium stands in Vat. Barb. 126, Saec. XIV.

5. *Clouds* 549 f, 584 f; note also the missing chorus at 888, the single epirrhema of the second parabasis, 1115 f, and the unmotivated exit of Socrates at 886. See Wilamowitz, "Der chor der Wolken," *passim*; the passages cited by Kaibel, *RE, s.v.* "Aristophanes," do not seem to me very convincing.

6. *Clouds* 1503; cf. 225.

7. Cf. *Clouds* 1483 f. One may at least question the morality of the act; though prompted by a deity, the deity is Hermes; and deities do not always instigate morally justified actions.

8. *Wasps* 1190 f; 1381 f.

9. *Clouds* 963–972, 1045–1059.

10. *Peace* 801; cf., for example, *Ach.* 1073.

11. *Clouds* 512 f.

12. *Clouds* 818 f.

13. *Clouds* 1298 f.

14. *Clouds* 1410 f, 1417; cf. Frag. 378.

15. *Clouds* 1406 f.

16. *Clouds* 1134, 1178 f.

17. *Clouds* 49 f.

18. Cf. *Clouds* 438 and 800.

19. *Clouds* 69 f.

20. *Clouds* 317 f, 331 f.

21. *Clouds* 275 f, 269 f.

22. *Clouds* 299 f.

23. *Clouds* 563 f, 595 f.

24. *Clouds* 581 f; 607 f.

25. *Clouds* 348 f.

26. *Clouds* 1457. The verb is ἐπαίρω, the same used to describe how he was trapped into his marriage, *Clouds* 42. The verb is frequently used by Aristophanes to denote a state of excitement, folly, and impending trouble; cf. *Clouds* 810; *Birds* 1448, 1657; *Wasps* 1024; *Frogs* 777.

27. *Clouds* 1458 f; cf. Herod. I, 158, 159, and the complex tempting of Xerxes in VII.

28. *Clouds* 1113, 1303 f.

29. H. Erbse, "Sokrates im Schatten der aristophaneischen Wolken," *Hermes*, 82 (1954): 385 f, esp. 400; Erbse thinks Socrates was also so motivated, but this untenable theory arises from the author's wish to show that Aristophanes never really meant to misrepresent Socrates.

30. In the whole following discussion I am much indebted to two recent works on the philosophical developments of the fifth century: E. A. Have-

lock, *The Liberal Temper in Greek Politics* (New Haven, 1957), and C. P. Segal, "Reason, Emotion and Society in the Sophists and Democritus," (unpubl. diss., Harvard, 1961).

31. See Segal, "Reason, Emotion and Society," chapters 1 and 2, esp. pp. 17 f, 24 f, 64 f, 84 f, 87 f, 96.

32. DK, *Vorsokr.*, II, 260 (Protag. A21).

33. DK, *Vorsokr.*, II, 346 (Antiph. B44, Col. 1, 10 f).

34. DK, *Vorsokr.*, II, 346 (Antiph. B44, 25 f). Cf. Segal's discussion, "Reason, Emotion and Society," chap. IV, and Havelock, *Liberal Temper*, pp. 267 f.

35. *Clouds* 1075, 1077 f. On ἀνάγκη, both human and in physics, cf. 377, 405, 437.

36. *Clouds* 1421 f; cf. the Sisyphus fragment of Critias, DK, *Vorsokr.*, II, 386 (Critias B25).

37. *Clouds* 1427 f.

38. Cf. also, on the foolishness of *nomos* and justice: *Clouds* 902, 1039, 1185 f, 1400.

39. Cf. Segal, "Reason, Emotion and Society," esp. p. 96.

40. See Wilam., "Wespen," p. 465. Cf. Mazon, *Essai*, pp. 63 f; and, by implication, Croiset, pp. 94 f; H. Erbse, "Sokrates im Schatten," pp. 385 f; N. Petruzzellis, "Aristofane e la sofistica," *Dioniso*, 20 (1957): 38 f. Kaibel's rather strange view was that the *Clouds* failed because it misrepresented Socrates, while Ameipsias represented him correctly in the *Konnos* of the same year, *RE, s.v.* "Sokrates."

41. See E. A. Havelock, "Why Was Socrates Tried?" *Studies in Honor of Gilbert Norwood*, M. E. White, ed., (Toronto, 1952), p. 105.

42. This clearly precludes interpreting the statement of Argument V, that the second *Clouds* was produced in the archonship of Ameinias (422); it may have been written then.

43. Cf. Süss, *Inkongruenzen*, p. 124, and Wilamowitz, "Der Chor der Wolken des Aristophanes," p. 738, for the view that the whole agon is new; on the other side, H. Erbse, "Sokrates im Schatten," pp. 395 f.

44. Presumably, he had to play one of the Logoi, and the song at 888 (now missing, if ever composed) would have given him time to change his costume. Yet, there is no song after the agon, and Socrates begins speaking at 1105 as if he had been there all along.

45. Cf. Edmonds, I, 680 f, n. c, to Aristophanes Frag. 378a, for the suggestion that something *similar* to the agon stood in the first *Clouds*; Schol. *ad Vesp.* 1037 seems to prove that the Weaker Discourse was in the play. This passage in the *Wasps* might be taken as supporting the theory that the first version was as moralizing as the second, but it may not refer to the *Clouds* at all; cf. M. Platnauer, "Three Notes on Aristophanes' *Wasps*," *CR*, 63 (1949): pp. 6 f, showing that the lines refer to the Ὁλκάδες, produced at the Lenaea in 423.

46. E. R. Dodds, *The Greeks and the Irrational* (Berkeley and Los Angeles, 1956), pp. 189 f; cf. Croiset, p. 122, on the situations later, during the Hermocopidae investigations.

47. Cf. Frag. 216.

48. *Clouds* 534 f.

49. Croiset, p. 33.

50. Mazon, *Essai*, pp. 179 f.

51. *Clouds* 264 f. See Gelzer, "Aristophanes und sein Socrates," p. 81 and n. 51, on the kinship between the language of natural philosophy and that of the theogonic and Orphic tradition.

52. See *Clouds* 377, 405; cf. 365.

53. *Clouds* 343 f.

54. *Clouds* 386 f; cf. 295.

55. *Clouds* 160 f; cf. 194, where an anus is learning astronomy all by itself.

56. *Clouds* 437.

57. See Gelzer, "Aristophanes und sein Socrates," p. 83, on air as a symbol of *alazoneia*; see pp. 68 f on Diogenes of Apollonia, and n. 14 for works identifying Socrates' physics with those of Diogenes (esp. H. Diels, "Uber Leukipp und Demokrit," *Verhandlung der 35 Philologenversammlung*, Stettin, 1880, pp. 105 f). See Gelzer, pp. 79 f on Aristophanes' use of air as a symbol of *alazoneia*. See also L. Edelstein, "Περὶ Ἀέρων und die Sammlung der Hippokratischen Schriften," *Problemata*, 4 (1931): 132 f; Newiger, p. 64; and Eupolis, Frag. 146b on Protagoras: ὃς ἀλαζονεύεται μὲν ἀλιτήριος περὶ τῶν μετεώρων, τὰ δὲ χαμᾶθεν ἐσθίει. Cf. n. 26 in this chapter.

58. *Clouds* 177 f.

59. *Clouds* 497 f, 719, 856 f.

60. *Clouds* 423 f. Cf. 260, 419.

61. *Clouds* 636 f.

62. *Clouds* 445 f. Cf. *Birds* 430 f.

63. Diminutives, expressive of λεπτολογία: cf. *Clouds* 144 f, 153, 179, 230, 320, 358, 740, 831, 1109, 1404, 1496.

64. *Clouds* 12 f.

65. *Clouds* 43 f.

66. *Clouds* 707 f.

67. See B. Marzullo, "Strepsiade," *Maia*, 6 (1953): 115 f, for a thorough study of the rolling and twisting images of the play.

68. For example, Murray, pp. 92 f; B. Snell, "Das frühste Zeugnis über Sokrates," *Philologus*, 97 (1948): 125 f; W. Schmid, "Das Sokratesbild der Wolken," *ibid.*, pp. 209 f; P. Mesnard, "La Verité transcendentale du Socrate d'Aristophane," *Mélanges Diès*, pp. 181 f; R. Stark, "Sokratisches in der Vögeln," *Rhein. Mus.*, 96 (1953): 83 f.

69. *Apology* 18b.

70. See Ehrenberg, p. 274 and n. 3.

71. Socrates is mentioned, outside of Aristophanes, in: Teclecleides, Frags. 39, 40; Eupolis, Frags. 352, 353, 361 (cf. Lucian, *Piscator* 25); Ameipsias, Frag. 9 (a rather complimentary remark).

WASPS

1. *Wasps* 341, 503 f, 720, 737 f, 1003 f, 1419 f, 1462 f.
2. *Wasps* 94 f.
3. *Wasps* 759, 1220; cf. 342. Cf. also Wilam., "Wespen," p. 485.
4. *Wasps* 281 f.
5. *Wasps* 106 f, 278 f.
6. *Wasps* 322; cf. 340.
7. *Wasps* 240 f.
8. DK, *Vorsokr.*, II, 355 (Antiphon, Frag. 44, Col. II, 25 f).
9. *Wasps* 1075 f.
10. *Wasps* 1073, 427.
11. *Wasps* 1114 f.
12. *Wasps* 1068 f.
13. *Wasps* 219 f.
14. *Wasps* 300 f.
15. *Wasps* 235 f, 354; cf. 357, 556, 1201.
16. Cf. Wilam., "Wespen," pp. 479 f, 482.
17. *Wasps* 725 f.
18. Note the verb νουθετέω, lines 732 and 743, and others indicating good sense and reason: ἔγνωκε, 744; λογίζεται, 745; σωφρονεῖ, 748.
19. *Wasps* 751 f.
20. *Wasps* 89.
21. *Wasps* 349.
22. *Wasps* 522 f, 713 f.
23. *Wasps* 508 f.
24. *Wasps* 548 f. With this claim, Croiset, pp. 105 f, compares Pseudo-Xenophon I, 18.
25. *Wasps* 622 f; cf. 571.
26. *Wasps* 671.
27. *Wasps* 1457 f.
28. Wilam., "Wespen," pp. 460 f.
29. *Wasps* 970; cf. *Knights* 1015 f on Cleon as watchdog of the people.
30. *Wasps* 922 f; cf. 896, 914 f.
31. *Wasps* 911.
32. *Wasps* 952 f; cf. 989.
33. *Wasps* 966.
34. *Wasps* 976 f.
35. *Wasps* 900 f.
36. *Wasps* 596 f; cf. *Knights* 59 f.

37. *Wasps* 672 f, 678 f, 684 f, 888 f, 917.
38. *Wasps* 1172; cf. *Birds* 804 f.
39. Wilam., "Wespen," p. 472.
40. *Wasps* 429, 1292.
41. *Wasps* 1304.
42. *Clouds* 1078.
43. *Wasps* 737.
44. *Wasps* 165; cf. 367 f.
45. *Wasps* 1066 f.
46. *Wasps* 354 f; cf. 396.
47. *Wasps* 1190 f.
48. *Wasps* 1198 f. With the Phaÿllus passage, cf. *Ach.* 213 f.
49. *Wasps* 1332 f.
50. *Wasps* 1351 f.
51. *Wasps* 1381 f.
52. Rogers, *ad loc.*, suggests that the whole scene, from 1250 to 1449, is an afterthought on the poet's part, designed merely to insure success through obscenity and slapstick.
53. *Wasps* 1356 f, 1370.
54. *Il.* XVI, 259 f.
55. *Wasps* 1336 f.
56. *Wasps* 1332 f, 1366, 1393, 1406, 1441.
57. *Wasps* 1253 f.
58. *Wasps* 1476 f.
59. *Wasps* 1503; Rogers' rendering of ἐμμέλεια κονδύλου.
60. *Wasps* 1486, 1489, 1496.
61. *Wasps* 1517, 1523, 1529 f.
62. Cf. *Clouds* 380 f.
63. *Wasps* 132.
64. *Wasps* 432.
65. *Wasps* 698 f, Rogers' translation.
66. *Wasps* 924.
67. *Wasps* 395.
68. *Wasps* 144 f, 184 f. Bdelycleon calls him *poneros*, 193.
69. *Wasps* 189, 1306, 1310.
70. *Wasps* 1408.
71. *Wasps* 1370; cf. *Clouds* 1273. The motif of second childhood also is common to both plays. Even Xanthias is rejuvenated by his beating, *Wasps* 1297 f.
72. *Wasps* 107 with 366 f, 129, 140, 207, 363, 778 (The octopus is said to eat himself for lack of other provisions, Pherecrates, Frag. 13), 704.
73. *Wasps* 155.
74. *Wasps* 15 f.

75. *Wasps* 31 f.
76. *Wasps* 1031 f.
77. *Wasps* 1507 f.
78. *Wasps* 1531 f. The "potent" is really τρίορχος.
79. *Wasps* 10.

V. *The Anatomy of Nothingness*

BIRDS

1. See J. W. Süvern, *Essay on the Birds of Aristophanes* (translated by W. R. Hamilton, London, 1835).

2. The view of A. W. Schlegel, *Vorlesungen über dramatische Kunst und Literatur* (Heidelberg, 1809), I, reiterated by many scholars, most recently by Van Leeuwen, *Aves*, Prolegomena; Q. Cataudella, *Aristofane* (Bari, 1934), pp. 143 f; M. Gigante, "La città dei giusti e gli 'Uccelli' di Aristofane," *Dioniso* 2 (1948): 17 f; E. M. Blaiklock, "Walking Away from the News," *Greece and Rome*, second series, 1 (1954): 98 f.

3. W. W. Merry, *Aristophanes, The Birds* (Oxford, 1904), Introduction, pp. 18 f.

4. *Birds* 119.

5. Walt Kelly, *Songs from the Pogo* (New York, 1956), pp. 144 f (© Copyright by Walt Kelly), quoted by permission of Simon and Schuster.

6. See, for instance, M. Heidegger, *What is Metaphysics?* in *Existence and Being*, trans. R. F. C. Hull and Alan Crick (London, 1949), pp. 359 f.

7. DK, *Vorsokr.*, II, 279 (Gorgias B3).

8. *Ibid.*, 282 (Gorgias B3, 83–84).

9. See C. P. Segal, "Gorgias and the Psychology of the Logos," *HSCP* 66 (1962), esp. pp. 100 f.

10. Democritus' "We know nothing correctly" (B9) negatively limits, from the point of view of epistemology, Protagoras' sanguine, anthropocentric definition of reality, DK, *Vorsokr.*, II, 262 (Protagoras B1).

11. Segal, "Gorgias," p. 110.

12. See also T. Rosenmeyer, "Gorgias, Aeschylus, and *Apate*," *AJP*, 76 (1955): 232.

13. Segal, "Gorgias," p. 120.

14. Compare also Eupolis Frag. 314 (note the image of wings), and Plato Comicus Frag. 53. These passages seem to indicate that Aristophanes was not alone in his awareness of the speech-reality issue. There is perhaps some rudimentary intimation of it in Hesiod, *Erga* 760 f. See also the remarks of Kayser, *Das Groteske*, pp. 110 f, on the demiurgic power of language.

15. *Birds* 27 f.

16. D. Fitts, *Aristophanes, The Birds* (New York, 1957).

17. The charade is, of course, of the same formal structure, as are also musical puns, such as Mozart's use of horns in *Figaro* and *Cosi fan tutte* to indicate cuckoldry. Analogous are the painted puns in a mural in a Cambridge restaurant: the picture represents a number of dogs sitting at a bar, a great Dane in a sailor suit flirting with a French poodle, and a long-haired beatnik mongrel making a speech. But the central group shows a demure cocker spaniel with a Martini glass; on one side of her stands a slick and leering doberman pinscher, who has just pinched her, while on the other side her husband, an angry-looking boxer, is about to punch the intruder in the nose. Words control the point, though not a word is printed.

18. *Birds* 156 f, with *double-entendre* on μύρτα; cf. also roses and parsley, for example, Cratinus, Frag. 111 (Edmonds); Pherecrates, Frags. 108, 28 f, 131; Plato Com., Frag. 174, 14.

19. *Birds* 114 f.

20. *Clouds* 1075 f. Cf. Chap. IV, "Clouds," n. 1, and pp. 119 f.

21. Cf. *Birds* 745 with 755 f; 1286 f.

22. *Birds* 162–184.

23. *Birds* 164 f, 185 f; cf. 1228.

24. *Birds* 188 f.

25. *Birds* 209 f.

26. *Birds* 228 f, 314 f.

27. *Birds* 284 f, 289 f.

28. *Birds* 300.

29. *Birds* 356 f.

30. Athenaeus, XIV, 629.

31. *Birds* 393 f.

32. *Birds* 430 f; cf. *Clouds* 260, 445 f.

33. *Birds* 466 f *passim*.

34. *Birds* 521; cf. Cratinus, Frag. 231.

35. *Birds* 608 f; cf. Hesiod, Frag. 171 (Rzach).

36. *Birds* 562 f. In the text Aphrodite's surrogate is the φαληρίς, "coot," supposedly a lustful bird.

37. *Birds* 547, 627.

38. *Birds* 649 f.

39. See above, pp. 108 f, 139 f.

40. *Birds* 35, 92.

41. *Birds* 199 f, 332, 353; cf. 39 f, where the winged creatures in the comparison are, however, cicadas, not birds. Perhaps κάδων should be read for δικῶν in 41.

42. *Birds* 1446 f; cf. Eupolis, Frag. 314. See above, note 14.

43. *Birds* 685 f.

44. DK, *Vorsokr.*, II, 316 (Prodicus B3, 4); cf. *Clouds* 360 f.

45. *Ibid.*, 310 f (Prodicus A9; 11; 13; 18, 5; 19).

46. On wind eggs see Schol. *ad Iliadem* A50, etc.; Aristoph., Frags. 186 and 969, 9 f (D. Page, *Greek Literary Papyri*, I, 222 f); Pliny, *N. H.* X, 79, 80, doubtless the source of Rogers' rendering; Athenaeus, 57e; Plato, *Theaet.* 151e, 161a, equating ἀνεμιαῖον and ψεῦδος.

47. *Birds* 729 f; "birds' milk" seems to be proverbial, see *Wasps* 508, and Eupolis, Frag. 379.

48. *Birds* 734 f.

49. *Birds* 737 f, 769 f.

50. *Birds* 757 f.

51. *Birds* 785 f.

52. *Birds* 745, 755.

53. *Clouds* 1075 f.

54. The term "decree seller" is probably a purely comic one for a venal politician, see C. N. Jackson, "The Decree-Seller in the *Birds*, and the Professional Politicians at Athens," *HSCP*, 1919, pp. 89 f.

55. Balanced symmetry of scenes and speeches is not in itself unusual in Aristophanes, but quite the rule; see Zielinski, *Die Gliederung der altattische Komoedie*, for the (somewhat exaggerated) theory of "syzygies," and the more moderate recent work of T. Gelzer, *Der epirrhematische Agon bei Aristophanes* (Munich, 1960). What is remarkable in the *Birds* is the union of outer with inner form, symmetry with plot movement, and the development of the fantasy through the demands of the impostors. Also, balancing scenes and speeches are not merely paired, but arranged in an elaborate order: the scene with Iris, crucial for the main plot, stands at the center of the second half of the play, flanked by two messengers' speeches, two choral passages, and two sets of impostors.

56. *Birds* 1071 f.

57. *Birds* 809 f.

58. *Birds* 822 f.

59. *Birds* 823 f.

60. *Birds* 848, 862; cf. 903. Gelzer, "Aristophanes und sein Sokrates," *Rhein. Mus.*, 13 (1956): 80, notes the similarity of terms in which the quack divinity of both the birds and the clouds is established, comparing *Birds* 690 with *Clouds* 228, 250. Gelzer also feels that in neither play would the apparent irreligiosity have been taken seriously (p. 88, n. 84); this is certainly true of the *Birds*, with its light touch and imaginative abandon, but it may not have been true of a play with less *vis comica* like the *Clouds*, especially if, as suggested earlier, the ending of the original version was left unresolved, and the Thinkery was not burned.

61. *Birds* 889 f, 899 f.

62. *Birds* 920 f.

63. *Birds* 934, 947.

64. *Birds* 950 f.

65. *Birds* 1000 f. Perhaps Antiphon, as well as Meton, is being satirized;

for Antiphon's squaring of the circle, see DK, *Vorsokr.* II, pp. 340 f (B13). The Shadow Feet who appear later in the play may also come most directly from Antiphon's Περὶ Ὁμονοίας, see B45. I am indebted to H. C. Avery for calling my attention to these passages.

66. *Birds* 1125 f.

67. *Birds* 1133 f.

68. *Birds* 1135, 1167.

69. *Birds* 1179.

70. *Birds* 1286 f.

71. *Birds* 1292 f.

72. *Birds* 1306; cf. the explicit 1228.

73. *Birds* 1218.

74. *Birds* 1238 f. Kock (*Die Vögel*, 2nd ed., Berlin, 1876, on *Birds* 1242) is surely right in seeing in the "Licymnian bolts" a reference to the pretentious Sicilian rhetorician Licymnius; cf. Plato, *Phaedrus*, 267 c.

75. *Birds* 1249 f.

76. *Birds* 1204; cf. 145 f.

77. *Birds* 1221 f.

78. *Birds* 1333 f.

79. *Birds* 1347 f; cf. 757.

80. *Birds* 1353 f.

81. *Birds* 1373 f.

82. *Birds* 1385, 1387.

83. *Birds* 1401 f.

84. *Birds* 1437 f; cf. n. 14 above.

85. *Birds* 1447 f; cf. Chap. IV, "Clouds," n. 26.

86. *Birds* 1462 f.

87. *Birds* 1470 f, 1553 f, 1694 f.

88. *Birds* 1470 f.

89. *Birds* 1458 f.

90. Actually the Triballian's speech is clear enough except for 1615, ναβαισατρεῦ, and this has been most plausibly explained as νὴ Βελσοῦρδον, "Yes, by Zeus Campestris"; see J. Whatmough, "On Triballic in Aristophanes," *CP*, 47 (1952): 26.

91. *Birds* 1656 f.

92. *Birds* 1680 f.

93. *Birds* 1709 f.

94. *Birds* 1731 f. With this whole scene, compare Cornford's theory of the comic hero becoming the new Zeus, pp. 20 f; the motif, if such it be, is unmistakable here, although the assertion that it is a survival of New Year or vegetation ritual cannot be supported by evidence from the other plays.

95. *Birds* 698.

96. *Birds* 1759 f.

97. *Birds* 548 f. On Βασίλεια, cf. Newiger, pp. 92 f, surely the right view.

98. *Birds* 1539 f.

99. *Birds* 826 f. On λιπαρὸς as a standard epithet of Athens, at least since Pindar, see *Ach.* 639 f.

100. *Birds* 832.

101. *Birds* 879.

102. *Birds* 1585.

103. Contrast, for instance, the quietist virtues of Nephelococcygia listed by the chorus at 1319 f.

VI. *The War between the Sexes*

LYSISTRATA

1. Animal images are scarce in the play, and none are applied to Lysistrata herself; cf. lines 353, 468, 476, 684, 695, 702, 1014 f.

2. *Lys.* 1105. This line is correctly explained by Ehrenberg, p. 180, n. 7, as an allusion to Spartan pederasty, with no reference to Lysistrata herself.

3. *Lys.* 7 f, 1110 f.

4. Hom., *Hymn to Aphrodite*, 7 f.

5. *Lys.* 99 f.

6. *Lys.* 155 f; she is perhaps paraphrasing Ibycus, cf. Eur., *And.* 629 f. See Schol. *ad loc.*

7. *Lys.* 149 f.

8. *Lys.* 249 f.

9. Sexual overtones are clear in the bolt and lock imagery of 408 f; cf. also 246, 264, 424 f, where μοχλὸs could have two kinds of secondary meaning corresponding to its two meanings of "crowbar" and "bolt." I cannot agree with G. Norwood, *Greek Comedy* (Boston, 1932), p. 249, that the combination of the two ideas, sex strike and seizure of the Acropolis, causes a "weakness of general effect," and "looseness of technical structure." The two ideas seem organically unified in the imagery.

10. *Lys.* 435 f. Cf. Rogers *ad loc.*

11. Cf. Stuart Atkins, *Goethe's Faust, A Literary Analysis* (Cambridge, Mass., 1958), p. 190, on the antithetical qualities of the northern *Walpurgisnacht* and the Classical *Walpurgisnacht* of *Faust* II, written under strong Aristophanic influence. See also S. Atkins, "Goethe, Aristophanes, and the Classical Walpurgisnacht," *Comparative Literature Studies*, 6 (1954): 64 f.

12. *Lys.* 16 f.

13. *Lys.* 507 f.

14. *Lys.* 593 f.

15. *Lys.* 328 f.

16. *Lys.* 640 f. Cf. R. E. Wycherley, "Aristophanes and Euripides," *Greece and Rome*, 15 (1946): 105, for the theory that the *Lysistrata* was influenced by the *Troades*.

17. *Lys.* 880 f, 889 f.

18. *Lys.* 748 f.
19. *Lys.* 895 f.
20. *Lys.* 898 f.
21. *Lys.* 729 f.
22. *Lys.* 735 f.
23. *Lys.* 723 f.
24. *Lys.* 519 f.
25. *Lys.* 567 f. C. T. Murphy, "Aristophanes and the Art of Rhetoric," *HSCP* 49 (1938), pp. 93 f, says the wool-weaving image is a παράδειγμα, associated with rhetoric; cf. Aristophanes, Frag. 638.
26. *Lys.* 586.
27. *Lys.* 1019 f.
28. *Lys.* 1182 f, 1275 f.
29. *Lys.* 870 f.
30. For the controversy, see *RE*, XXI, 1219 f (Körte); Pickard-Cambridge, *Dithyramb*, 2nd ed., pp. 133 f and *passim*; Pohlenz, p. 32; T. B. L. Webster, "The Costume of the Actors in Aristophanic Comedy," *CQ*, 49 (1955):94 f; W. Beare, "Aristophanic Costume Again," *CQ*, 51 (1957):184 f; and Webster, "A Reply on Aristophanic Costume," *ibid.* 185.
31. *Lys.* 124.
32. For the theory that Myrrhine and Lysistrata were real persons, identifiable in contemporary inscriptions as priestesses, respectively, of Athena Nike and Athena Polias, see D. M. Lewis, "Notes on Attic Inscriptions (II)," *Annual of the British School at Athens* 50 (1955): 1 f.
33. *Lys.* 619.
34. Cf. *Lys.* 60, 192, 676 f.
35. *Lys.* 632 f; on myrtle, cf. above, Chap. V, n. 18.
36. *Lys.* 985.
37. *Ion* 843.
38. *Lys.* 203, 551 f, 823 f, 1290.
39. *Lys.* 113 f, 195 f.
40. *Lys.* 87 f, 91 f.
41. *Lys.* 9 f.
42. Cornford, pp. 128 f.
43. *Lys.* 274 f, 285.
44. *Lys.* 381 f.
45. *Lys.* 372, 378, 384.
46. *Lys.* 1029 f.
47. *Lys.* 298.
48. *Ach.* 17.
49. *Lys.* 1289 f.
50. *Lys.* 529 f.
51. *Lys.* 599 f.
52. *Lys.* 551 f.

53. *Lys.* 1011 f.
54. DK, *Vorsokr.*, II, 272 (Gorgias A1), 287 (Gorgias B7–8a); cf. Croiset, *Aristophane*, pp. 139 f, on the Hellenic (Panhellenic) sentiment in *Lysistrata*; the theory of W. M. Hugill, *Panhellenism in Aristophanes* (Chicago, 1936), esp. pp. 39 f, seems to me overcontrived, and too inclined to find practical recommendations in the poet.
55. *Lys.* 1137 f, 1250 f.
56. Cf. Gorgias, DK, *Vorsokr.*, II, 272, A1; Isocrates, *Panegyricus*. See the remarks on Panhellenism by W. Jaeger, *Demosthenes* (Berkeley, 1938), pp. 152 f.
57. *Lys.* 1306 f.
58. *Lys.* 1043 f; 1189 f.

THESMOPHORIAZUSAE

1. The date seems to depend on whether *Thesm.* 808 f refers to the appointment of the Probouloi in 413 or the oligarchic *coup d'état* in 411; but Croiset, p. 146, thinks it need not refer to either; cf. also Rogers' Introduction.
2. For example, *Birds* 137 f.
3. Murray, p. 117.
4. *Thesm.* 804 f. Cf. above, n. 1.
5. *Thesm.* 9 f.
6. For example, lines 87, 93 f, 926 f, 1128 f, 1202.
7. For the theory that Euripides, Socrates and others in Aristophanes are stock masks, see Cornford, pp. 154 f; W. Süss, *De personarum antiquae comoediae Atticae usu atque origine* (Bonn, 1905).
8. *Thesm.* 149 f.
9. *Frogs* 1058 f.
10. *Thesm.* 159 f.
11. *Thesm.* 100, 130 f.
12. *Lys.* 801 f, 825 f.
13. *Thesm.* 218 f.
14. *Thesm.* 191 f.
15. *Thesm.* 52 f; cf. *Kn.* 461 f.
16. *Thesm.* 66 f.
17. *Thesm.* 142; cf. 643 f.
18. *Thesm.* 389 f.
19. *Thesm.* 400 f, 405 f, 418 f.
20. *Thesm.* 410 f; cf. *Lys.* 595.
21. *Thesm.* 407 f, 502 f, 564 f.
22. *Thesm.* 689 f.
23. *Thesm.* 275 f.
24. *Thesm.* 768 f.
25. *Thesm.* 879 f.

26. *Thesm.* 1111 f.

27. DK, *Vorsokr.*, II, 282 (Gorgias B3, 82).

VII. *Death and Life*

FROGS

1. Mazon, *Essai*, p. 180, calls the *Frogs* "une pièce incohérente et informe"; But see C. P. Segal, "The Character and Cults of Dionysus and the Unity of the *Frogs*," HSCP 65 (1961), pp. 207 f, for an excellent defense of the play's structure and meaning; the present discussion owes much to this article.

2. *Frogs* 354 f.

3. *Frogs* 47. For a study of the relation between Aristophanic quests and the heroic journeys to distant lands and to the other world, see Jacqueline Duchemin, "Recherche sur un thème aristophanien et ses sources réligieuses," *Les Etudes Classiques*, 25 (1957): 273 f; cf. also Joseph Campbell, *The Hero with a Thousand Faces* (New York, 1949), pp. 245 f, for the general shape of the heroic plot and the journey into Hell.

4. Eupolis, Frags. 90 f; Aristophanes, Frags. 149 f.

5. Pherecr., Frags. 94, 108. Other fragments of Aristophanes perhaps relevant to the theme of death and life are those of the *Niobos*, Frags. 278 f; also 488, 677, and 678. Cf. also Plato Com., *Laconians*, Frags. 67, 68, 69, apparently imitating the *Frogs*.

6. *Frogs* 1482 f.

7. Segal, "The Character and Cults of Dionysus," esp. pp. 215 f.

8. Schol. *ad Ran.* 330; Paus., II, 37, 5; Diodorus Sic., IV, 25, 4; Apollodorus, III, 5, 3. Cf. Cornford, p. 85.

9. Pindar, *Ol.* II, 26; cf. *Pyth.* III, 99.

10. Cf. Sir J. G. Frazer *ad Apollod.*, *loc. cit.*, Loeb Classical Library, (Cambridge, Mass. and London, 1954).

11. *Frogs* 112 f.

12. Plutarch, *De sera num. vind.* 27.

13. *Frogs* 186.

14. Apollodorus, II, 5, 12; [Plato], *Axiochus* 371e; Plutarch, *Theseus* 30, 5; Schol. *ad Plut.* 1013; Diodorus Sic., IV, 25, 4; Xenophon, *Hellenica* VI, 3, 6.

15. G. E. Mylonas, *Eleusis and the Eleusinian Mysteries* (Princeton, 1962), pp. 275 f, denies Dionysus any formal connection with the Mysteries beyond his initiation and the confusion of his identity with Iacchus.

16. Soph., *Ant.* 1151; cf. Segal, "The Character and Cults of Dionysus," pp. 217 f.

17. *Frogs* 417 f.

18. *Frogs* 270, cf. Rogers *ad loc.*; doubtless also with some reference to the *diobelia* of Cleophon, cf. 142 f.

19. *Frogs* 455 f.
20. Cf. Segal, "The Character and Cults of Dionysus," pp. 212 f.
21. *Frogs* 16 f.
22. *Frogs* 20, 30, 479.
23. Cf. *Frogs* 38, where it is specifically said that he knocks on the door "like a centaur."
24. *Thesm.* 138.
25. *Frogs* 96 f.
26. *Frogs* 494 f.
27. *Frogs* 503 f.
28. *Frogs* 635 f.
29. *Frogs* 33 f; cf. 190 f.
30. See Appendix.
31. *Frogs* 179; 640.
32. *Frogs* 739 f.
33. *Frogs* 693 f. Croiset, pp. 155 f, is surely right in divesting this parabasis, and the *Frogs* in general, of any practical political platform. Rather it is a reflection on the nature of citizenship.
34. *Frogs* 1455 f.
35. *Frogs* 750, 756.
36. *Frogs* 745.
37. *Frogs* 288 f.
38. *Frogs* 298 f.
39. *Frogs* 694.
40. *Frogs* 534 f; cf. 967.
41. *Frogs* 1069 f.
42. *Frogs* 1078 f.
43. *Frogs* 948 f.
44. *Frogs* 1008 f; 1055.
45. *Frogs* 967.
46. *Frogs* 832.
47. *Frogs* 911 f.
48. *Frogs* 923 f.
49. *Frogs* 886 f.
50. *Frogs* 890; cf. 725 f.
51. *Frogs* 892 f.
52. *Frogs* 1391 f.
53. *Frogs* 1402 f.
54. *Frogs* 1301 f.
55. *Frogs* 1327. Cf. Pherecrates, Frags. 144b, 145, where the δώδεκα ἁρμονίαι, according to Süss, "Inkongruenzen," pp. 118 f, are modes of intercourse; cf. also Plato Com., Frag. 134.
56. *Frogs* 1469 f.
57. Eurip., *Hipp.* 612.

58. *Frogs* 1474 f.
59. Eurip., Frag. 19 (Nauck).
60. *Frogs* 1305; cf. Hermippus, Frag. 31.
61. *Frogs* 771 f.
62. *Frogs* 1491 f.
63. *Frogs* 1419.
64. *Frogs* 154, 313.
65. See esp. lines 359, 457 f.
66. *Frogs* 372 f.
67. *Frogs* 388 f.
68. *Frogs* 729.
69. *Frogs* 675; cf. 356, 386.
70. *Frogs* 356 f.
71. *Frogs* 202 f.
72. Cf. Eurip., *Ion* 161 f.
73. *Frogs* 211 f.
74. *Frogs* 221 f.
75. *Frogs* 1071 f.
76. *Frogs* 236 f; cf. *Wasps* 1119 for blisters as a symbol of fighting qualities.
77. *Frogs* 217; cf. 316, 357.
78. *Frogs* 145 f, 273 f; cf. Mylonas, *Eleusis*, pp. 266 f; W. K. C. Guthrie,
Orpheus and Greek Religion (2nd ed., London, 1952), p. 160; I. Linforth,
The Arts of Orpheus (Berkeley, 1941), pp. 75 f.
79. *Frogs* 155, 313 f; see in general G. W. Elderkin, *Mystic Allusions in
the Frogs* (Princeton, 1955).
80. *Frogs* 340 f.
81. *Frogs* 455 f.
82. Pindar, *Ol.* II, 61 f; cf. Frag. 114.
83. *Frogs* 851, πολυτίμητος; cf. 324, 337, 399.
84. *Frogs* 1087 f.
85. *Frogs* 1089 f.
86. *Frogs* 1524 f.
87. On the use of poets and the idea of true versus false poetry as cultural
indexes, cf. W. Jaeger, *Paideia*, I, 380.
88. *Frogs* 851 f.
89. Murray, pp. 122 f.
90. *Frogs* 33, 49, 190 f, 693 f.
91. *Frogs* 704, 1419.
92. *Frogs* 1427 f.
93. *Frogs* 1446 f. It is a question whether this suggestion implies a return
to the limited polity of Theramenes, here represented as the "pupil" of
Euripides, who is himself represented as slightly antidemocratic, 952 f.
94. *Frogs* 1431 f.

95. Aesch., *Agam.* 717 f, 727 f.
96. Cf. Ennius, *Alexander*, Frags. 35 f (Vahlen), esp. Hyginus, *Fab.* 91.
97. *Frogs* 1463 f.
98. Thuc. I, 143, 4–5.
99. Cf. *Frogs* 1458 f, which seems to imply that there can be no salvation.
100. *Frogs* 1466; cf. Rogers, and W. W. Merry (*Aristophanes, The Frogs,* Oxford, 1905), *ad loc.*
101. See Croiset, pp. 161 f, comparing *Ach.* 484.
102. *Frogs* 1528 f; other hexameters occur in 814 f, 876 f.
103. *Frogs* 1477.
104. *Frogs* 176 f.
105. *Frogs* 155.
106. *Frogs* 142.
107. *Frogs* 783.
108. *Frogs* 424.
109. *Frogs* 455 f.
110. *Frogs* 866 f.

VIII. *Discourse of Fantasy*

1. *Poetics* 1451b27 f.
2. For a concise account of Dali's development, see J. T. Soby, *Salvador Dali* (Museum of Modern Art, New York, 1946). See also S. Dali, *The Secret Life of Salvador Dali,* trans. H. M. Chevalier (New York, 1942), and *Fifty Secrets of Magic Craftsmanship* (New York, 1948); R. Descharnes, *The World of Salavador Dali* (New York, 1962).
3. Dali has himself given different accounts at different times of the limp watches (see below, n. 12); one may be permitted yet another.
4. See Wilam., "Wespen," p. 481, on comedy's mad disregard of place and time. Mazon's attempt, *Essai,* p. 18, n. 1, to rationalize a comic *mise en scène* (*Acharnians*) seems to miss the point.
5. Huizinga, *Homo Ludens, passim,* esp. chap. 1.
6. *Frogs* 242 f.
7. *Birds* 1105 f.
8. *Peace* 796 f.
9. Harpo is, presumably, "sympathetic" to giraffes; see Dali's discussion of "sympathy" and "antipathy" in objects, *Fifty Secrets,* pp. 48 f; for a reproduction, see Soby, *Salvador Dali,* p. 86.
10. *Wasps* 42 f.
11. See Soby, *Salvador Dali,* p. 20.
12. See Soby, *Salvador Dali,* p. 14. The quotation, describing limp watches, is from Dali's *The Conquest of the Irrational*; elsewhere Dali calls the limp watches masochistic symbols.

INDEX

329